A HISTORY OF FASCISM IN FRANCE

A HISTORY OF FASCISM IN FRANCE

FROM THE FIRST WORLD WAR TO THE NATIONAL FRONT

Chris Millington

BLOOMSBURY ACADEMIC
LONDON • NEW YORK • OXFORD • NEW DELHI • SYDNEY

BLOOMSBURY ACADEMIC
Bloomsbury Publishing Plc
50 Bedford Square, London, WC1B 3DP, UK
1385 Broadway, New York, NY 10018, USA

BLOOMSBURY, BLOOMSBURY ACADEMIC and the Diana logo are trademarks of
Bloomsbury Publishing Plc

First published in Great Britain 2020

Cover design: Tjaša Krivec
Cover image: Propaganda of the Cross of Fire and Briscards, National Volunteers,
National Regroupement. French choose! About 1935 (© Collection Jean Jacques
Allevi / Bridgeman Images)

A catalogue record for this book is available from the British Library.

A catalog record for this book is available from the Library of Congress.

ISBN: HB: 978-1-3500-0654-6
PB: 978-1-3500-0653-9
ePDF: 978-1-3500-0655-3
eBook: 978-1-3500-0656-0

Typeset by Deanta Global Publishing Services, Chennai, India

For Mum and Dad

CONTENTS

Acknowledgements   ix
List of abbreviations   x

Introduction: What was fascism?   **1**

1   Searching for a French Mussolini during the 1920s   **13**
The Jeunesses Patriotes   14
The Faisceau   20
Fascism and the leagues   24
The decline of the leagues   27

2   Bloodshed in the City of Light: 6 February 1934   **29**
France in the doldrums   31
Lighting the fuse: The Stavisky Affair   35
The 6 February crisis   37
'An attempted overthrow of the Republican regime'   41

3   The army of the death's head: The Croix de Feu   **45**
Origins   48
1934: Development into a mass movement   51
The Croix de Feu and the Republic   55
Anti-Semitism and race   57
Fascism and violence   61
1936: Dissolution   65

**4   Fascism defeated? The Parti Social Français and the
Parti Populaire Français**   **69**
'[The] PSF is the CF plus electoral politics'   71
The PSF and the Republic   79
The Parti Populaire Français   83
The PPF, the Freedom Front and Fascism   87
The PSF and the PPF at the end of the 1930s   91

5   Bombs, bullets and bloody murder: The Cagoule   **93**
The OSARN   94
Who were the Cagoulards?   97

Contents

Exposure   101

Anticipating Vichy?   105

6 National Revolution, 1940–4   **107**

The single party project   109

The National Revolution   112

From the Légion to the Milice   115

Collaborationism in Paris   119

Vichy and fascism   124

7 The Front National   **127**

The wilderness years: 1944–81   129

Breakthrough: The 1980s   133

Consolidation and division: The 1990s   137

2002–11: At the gates of power   139

2011–18: A *Bleu Marine* Revolution?   141

Conclusion   **145**

Appendix: The French allergy to fascism   149

René Rémond's founding work and the 'orthodox' school   149

The 1980s I: The Sternhell controversy   152

The 1980s II: Battle lines are drawn   154

The 1990s: Obsession   156

The twenty-first century: Directions both old and new   159

Notes   165

Select bibliography   221

Index   229

ACKNOWLEDGEMENTS

My interest in fascism in France began in 2003 when, as a final year undergraduate student at the University of Liverpool, I wrote an essay in response to the question, 'Can we define a French fascism in interwar France?' That choice of essay question has to a great extent defined my career thus far as a historian. I have worked on the French extreme right both directly (with Brian Jenkins on the riot of the *six février* 1934) and indirectly, through my PhD research (under Kevin Passmore) on the *anciens combattants* of the First World War and a postdoctoral project on political violence during the 1920s and 1930s. I have therefore conducted research for this book over a long period, largely thanks to generous funding from a number of institutions, namely the Arts and Humanities Research Council, the Institute of Historical Research, the British Academy and the universities of Cardiff and Swansea. Generous funding from the Gerda Henkel Stiftung allowed me to enrich the chapters on the Cagoule and Vichy at a late stage in the writing process.

Thanks are due to a number of people. I thank Julian Jackson who suggested that I write this book. It was a pleasure to work with the staff at Bloomsbury Academic, and I thank them for this experience. Thanks are owed to the readers who commented on the manuscript: Caroline Campbell, Sean Kennedy and Kevin Passmore. The book is better for their valuable input. I thank the students of Swansea University for their interest in French history and the enjoyable discussions that I have had with them about it, in and out of the classroom. I thank the staff in the Department of History at Swansea University for providing a friendly environment to teach and research. The College of Arts and Humanities granted me sabbatical leave in 2018 during which I finished the manuscript; I am grateful for this. Colleagues in the Department of History, Politics & Philosophy at Manchester Metropolitan University provided a welcoming atmosphere to complete this project.

My wife has listened to me speak about French history for many years. She has read my work, commented upon conference papers and tolerated long absences while I researched abroad. Thank you for your love, patience and unwavering support, Alexandra. Time spent with my daughter Madeleine is so full of happiness that it is difficult to believe that evils such as fascism could exist in the world. The current state of our country makes me more determined than ever to raise a daughter who sees beyond borders, nationalities and other such artificial divisions to embrace and enjoy foreign cultures, languages and histories. For your love of life, I thank you Madeleine.

Finally, I thank Ron and Jean Millington. For your unconditional love and support and the example that you have set me as a parent, this book is for you, mum and dad.

ABBREVIATIONS

ARAC	Association Républicaine des Anciens Combattants
CAUR	Comitati d'Azione per l'Universalità di Roma
CGT	Confédération Générale du Travail
CVIA	Comité de Vigilance des Intellectuels Antifascistes
EVP	Équipes Volantes de Propagande
FN	Front National
FNJ	Front National de la Jeunesse
GRECE	Groupe de Recherche et d'Etude pour la Civilisation Européenne
LICA	Ligue Internationale contre l'Antisémitisme
MSR	Mouvement Social Révolutionnaire
OSARN	Organisation Secrète d'Action Révolutionnaire Nationale
PPF	Parti Populaire Français
PRNS	Parti Républicain National et Social
PSF	Parti/Progrès Social Français
RNP	Rassemblement National Populaire
RPF	Rassemblement du Peuple Français
STO	Service du Travail Obligatoire
UCAD	Union des Comités d'Action Défensive
UDCA	Union de Défense des Commerçants et Artisans
UNC	Union Nationale des Combattants

INTRODUCTION: WHAT WAS FASCISM?

This book examines the principal movements, parties and militias of the French extreme right from the end of the First World War until the early twenty-first century. It explores their political doctrine and action, their leadership and membership, their competition with rivals and enemies and their influence upon the politics of their era. Few of the groups under consideration here readily declared themselves fascist. Fascism was generally perceived to be a foreign phenomenon which, though much admired on the extreme right, was not suitable for France. Nonetheless, the organizations in this book adopted (and adapted) aspects of the content and form of fascism for their own purposes. In this sense, the reader might perceive a French variant of fascism in the pages that follow.

Historical study of French fascism has been mired for decades in a bitter and acrimonious controversy over the strength of the phenomenon in interwar France. Scholars are divided on the scale and significance of the fascist threat to the democratic French Third Republic. The origin of the debate may be located in the work of Sorbonne graduate René Rémond who in 1954 published *La Droite en France de 1815 à nos jours*. In this book, Rémond traced the development of French right-wing politics since the end of the Napoleonic era. At the time of writing, barely a decade had passed since the liberation of France and the collapse of the collaborationist Vichy state, a regime widely associated with the right. The conservative Rémond sought to detoxify right-wing politics and disentangle it from fascism. His analysis of Vichy was brief; in just four pages Rémond concluded that the conservatism of Marshal Philippe Pétain's administration had rendered it 'the very opposite of fascism'. *La Droite en France* devoted considerably more attention to the extreme right-wing antiparliamentarian leagues and parties of the interwar years. Rémond admitted that the men and women of these groups had a penchant for wearing uniforms and marching in the style of Italian Fascism[1] and German Nazism but their fascism was only skin deep, merely a 'Roman whitewash'. At their core, these groups were socially and economically conservative. Fascism, on the other hand, based its appeal on the primacy of popular sovereignty and the desire to overthrow the status quo. Rémond admitted that there *were* some smaller authentically fascist groups yet their size rendered them insignificant; after all, he asked, 'What are twenty thousand recruits, even devoted ones, in a nation of forty million!' He concluded subsequently that 'there was no true French fascism: France experienced only a fascism of poor imitations, of dull forgeries, of plagiarists with neither talent nor honour. It had its Mosley, [but] it did not find its Mussolini'.[2] The country had simply not provided the social and economic conditions propitious to the development of an indigenous fascist movement. Deep down, the 'wisdom of the French people' and their 'political maturity' rendered them resistant to this distinctly foreign ideology.[3]

Almost thirty years later, Zeev Sternhell, Professor of Political Science at the Hebrew University of Jerusalem (and graduate of Paris's prestigious Sciences Po), published *Ni droite ni gauche. L'idéologie fasciste en France*. This book built upon Sternhell's previous research into the French fin de siècle 'revolutionary Right', a synthesis of left- and right-wing ideas in which he perceived the ideological building blocks of fascism.[4] In *Ni droite ni gauche*, Sternhell argued that far from being a minor political curiosity, fascism in fact penetrated French society deeply during the 1930s. He identified a very real threat to democracy in contemporary intellectual circles that rejected stale parliamentarianism in their search for a new course for France; their work towards a third way between Bolshevism and capitalism facilitated the spread of fascist ideas. Most controversially, Sternhell claimed that the fact that fascism had not come to power in France rendered its French variant free from the inevitable compromises of power. Fascism, in its purest form, was French.[5]

The works of Rémond and Sternhell demarcate the rudimentary battle lines in one of the fiercest debates in modern French historiography, that on the strength of fascism in France. After decades of research, the differences between the 'Rémondians' and the 'Sternhellians' seem irreconcilable, and they have prompted not a few bad-tempered exchanges more suited to the schoolyard than the work of professional scholars. So protracted is the disagreement that the debate has itself become an object of study.[6]

The bitterness of the argument stems in part from high stakes of the debate. Under the shadow of the Occupation, research into French fascism speaks to France's relationship to its past and its status as the birthplace of Western European democracy. After the Second World War, Vichy was routinely dismissed as a measure of expediency implemented in the extraordinary atmosphere of defeat, a holding operation forced to do the Germans' bidding while awaiting liberation from abroad. The worst excesses of the French state were thus attributed to irresistible pressure from the Third Reich, not to mention a handful of fanatical Germanophiles, traitorous extremists and political opportunists. The French public, so the story went, were sympathetic to the Resistance and General Charles de Gaulle's London-based Free French, both of which incarnated the 'true' France of democracy and democratic Republicanism. This was a comforting narrative for a nation that looked to heal the divisions of wartime in the uncertain waters of the emerging Cold War.[7]

This version of France's wartime past was all but destroyed during the early 1970s. In 1971, Marcel Ophüls's landmark documentary about the Occupation, *Le chagrin et la pitié*, exposed the venality of a nation which, rather than supporting the resistance, preferred *attentisme* ('to wait-and-see') until finally throwing its lot in with de Gaulle at the eleventh hour. In 1972, American historian Robert O. Paxton's bombshell of a book, *Vichy France: Old Guard and New Order*, documented convincingly the extent to which Vichy had collaborated closely with the Nazi administration, in many cases going above and beyond what was required. Paxton further revealed that Vichy was more than just a temporary measure: its programme for 'National Revolution' drew upon long-established French political concerns in an attempt to undo decades of Republican democracy. If Vichy was not a fully fledged fascist state, it was perilously close to being so. As for the French people, though not entirely supportive of Pétain's regime, many had supported the marshal to the bitter end.[8] Scholars inside and outside France came to accept that right-wing authoritarianism had caused more than a handful of French to break with the country's democratic tradition during the war.

There was no such reversal in the historiography of the interwar years. In the wake of Sternhell's path-breaking work, it was only during the 1980s and 1990s that historians came to challenge the belief that fascist ideology held little interest for a nation wedded to democracy. Yet revisionists such as William D. Irvine, Kevin Passmore and Robert Soucy met with strident resistance from the likes of Serge Berstein and Michel Winock who steadfastly clung to Rémond's thesis. So systematic was the defence of the long-established Rémondian orthodoxy that French political scientist Michel Dobry (a partisan of neither school) coined the term 'immunity thesis', to describe France's alleged allergy to fascism.[9]

To group historians into two opposed 'camps' erases and obscures significant differences between scholars *within* each camp, as well as points of agreement and convergence *between* camps. The intricacies of the debate are explored in the Appendix to this book. Suffice it to say here that the principal sticking point in the debate is the definition of fascism itself. The work of historians on all sides of the question has for decades been predicated on a shared approach. This approach, which Dobry termed the 'classificatory logic', entails the formulation of a definition of fascism and the subsequent application of this definition to history in order to 'classify' which leagues, movements, parties and personalities were, or were not, fascist.[10] Scholarship on fascism in France has produced a number of competing definitions of the ideology. French historians are not alone in this endeavour. The search for the essential characteristics of fascism – a generic fascist minimum – that can be applied to movements and regimes across borders and time periods has spawned a huge amount of literature in the field of fascist studies.[11] Problems arise from disagreements over matters of definition. The study of fascism encounters difficulties when the classificatory logic is allowed to take precedence over past understandings of fascism. Too often historians have used their definition of fascism to decide which groups were or were not fascist, regardless of the views of contemporaries. The strive to classify groups has also led to a false dichotomy that pitches the 'fascist' against the 'moderate'. Yet groups could be non-fascist and still pose a threat to democracy. Historical actors – some of whom self-identified as fascist – understood the phenomenon in a variety of ways. Like historians, they perceived 'essential' characteristics in fascism. And, like historians, they disagreed on exactly which characteristics these were.

Fascism was a new force in European politics and contemporaries strove to understand it. Early French attempts to comprehend Fascism were framed according to the context of post-war Italian politics. For French diplomats, Fascism was above all a counter-revolutionary force. French ambassador to Rome Camille Barrère identified the movement as one of 'order, patriotism and security'. He reported approvingly on the actions of the *squadristi* against the forces of the left, at once praising their 'energetic and resolute attitude' and their 'work of purification'. Barrère recognized that the Fascists were prone to committing acts of excessive violence, yet he considered Mussolini to be just the 'moderate' needed to channel the movement in a more peaceful direction. The French embassy in Rome generally looked favourably upon the Fascist leader in light of his wartime interventionist campaign (which the embassy partly funded during 1914–15) and his critical attitude towards Germany.[12]

News from across the Alps trickled into the French press. In November 1919, Parisians were informed of the violence between, on the one hand, the 'Fascio' of ex-servicemen, the *arditi*[13] and nationalists and, on the other hand, the 'reds'.[14] The Parisian press first mentioned Fascism only in early 1921, two years after Mussolini founded the *Fasci di Combattimento*. Right-wing newspapers were most celebratory of the movement and its actions. *Le Figaro* reported that the movement was one of war veterans determined to combat those who sought to undermine the victory.[15] *Le Matin* praised 'the new national forces thrown into the struggle against socialism and against the old political caste which abandoned the State to the mercy of socialism'. When Mussolini was invited to form a government in October 1922, there was much optimism in the French conservative press for future relations between France and Italy, the 'two Latin sisters'.[16]

French academics looked to analyse the new force in Italian politics. In August 1922, Emile-Guillaume Léonard, a historian at the Ecole française de Rome, asked in *La Revue hebdomadaire*, 'What is Fascism?' He responded that Fascism developed as a reaction to the threat from communist revolution in Italy. Its 'punitive expeditions' and 'surgical operations' (described by Léonard as 'murder pure and simple') revealed that Fascism was little more than a means to exact reprisals against the left; it was a physical manifestation of the *lex talionis*. Léonard perceived little of substance in the movement: Mussolini concerned himself with a political programme only once he looked to make electoral gains, declaring that Fascism was Republican to better distinguish it from monarchism and nationalism. However, Léonard recognized, too, that there were numerous tendencies within fascism, from royalism to radicalism.[17] Pierre Dominique agreed with Léonard's analysis in the pages of the same publication in November 1922. Fascism was merely a 'demonstration', and a 'sweep of the broom' that lacked a specific doctrine.[18] By early 1923, 'Fascism' had appeared in a French dictionary for the first time. *Larousse mensuel illustré* defined the word as 'a movement of ideas and a political party aiming to unite all Italians to fight against the forces of social disaggregation (in particular Bolshevism)'.[19]

Despite the ostensible specificity of Fascism to Italy, comparisons with historical French movements seemed to offer further clues as to its nature. In 1925, the centre-left *L'Oeuvre* mused upon the political candidates for the title of the 'French Mussolini'. What was needed was 'a photogenic Boulanger, who really knows how to ride a horse [and], salute in the Italian style'; only then would the 'castor oil and the grenade [be] let loose'.[20] During 1889, General Georges Boulanger had led a populist campaign for a radical revision of the Third Republic. His combination of fierce nationalism, antiparliamentarianism and a form of socialism, not to mention his innovative campaign tactics, foreshadowed aspects of interwar politics.[21] Meanwhile, editorialist Ludovic Naudeau wrote in *L'Illustration* that Italy was now 'governed by the Ligue des Patriotes'.[22] Paul Déroulède's Ligue des

Patriotes was a late nineteenth-century nationalist and anti-Republican movement that combined a radical appeal to the people with street violence.[23]

Italian Fascism had a physical presence on French soil. Both Mussolini and his antifascist opponents courted the Italian community in France, the largest outside the peninsula. During 1923 Mussolini's Grand Council of Fascism founded the *Fasci all'estero*, with the aim of defending Italian interests and assisting foreign nationals abroad. Several French *fascio* were founded in urban centres with significant Italian populations.[24] The French intelligence services identified numerous agents of the Italian government and Mussolini's Organizzazione per la Vigilanza e la Repressione dell'Antifascismo (OVRA) in France.[25] The Italian veterans' group, the Associazione Nazionale Combattenti (ANC) had sections in France. The ANC acted as a conduit for Italian Fascist propaganda.[26] Meanwhile, the Communist Party made efforts to organize Italian workers into proletarian antifascist committees that would, with French workers, combat Italian and French fascism within France.[27] French police reported that Italian antifascists had formed a combat group, the Garibaldi Legion, while several prominent antifascists, such as the founder of the antifascist Giustizia e Libertà Carlo Roselli, took refuge in the country. Conflict was exported, too; between 1923 and 1933, twenty-eight Italian Fascists were murdered in France at the hands of their antifascist countrymen.[28]

French interest in the Italian movement remained constant during the 1920s. Between 1922 and 1932, forty books on Mussolini and Italian fascism were published in France.[29] The politics of Mussolini's regime was even the subject of doctoral theses.[30] Yet French observers of Fascism recognized that a wholesale transposition of the ideology into France was not viable.[31] Fascism was widely considered a 'foreign phenomenon, emergent from a peripheral power inhabited by *bravacci* (braggarts) [and] held quite in contempt, despite the wartime alliance [between France and Italy]'.[32] It was often suggested that while Fascism suited the Italians, it was not possible to transpose it wholesale onto the French. 'It's a matter of temperament', stated journalist Louis Latzarus in 1922.[33] Mussolini himself declared that Fascism was not an ideology that could be exported beyond Italy's borders.[34] However, if Fascism was not suitable for export, it remained a model that could be adapted if not imitated. Former socialist Gustave Hervé wrote in October and November 1922, for example, that the March on Rome provided lessons for the French government about how to deal with domestic subversion.[35]

In November 1925, the spectacle of blue-shirted men marching in Paris announced to many observers the birth of a French fascism. These men belonged to the Faisceau, a league that lionized Mussolini's Fascism and denounced communism and democracy. 'We vomit on parliamentarianism', declared leader Georges Valois.[36] Valois, a former member of the monarchist league, the Action Française, had established contact with French business interests 'searching for a French Mussolini' shortly after the March on Rome. His league sought the violent overthrow of the Third Republic and its replacement with a fascist-style dictatorship called the 'Combatants' State'.[37] The Jeunesses Patriotes, founded in November 1924, likewise sympathized with elements of Fascism though it stopped short of declaring itself fascist. The league's leader, deputy Pierre Taittinger, spoke in favour of authoritarianism, stating in December 1925 that to install such a regime in France would perhaps require violence. His uniformed shock squads fought their opponents and police in the street; a handful of Jeunesses Patriotes died in these confrontations during the 1920s.[38]

The phenomenon of the leagues – 'extra-parliamentary formations that privileged the mass demonstration and the use (or at least the threat) of physical force over electoral politics' – was not novel to 1920s France. The Jeunesses Patriotes was itself an auxiliary of Déroulède's older Ligue des Patriotes. However, the experience of the First World War and the emergence of paramilitary groups across Europe, not least the Italian *squadristi*, exerted an influence on the post-war French groups.[39] In some cases, leaguers acted in direct imitation of Italian Fascists. In June 1923, the Action Française's *camelots du roi* street fighters – a group that predated Italian Fascism – attempted to force-feed castor oil to deputy Marc Sangnier. *Time* magazine called the attack an imitation of 'Facismo' in France.[40] Sympathetic commentators presented both French leaguer and Italian Fascist violence as defensive responses to left-wing provocation. Mussolini himself was in fact careful to frame *squadristi* attacks in this way, concerned both to avoid legal sanction and to legitimize the violence in a culture that considered offensive action as rash, uncontrolled and unbecoming of a man.[41] French leaguers likewise presented their own violence as defensive. Conservatives and some moderate left-wingers shared such an understanding of leaguer violence.[42] The boundaries between formations on the right, from the extremes to the centre, generally remained fluid. Political meetings saw members of the conservative parliamentary parties the Fédération Républicaine and the Parti Démocrate Populaire sit alongside the centuries of the Jeunesses Patriotes and the Action Française's *camelots du roi*.

The founding of the French leagues prompted the birth of a French 'antifascism'. Originally, the term was applied only to opposition to Mussolini within Italy. By the mid-1920s French left-wingers had witnessed the violent destruction of the Italian left and set about organizing their own defence.[43] The Communist Party monopolized the cause of 'antifascism' and the Radical and Socialist parties rarely used the term.[44] The extreme left's response to fascism was embodied in the paramilitary Groupes de Défenses Antifascistes, founded in spring 1926.[45] Activists targeted right-wing meetings with counter-demonstrations that tended to descend into violence between antifascists and the police. When antifascists managed to gain entry to the meeting venue, they disrupted speakers with boos, chants and singing, often drawing retaliation from the leagues' security forces. As the leagues declined after 1926, the cause of antifascism was once again understood as the struggle against Italian Fascism alone.[46] Communist opposition to fascism took on a new meaning in the final years of the decade when Moscow declared class warfare on all 'bourgeois' parties. The fight against the 'social-fascism' of any formation to the right of the communists (including the Socialist Party) subsequently dominated the French party's political agenda.[47]

If the leagues of the 1920s admired, appropriated and adapted elements of Italian Fascist doctrine and practice, they did not wish to be understood merely as pale imitations of a foreign ideology. Dobry has termed this the 'dilemma of the authoritarian nationalist', who seeks to emphasize the indigenous roots of a political programme.[48]

Hitler was not above such concerns, and he proceeded cautiously in his relationship with Mussolini. Only after 1933 did contacts with Rome develop in a meaningful way; prior to that point the Nazis were wary of being publicly associated with a foreign movement.[49] In France, even Valois suggested that he would use French rather than Italian 'methods' in his assault on the Third Republic.[50] The majority of French right-wingers cast doubt on the universality of fascism, and this attitude persisted into the 1930s.[51]

Political developments in Italy and Germany during the 1930s rendered French attitudes to fascism more complex. In Italy, Mussolini aimed to reinvigorate the Fascist revolution while developing a potential counterweight to the revival of Germany on the continent. Consequently, he declared that his ideology *could* succeed abroad: 'In a decade Europe will be fascist!' he thundered during a speech in Milan in October 1932.[52] The following year he established the Comitati d'Azione per l'Universalità di Roma (Committees of Action for the Universality of Rome, CAUR). The French authorities came to understand the CAUR as a further means to help 'crush the democracies' in Europe.[53] The body organized the Fascist International Congress at Montreux in 1935; Marcel Bucard, former Faisceau member and now leader of the Francistes league, represented France.[54]

Italian money and weapons flowed into France. Bucard's Francistes and Jacques Doriot's PPF (founded in 1936) both benefited from regular injections of Fascist cash. Meanwhile, the underground Cagoule movement received arms from Rome during the late 1930s. By August 1939, the French government believed that the Fascist authorities were preparing terrorist attacks in France in the event of war.[55] Yet the leagues and parties of the extreme right, not to mention conservatives and a number of civic associations, encouraged good relations with Mussolini. Right-wing political journalist Henri de Kerillis admired Mussolini's pragmatism for it had allowed him to come to an understanding with diverse sections of society such as the church and the monarch. He regarded Fascism as a 'dangerous tool' yet simply lamented that circumstances had constrained Mussolini to use it. Enamoured with the Duce, de Kerillis hoped that France would soon find 'its Mussolini'.[56] On several occasions delegates from the French veterans' movement were granted audiences with Mussolini. Following a visit to Italy in 1933, one such delegate was moved to declare that 'the blackshirts of the March on Rome … were our comrades of the war'.[57] The warm relations between French and Italian ex-servicemen helped further spread fascist discourses in France.[58]

As for Germany, long-held suspicions of the hereditary enemy coloured French understandings of Nazism. In *Mein Kampf*, Hitler had attacked France as the 'mortal' and 'ruthless' enemy of the German people and a nation comparable to the Negro race.[59] There seemed little difference between the Nazis and a longer tradition of German Francophobia and militarism. Hitler was the successor to Bismarck and the Kaiser, 'the incarnation of eternal Germany, militarist, expansionist, [and the] hereditary enemy of France'.[60] The publication of *Mein Kampf* in France during 1934 reinforced such beliefs and few on the right perceived any novelty in Nazism. Rather, Hitler's expansionism was situated in the tradition of Prussian militarism: nationalist intellectual Charles Maurras considered the Nazis to be descended from the Prussians and Uhlans.[61] French admirers of fascism thus rarely applied the label to the German Nazis, preferring 'racists' instead.[62]

Within France, the 1930s saw the emergence of new paramilitary leagues and parties including Jean Renaud's anti-Semitic Solidarité Française and Doriot's PPF. The most important of these new groups was Lieutenant-Colonel François de La Rocque's Croix de Feu (later renamed the Parti Social Français or the PSF). The Croix de Feu was founded as an association for decorated veterans in 1927.[63] La Rocque took over the leadership in 1932, subsequently reorienting it towards paramilitarism and expanding the movement's membership (the league would have 500,000 members by mid-1936 when it was dissolved by the left-wing Popular Front government). La Rocque's stance on the Republic was ambiguous to say the least. He declared his loyalty to the regime on several occasions while condemning its gangrenous institutions and the parasites and eunuchs within them.[64]

Attitudes to fascism on the extreme right remained complex. Belief in a French 'nature' that rendered fascism unsuitable in France was still popular.[65] Consequently, in 1935, Jacques Bainville, historian and member of Action Française, determined that 'the French cockerel is not suited to suckle at the teat of the Roman she-wolf'.[66] Likewise, in the 1937 newspaper article, 'No fascism', La Rocque determined that the doctrine could not succeed in France for it was 'contrary to the French temperament'.[67] The renunciation of the fascist label usually accompanied a rejection of 'totalitarianism', understood as the deification of the state to the detriment of the Catholic Church and Western Christian culture.[68]

The concept of a 'Latin civilisation' rendered the imperviousness of national boundaries less certain. Renaud hailed the strong 'spiritual ties' between the Latin cultures of France and Italy while La Rocque claimed that the Germans, unlike the Italians, lacked the 'Latin sense of measure'.[69] In 1939, right-wing essayist Henri Massis suggested that only a 'Catholic and Latin' political alliance with Italy could halt the westward march of Germany and the Slavic nations, Europe's 'new barbarians'.[70] Massis warned that to understand all totalitarian regimes through the lens of Nazism would be 'blind' and 'unjust': the regimes in Italy, Spain and Portugal were 'united by their Latin fundament, the affinity of language and culture, the same faith and a similar zeal for Western Christian civilisation'.[71]

If such arguments permitted borrowings from Italian Fascism while distancing oneself from the politically toxic German Nazism, they also facilitated favourable exchanges with other Latin dictatorships. António de Oliveira Salazar's authoritarian regime in Portugal drew admiring glances from the broad sweep of the French right. Salazar, who cultivated an image at home and abroad as a 'reserved puritanical and provincial dictator', represented a respectable model, especially after 1934 when he publicly rejected totalitarianism.[72] Richard Griffiths writes that 'most contemporary commentators in the Thirties distinguished between Mediterranean fascism, based on the eternal principles of Catholicism, and German paganism'.[73] Indeed, Bainville described the Portuguese as the 'most honest, most wise, and most measured dictator', in Europe.[74] Yet Salazar, too, borrowed from Italy, and his rejection of fascist totalitarianism was not so straightforward, informed as much by domestic political rivalry with Portuguese fascists than a simple rejection of the ideology.[75]

The French left subscribed to similar well-established anti-German stereotypes, yet it invested them with class politics. Hitler was in league with the bourgeoisie and the war profiteer, two stereotypes that differed little from his French counterparts.[76] There were of course national peculiarities: mentions of Hitler's movement were more likely to involve incidents of racism.[77] The Socialist Party's *Le Populaire* reported an anti-Semitic demonstration by the Action Française as an attempt 'to outdo, without doubt, the methods employed in Germany by Hitler'.[78] Nevertheless, the left's use of the word 'Nazi' to label the French extreme right was rare.[79]

The growth of the French leagues during the 1930s worried antifascists. Communist leaders depicted the leagues as heirs to the Versaillais, the government troops who had massacred thousands in Montmartre during the Commune of Paris. Antifascists were likewise associated with the bravery and martyrdom of the communards and the 'glorious traditions' of the left, such as the erection of barricades.[80] Boulangism remained a historical reference point, yet it was now used to place the threat from the extreme right into sharp relief. If Boulanger had introduced insults and street quarrels to French politics, the leagues had made 'mortal aggression a new method of permanent activism'.[81]

In 1935, the left-wing Comité de Vigilance des Intellectuels Antifascistes (CVIA) published an information booklet entitled *What Is Fascism?* The question was a perplexing one for, as the CVIA explained, 'amongst those [political groups] that the popular voice designates as fascist, no important group recognises itself as such'.[82] The CVIA warned that the 'ambiguity', 'obscurity' and myths surrounding the word obstructed understanding of its meaning. The result was that a great many members of fascist organizations at home and abroad – most members even – were 'fascists-without-knowing-it'.[83] To better define fascism, the CVIA looked to distinguish the 'common and essential elements' of the regimes in Austria, Germany and Italy. The conclusion was that fascism was the 'desperate attempt to stabilise by force a degenerate capitalism'. Its aim was to 'bring to heel the unemployed and the impoverished masses and shore up the power of the privileged, capitalists and rulers alike'; it could take root in any country where capitalism reigned.[84]

Given the violent fate of foreign antifascists, the Communist Party decided that to fight fascism in the realms of political theory would not be sufficient. It was necessary to 'represent it as an immediate and fearful danger to working-class liberties'; the violence of fascism dominated antifascist propaganda.[85] A pamphlet in May 1934 called on workers of all political stripes to demonstrate against a planned fascist meeting in Saint-Quentin and 'nip in the bud the regime of the axe and castor oil'.[86] Translated texts from Germany reinforced the left's construction of the violent threat from fascism: Werner Hirsch's 1935 *Leçons de courage* recounted the author's experience of incarceration, interrogation and torture in the Nazi prison system.[87] Antifascists transposed the vocabulary of foreign fascism onto French movements: the leagues took part in 'punitive expeditions' in which their shock squads subdued the proletariat 'in the Mussolinian and Hitlerian fashion'.[88] The left therefore understood fascism as a transnational phenomenon. There were some exceptions to this line of thinking: socialist Jean-Maurice Hermann recognized that for fascism to succeed, it would need to be 'adapted to the temperament and deep sentiments of the French masses'.[89] Yet left-wing propaganda usually tarred all French and foreign 'fascists' with the same brush. A political sticker from 1935 pronounced:

The Croix de Feu

The Solidarité Française

The Jeunesses Patriotes

The Camelots du Roy

The Francistes

Are all 'FRENCH NAZIS'.

Their strong State is a Hitler State

Join us boys who wish to

LIVE IN FREEDOM

Join Antifascist Organisations.[90]

Antifascists generally considered Hitler to be fascist as it did Mussolini and the French leagues: all were 'the swirls of the same current flowing to disaster'.[91]

The meaning of fascism was therefore contested. Laurent Kestel is right to claim that fascism 'is less an analytical concept than a social word, subject to a wide variety of meanings and interpretations'.[92] Maurice Tournier is equally correct to stress fascism's 'culturally multilingual' nature: it means different things, to different people, in different contexts.[93] In France, 'fascism' was (and is) a political label that drew on French and foreign precedent. Features of foreign fascist movements could be borrowed and adapted, or rejected, depending on the circumstances of the time and the predilections of actors. To claim or reject the fascist label was a means for a group to distinguish itself from its rivals on the extreme right. Interactions between competing groups further influenced their efforts to position themselves on the political spectrum.[94]

I offer no new definition of fascism to add to the plethora in the scholarly literature. My refusal to engage in the classificatory logic does not mean that fascism *cannot* be defined; the voluminous literature on the subject suggests the opposite.[95] However, problems arise when definitions are applied to historical cases. A movement, league or party that does not fulfil the requirements of a definition may be dismissed as 'not fascist'. Where differences exist between two or more movements classified as fascist, these may be determined to be of secondary importance in relation to the fascist 'core' or 'essence'. The historian can neither determine which features of a movement were considered primary or secondary nor whether contemporaries in fact perceived such a dichotomy. Even if we measure French movements against the fascism par excellence of the Italian and German varieties, we must admit that there were points of convergence and divergence between these ideologies.[96]

Whether or not one considers the groups examined in this book to be fascist should not diminish the real threat to democracy that they represented. Each proposed an authoritarian vision for the future of France that severely curtailed democratic Republican liberties, effaced political pluralism and looked to build an ethnically homogenized nation in the sense that white, Christian French would be at the head of a racial hierarchy. How a future regime would be installed differed from group to group, from a violent seizure of power to the expectation that the Republic would collapse under the weight of its own contradictions. The new regime – whether a Combatants' State, a Social State, a Popular State or a National Socialist State – would be based on the masculine and martial values of order, hierarchy and discipline. A strain of violent hypermasculinity ran throughout all groups under consideration here. Their plans were represented as the antidote to a democratic regime that had ruined the country and devirilized the nation. Women were afforded little consideration beyond their roles as faithful wives and loving mothers to the coming generations. In this sense, the leagues and parties of the extreme right reflected contemporary thinking about women and their 'duty' to 'give birth, to give birth again, to always be giving birth'.[97] It would be wrong to assume that the extreme right ignored female political activism. On the contrary, several organizations offered women the chance to enter the public sphere through social work. This work was highly politicized and represented an important means to exert influence over communities that were otherwise difficult to reach. Fascist or not, the leagues and parties of the extreme right drove a process of 'incremental drift towards authoritarian government, against a background of institutional decay and political radicalisation' that paved the way for the Vichy regime of the war years.[98]

CHAPTER 1
SEARCHING FOR A FRENCH MUSSOLINI
DURING THE 1920s

On the night of 23 April 1925, two men waited in the shadows on the rue Damrémont in the eighteenth arrondissement of Paris. Jean-Pierre Clerc, a thirty-seven-year-old engraver, and Joseph-Marie Bernardon, a varnisher ten years Clerc's junior, were members of the Communist Party. Armed with revolvers, they were about to commit murder. A short distance away, a company of activists belonging to the extreme right-wing Jeunesses Patriotes disembarked the metro at Jules Joffrin and made their way towards the communists' position. The young leaguers had received word that their leader, Pierre Taittinger, had been threatened with violence during an electoral meeting in the vicinity. Their mission was to protect Taittinger as he exited the gathering. The men marched in a column and sang the Marseillaise as they approached the meeting venue on the rue Championnet. Informed upon their arrival that their services were no longer needed, the column trooped up the rue du Poteau, harassed by a crowd of communists. The leaguers held their formation and continued to sing as they turned left onto the rue Damrémont. At this moment, Clerc and Bernardon unleashed a volley of bullets. Three leaguers fell to the cobblestones, all mortally wounded in the back. The communists fled. Unfamiliar with the geography of the district, they ran towards the police station on the rue Belliard, and into the arms of waiting constables.

Taittinger left the meeting at midnight. Surrounded by thirty bodyguards, he walked towards the Simplon metro station. As the group passed 109, rue Championnet, a man stepped out from the darkness and opened fire, fatally injuring a leaguer. Communist street brawlers chased the Jeunesses Patriotes to the metro where a fight ensued. The leaguers managed to escape on a train, leaving behind them 'quite large pools of blood'; they had beaten back their attackers with canes, truncheons and a fire axe. Similar violence was witnessed at the Jules Joffrin station, where police reported that a Jeunesses Patriotes blinded a communist with his bare hands.[1]

A year later, Clerc and Bernardon stood trial for murder at the assizes court of the Seine. Police had confirmed that the bullets removed from the victims were fired from the Browning revolvers found on the two men. Clerc and Bernardon's defence – that they had fired to protect themselves from a beating – seemed unlikely given that the fatal wounds were inflicted from behind. The lawyers for the defence thus attempted to turn proceedings to their advantage and put the political doctrine of the Jeunesses Patriotes on trial. Jean Piot, editor of the newspaper *L'Oeuvre* and a witness for the defence, summed up this tactic in his deposition: 'For certain simple men, it is evident that ideas are inseparable from the men who represent them. If Clerc and Bernardon fired, it was not on men, nor on Frenchmen, [but] on Fascism.'[2]

Had fascism travelled across the Alps and taken root in France? Historian Robert Soucy believed so; he termed the extreme right-wing movements of the mid-1920s the 'first wave' of French fascism. The Jeunesses Patriotes, founded by deputy and businessman Taittinger in November 1924, was an offshoot of the nineteenth-century Ligue des Patriotes. The league proposed to launch a 'National Revolution' to end parliamentary decadence while in the street and meeting halls of France its uniformed 'centuries' engaged in political violence. Georges Valois's Faisceau, established in November 1925, celebrated Mussolini and sought to imitate its Italian counterparts with blue-shirted legions and a plan for an authoritarian 'Combatants' State'. Meanwhile, the Action Française's ruffians plied their violent trade in the Latin Quarter. The *camelots du roi* street fighters ransacked left-wing newspaper offices and threatened their enemies with purgation with castor oil. In total, at least 100,000 French held a membership to the leagues of the 1920s.[3]

The French left perceived fascism in the leagues. The violence of fascism was central to this understanding. In 1926, the Secours Rouge International, a communist aid organization, published *L'Italie sous la terreur*. The book described the 'pogroms' and the 'orgy of violence' in Italy that had seen hundreds of workers killed. It reprinted quotations from Mussolini that endorsed physical aggression against the left.[4] Communist Marcel Cachin drew a comparison between the French leagues and Italian Fascism, describing the 'punitive expeditions' of leaguers as an attempt to 'bring to France the customs of Italian fascism'.[5] Communist newspaper *L'Humanité* condemned these 'imitators of the Black Shirts' and promised that the party would organize its own defence in the face of the lassitude of the police.[6]

The leagues understood 'fascism' in a variety of ways. The Faisceau emphasized the aspects of Italian Fascism that suited best its own domestic agenda, notably (for Valois at least) the heritage of revolutionary syndicalism. For similar reasons the monarchist Action Française, on the other hand, underscored the reactionary elements of Mussolini's doctrine and drew attention to the role of the king in the Duce's assumption of power.[7] The Jeunesses Patriotes likewise conceived of Fascism as a counter-revolution in the name of order; it distanced itself from the more revolutionary aspects of the ideology.[8] The word, while imported from Italy, was invested with meanings that drew not only upon understandings of the Italian experience but also on long-held values and ideas in French extremist politics.[9]

The Jeunesses Patriotes

In May 1924, the left-wing Cartel des gauches won 286 seats out of a possible 584 in the Chamber of Deputies. The Bloc National – the right-wing alliance that had swept to power in November 1919 – was reduced to 205 seats.[10] The conservative coalition had come to power on a wave of patriotism and a promise to hold Germany to the punitive peace terms formulated at Versailles. The murderousness of the First World War left an indelible mark on France. With over two million men dead or permanently disabled and a further six million veterans having survived the conflict, the war loomed large in political, cultural and family life and few French were willing to forgive and forget. The emergence of Bolshevism in Russia sharpened fears of home-grown revolutionaries especially during the huge strike waves of the early 1920s. The Bloc National was therefore elected on the promise that it would secure French recovery at home and its rightful rewards abroad by administering a dose of authority to the Republic.

The experience ultimately proved frustrating for the right. The government failed to undertake any reform of the regime, missing the opportunity in the eyes of some right-wingers to render the Republic more 'efficient'. Poincaré's invasion of the Ruhr in January 1923 split right-wing and centrist elements in the parliamentary coalition. By the general election in 1924, many right-wingers were disappointed. From the vantage point of 1925, nationalist Jean Binet-Valmer scoffed at the legislature of 1919: 'The *Sky-Blue* Chamber? Oh! How we were naïve, ready for sacrifice, but so unprepared for the exercise of power!'[11] The election result in 1924 and its repercussions – the eviction of Poincaré and the subsequent resignation of President Alexandre Millerand – represented no less than the vacation of power by the right.

Worse still for conservatives, twenty-six communist deputies for the first time took up their seats in parliament. In December 1920, the Communist Party was founded at the Congress of Tours. The Third International seemed even more terrifying than its socialist counterpart and the Bloc National had been intransigent in its anti-communism.[12] The government had sanctioned the use of 'civic unions' against strikers during 1919–20. With the official status as an 'auxiliary' police force the parallels between the unions and the later paramilitary leagues were striking. It was even suggested that 'Civic Guards' wear a sky-blue uniform and be equipped with firearms.[13] The strikers were ultimately defeated, but conservative fear of communism continued unabated. It centred on the impoverished suburbs of Paris, where approximately one million workers and their families lived. Rapid and unplanned urbanization in the wake of the First World War saw the suburbs grow exponentially into 'great working-class ghettos'. This 'Red Belt' was feted in communist circles as the 'citadel of the working class'. Yet for the terrified bourgeoisie, it was the 'nerve centre of French communism'; the capital was caught in the stranglehold of the revolutionary left.[14] The policies of the Cartel – perceived as the 'thin end of a Marxist wedge' – threatened causes that the right held dear.[15] In domestic affairs, new Prime Minister Edouard Herriot announced his intention to extend secularism to Alsace and Lorraine, a move that seemed to target Catholics. In foreign policy, the government recognized the existence of the Soviet Union while withdrawing its ambassador to the Vatican and seeking reconciliation with Germany. In conservative eyes, the Republic was in thrall to the left.

Right-wingers looked to new methods to combat the perceived revolutionary threat. In November 1924, former president Millerand established the Ligue républicaine nationale with a view to creating a mass conservative movement. The league addressed its appeal to 'Republicans of all colours', including those of the Catholic faith.[16] Catholics who feared a new wave of anticlericalism from the secularists in government founded their own defence groups. These were eventually federated in General Edouard de Curières de Castelnau's Fédération nationale catholique (FNC), founded in February 1925. The FNC aimed to 'restore Christian Order to the individual, the family, society, and the nation'; by September 1926 it had 1.8 million members.[17]

A number of extra-parliamentary groups opposed the Cartel. The Action Française took up once again its campaign against the Republic. This was a successful period for the league with approximately 30,000 members across France and its North African territories; its eponymous newspaper sold 100,000 copies per day. The league had shown signs that it was ready to compromise with the Republican system: in 1919, it ran candidates for election, Action Française lieutenant Léon Daudet won a seat in Paris. Furthermore, Maurras had enjoyed warm relations with Bloc Prime Minister Poincaré, notably supporting the latter's hard-line foreign policy on Germany.[18] Some moderate politicians evidently saw practical use in *camelot* violence against the left. In June 1921, for example, an unnamed Radical politician apparently called upon the young brawlers to help prevent a socialist-organized celebration of Joan of Arc.[19]

The movement turned more forcefully to violence after the killing of leaguer Marius Plateau by anarchist Germaine Berthon in January 1923.[20] The *camelots* underwent paramilitary training under the supervision of Colonel Georges Larpent.[21] Police noted that these young street fighters were reshaped into 'a disciplined troop … called upon to play, according to circumstance, an offensive or defensive role in the style of the Italian fascists'. Comprised of men aged over sixteen years, they were grouped into teams of 100, which were themselves divided into squads. Armed with a cane, a knuckleduster, sometimes a revolver and 'blindly obedient', the squads could be mobilized in secret and at very short notice to commit violence against enemy activists or property.[22]

New formations emerged. Antoine Rédier's Légion, founded in June 1924, proposed the replacement of the weak and effeminate Republic with a regime built on order, discipline and hierarchy that prioritized fatherhood and virile masculinity.[23] The largest of the new leagues was the Jeunesses Patriotes. The league was founded in the wake of the transfer of the ashes of socialist luminary Jean Jaurès to the Panthéon in Paris. The ceremony, which took place on 23 November 1924, profoundly worried nationalist observers. *Le Matin* noted that, of the ten flags that flew around the coffin of Jaurès, a lone tricolour fluttered next to eight red flags and the sky-blue flag of the masonic lodges.[24] The presence of communist marchers in the procession implied that the Cartel had accepted Bolsheviks into its camp. The Catholic and nationalist right now feared that revolution was imminent, and with anti-*cartelliste* deputies in a position of relative weakness in parliament, street politics became attractive. As Jean Philippet notes, 'Within weeks [of the Panthéonisation of Jaurès], the right abandoned the parliamentary terrain and gave the impression of recanting on parliamentarianism.'[25]

In December, the Jeunesses Patriotes was launched officially as an affiliate of the Ligue des Patriotes by nationalist deputy and businessman Pierre Taittinger.[26] Taittinger was born in Paris in 1887. His family – committed Catholics nationalists – had moved to the capital from Lorraine after the defeat of 1871. As a young adult, Taittinger worked as a shop clerk and salesman before marrying into money. His wife's fortune enabled him to set up a successful business empire. Her connections further opened the world of right-wing politics to Taittinger, especially those of the monarchist and Bonapartist brand. In 1919, he joined the ranks of his fellow veterans in the so-called Sky-Blue Chamber as a supporter of the Bloc National and the Fédération Républicaine. Re-elected in 1924 and dismayed at the victory of the Cartel, Taittinger sought to unite the disparate forces of the counter-revolutionary right into the Jeunesses Patriotes. The new group benefited from the support of the *Echo de Paris* and *La Liberté* (owned by anti-Semite François Coty); police suspected that several large banks and business interests financed the movement, too.[27]

The Jeunesses Patriotes drew on the same nationalist and plebiscitary politics as the Ligue des Patriotes. Its plan for a 'National Revolution' entailed the curtailment of the legislative powers of the Chamber. Ministers would be recruited from outside parliament while legislation would be drawn up not by deputies but by a Council of State. The league's vision of the future French regime was highly gendered, resting on a martial manliness expressed in military values and a strong executive that would put an end to the chaos of 'king parliament'.[28] The league's propaganda was couched in the lexicon of muscle, might and willpower. To describe such plans as merely a strengthening and modernization of the regime is to both accept that the regime required such action to render it more efficient (a political statement itself) and to ignore the authoritarianism inherent to this reform.[29]

Taittinger pursued a dual strategy in his attempt to build a broad anti-*cartelliste* coalition of the right. Deputies sat on the leadership committees of the league at local and national level. Relations were particularly strong with the conservative Fédération Républicaine; Fédération deputy Désiré Ferry spoke at the first congress of the Jeunesses Patriotes at Luna Park in November 1925.[30] The party – to which some Jeunesses Patriotes referred to as their 'big sister' – looked to harness the league's ability to mobilize the public. In March 1926, Fédération deputy Edouard de Warren wrote to Party Chief Louis Marin that 'we must help the developing Jeunesses Patriotes group to become a force that could prove useful at a certain point [and] which has already been of service [to us]'.[31] During electoral periods, Taittinger's leaguers supported Fédération candidates, providing stewards at meetings, sticking up electoral posters, delivering leaflets and disrupting the gatherings of the Fédération's opponents.[32] The league even courted the support of Radicals with a centrist economic policy that promised to defend small businessmen from communism and unfettered capitalism.[33] By the end of the decade, over seventy deputies in the Chamber claimed an affiliation to the Jeunesses Patriotes; the league's collaboration with right-wing members of parliament persisted into the 1930s.[34]

Simultaneously, Taittinger was prepared to countenance violent street politics. This tactic did not necessarily displease the league's conservative allies. The Fédération Républicaine liked the leaguers' muscular antisocialism, and Taittinger's troops provided stewards for meetings of the party.[35] The Jeunesses Patriotes was organized along paramilitary lines. Paris was divided into sectors with each sector the responsibility of a designated group.[36] Mobile groups, 'shock' centuries and the elite 'iron brigade' were all intended for rapid mobilization in the event of action.[37] Their uniform comprised a blue shirt, a beret and an insignia.[38] Taittinger promised that his 'centuries' were ready to defend France from the threat of leftist insurrection; to this end, mobilizations were staged in Paris as a rehearsal for the coming day of action.[39] The league's associated student group, the Phalanges Universitaires, possessed its own free groups who were often at the forefront of fighting in the Latin Quarter.[40]

Preparedness for violence was a desirable quality in the league's recruits. Members were to be 'young men, determined and ready for possible action, [and] not afraid to resort to violence'. Often recruited from sporting and military societies, they also took physical exercise and shooting classes put on by the league. Police suspected that Jeunesses Patriotes leaguers were armed with firearms (against the desires of the leadership) though it was more likely that leaguers carried clubs and canes, something which Taittinger endorsed.[41]

The Jeunesses Patriotes collaborated with other violent organizations. Leaguers attended the meetings of their ostensible rivals and held multiple memberships.[42] Action in the street could be undertaken jointly, too. On 20 March 1928, a combined force of the Phalanges Universitaires and *camelots* attacked a column of socialist students marching on the rue de la Sorbonne.[43] The divisions between the leagues on the extreme right were surmountable. It is true that the leagues jealously guarded their memberships and stressed the differences between themselves and their rivals. However, such differences could be overcome when necessary. Taittinger stated that though he was a Republican and he did not share the ideas of the Action Française, when the time for action came, his troops would descend into the street and 'fuse' with the royalists.[44] Given Taittinger's hatred of the Cartel, it is difficult to imagine his league defending the Republic with the left still in power.

The violent interplay between the Jeunesses Patriotes and the left contributed to the success of the league. Clashes were common, especially in Paris, and these encounters allowed Taittinger to highlight the threat of violent revolution that communism posed and, at the same time, to herald the bravery of his faithful. Following the killings at the rue Damrémont, Taittinger spoke in the Chamber of Deputies of the 'unheard of savagery' of the communists who had attacked unarmed leaguers and who were ordered to 'fire into the crowd' (*tirez dans le tas*).[45] The killings were the latest incident in a continuum of violence since the turn of the year: right-wing strike-breakers had fired on striking workers at Douarnenez in January; two men were killed outside a meeting of the FNC in Marseilles in February; in April, the Jeunesses Patriotes mobilization at Sèvres had drawn protests from the left. The violence on the rue Damrémont proved a boon for the league, which posed itself in the aftermath as 'the vanguard of the Army of Order [and] its shield'.[46] The membership grew as tens of thousands attended the funerals of the leaguers at Notre Dame.[47] Some activists advised their comrades to carry firearms in the event that self-defence would be necessary.[48] Taittinger counselled against such a course of action, wary of the bad publicity and legal sanctions that violence could bring to the group. But the league continued to hold meetings in working-class districts, a fact that both irked and worried the left.

By mid-1926 the Jeunesses Patriotes had up to 65,000 members, mainly drawn from the urban petit bourgeoisie.[49] Its broad support base attested to the porous nature of the boundary between the extreme and conservative right.[50] The league recruited from a variety of sources; it appealed to students, artisans, white-collar workers and the owners of small businesses.[51] The veteran community provided particularly fertile ground for recruitment, especially right-wing groups like the Union Nationale des Combattants (UNC) and the Ligue des Chefs de Sections.[52] Taittinger was a member of the UNC and the association's veterans frequented his league's meetings. Posts of special responsibility within the Jeunesses Patriotes were reserved for men with military experience. Leadership positions in the centuries were given to former officers, and the elite iron brigade recruited only veterans who had seen active service during the war.[53]

The league's metropolitan success was not replicated overseas, and the Jeunesses Patriotes foundered in France's North African territory. Taittinger took a serious interest in matters of French colonialism, and he rose to become president of the colonial commission in the Chamber of Deputies.[54] He hailed the French civilizing mission while pointing to the enormous economic benefit to be gained in exploiting overseas territories.[55] Taittinger spoke in favour of limited indigenous rights, calling for suffrage to be granted to Algerian Muslim veterans of the Great War; his league founded a Muslim section in 1930.[56] However, the Jeunesses Patriotes' attempt to transpose its political agenda unchanged from the mainland gravely neglected matters of concern for the settler communities. The league was not alone in experiencing such difficulties: the Action Française likewise failed to expand its influence beyond several small sections in Oran, Mostaganem and Blida.[57] Ignorance of colonial politics thus hampered the metropolitan leagues and such mistakes proved fatal given the popularity of Jules Molle's Unions Latines.[58] Molle appealed to the European population of Oran on the basis of *algérianité*, a specifically settler identity grounded in notions of racial superiority. In 1924, he joined with other conservatives to found the anti-Semitic Unions Latines. The group exploited the deep economic and cultural anti-Semitism of the department's settler community. Molle targeted the Jewish community with violence in the street and legal sanction (he was elected mayor of Oran in 1925.) The Unions Latines also sought to cast off the rule of the French Republic in favour of a French Algerian authoritarian regime tailored to the racial hegemony of the Latin races – French, Spanish, Italian and Maltese – of the territory. Molle's death in 1931 hobbled the group, yet the Union Latines had blazed a trail for the North African extreme right.[59] The success of Molle's 'colonial fascism' meant that by the end of the decade Taittinger's league in Algeria was effectively defunct.[60]

While the paramilitary culture of the Jeunesses Patriotes doubtless spoke to young men desirous to test their mettle, the league admitted women members, too.[61] It is difficult to estimate the size of women's involvement in the league. In 1928, the league counted 3,000 women members and 4,000 female Phalangeards in Paris.[62] Yet Daniella Sarnoff suggests that as much as one-third of the membership was female.[63] In one respect, the league's paramilitarism implicated female recruits for they were charged with taking care of the medical treatment of injured male comrades; some even possessed the *brevet infirmière* to this end.[64] Women were employed generally away from the male domain of the street. Under women's section leader Marie-Thérèse Moreau, they engaged in recruitment drives and social work.[65] Their charitable enterprises were deeply political. It was believed that women could better penetrate working-class milieus than men, bringing the message of the Jeunesses Patriotes to hard-to-reach areas.[66] This political role seemed to jar with the league's discourse on female domesticity; Taittinger said that women should be the 'smiling queens of the home', because 'we have no need for amazons'.[67] However, unlike other groups on the right, the Jeunesses Patriotes offered women a chance for activism even if this was defined according to their 'natural' attributes.[68] Moreau argued that 'people who claim that politics is the reserved domain of men, and the home life is that of women, commit a grave error. The life of the *patrie* is that of a *grande famille* and there is not a firm divide between the two domains.'[69] The family was central to the Jeunesses Patriotes' conception of a renovated France. The future France would reject the selfish and childless individualism of the Republic.[70] The league's conception of the nation as a family broke down the barrier between the public and the private sphere, giving women (as mothers) an important role that was compatible with intervention in public life.[71] The enfranchisement of women was a frequent subject of discussion in the league's press and meetings, and it was bound up in concerns about the family.[72] Leaguers argued that women deserved the opportunity to vote to protect their concerns. Equality was not the goal. Women's concerns were framed as 'moral', and it was believed that, given the chance, they would vote to protect the future and health of the family.[73] Family matters were politicized thus, and they came to encompass the future of French youth and the quality of the race, too.[74] The involvement of women in the Jeunesses Patriotes, which offered right-wing women a political outlet that the parliamentary right did not, harbingered the importance of female members to the 1930s extreme right, as evidenced in the Croix de Feu.[75]

By January 1926, the Jeunesses Patriotes had developed into a successful paramilitary movement. In this month, Taittinger split from the Ligue des Patriotes, having decided to place the Jeunesses Patriotes on a more offensive footing.[76] The move suited General de Castelnau, president of the Ligue des Patriotes, who did not wish to associate his organization with such overt activism. Taittinger's decision owed no small part to the emergence of a new league, the Faisceau. The Faisceau's blue-shirted paramilitary units and its self-conscious identification with fascism appeared more energetic than its older counterparts, and Taittinger feared losing members to the group.[77] Consequently, he quit the Ligue des patriotes, taking its most dynamic element with him.

The Faisceau

'Yesterday, on the stroke of midday, fascism officially came to life in Paris,' *Le Matin* thus reported the founding of the Faisceau on 11 November 1925.[78] On that day, 6,000 people crowded into the Salle Wagram, a ballroom in the seventeenth arrondissement of Paris that was a popular venue for political meetings. The audience listened in silence as Jacques Arthuys spoke first. Arthuys proclaimed that, with France on a path to destruction, now was the time to rally the forces that had brought victory in 1918. Salvation lay in fascism, not undisciplined Italian Fascism but a 'measured and thoughtful' variant, more suited to the French national character. Next, Philippe Barrès, son of legendary nationalist author Maurice, told listeners that only the Faisceau could guarantee the survival of the spirit of victory because its young 'legionnaires' were motivated by faith in the nation, a taste for discipline and a deep disgust with parliamentarianism. Finally, Georges Valois took to the stage. He condemned the folly of communism and explained that the path to greatness lay with fascism. The Faisceau's mission was to suppress parliamentarianism and deliver a true leader, a *chef*, to the state. When Valois finished his speech, the meeting broke up to the sound of the Marseillaise. Six hundred men of the league's blue-shirted legions formed into companies and, in rhythmic step, marched to the Tomb of the Unknown Soldier.[79] The striking parade spoke to both the league's imitation of Italian Fascist paramilitarism and its vision for the future of France as a dictatorship of war veterans. Seven years after the armistice, France's first avowedly fascist movement, the Faisceau of Combatants and Producers, was founded.

The founding of the Faisceau caused a stir. André Kaminker in *Le Rappel* noted, 'Blue shirts [and] blue ties, fair enough. A little childishness is welcome these days. But, all the same, six thousand young people, four by four, in compact ranks, six thousand young people who want nothing else than to be the first Faisceau, whatever you think of blue shirts, is really something.'[80] In a similar vein, the anarchist newspaper *Libertaire* reported that if up to that point French fascism had been a subject of ridicule, the meeting proved that this movement of 'bludgeoners' was serious.[81] In relating the news to their readers, the press made frequent mention of Mussolini. René Thévenin in *Ere nouvelle*, for example, called Valois the 'French Mussolini'. For commentators such as Thévenin, the connection between the Faisceau and Italian Fascism was evident.[82]

The roots of the Faisceau in fact lay in the Action Française. The former's founder, Valois, had been a leading member of the monarchist league along with several other prominent members of the Faisceau. Valois was born Alfred Georges Gressent in 1878 to a Parisian butcher and his seamstress wife. Raised in the village of Jouarre (Seine-et-Marne), Valois's childhood was dominated by his Republican grandfather and his nationalist and devoutly Catholic grandmother.[83] As a young man he returned to Paris in 1897 where he mixed with anarchists and revolutionary syndicalists in the Latin Quarter and was greatly influenced by the likes of Georges Sorel and Lucien Jean.[84] However, by 1906 he had shifted to Catholicism and royalism, a result of a spell spent in Tsarist Russia, in military service, and a growing disenchantment with left-wing visions of a post-revolutionary world. His personal transformation was startling; Valois changed from 'a free-thinking, anarcho-syndicalist without ties to job or family into a married, Catholic, authoritarian antidemocrat'.[85] That same year Valois joined the Action Française and published *L'Homme qui vient*, a book in which he denounced democracy and socialism while calling for the restoration of the king as the head of a paternalist and authoritarian state. A talented propagandist, he rose to the league's central committee and was appointed head of its publishing operations.[86]

Valois's post-war work for the Action Française moved him further from monarchism and closer to fascism. His interests lay in questions of economics, especially corporatism, and social transformation. In February 1924, he attempted to convene an estates general of business and financial interests to demand the postponement of the May elections and the installation of a new government with full powers to tackle the burgeoning economic crisis.[87] At the same time, Valois's attention turned to Italy; he visited the country in January 1924 and met with Mussolini. He admired what he saw as fascism's 'revolt of workers, peasants, intellectuals and war veterans against a liberal and democratic bourgeoisie'.[88]

Valois grew increasingly frustrated with what he perceived to be the lack of dynamism in the Action Française. He would later describe his disappointment with the league's 'complete lack of a will to action … [its] salon atmosphere and royalism … [its] squirearchy, [its] cavalry officers and [its] Lady Bountifuls'.[89] He contrasted the league's lethargy with the perceived masculine dynamism of the French veterans. Valois served with distinction during the First World War, and the experience reinforced his belief in military values, hierarchy and strong leadership, as well as in the fraternity of the trench soldiers.[90] He came to consider veterans of the conflict a new source of power and authority in post-war France, above that of the pretender to the throne, and his plan for a 'Combatants' State' began to take shape.[91]

In February 1925, Valois launched the Légions pour la politique de la victoire. In April, he founded Le Nouveau Siècle, the newspaper that would later become the mouthpiece of the Faisceau. Both initiatives benefited significantly from the financial support of right-wing industrialists and businessmen such as Coty, and the Italian government.[92] Valois stressed to Maurras that his new ventures were not intended to compete with the Action Française. However, the die was cast and Valois quit the league's leadership in October 1925. Soon after the founding of the Faisceau, he criticized his former group in the Italian press.[93] In turn, Maurras accused the Faisceau of trying to steal its members, and he forbade anyone from attending the Armistice Day launch or any subsequent Faisceau meetings.[94] By spring 1926, the monarchist league had lost up to 1,800 of its most combative and active members in Paris to the upstart rival, and it haemorrhaged leaguers in other parts of France, too. The Action Française was not the only league to suffer in comparison with the new and apparently most dynamic group on the extreme right. The Jeunesses Patriotes, which up to that point had been cautious in its attitude to fascism, lost 4,000 members in Paris alone to the Faisceau.[95]

The Faisceau comprised a number of distinct sections. The paramilitary legions recruited veterans both of the First World War and the colonial campaigns, as well as men who desired to test their mettle in street violence. The legions wore a blue uniform and carried a cane; their security guards at meetings were armed with short whips and pepper to throw in the eyes of an assailant.[96] Legionnaires received orders to pull down the trousers of opponents and whip them.[97] There were also sections for young French, 'producers' from the industrial and business sectors and a 'civic' Faisceau, which women could join.[98] At its height in November 1926, the Faisceau had as many as 60,000 members. The league was able to organize impressive rallies. In February 1926, the Faisceau staged a large rally at Verdun, a highly symbolic event that was framed as a 'pilgrimage' in honour of the lost generation of the war; 4,000 attended. The Verdun meeting was followed in June by a meeting in Reims that attracted perhaps 100,000 attendees.[99] Its intellectual reach, however, was narrower than that of the Action Française; *Le Nouveau Siècle* had only 4,700 subscribers by mid-1925 compared to the 40,000 who subscribed to the monarchist newspaper.[100]

The Faisceau desired the overthrow of the Republic and the installation of a dictatorship of war veterans. Valois lauded the experience of the war: 'For all of us, the war was a prodigious school … a bath in the deep waters of our people', from which had emerged 'a youthful vanguard for the fight against Republican decadence and [for] the fascist future'.[101] Faisceau leaguer Marcel Bucard – who would found the Francistes during the following decade – spoke of the 'heroic' times of the war and the fraternal links that united all French; it was the Faisceau's goal to reunite the 'willing' (*bonnes volontés*).[102] The Faisceau claimed to speak to the regret of 'true' veterans who had seen the fruits of the victory sabotaged under the Cartel.[103] Unsurprisingly, the league recruited strongly from the veterans' community, especially the UNC, which provided some of the 'most enthusiastic' propagandists to the league.[104]

Like Taittinger, Valois drew on masculine values in his articulation of the future of France. Indeed, the very means by which the Faisceau threatened to overthrow the regime – the mobilization of its paramilitary legions – focused on the figure of the virile veteran and his young disciples.[105] The new state would be a 'dictatorship of the combatant', in which, under a supreme leader, the men of the First World War, having proved their masculine worth in combat, would bring their sense of action, sacrifice and creativity to government.[106] The dictator (not Valois himself but probably a military figure) would enjoy powers to choose members of a new assembly from the ranks of the war generation and France's professional communities.[107] Faisceau members were forbidden from serving in parliament, a fact that differentiated the movement from its leaguer competitors (Valois had himself run unsuccessfully in 1924).[108] Corporations of bosses and workers would manage the economy in the national interest.[109]

Valois was the most prominent political thinker in the league. A 'utopian moderniser', his taste for a technocratic state, fit for the 'age of electricity', in which ideas were drawn from left and right, featured throughout his writing.[110] Other leading theoreticians in the league such as Hubert Bourguin, Jacques Arthuys and Philippe Barrès showed little interest in such new-fangled theories of organization; instead they stressed the nationalist and Catholic virtues of hierarchy and discipline. What united men such as Bourguin and Valois was a shared hatred of communism and democracy, and a love of Catholic values and the family.[111] The Faisceau thus 'advanced designs for an authoritarian corporative state, in which representative assembles of families and producers advised an all-powerful dictator on political, economic, and social needs and desires'.[112]

The Faisceau's plan for a thorough reorganization of the state and the economy, combined with its taste for tradition and authoritarianism, attracted an array of groups, especially technicians, engineers, middle-management and other white-collar workers along with industrialists and businessmen. For these groups, the Faisceau's corporatism seemed to evidence a dynamism and an energy lacking in the other leagues.[113] The league was less successful in attracting working-class supporters despite its anti-bourgeois rhetoric. Valois was serious about attracting workers to his movement. However, lack of funds and the success of left-wing antifascism meant that working-class membership of the Faisceau's corporations lay somewhere between 10 per cent and 20 per cent.[114] It did score a few high-profile successes in securing the membership of some former socialists and communists, in particular that of the former communist mayor of Périgueux Marcel Delagrange.[115] However, for young working-class men looking for a fight, the Communist Party offered its own paramilitary units.[116]

The French family was central to Faisceau ideology.[117] The group conceived of the family as the basic cell of the nation; such importance was placed upon the family that one of the Faisceau's future corporative assemblies would be populated by fathers. The league was, however, concerned with more than the private lives of French families. The nation was a family, a living organism, whose health depended on the sum of its parts. In this respect, Faisceau familial policy extended to concerns for racial health, eugenics and, if necessary, medical intervention.[118] Women were encouraged to join the civic section of the league until late 1926 when a Faisceau féminin was founded. They generally worked in propaganda and administrative roles.[119] Women also contributed contribute articles to *Le Nouveau Siècle*'s family page, but this feature did not appear on a regular basis.[120] The Faisceau's focus on the virile veteran and father left little room for women. The league mixed a progressive rhetoric on the participation of women in the workplace and society with more conservative discourse on the place of women in the home.[121] It devoted little attention to women's political rights, framing female suffrage as a component of the Communist Party's project to seize power. Feminism and communism were considered twin indicators of moral decay.[122] Women in the Faisceau were marginalized thanks to 'the original matrix of war veterans, pronounced hyper-virility and the significant paramilitary dimension of the group' and the conservative and gendered hierarchy of the organization.[123] Mention of women in reports of Faisceau meetings is rare, and the league considered the civic Faisceau as a repository for paper members.[124]

Fascism and the leagues

Shortly after the founding of the Faisceau, the Action Française launched a bitter campaign against the new league. Maurras accused Valois of treachery while alleging that his former colleague now worked for the Ministry of the Interior. Action Française lieutenant Maurice Pujo likewise attacked Valois, labelling him a 'wooden dictator' who had sullied the 'glorious name of Fascism'.[125] Threats of violence accompanied the accusations: Maurras's right-hand man, Léon Daudet, promised to slap Valois 'like the simple servant that he is'.[126] On 14 December 1925, the *camelots* attacked for the first time a Faisceau meeting at the Salle d'Horticulture on the rue de Grenelle. The meeting was intended to mark the launch of the Faisceau's student group, the Faisceau Universitaire. Hardly had Hubert Bourgin opened the meeting when a man in the audience rose to his feet and asked, 'Is M. Valois an honest man?' The question was the signal for an assault. Action Française students in the room immediately started to boo and chant. A fight broke out during which the monarchists let off smoke bombs and the room had to be cleared.[127] 'Between fascism and the king, the fight is on', declared one young man leaving the meeting venue.[128]

In the aftermath of the attack, *Le Nouveau Siècle* struck a conciliatory tone. The newspaper stressed that the Faisceau desired unity and an end to the political and economic crisis in the country. This resolution would not be achieved either by throwing smoke bombs or by fighting between French patriots.[129] Nevertheless, Valois formally severed ties with the Action Française the day after the attack, and he threatened to use the legions against his former comrades if they repeated their attack.[130] A cycle of attack and revenge was set in train. Violence between the groups escalated until the Faisceau's ill-fated attack on the Action Française offices on the rue de Rome in November 1926.[131]

The Action Française's campaign against the Faisceau did not stem from irreconcilable ideological differences. It is true that Maurras and Valois formulated different plans for the overthrow of the Republic and the future of France. Yet later court cases between Maurras and Valois revealed 'more a clash of personality than intellectual differences'.[132] In the provinces, leaguers from the Action Française and the Faisceau continued to collaborate.[133] Rather, competition between the two groups brought them into conflict. It cannot have escaped Maurras's notice that the press had heralded the Faisceau as a new dynamic force in French politics. Meanwhile, since 1924, the monarchist league had suffered a series of setbacks, from the loss of Daudet's parliamentary seat in May 1924 to the failure of Maurras to be elected to the Académie Française.[134] The new league's ability to attract members away from both the Action Française and the Jeunesses Patriotes seemed to suggest that the Faisceau had risen to a position of leadership on the anti-Republican extreme right.

The Faisceau's appropriation of fascism clearly irked Valois's rivals; as a result, the Jeunesses Patriotes rejected the label, perceiving the doctrine as specifically Italian.[135] Nevertheless, fascism could serve as a model for the defeat of French communism, and Taittinger expressed admiration for the dynamism and energy of Mussolini's movement; the Jeunesses Patriotes' rhetoric and organization owed something to his perception of Italian fascism as an army of order.[136] Sections of the league celebrated fascism and desired a wholesale adoption of the ideology. In the Rhône, the Jeunesses Patriotes praised the Italian *squadristi* while advocating a 'Republican fascism'. The more radical sectors of the movement at times grew frustrated with what they perceived to be the moderate stance of the leadership, some of whom were parliamentarians themselves. Was the league simply an 'auxiliary police force for the maintenance of civil peace'?[137] In response to the challenge from the Faisceau and the concerns of members, Taittinger toughened up his stance. The first congress of the Jeunesses Patriotes on 15 November 1925 opened in paramilitary style with troops taking an oath to the dead of the rue Damrémont: 'We will avenge them for all to see, proudly, in the French way, [with] chests thrust forward'. A parade saw eighty-three sections present their standards to the leadership. A number of barnstorming speeches elicited enthusiastic cries of 'Dictatorship! Dictatorship!' from the throng.[138]

Upon the emergence of Fascism in Italy, the Action Française had stressed the kinship between itself and Mussolini's movement, claiming that the former had exerted a formative influence on the latter: 'Before the war and the *fascio* there were in France the *camelots du roi*.'[139] The violence of Italian fascism and of the *camelots* seemed to be a site of convergence in understandings of the doctrine on the right and left. Thus, in 1923, in a self-conscious imitation of the Italian *squadristi*, the *camelots* sent Radical deputy Fernand Buisson a gift of castor oil, with a message: 'We hope to cure your gastric embarrassment by administering this Roman medicine that has succeeded so well beyond the Alps.'[140] Daudet heralded the Blackshirts' repression of the left and Mussolini's returning of the country 'to its origins', something that would be effected in France by the Action Française.[141] The French left, in turn, had levelled its own accusations of fascism at the monarchists. The Socialist Party had referred to the Action Française's 'fascism' when, in the aftermath of Plateau's killing on 22 January 1923, the *camelots* sacked the headquarters of *L'Oeuvre*, *Le Populaire* and *L'Humanité*.[142]

As the rift opened between the Action Française and the Faisceau, Maurras sought to distance himself from fascism, a label now claimed by his bitter enemy Valois. Still expressing admiration for Mussolini, the Action Française declared that Italian-style Fascism was not suitable for France. It now pointed to doctrinal differences between the two movements, as well as posing its own doctrine as superior to that of its brothers across the Alps. Maurras worked to position his league as the true defender of French nationalism in contrast to his foreign-influenced rival. This strategy culminated in the Action Française's attack on Mussolini's claims on south-eastern France in November 1926.[143] Maurras's attempts to differentiate his politics and his movement from both the French and Italian variants of fascism stemmed from the competition between his movement and Valois's rather than an incompatibility of doctrine.[144]

Valois's embrace of the fascist label immediately distinguished the Faisceau from its competitors on the extreme right. He stressed that fascism was not simply a project for Italians but an international phenomenon. Yet it would still require some adaptation to the French context: 'Italian fascism saved Italy by employing methods consonant with the Italian nature Italian; French fascism will use the methods consonant with the French nature.'[145] This would mean using different methods to that of Mussolini in order to remedy French problems. Speaking to a meeting in Strasbourg in April 1926, Valois claimed, 'As a veteran, I condemn violence and I am keen to state that by no means do we intend to use it to reach the goal that we pursue. French fascists do not need to employ the same methods as Italian fascists.' Unlike their Italian counterparts, he continued, Faisceau members were confronted not with the forces of communism or anarchism as in Italy, but with parliamentary impotence.[146]

The Faisceau's desire to distance itself from its rival forced Valois into some uncomfortable policy decisions. The association with Italy hurt the league during a spate of border incidents between Italy and France in late 1926.[147] Furthermore, the issue of monarchism was a thorny one. Valois had privately retained his royalism and enjoyed close relations with the pretender to the throne, the Duc d'Orléans, in exile in Belgium. Yet the Action Française's monopoly on monarchism prompted the Faisceau to take up an increasingly anti-monarchist position. This upset a number of members who resigned in protest. Valois broke definitively with monarchism only after the death of the Duc in

April 1926. If the Action Française had lost some of its more dynamic members following the Faisceau's appropriation of the fascist label, the Faisceau likewise was damaged by its attempt to separate itself from monarchism. Maurras's decision to allow the readmission of former members who had defected to his rival further weakened the Faisceau's position.[148]

To a certain extent, the conflict with the Action Française worked to the benefit of the Faisceau. Following an incident in Lyon in April 1926, during which a *camelot* threw a pot of mustard at Barrès and Arthuys, Valois flew into a rage and declared his intention to 'flog' (*cravacher*) Pujo. Barrès dissuaded his comrade from taking such rash action, explaining to Valois that though the monarchist campaign was a nuisance, the very existence of the Action Française served the cause of the Faisceau. Maurras's league seemed more extreme than the Faisceau and Barrès believed that the public would not rally to the fascist party if it was the most extreme party in France.[149]

Barrès was right to counsel caution for, when Valois did eventually order an offensive against the Action Française, the results were damaging to the fascist league. On 14 December 1926, Faisceau leaguers gained entry to the offices of the monarchist league situated on the rue de Rome. A brawl ensued between fascists and royalists and revolver shots were exchanged. The attack, though much to Valois's delight for he had finally avenged the attack at the Salle d'Horticulture, sparked a wave of resignations of members who disliked such disorderliness and those who were tired of the dispute between the brother-enemies of the extreme right. Several financial backers withdrew their money and the league was crippled.[150]

The decline of the leagues

In the mid-1920s, the extreme right-wing leagues attracted tens of thousands of French to their various projects for the reform or removal of the Republic. At the other end of the political spectrum, the Communist Party had approximately 76,000 members by the end of 1924.[151] The backing of a portion of conservatives, many of whom were parliamentary deputies, indicated that right-wing support for the Republic was tenuous. The perceived threat from the revolutionary left and the apparent weakness of the Cartel government created a situation that echoed not a little that of Italy before the March on Rome. Nonetheless, French democracy survived the 'first wave' of French fascism. In July 1926, conservative Raymond Poincaré returned as prime minister when a financial crisis caused the collapse of the Cartel government. Right-wingers were now reassured that their interests could once again be pursued through parliamentary channels. A government clampdown on the extreme left further endeared conservatives once again to the Republic.[152] With the right back in power, the leagues went into decline.

Taittinger expressed support for the Poincaré government and his league backed conservative candidates running for parliament in 1928.[153] Taittinger was himself elected along with seven other Jeunesses Patriotes candidates.[154] The Jeunesses Patriotes' backing for the Poincaré government revealed its dual strategy rather than its inherent Republicanism. Taittinger was nevertheless required to walk a difficult path between members who backed this policy of parliamentary engagement and more radical activists who demanded action rather than compromise.

In 1926, the Action Française ran into serious difficulties in its relationship with the Catholic Church. The league had long been the refuge of hard-line Catholics who had refused to reconcile themselves to the secular Republic. In December 1926, the Vatican condemned the Action Française, its newspaper and Maurras's writings; all were added to the Index Librorum Prohibitorum, a list of banned publications. The move dealt a severe blow to the league.[155] Worse was to follow for members. In March 1927, the pope threatened with suspension all priests who belonged to the movement. The following year, Action Française members were denied the right to Catholic marriages and funerals. By 1930, the league's membership stood at 30,000, half of its size in 1925.[156]

The Faisceau's decline made itself felt only months after Poincaré became prime minister. In fact, the league was still growing fast even by November 1926.[157] However, the Reims rally in June 1926 had emptied the Faisceau's coffers, leaving it unable to act when the ministerial crisis struck a month later. A third meeting planned for Meaux, at which the 'National Revolution' would be launched, was abandoned.[158] Activists grew impatient while waiting for 'D-Day' and Valois's vagueness on when this would be achieved further fanned the flames of discontent. Cost-cutting measures saw Le Nouveau Siècle move from daily to weekly publication; it stopped printing altogether on 4 December.[159] The following year, beset by court cases, disputes with funders and infighting, the Faisceau folded.[160]

The leagues' disagreements about fascism were as much about labels and political positions as about the finer points of doctrine. Maurras and Valois did understand fascism in different ways. The Action Française hailed the reactionary elements of the Italian's programme, underlining the importance of the king of Italy to Fascism's accession to power and Mussolini's ostensible commitment to Catholicism.[161] On the other hand, Valois placed the emphasis on the revolutionary and 'modern' aspects of Mussolini's programme; for him fascism was both an economic and a political project.[162] He feted what he perceived to be fascism's technocratic approach to the state and economy, especially its use of new technologies such as hydroelectric power and production line techniques. Valois's belief that Mussolini was a 'left-fascist' spoke to the Frenchman's own agenda for domestic reform; he would likewise abandon fascism once Mussolini took a perceived reactionary turn.[163] Ultimately, while Mussolini drew admiration in France from across the right, and prompted revulsion on the left, the meaning of fascism was in the eye of the beholder. Contemporaries 'interpreted Fascism in their own, divergent ways, and did not necessarily believe that it was appropriate to France'.[164]

CHAPTER 2
BLOODSHED IN THE CITY OF LIGHT:
6 FEBRUARY 1934

The night of 6 February 1934 in Paris was cold. The sun set a little before five o'clock, and as darkness descended on the City of Light the temperature dropped to freezing point. Parisians out on the street wrapped themselves up in overcoats, hats and gloves; a strike by taxi drivers meant that more people than usual were braving the icy chill of the capital. In another sense, Paris was ablaze. Anger, passion and hatred heated the bodies of the mob on the Place de la Concorde, the square that lies across the Seine from the Chamber of Deputies. A crowd of thousands, made up of leaguers, war veterans and a smattering of communists, had gathered to demonstrate against the investiture of new premier Edouard Daladier. For six weeks, a poisonous mood had gripped the country. The revelations of government corruption and cronyism in the so-called Stavisky Affair had engulfed the administration of Daladier's predecessor, Camille Chautemps. The press, under the influence of the ferociously anti-Republican campaign of the Action Française, had printed day after day accusations, scandalous revelations and angry demands for retribution. Violence was not limited to the columns of the Parisian dailies: several demonstrations of leaguers throughout January had led to confrontation with the police. When, on 3 February and after only a few days in office, Daladier sacked Prefect of Police Jean Chiappe – a man well liked on the right for his relentless communist bashing – nationalists caught a whiff of conspiracy. Was Chiappe the first victim of a left-wing coup?

The extreme right-wing leagues called for a demonstration against the government on 6 February. Well-established groups made appeals to their members, the Action Française condemned the 'socialist anarchy' and 'masonic swindlers' in government, while the Jeunesses Patriotes warned of a coming purge of patriots. Newer leagues added to the calls for action: the anti-Semitic Solidarité Française demanded action against the Jewish conspiracy in government; the Croix de Feu warned the French that soon they would be living under the sign of the red flag. The leagues were not alone in their appeals to protest: two veterans' associations – the right-wing UNC and the communist Association Républicaine des Anciens Combattants (ARAC) – and a group of Parisian municipal councillors also called on the people of France to descend into the street.[1]

On the evening of the sixth, it did not take long for the mood on the Place de la Concorde to turn ugly. Cries of 'Down with the thieves!' and 'String up the deputies!' rang out in chorus from the thousands of demonstrators. The familiar refrains of the Marseillaise – 'To arms, citizens!' – could be heard alongside the rousing call of the communist International, 'Arise damned of the earth!' Police and riot control officers –

the Mobile Guard – blockaded the Pont de la Concorde, the bridge that linked the square to the Chamber. Further barricades were erected along the main arteries to the parliament building. It was rumoured, too, that the government had requisitioned infantrymen, machine guns and tanks, held in reserve until the protesters looked likely to invade parliament. As the anger of the crowd grew, determined leaguers attacked police officers guarding the bridge. They smashed their fists into the faces of constables and beat their arms and legs with canes. Cobble stones and pieces of iron street furniture rained down on police lines. Rioters cut the bellies of police horses with razor blades affixed to the end of their canes. Frightened policemen responded with baton charges and sabre thrusts. The mood of the crowd verged on insurrection. William Shirer, an American journalist with the *Paris Herald*, described the scenes of violence:

> The square was packed with several thousand demonstrators who were standing their ground against repeated charges of mounted, steel-helmeted Mobile Guards. Over by the obelisk in the centre a bus was on fire. I worked my way through the Mobile Guards, who were slashing away with sabres, to the Tuileries. … A mob of several thousand men were crowded behind the railings, pelting the police and guards with stones, bricks, garden chairs and iron grilles ripped up from the base of trees. … Down on the broad square itself the fighting continued, with the crowd advancing and then retreating before charges of the mounted Guards. It was by no means an unequal fight. The rioters were using sticks with razor blades attached to one end to slash away at the horses and the legs of men mounted on them and they were throwing marbles and firecrackers at the hooves. A number of horses went down and their riders were mauled.[2]

New Prefect of Police Adrien Bonnefoy-Sibour had ordered his forces to defend the Palais-Bourbon, 'at all costs' and to obstruct the demonstrators 'by all [necessary] means'.[3] Police twice opened fire on the crowd, killing two and mortally wounding a further sixteen. Over 2,000 people were injured. The forces of order counted many casualties. Between 5.00 pm and 7.30 pm, half of the police on duty were removed due to injury. An officer of the Mobile Guard received a fatal injury when he was struck in the face by a lump of metal. The doctors and nurses who treated the injured police noted that wounds were in general inflicted by pieces of asphalt, rubble, stones, cast iron, bottles and sticks. Several police had bullet wounds.[4]

As midnight approached, mounted Guards charged the crowd while their comrades on foot beat back the most tenacious leaguers; the square was at last cleared. The Republic had survived and Daladier seemed resolved to defend its institutions from further attack. However, by early afternoon the following day, the premier had resigned, having lost the support of senior ministers and President Albert Lebrun, all of whom feared a repeat of the violence. Daladier's successor, the conservative former president Gaston Doumergue, formed the ninety-sixth government of the Third Republic. Lebrun hoped that seventy-year-old Doumergue – known affectionately as 'Papa' Doumergue, the 'wise man of Tournefeuille' – would be a consensus candidate as the head of a 'truce' government that would satisfy the restive extreme right and bring an end to the threat of further bloodshed.

Lebrun underestimated the leagues' political objectives. The removal of Daladier was only the first step in a desired authoritarian transformation of the regime. In winter 1934, the drawn-out crisis had served further to undermine the perceived legitimacy of the Republic; to many, the regime was in dire need of reform. The right cited the Stavisky Affair and the bloody police violence of the sixth – depicted disingenuously as a massacre of unarmed veterans – as evidence of the rot in the regime. The night was a watershed moment for the extreme right. Polemicist Henri Béraud heralded the *six février* (as it came to be known) as the 'dawn of fascism' in France.[5] A misty-eyed Pierre Drieu la Rochelle was in awe of the unity of the rioters, in an otherwise divided nation: 'In the crowd that rushed toward the Place de la Concorde to experience the great 11 o'clock fusillade, people were singing the *Marseillaise* and *L'Internationale* interchangeably. I wish that moment could have lasted forever.'[6]

The *six février* took on meaning for the left, too. On the one hand, in the immediate aftermath of the riot there was relief on the left: 'The fascist coup has failed', *Le Populaire* reported on 7 February. The Communist Party hailed its demonstration on 9 February as true to the 'tradition of the Communards'.[7] Relief was mixed with apprehension about the threat from the extreme right, and this brush with 'fascism' prompted a reconciliation between the Communist, Socialist and Radical parties that led to the formation of the Popular Front alliance in July 1935. In the long term, and from the perspective of the war years, left-wingers considered the February 1934 riot the beginning of a fascist plot against the Republic. In 1944, socialist Jean Glaive argued, 'If one retraces link by link the chain [of events from 1940], one arrives at the *six février*'; the riot had marked 'the beginning of the sundering of France.'[8]

France in the doldrums

The great Crash of 1929 and the resultant global downturn were felt later in France than elsewhere.[9] Only in September 1931 did the overall level of industrial production begin to decline. To that point, while foreign economies teetered on the edge of the abyss, the French led a charmed life. It was not without some self-congratulatory arrogance that ministers looked to the worsening financial situation abroad and hailed their own financial 'policy of prosperity'.[10] France could not shelter forever from the crisis. By May 1932, industrial production was down 20 per cent compared to the level in 1928.[11] Official unemployment figures grew to several hundred thousand; the real number of men and women out of work was likely at least double that. The 'delayed crisis meant delayed recovery', and as British and German industrial output climbed back in 1934 to the levels of 1929, France would not recover until 1939.[12]

The right-wing government elected in 1928 had responded to the economic crisis with a programme of cuts to public expenditure. Its inability to turn the economy around prompted voters to elect a new Cartel des gauches in the elections of May 1932.

This election represented the biggest success for the left since 1918. While the Radicals and the socialists – with 160 and 132 seats respectively – had worked together during the campaign, it proved more difficult to agree upon a governing coalition after the election. The Socialist Party maintained its policy of non-participation in government. Ministers were drawn mainly from the upper echelons of the Radical Party, the moderate right and a number of socialists who had split from the main party. The passage of legislation to put right the economic problems in France became precarious. The first government of the parliamentary session under Edoaurd Herriot did not break with the financial orthodoxy of its conservative predecessor. Spending cuts and tax increases were implemented in an attempt to balance the budget. A few meagre green-shoots of recovery were perceptible: levels of production improved and unemployment declined. Herriot's government fell in December 1932 over the issue of war debt repayments to the United States rather than its management of the country's finances. Meanwhile unrest grew throughout France with farmers, veterans, shopkeepers and civil servants all voicing anger at their declining fortunes.[13]

The succession of governments that followed tried to cut their way out of the crisis; Keynesian economics received short shrift in France. Few areas were spared: schools, social housing, shipyards, arsenals, ironworks, hydroelectric power production, civil servants – the axe of austerity fell upon them all. The relative recovery seen under the Herriot government was choked off. Real unemployment crept towards one million. Many workers were underemployed, suffering a reduction in their working hours to allow their employers to remain solvent. Town and country were hit hard. Urban workers were stretched intolerably. In the early 1930s, for example, unemployment relief in Clichy totalled over 1,000,000 francs; in 1929, the sum was a mere 1,839 francs.[14] In the countryside, prices of produce fell by half between 1930 and 1935; government attempts to fix the market could not alleviate the desperate poverty of many peasants. Homelessness, suicide and starvation became newsworthy stories. In late 1933, Prime Minister Camille Chautemps was faced with falling output, rising prices and unemployment. A large budget deficit and the declining value of exports, along with a fetishistic obsession with balancing the budget, added to a 'prevailing gloom' by the end of the year.[15] The dire economic outlook, combined with apparent government incompetence in monetary matters, served to exacerbate antiparliamentarian sentiment. In January 1934, a police superintendent in Cannes reported that the public held politicians 'responsible for the [present] state of moral and material anarchy. ... Nothing good will ever be achieved while universal suffrage continues. The public believes in the Republic but only on condition that it reforms and cleans itself up.'[16]

The growth in antiparliamentarian sentiment throughout France revived the fortunes of the leagues. Since the 'first wave' of French fascism had come to an end in the late 1920s, the Jeunesses Patriotes and the Action Française had continued to operate on a reduced scale, roughing up opponents (and, on occasion, each other) in the street, while providing security for right-wing political meetings. The crisis of the early 1930s reinvigorated these leagues, giving new resonance to their campaigns against the Third Republic.

Several new leagues emerged. In June 1933, the Solidarité Française, led by Jean Renaud, was founded with the support of perennial right-wing financier Coty. Coty had launched the cheaply priced newspaper, *L'Ami du peuple*, in 1928 with the intention of shaping a new populist right-wing movement; the publication became the mouthpiece of the Solidarité Française. Renaud threatened to violently bring down the Republic and replace it with an authoritarian and corporatist state. He promised that on the coming D-Day, 'if at seven in the morning [we] attack and take power … at eight o'clock [communist newspaper] *L'Humanité* will be gotten rid of, [socialist newspaper] *Le Populaire* will be banned, Freemasonry expelled. … And at nine o'clock, [socialist leader Léon] Blum will be court martialled.'[17] In early 1934, the league claimed to have 250,000 members, a number that would have made it one of the most successful movements on the French extreme right. The actual size of its membership was closer to 20,000.[18] In the main, members were war veterans and right-wing journalists, with a handful of representatives from the liberal professions.[19]

The Solidarité Française's muscular street politics recalled that of the Faisceau. Renaud possessed a contingent of 3,000 shock troops in Paris that it could mobilize at short notice.[20] These men dressed in blue shirts, dark berets and leather boots, and were fond of the fascist salute. In a 'subtle mix of transalpine imitation and national identity', the blue of their uniform was intended to emphasize their Frenchness. These paramilitaries were the embodiment of strength, virility and devotion to Renaud.[21] Their use of punitive expeditions and their admiration for purgation with castor oil suggested further similarities with fascism abroad. Renaud, however, rejected the term 'fascism', for it had 'no meaning in France'. He further saw in Nazism a biological theory of racial purity and the state that was alien to France. Renaud did not reject racism – the league was thoroughly anti-Semitic – but he preferred to formulate a 'specifically French national-socialism' rather than copy models from abroad.[22]

In September 1933, former Faisceau leaguer Marcel Bucard founded the Francistes. Bucard was a war hero who had been profoundly affected by his experience of the conflict: it 'completely shattered, to the point of absurdity, my idea of life', he wrote, 'did we ever come back from [the front]?'[23] The Francistes were a small group whose implantation throughout France was patchy. The league was strongest in Paris and its surrounding region. It counted a good number of sections in Lorraine. Compared to its rivals, the league was small and its ability to self-publicize was greater than the size of its 1,500-strong membership.[24] Nevertheless, the group caused alarm on the left because of its predilection for, and celebration of, violence, its indulgence in racism and anti-Semitism and its open admiration for foreign fascism (in turn Mussolini provided the Francistes with 50,000 francs each month by the mid-1930s).[25] Left-wing groups perhaps feared, too, Bucard's attempt to break the grip of the socialists and the communists on the French working class. His strategy in this area mixed violent paramilitarism and social work in a way typical of other leagues of the period. On the one hand, the Francistes leaguers struck at the left in some much-publicized incidents of political violence.[26] On the other hand, the league distributed clothing to the impoverished, set up a soup kitchen and ran youth camps for children and young people. The two prongs of the strategy were not altogether distinct from each other. According to Henri Noguères, who was active in the interwar socialist movement, young holidaymakers at the Francistes camps were trained not only in physical exercise but also in the best means to strangle and break the neck of an opponent.[27]

The most successful league of the 1930s was the Croix de Feu. Founded in November 1927, the Croix de Feu appealed to an elite of war veterans who had won medals for action under fire. Like most other veterans' associations, it professed a strident and apolitical antiparliamentarianism. Unlike its veteran counterparts, the Croix de Feu was a paramilitary group. The league came to national attention when in November 1931 a contingent of Croix de Feu leaguers led by Lieutenant-Colonel François de La Rocque stormed the stage at the Trocadero disarmament conference.[28] La Rocque took over the reins of the league in May 1932. By winter 1934, the colonel could count on 35,000 faithful followers. Certainly, this number was far from the half a million members that the league would claim in 1936, but in 1934 it made it one of the leading forces on the extreme right.[29]

While the extreme right-wing leagues were the most vociferous critics of the parliamentary regime, antiparliamentarianism spread to ostensibly more moderate groups. Disdain for parliament and politics united the diverse associations of the veterans' movement. Dominated by the centre-left Union Fédérale and the conservative UNC – each had close to one million members – the veterans juxtaposed the virtuous ex-serviceman who had shed his blood for France with the corrupt and self-serving politicians. A new assertiveness took hold of sections of the veterans' movement during 1932. When the Herriot government threatened a reduction in their allowances, the three-million-strong *anciens combattants* movement launched a 'battle for pensions'. Deputies several times voted down the government's project but the damage was done: the veterans were a large cross-party constituency and the threatened cuts sharpened their already bitter antiparliamentarianism.[30] In October 1933, the UNC published its so-called Wagram manifesto, which was read by many as a declaration of the association's desire to intervene in politics. At the same time the inter-associational veterans' Confederation outlined 'plans for taking over the railways, marching on the prefectures, occupying telephone centres and disrupting communications and creating and arming groups capable of rapid movement'.[31]

On the eve of the *six février*, dissatisfaction with the Third Republic was broad, touching sectors of society beyond the immediate constituencies of the leagues. The movement against the parliamentary regime was ostensibly fractured. The leagues guarded their memberships with a ferocious jealously while seeking to tempt French men and women away from their rivals. Men like La Rocque, Taittinger, Renaud and Bucard desired to taste power for themselves alone; a power-sharing arrangement could not be countenanced. In any case, were not the aims of the leagues incompatible? The monarchist Action Française demanded the return of the king of France, a prospect that a fascist like Bucard would hardly have found appealing. However, though the leagues may have professed the incompatibility of their programmes, such claims owed more to the hard-nosed reality of political competition rather than to profound ideological differences.[32] It was not unusual for members to belong to several leagues simultaneously, playing 'musical chairs' between them.[33] Meanwhile, moderates and conservatives flirted with the leagues. Veterans from the UNC and other right-wing groups held memberships to the extreme right-wing formations. The conservative press indulged in antiparliamentarianism even if its language was less extreme than that of the extreme right.[34] During the crisis of 1934, the campaign against the rotten Republic was vigorous.

Lighting the fuse: The Stavisky Affair

The Stavisky Affair exploded into this context of economic crisis and political activism. In December 1933, *L'Action Française* revealed for the first time the shady connections between prominent members of the governing Radical Party and the fugitive fraudster Stavisky.[35] The Republic was no stranger to political scandal. In the previous six years alone, the Hanau, Oustric and Aéropostale affairs had seen leading politicians implicated in some decidedly insalubrious politico-financial dealings.[36] Affairs, wrote author and far right sympathizer Robert Brasillach in 1941, were the common practice (*monnaie courante*) of the parliamentary regime. 'But', he added, 'we had not yet known a drama quite as vast, as rich, as mysterious [as the Stavisky Affair], to shake up the whole country'.[37]

Serge Alexandre Stavisky was a man of Ukrainian-Jewish descent. After conducting a number of shady deals, he was arrested in July 1926 and spent over a year in police custody awaiting trial. However, before he could come to trial, Stavisky was released from prison, ostensibly on the grounds of his deteriorating health, to await his court date in more comfortable surroundings. Stavisky was still at liberty seven years later, his court date having been postponed an astonishing nineteen times despite the eighty files on him held by various branches of the national and Parisian police forces.[38] Stavisky's brush with the law had not deterred him from his lucrative (and criminal) pursuits, and he had built up a substantial network of contacts in the press and political establishments. His business empire included newspapers, a Parisian theatre and race horses; in his pockets were not a few policemen, too.[39] Unafraid to flaunt his wealth, the 'delightful scoundrel' Stavisky could be found at the door of his Parisian night club, 'the perfect host in evening-dress, orchid in his buttonhole and calculated smile on his face'.[40]

The game was up for Stavisky in 1933 when his latest scam involving the Bayonne municipal pawnshop emerged. In setting up the swindle, it appeared that Stavisky had benefited from the support of Radical deputy Joseph Garat. Radical involvement in Stavisky's affairs ran deeper. The responsibility for the repeated postponement of Stavisky's trial lay with the office of the Parisian public prosecutor Georges Pressard. Pressard happened to be the brother-in-law of Radical Prime Minister Camille Chautemps. He had ordered assistant prosecutor Albert Prince to turn a blind eye to the swindler's mushrooming business empire on more than one occasion.[41] For *L'Action Française*, the story of a Jewish immigrant fraudster and his sordid con-jobs facilitated by the connivance of the upper echelons of the masonic Radical Party – Pressard and

Chautempes were both Freemasons – was almost too good to be true. The newspaper broke the news during Christmas 1933 and Stavisky fled.

The press played a central role in the spread of scandal, often with the intention of impugning Republican governments, if not the regime itself. In a climate of declining sales and meagre incomes from advertising, 'most papers [and journalists] sold their news columns to anyone that paid'.[42] Stories of plots and conspiracies abounded, and the Affair took on a momentum of its own. The Action Française led the charge against the government.[43] Its newspaper conducted a relentless campaign against the corruption of Stavisky, the Radical Party and the Republic; 'All the tricks of rabble-rousing and provocation were given free rein in the most extravagant form'.[44] On 7 January 1934, it launched the slogan, 'Down with the thieves!', aimed squarely at the Republican political class. Just as the Action Française campaign was reaching fever pitch, the situation took a turn for the worse. Stavisky was located at the Vieux Logis chalet in Chamonix on 8 January. About what happened next, there are two versions. According to police, Stavisky invited them to enter the chalet. As officers made their way inside, the fugitive placed a revolver to his head and blew out his brains. The press reported a different story: police had executed Stavisky on the orders of the Radical Party, thus preventing further damaging revelations. Significantly, this allegation was not limited to the Action Française ('Down with the murderers!', the league now raged); it was taken up by moderate right-wing and left-wing newspapers, and the press campaign against alleged Republican corruption widened. On 10 January, *Le Canard enchaîné* famously reported that Stavisky had committed suicide 'with a bullet fired at him from point-blank range'.[45] The paper continued: 'Upon hearing the news of the revolver shot in Chamonix, there was a moment of surprise in the corridors [of the Chamber of Deputies]. Then, little by little, one saw faces relax, colour return to cheeks, people who for four days had been on tenterhooks could now miraculously breathe again.'[46] The death of Stavisky seemed to indicate to right-wingers that the Republic was prepared to silence anyone that threatened its authority. For the left, the whole scandal was orchestrated in the right-wing press to cause maximum damage to the regime. The government refused to open an inquiry, fanning the flames of public anger.[47]

Street violence accompanied the press campaign. Between 5 January and 5 February, the leagues staged ten demonstrations in Paris, half of which were aimed at the Chamber of Deputies. During the month, police made over 1,600 arrests and 148 officers were injured. On several occasions the leagues worked together during demonstrations. On 11 January, 4,000 activists from the Action Française, the Jeunesses Patriotes and the Solidarité Française demonstrated on the Boulevards Saint-Germain and Raspail; there were 238 arrests and 22 police injured. On 27 January, the three leagues once again took to the streets in concert; on this night, police arrested 317 and 83 officers were wounded.[48] La Rocque held the Croix de Feu aloof from the January protests. He had, however, ordered his followers to sermonize on the recent scandal in the street, in cafes, in shops and in waiting rooms, while promoting the Croix de Feu as the solution to France's current ills.[49]

By the end of January 1934, what had begun as a run-of-the-mill scandal had escalated into a national crisis. Whatever the truth behind the Stavisky Affair, the press campaign and the rioting in the street had created a climate of emergency, driven on left and right by a belief in the conspiracies of the enemy. Amid the chaos, Chautemps clung to power until 28 January. Neither the tenacious press campaign against his government nor the violence of the leagues brought down his government. It was another financial scandal, this time involving the minister for justice, that forced the premier's hand. Within two days, President Lebrun appointed Daladier to form a new government. Daladier had, in fact, served as the prime minister for much of 1933, his government falling victim to the toxic financial situation.[50] The son of a baker, a student of history, a war veteran and nicknamed the 'Bull of Vaucluse' for his thick neck and broad shoulders, Daladier enjoyed the reputation of a 'tough, intelligent, straightforward and utterly uncorruptible [*sic*]' man.[51] The immediate priority for his second term as prime minister was to bring an end to the Stavisky Affair. Daladier fixed his sights on Paris Prefect of Police Jean Chiappe.

The 6 February crisis

Chiappe, a native of Corsica, was appointed Prefect of Police in 1927. The post of prefect was invested with a good deal of power: he was a 'civic colonel', whose control over the forces of order in the capital was unparalleled.[52] During his tenure as prefect, Chiappe made a name for himself as an intransigent anti-communist, something that ingratiated him into right-wing circles. Consequently, Chautemps had hesitated to remove the Prefect from office, believing that such a move would be interpreted as a concession to the Socialist Party. Chiappe instead fell victim to Daladier's reshuffle. The prime minister decided that France's premier policeman was to take the fall for Stavisky's repeated evasion of justice. On 3 February, he offered the prefect the governorship of Morocco, hoping to save Chiappe's blushes with a transfer. When Chiappe refused, Daladier sacked him.[53] The following day, the right-wing press railed against the government. Chiappe's removal was interpreted at best as a backhander to the socialists and at worst as the first indication that a left-wing coup was in the offing. The UNC called its members to demonstrate on the evening of 6 February, the day of Daladier's investiture. The association felt particularly aggrieved: it had already postponed a demonstration scheduled for that day upon Chiappe's special request. Yet the UNC's decision to act was perhaps inspired, too, by the desire to disentangle itself from the scandal: its president Henry Rossignol had resigned following allegations that he was an acquaintance of Stavisky.

Inspired by the UNC's lead, the leagues followed suit. Calls to demonstrate on the evening of the sixth flooded the newspapers and the public noticeboards of Paris. Action Française called on the French people to demonstrate their disgust at the government and 'this despicable regime'. In its newspaper, the league promised that the guilty would be 'struck down as they deserve to be'.[54] The Solidarité Française and the Jeunesses Patriotes warned that socialist dictatorship and civil war were imminent; the French must not forget that they were 'the sons of 1789' and duty bound to take direct action. A group of right-wing municipal councillors produced a poster that drew, too, on the revolutionary heritage of the capital: 'People of Paris, your representatives have not forgotten that the tricolour flag and the Republic itself were first conceived in the Hôtel de Ville.' On 3 February, La Rocque had placed all sections of the league in a state of alert should the Croix de Feu be required to intervene if the 'various initiatives' of the extreme left bore fruit.[55] A Croix de Feu poster displayed on the streets of the capital on the morning of the sixth alerted readers to the threat from a government 'whose sign is the red flag'. The league was determined to 'establish a Government of good Frenchmen who are free from political chicanery'.[56]

The groups did not call explicitly for the destruction of the Third Republic in their appeals to the people of Paris. Their anger seemed directed instead at the Daladier administration while their goal was a change of government rather than a change of regime. Yet the appeals were ambiguous. What did the Solidarité Française mean when it urged the French to be 'masters in their own house, with brooms in their hands!'? Could the promise of the Jeunesses Patriotes to 'silence the political factions and give the nation the leader it deserves' be interpreted as a threat to the Republic itself? How exactly would the Croix de Feu 'sweep away [the] shameful divisiveness' of politics?

The leagues and the UNC selected neither a single meeting place nor time. The Action Française requested that its members and sympathizers gather on the Place de la Concorde at the close of business. Taittinger convened the Jeunesses Patriotes to the Hôtel de Ville at 7.00 pm. The Solidarité Française summoned its followers to meet at the same time on the boulevards around the Opéra and Richlieu-Drouot. Veterans from the UNC would meet near the Grand Palais at 8.00 pm, with their rivals in the communist ARAC gathering close by. Lastly, the Croix de Feu was the only group to call its members to meet on the left bank, in the streets to the rear of the Chamber of Deputies.[57] It thus appeared that the leagues would not work together on the night of the sixth as they had done several times in January. However, the groups' diverse rallying points formed a circle around the Chamber of Deputies. French democracy would be gripped in a stranglehold.[58]

At 3.00 pm on 6 February, the parliamentary session commenced. Daladier took to the tribune. The prime minister had barely uttered a sentence when the Chamber descended into uproar. Deputies hurled insults at each other, whistled and booed. Communists and nationalists bellowed their respective anthems. Deputy Marcel Déat described Daladier: '[He was] crimson, flushed, staring into the distance, face tense, after having read aloud his statement during the tumult, [he] seemed unable to continue the debate.' Barely twenty minutes after its opening, the session was suspended. When proceedings began again an hour later, the government carried a motion of confidence.[59]

Outside, the forces of order were preparing the defence of the Palais-Bourbon. A line of police vans formed a barricade across the bridge, in front of which was stationed the bulk of the men on duty. Rather than take a position of forward defence and occupy the square, it was decided that the best means of defence would be to obstruct the main artery to the Chamber across the river. This fact indicated that the police leadership was not prepared for the task ahead of it. Prefect Adrien Bonnefoy-Sibour was new to his post and could not rely on the head of the municipal police Paul Guichard, who had taken sick leave. Bonnefoy-Sibour oversaw operations on the Pont de la Concorde, worried, isolated and chain-smoking.[60] Combined with this inexperience at the senior levels of the police on the night, intelligence services underestimated both the size and mood of the demonstration. There was also confusion as to who was directing the Mobile Guard, technically a part of the army, but under civilian control on the night.[61] Events were about to turn ugly. Scuffles between police and protesters – mainly Action Française toughs whose number was swelled by curious onlookers – began at about 6.00 pm as officers attempted to clear the southern section of the square closest to the bridge. Angry leaguers halted a bus, smashed its windows and set it ablaze with a flaming copy of *Le National*, the newspaper of the Jeunesses Patriotes.[62]

A short distance away at the Place du Châtelet, the Jeunesses Patriotes began to assemble. Police had denied the group access to the agreed meeting place in front of the town hall, fearing the insurrectionary potential of the location. The Parisian municipal council was an important force in the capital's politics. When the left was in power, conservatives considered the council a formidable means by which to combat their opponents.[63] Right-wing councillors had fomented the street agitation throughout January 1934, depicting the Hôtel de Ville as in touch with the mood of the capital in contrast to the aloofness of the Radical government.[64] Leading members of the council were sympathetic to the protesters. Georges Lebecq, president of the UNC and a member of the Jeunesses Patriotes, sat on the council for the St Victor district.[65] Leader of the Jeunesses Patriotes, Taittinger, also held a seat on the council.[66] On the evening of the sixth, he led the Jeunesses Patriotes leaguers and several nationalist councillors across the river to approach the Palais-Bourbon from the east. Later in the evening, this self-styled 'Committee of Public Safety' managed to reach the Chamber, albeit reduced in number thanks to their encounters with several police barricades along the riverside. The group demanded to meet with Daladier in order to secure the resignation of the government. They met the premier, but their plan failed.[67]

To the rear of the Palais-Bourbon, the Croix de Feu gathered. La Rocque was not present. The lieutenant colonel spent the evening in an apartment in the Ternes district of Paris in regular communication with his troops. Leaguers provided La Rocque with updates on developments in the street while Etienne Riché, deputy for the Ardèche, kept the lieutenant colonel abreast of developments in the Chamber via telephone.[68] Two thousand Croix de Feu leaguers met on the Boulevard des Invalides. Their plan was to march north along the rue de Bourgogne and approach the Chamber of Deputies from the rear. Along the way they encountered police barricades at which there were heated exchanges with officers. La Rocque soon gave the order, relayed by telephone, for his troops to disperse. A number crossed the river and joined the demonstration on the right bank.[69]

At 7.25 pm, Daladier's government won a second motion of confidence. The situation on the Place de la Concorde was one of anger, fear and confusion. Street lamps had been smashed and, while the bus that was ablaze provided some light, the darkness made it difficult to see what was happening.[70] The pressure on police lines was immense thanks largely to the arrival of the Solidarité Française on the scene. The leaguers had gathered between Richelieu-Drouot and the Opéra at 7.00 pm and had then marched to the Place de la Concorde. They swarmed towards the Chamber, unleashing a hail of projectiles, throwing ball bearings and firecrackers at mounted officers and pummelling officers on the front line with their canes and their fists. Policemen on the bridge – cold and exhausted from several hours' duty – now feared being crushed between the enraged crowd and the line of vans stationed behind them. Suddenly, a volley of gunfire sent the rioters fleeing for their lives.[71] The violent defence of the bridge deterred some leaguers. Solidarité Française lieutenant Vinceguide decided to pull his troops back to the rue Royale.[72]

As news from the Place de la Concorde reached parliament, pandemonium reigned in the Chamber of Deputies. 'Government of murderers!', shouted Georges Scapini, a nationalist deputy and blind war veteran.[73] Cries rang out from the right ('Resign!') and from the far left ('Soviets! Soviets!').[74] Angry deputies several times came to blows with each other.[75] In spite of these divisions, the government carried a third and final vote of confidence at 8.15 pm, with the support of the Socialist Party. As the noise of the mob grew louder, several members slipped away, some disguised in the clothes of working men, fearing a lynching should the demonstrators break in. From the Ministry of the Interior, Eugène Frot directed the defence of the Palais-Bourbon: 'Nearly without interruption, I was called by telephone [by deputies] from the Chamber; Daladier's entourage bombarded me with questions, asking what was happening with the demonstration, what the security force was doing, if every measure had really been taken to defend the Palais-Bourbon.'[76] On the door of the press room, panicked journalists scrawled a sign: 'Notice to demonstrators: No deputies in here!'[77]

The riot on the Place de la Concorde was about to reach a critical moment with the arrival on the square of the UNC. At the head of the column were seven Parisian councillors, led by Lebecq. Police estimated the size of the UNC column to be 8,000-strong, made up of veterans of the UNC and ARAC, members of other groups, notably the Croix de Feu, and bystanders.[78] As the column marched along the Avenue des Champs-Elysées, its members sang the Marseillaise and popular songs from the war such as the Madelon. At the head of the column a large banner proclaimed: 'We want France to live in honour and purity.' The march of the war veterans, their medals glinting, walking canes aiding their passage and the empty sleeves of the *mutilés*, presented so formidable a sight that police officers reportedly saluted.[79]

Upon reaching the square, voices in the UNC procession cried, 'To the Chamber!' and a contingent of marchers, likely leaguers and angry veterans, broke away and rained projectiles down on the bridge. However, the bulk of the column turned away from the Chamber of Deputies and proceeded towards the Madeleine. As it reached the square to the north of the Place de la Concorde, the column split once again. Lebecq led a group down the rue du Faubourg Saint-Honoré, at the end of which lay the palace of the president. Along this narrow street the veterans encountered fierce police resistance.

Three barricades blocked the way; the veterans of the UNC overcame them all. Only when the marchers were within sight of the presidential residence did officers manage to force them back, thanks to repeated blows from their truncheons and sabres. Lebecq was injured in this fighting; a photograph of his bloodied face was reproduced in several publications in the days following the riot.[80]

By 10.00 pm, police officers and guards were exhausted, and Bonnefoy-Sibour feared that a further charge towards the bridge from the rioters might break through police lines and into the Palais-Bourbon. The situation became critical when, shortly after the hour, a mass of demonstrators gathered once again on the square. This mob contained a diverse array of individuals, from enraged veterans who had been brutalized on the rue du Faubourg Saint-Honoré to youths looking for a fight. Leaguers from all associations were spread throughout its ranks. The mass pushed towards police lines, breaking through one barricade and threatening the last line of defence on the bridge. This was the most critical moment of the night, thought Camille Marchand, deputy director of the municipal police. Officers came under intolerable pressure and many were injured. Police chief Louis Ducloux described the scene: 'The frenzy of the assailants was at its height. … Wedged against the lorries drawn up behind them, the police were crushed, lifted off the ground and in danger of being thrown into the Seine.'[81] Officers responded with brutal violence. Some constables and guards opened fire once again while their comrades chased down rioters and beat them unconscious. The forces of order at last gained the upper hand. A final charge by the mounted Mobile Guards with their comrades on foot in pursuit cleared the square.[82]

On the cold streets of Paris at the height of the riot the semantics of the league's calls did not limit the scope of their action. The literal 'exchange of blows' – Dobry's term – raised the stakes repeatedly as the riot developed its own momentum.[83] The anger of the mob threatened to carry away all before it. This anger sharpened once the police had opened fire on the crowd, and it united the demonstrators in a single cause. In the heat of the riot contagion spread and demonstrators broke out of the narrow confines of their associations to mingle in the street.[84] Bruised, beaten and shot at, their reason for protesting – to bring justice to the Stavisky criminals – seemed unsatisfyingly limited. What good would a mere change of government now do? The whole sorry Republic was rotten.[85]

'An attempted overthrow of the Republican regime'

Daladier released a statement to the press at 11.15 pm. The premier commended the veterans for their sangfroid and for refusing to become mixed up in the schemes of professional agitators. He condemned 'certain political leagues' that had 'attempted an overthrow of the Republican regime', with 'gangs, armed with revolvers and knives [who] attacked constables, Republican Guards and Mobile Guards', and injured numerous officers. Daladier continued that the identity of the arrested men, and the groups to which they belonged, proved that the riot had constituted 'an armed attempt at the security of the State'. When the prime minister made this statement, the full extent of the violence was not yet known. In fact, three people were killed outright during the violence, while a further twelve would succumb to their injuries in the following week.[86]

Though the violence was over by midnight, the state of political emergency continued. Daladier met with ministerial colleagues in the early hours of the morning to discuss a course of action. Frot counselled in favour of taking decisive measures against the leagues, including the declaration of a state of emergency and the arrest of ringleaders to prevent a repeat of the violence. Despite the reservations of Attorney General Donat-Guige, Frot and Daladier decided to act quickly and firmly in order to remain in power and to save the Republic. Preventive arrests were ordered, and cavalry, infantry and army vehicles requisitioned. However, by mid-morning on 7 February, Daladier's resolve had weakened, undermined by voices – including Frot's (who had had a change of heart), the presidents of both parliamentary assemblies, and allies in the Radical Party – that advised him to resign. These men were motivated not only by the threat of renewed violence from the extreme right but also by the desire to save their own skins from association with the unpopular 'government of murderers'. Daladier resigned later that day.[87] It was not a democratic political culture that 'saved' the Republic but the 'naked self-interest' of a handful of senior politicians.[88]

There was further street violence that week. A handful of men died in fighting with police on 7 February, while a communist demonstration on 9 February resulted in fatalities, too. The latter date saw the formation of a new government under septuagenarian Gaston Doumergue, a 'vain, mediocre, and … senile old man', according to Shirer.[89] Nicknamed the 'Mona Lisa' for his permanent smile, 'Papa' Doumergue had held the office of president from 1924 until 1931. His cabinet in 1934 reversed the left-wing electoral victory of 1932. It included men from the right wing of the Radical Party to conservatives such as Louis Marin, leader of the conservative Fédération Républicaine.[90] The left regarded the government as 'pre-fascist'.[91] President Lebrun's hopes for a 'truce' government looked to have been stillborn. Indeed, Doumergue's first address to the Chamber of Deputies on 15 February 1934 as prime minister was greeted from the communist benches with hoots and catcalls: 'Down with the national union! Down with the murderers' government! Murderers! Murderers!'[92]

With Dourmergue in government, the leagues stood their troops down. Yet they were not satisfied simply with the appointment of a new government despite the administration's right-wing bent. The new government was hardly the picture of dynamism that some on the extreme right desired. With men such as seventy-two-year-old Louis Barthou as foreign minister and seventy-eight-year-old Marshal Philippe Pétain at the Ministry of War, the administration was a 'geriatrist's dream'.[93] Many hoped that the wise-man from Tournefeuille would enact an authoritarian reform of the regime; 'There was much still left to play for.'[94] The Jeunesses Patriotes' newspaper Le National informed readers on 8 February, 'We have achieved one of our objectives.' Charles des Isnards, a vice president in Taittinger's league and a member of the Paris town council, confirmed this attitude when he informed the parliamentary commission of inquiry into the riot that a change in government had been merely one of the league's objectives. Had the rioters succeeded in entering the Palais-Bourbon it is likely that the Republic would have been overturned and replaced with a nationalist regime based in the Hôtel de Ville.[95]

Lieutenant-Colonel de La Rocque – who described Doumergue's cabinet as merely 'a poultice on a gangrenous leg' – informed his section leaders on 7 February that the 'first objective' had been achieved yet the 'state of alert' should be maintained; instructions would soon follow. Speaking to the parliamentary commission, the lieutenant colonel denied any desire to supplant the government through illegal action: 'If we had wanted to, we would have on the 5th, at 7.40pm, occupied the Ministry of the Interior, [and] on the 6th, at 8pm, occupied the Chamber. We didn't want to because we are pursuing the re-establishment of order and not the carrying out of a coup.' His intention had been to make a 'demonstrative' display, rather than an 'offensive raid'.[96] La Rocque would later claim that to have invaded the Chamber would have been a short-lived enterprise. Beyond Paris, the French had little understanding of the seriousness of the situation, and the league's action was necessarily limited to forcing the resignation of the Daladier government.[97] La Rocque's rivals came to the same conclusion. Throughout 1934 the leagues made a concerted effort to nurture provincial support through a series of meetings. These gatherings frequently resulted in violence with left-wing counter-demonstrators.[98] The leagues' failure to capitalize upon their political advantage once Daladier was out of power rested on their lack of parliamentary representation. While there were extreme right-wing sympathizers in parliament, leagues rejected electoral competition. They therefore lacked men on the inside who could have turned the situation to their advantage.[99]

The *six février* soon passed into the mythology of the right.[100] In the weeks, months and years after the riot, right-wing opinion understood the night as a massacre of unarmed war veterans at the hands of a corrupt government in hock to Moscow. This myth drew conservatives and leaguers closer together. Deputy Paul Reynaud spoke for many on the right when in March 1934 he told a political meeting, '[M.] Daladier spilled the blood of Verdun [on the *six février*]'.[101] The Fédération Républicaine praised the rioters for their service to the nation. Indeed, a number of the party's members and deputies had been at the centre of the night's political violence: Taittinger, Edouard Frédéric-Dupont, Jean Ferrandi, Charkes des Isnards and Félix Lobligeois.[102] The night provided images and symbols with which the enemies of the Republic would continue to lambast their opponents.

For many individuals, the riot was a formative experience. Vichy's future minister of the Interior Pierre Pucheu claimed that the *six février* sparked his interest in politics; he subsequently joined La Rocque's league and revelled in its spirit of abnegation and enthusiasm.[103] Jean Filiol and Eugène Deloncle, who would go on to found the extreme right-wing Cagoule, were involved in the thick of the fighting on the Place de la Concorde.[104] Louis Darquier de Pellepoix was injured on the night and later founded the Association des Blessés et Victimes du 6 Février; in May 1942 he took over Vichy's General Commissariat on Jewish Questions.[105] Of course, not all leaguers had taken part in the riot. But the night acted as a mobilizing myth to which all leagues laid claim, each alleging to have left more bodies on the 'battlefield' of the Place de la Concorde than their rivals.[106] The victims were accorded the same rhetorical honours as the fallen of the First World War. During the parade to commemorate Joan of Arc in May 1934, a delegation from the Action Française, the Jeunesses Patriotes and the Solidarité Française carried a wreath dedicated to 'The Dead of the 6 Février'. During a ceremony before the monument to the 'Maid of Orléans', the names of the fallen were called aloud. To each one, a single voice responded: 'Died on the field of glory.'[107]

The crisis of February 1934 sparked a radicalization in French politics. Hundreds of thousands of French men and women began to look to extra-parliamentary groups for salvation. On the extreme right, the main beneficiary of this reconfiguration of politics was the Croix de Feu, examined in Chapter 3. On the left, the Communist, Socialist and Radical parties formed the Popular Front coalition in July 1935 to defend the Third Republic against the 'fascism' of the leagues. Political combat moved increasingly from the institutions of the parliamentary Republic to the street where activists confronted each other in ever greater numbers with each fight seemingly raising the stakes. The leagues may not have succeeded in overturning the regime on 6 February 1934, yet the Republic was weakened.[108]

CHAPTER 3
THE ARMY OF THE DEATH'S HEAD:
THE CROIX DE FEU

On 14 July 1935, a man walked silently along the Avenue des Champs-Elysées towards the Arc de Triomphe. In his black suit, upon which were pinned several medals, he cut a solemn but proud figure on his way to a ceremony at the Tomb of the Unknown Soldier. This man was Lieutenant-Colonel François de La Rocque, leader of France's largest extreme right-wing paramilitary league. 'The Croix de Feu, here come the Croix de Feu!' onlookers whispered. Behind the lieutenant colonel marched row upon row of his followers, death's head insignia fixed to their lapels. The procession spread out across the wide avenue, flowing forward like an 'irresistible tide'. A military band played as cries rang out: 'Vive les Croix de Feu! Vive La Rocque!' For admiring onlookers, the fête nationale parade proved the 'magnificent force' of the Croix de Feu, which nothing could resist. La Rocque was the man who would save France from communist revolution and the decadence of the Third Republic.[1] Conversely, the communist L'Humanité remarked, 'One easily imagines greatcoats on their backs, rifles on their shoulders, and in the wink of an eye an army of civil war is ready.'[2]

That same day, barely five miles away at the Place de la Nation, the Communist, Socialist and Radical parties sealed the Popular Front alliance with an oath to defeat fascism in the name of peace. Leading Radical Edouard Daladier shared the platform with socialist chief Léon Blum, his comrade Roger Salengro, and a beaming Maurice Thorez, secretary general of the Communist Party. A crowd of thousands celebrated the new coalition; this great 'human sea' resolved collectively to wash away the forces of French fascism.[3]

In summer 1935, over a year since the six février riot, France was still mired in political and economic strife. The 'truce government' had fallen in November 1934 before 'Papa' Doumergue could realize his reform project. By early June 1935, two more prime ministers had come and gone. A semblance of stability returned (for six months, at least) when Pierre Laval took up the premiership with the support of the Radicals. Laval persisted with his predecessors' policy of deflation. He made extensive use of decree powers – 549 times, in fact – to stimulate economic growth through a reduction in government spending. The decrees led to a meagre improvement in living standards (for they simultaneously cut wages and drove down prices), yet they caused much discontent among civil servants, rentiers and war veterans on a fixed income.[4]

Meanwhile, French eyes looked anxiously across the Rhine with Hitler's intentions towards France in mind. The German chancellor had consolidated his position as dictator following the death of President Hindenburg in August 1934. The slow erosion of the Versailles European order was underway. In January 1935, the people of the Saar, an international territory since the First World War, opted for unification with Germany rather than France. Six months later, Britain agreed to an expansion of the German navy.[5] The image of a Bismarckian and imperialist Germany, 'the anti-France incarnate', still informed the idea that many French had of their eastern neighbour.[6]

Hitler's hostility to the French was well known. Unguarded comments to the press laid bare his hatred of Germany's hereditary enemy. In 1930, for example, he had remarked to the Italian publication *Messagero*: 'We hope that the present face of Europe will change, thanks to a system of alliances with the enemies of France.'[7] Nationalist political groups sought to sensitize their followers to the Nazi threat: in September 1933, the Jeunesses Patriotes published 100,000 copies of a leaflet that warned of Hitler's anti-French agenda.[8]

The first French edition of *Mein Kampf* was published (as *Mon Combat*, My Struggle) in 1934 by the Nouvelles Editions Latines publishing house, under the Maurassian and Germanophobic Fernand Sorlot. Remarkably, the Ligue Internationale contre l'Antisémitisme (LICA) helped to fund the book's French publication, promising to buy the first 5,000 copies with the intention of exposing a French audience to the dangers of Nazism. This unabridged edition was printed without permission and included many remarks injurious to Franco–German relations. In June 1934, Hitler succeeded in having the publication banned in France though Sorlot continued to publish the book illegally. By 1939, it had sold 20,000 copies. An abridged version of *Mein Kampf* appeared in 1938, entitled *Ma doctrine*, with the most controversial sections on France redacted.[9]

To allay French concerns, Hitler accorded several interviews to the French press during the 1930s. On 16 November 1933, Fernand de Brinon interviewed the chancellor for *Le Matin*. De Brinon was only the second Frenchman to be received by Hitler, behind the French ambassador. His conversation with Hitler revealed a man who desired good relations with France.[10] Similar sentiments were expressed in an interview in *L'Intransigeant* in September 1934.[11] Two months later, French veteran leaders Jean Goy and Robert Monnier met with the German leader in Berlin. Hitler reassured the men of his goodwill towards the French and spoke of the mutual experience of French and German veterans, concluding that these men could 'bring peace to the world'.[12]

French relations with Mussolini gave greater cause for optimism. Laval (in his capacity as foreign minister) visited Rome in January 1935 to launch a new era of Franco-Italian relations. The sympathetic press hailed the collaboration of Europe's Latin sister countries. Self-declared French fascists looked to Italy as an ally against Germany: the Franciste René Fery suggested that Paris and Rome erect 'a moral and Latin barrier to barbarous Kultur'.[13] However, later that year Mussolini's pursuit of an African empire with the murderous campaign in Abyssinia saw the agreement break down (although London and Paris were later revealed to be complicit in Italy's imperial venture). By the mid-1930s, the Third Republic seemed threatened from within and without on a variety of fronts. Small wonder that Ray Ventura's song *Tout va très bien madame la marquise* became a hit. The blind optimism – or knowing self-deception – of the lyrics encapsulated the national mood, and the title entered the popular vernacular to be deployed with no small amount of irony.

Following the *six février* crisis, Lieutenant-Colonel de La Rocque appropriated the plaudits for the fall of the Daladier government even though the Croix de Feu had played a relatively minor role in the demonstration. La Rocque vaunted the discipline of his leaguers who had, according to his story, held parliament in the palm of their hand but had decided to act with restraint. The image of an orderly but powerful league ready to strike at a moment's notice appealed to many conservative French especially in light of the emergence of the left-wing Popular Front alliance.[14]

For the left, the Croix de Feu embodied a French fascism. Left-wing parties had watched developments in Germany with unease yet the cause of French antifascism gathered pace only after the riot of February 1934.[15] The example of foreign fascism proved instructive to the left's understanding of the French variant. References to Hitler and Mussolini's regimes appeared in the antifascist press as the left attempted to understand the purpose of the February violence.[16] The 'fascist' uprising in Austria that occurred within days of the *six février* nurtured the belief that fascists took power through armed insurrection. It appeared to confirm, too, the international character of fascism and the transnational portability of its methods. The French leagues' paramilitarism was understood not only as an attempt to break the working class but also as a rehearsal for a coming fascist seizure of power. The Croix de Feu's mass mobilizations and huge motorcades, often directed at towns where working-class organizations dominated local politics, drew comparison with the tactics of Mussolini and Hitler. Within weeks a group of the *six février* left-wing intellectuals founded the CVIA to coordinate propaganda against the fascist threat in France.

The task of understanding what the Croix de Feu wanted is not easy, not least because of the multitude of ambiguous statements that issued from La Rocque and his followers. When, in the wake of the *six février*, the newspaper *L'Oeuvre* asked the lieutenant colonel to explain his Republicanism, he responded, 'I am loyal to the presently existing constitution.'[17] One might rest one's case there, if it were not for the fact that at that very time La Rocque was under parliamentary investigation for his role in the February riot. Furthermore, several months later, in his book *Service Public* (1934), La Rocque outlined his plans for a future authoritarian French state that little resembled the Third Republic. The lieutenant colonel often made cryptic statements. In 1935, for example, he told Bertrand de Jouvenel in the pages of the magazine *Vu*, 'I desire nothing as much as to see a disciplined association seize power [and] to exercise it in a male way but I have one condition: *provided that it works to realise a fairer society*.' How would such an association 'seize' power? And what was this 'fairer' society, in pursuit of which it was worth circumventing – and perhaps sacrificing – the democratic process? La Rocque's pronouncements of a coming day of reckoning with the left – which he termed D-Day and H-Hour – further convinced antifascists that a coup against the Republic was in preparation.

Origins

The Croix de Feu was founded in November 1927 under the leadership of Maurice d'Hartoy and with the financial aid of Coty. The league emerged from the rich associational culture and networks of the First World War veterans' movement. D'Hartoy was a member of the Association des Ecrivians Combattants, which he patronized with right-wing veterans such as Jacques Péricard (a founding member of the Catholic Droits du Religieux Ancien Combattant, and a leading member of the UNC), Ernest Pezet (UNC member and FNC activist), Jean Renaud and Georges Valois.[18] The group's connection to the war and the dead was conveyed in the Croix de Feu insignia: a flaming death's head set upon swords and a Maltese cross.[19] The Croix de Feu consistently re-forged its links to the veterans' movement through participation in the calendar of commemorative events each year; these links gifted the league a certain amount of moral legitimacy. The claim to this 'veterans' mystique' formed the backbone of the group's plans for a renovated French state until its dissolution in 1936.[20]

Veterans were certainly attracted to the movement, perhaps for its promise that the comradeship of the front could be relived in the ranks of the association.[21] However, the Croix de Feu did not cast its net widely in the ex-servicemen's world. Membership was initially confined to an elite of veterans who had won the Croix de Guerre for acts of bravery under fire. This restrained membership was central to the league's aim to form a muscular and masculine 'knighthood' based on military courage.[22] The Croix de Feu's belief in the 'aristocracy' of its members within the veterans' movement saw it hold itself above rival groups, admitting only 'authentic *poilus*' and 'true' combatants – read 'real men' – rather than men who had been mobilized yet who had seen no action.[23] The perceived moral authority of the league drew admiration from abroad: in 1929, Winston Churchill contacted the group, writing, 'I would so much have liked to come to speak to your splendid association.'[24]

In 1929, the league expanded its membership: men who had served on the frontline for a period of at least six months (termed 'Briscards') could now join. The addition of the Briscards saw the membership of the movement increase from 500 in 1928 to 12,000 the following year.[25] The league also founded the Fils et Filles des Croix de Feu (FFCF) for children and adolescents, under the leadership of Duke Pozzo di Borgo. Boys took part in sport and outdoor pursuits akin to those of the scouting movement. Girls were prepared for their future vocation of housewife and mother. By August 1933, the youth group boasted 10,000 members.[26]

D'Hartoy's leadership of the league was short lived. Following a dalliance with Coty's secretary, he was replaced in July 1929 by an interim leader, Maurice Genay. In May 1932, when Genay was recalled to active service, Lieutenant-Colonel de La Rocque took over the reins of the association.[27] A native of Lorient and son of a general, the aristocratic lieutenant colonel was a graduate of the Saint-Cyr officer training academy. He served with distinction in several bloody campaigns in North Africa, growing close to Marshal Hubert Lyautey in the process. La Rocque fought on the Western Front during the First World War, too, and by 1918, the thirty-two-year-old was the youngest major in the army.[28]

The lieutenant colonel withdrew into civilian life after 1926, a *mutilé de guerre* with a distinguished record, mentioned in dispatches no less than eleven times. La Rocque worked for a time at the Câble de Lyon, a subsidiary of the Compagnie Générale d'Electricité, yet he maintained a keen interest in French military and political affairs, growing increasingly disillusioned with the latter as the 1920s drew to a close. His experience in the armed forces influenced his vision of a future France. The lieutenant colonel told his wife in 1929,

> I hear still the marching step of my battalion, alas! ... you heard only one step, only one, such was the unity of my men, a dynamic step despite the hardship, the step of brave men who return home [with] their job done. ... France is growing weak, decaying, we must create elites at every level for her. The horizon is dark. Will we have the time [to act]?[29]

La Rocque joined the Croix de Feu soon after its founding and rose rapidly through its ranks, penning articles on a range of issues for the league's monthly newspaper *Le Flambeau* and giving vent to his evident disdain for politicians and parliamentarians.[30]

Once leader of the Croix de Feu, La Rocque consolidated his control of the movement through the appointment of loyalists to key posts. At the same time, a leadership cult began to develop around the lieutenant colonel. Despite Shirer's rather cutting appreciation of La Rocque – 'he was the idol of the elderly upper-class women in the Boulevard St. Germain' – it was reported in 1935 that for members, '[La Rocque's] voice is their rallying point, his words are their gospel. His name, a magic syllable that electrifies them.'[31] The league's orators were instructed to eulogize incessantly their leader's virtues; the lieutenant colonel himself framed his mission to save France as a crusade in which his 'faithful' were implicated.[32]

Under La Rocque, the antiparliamentarianism of the Croix de Feu sharpened. It is true that the league had indulged in criticism of politicians and their alleged self-interest long before the lieutenant colonel took over. A propaganda brochure distributed in January 1928 stated that the league represented the cream of the *anciens combattants*, who were alone capable of expressing the desires of the victorious nation. Suffused with an antiparliamentarianism that was common to all veterans' associations, the Croix de Feu rejected party politics in favour of 'action by all means', to maintain order in France. It was further prepared to 'descend into the street', in support of the army and police, when the time came to put down communist revolution.[33] The veterans of the Croix de Feu would thus stand at the heart of a national revival in which the threats of Bolshevism and pacifism would be defeated and the French political system reordered.[34] With La Rocque in charge, the league did not shrink from direct action, and it won valuable publicity through several high-profile public interventions. On 27 November 1931, for example, the lieutenant colonel and hundreds of Croix de Feu leaguers disrupted the closing session of the international disarmament conference at Trocadéro in Paris. La Rocque stormed the stage and delivered a short speech while his troops scuffled with members of the audience. Later, he would state that from that moment on, the

Croix de Feu's demands would be heard; indeed, the tumult had been broadcast live on the radio.[35]

Muscular displays of paramilitarism now became central to the Croix de Feu's propaganda. These mass mobilizations and parades were intended to demonstrate the vigour of the league and intimidate the left-wing enemy.[36] The group's paramilitary wing was called the *Disponibles* or *Dispos* for short. Unveiled at a meeting in April 1932,[37] the *Dispos* acted both as a security team to protect Croix de Feu meetings and marches and as a strike force that could sabotage enemy meetings.[38] They were organized into 'hands', each comprising one leader and four subordinates; the hands were in turn organized into divisions.[39] Each section of the league had its own *Dispo* group, with 12,000 in Paris alone by spring 1936.

Members of the *Dispos* were prepared to commit acts of physical intimidation and violence when necessary. Indeed, combativeness was central to the organization; its members were 'the youngest and the quickest to throw a punch [*les plus prompts à la bagarre*] … [and] aware of their mission to protect others. Feeling themselves the most activist, the most devoted to the "boss", they formed themselves instinctively into an elite corps, ready to affirm themselves the most faithful to the "Croix de Feu mystique".'[40] The *Dispos* were forbidden from carrying firearms though some reservists possessed them at home.[41] La Rocque credited the *Dispos* with giving the broader movement its 'aspect of permanent strength'.[42] In November 1933, he reported proudly in the pages of *Le Flambeau* the disruption of a meeting of conscientious objectors at Laon, achieved, 'at the cost of several blows'.[43] The following month, members of the Croix de Feu gave a group of pacifists 'an all-out thrashing', in Normandy.[44] However, like the physical aggression of the other leagues, the violence of the *Dispos* was usually framed as defensive. La Rocque himself wrote that violence was 'the sign of intellectual and social disorder'; it was not the deed of 'courageous individuals'.[45] The defensiveness of Croix de Feu violence was defined broadly and could be perpetrated in response to an immediate or a long-term threat. The league's use of violence became evermore frequent as the 1930s progressed, especially when large left-wing counter-demonstrations aimed to disrupt Croix de Feu meetings.

La Rocque sought to diversify the membership of the league. In 1933, two new groups were formed: the Regroupement National autour des Croix de Feu (for sympathizers and subscribers to the league's newspaper *Le Flambeau*) and the Volontaires Nationaux (for young men under twenty-one years of age, but who were too old to belong to the FFCF). In the wake of the February 1934 riots, the league established the Section Féminine under the guidance of La Rocque's relative and close adviser Antoinette de Préval. Women who had been decorated for their roles as frontline nurses had always been able to join the movement, though there were only 120 such members by mid-1933. In 1934, the new women's sections aimed to better coordinate and organize female participation. The move was a success and, at its peak in 1939, women's membership of the movement stood as high as 400,000.[46]

The geographical and social reach of the league grew in tandem with the size of its membership. From its beginnings as a group based mainly in Paris, by November 1931 half of the Croix de Feu's members belonged to sections outside the capital, particularly in large industrial towns and ports such as Lille and Marseille. The group also attracted significant support in the three departments of French Algeria, with 7,000 members across Alger, Oran and Constantine in 1933; this number more than doubled by 1936.[47] Like other extreme right-wing groups, the Croix de Feu was weaker in Morocco and Tunisia (where the European population was smaller) though it maintained a presence there.[48] As for the social composition of the league, members were drawn predominantly from the aristocracy and the middle class (businessmen, managers, landlords, people of independent means and professionals), that is, according to historian Albert Kéchichian, the social strata who had most to lose in the event of communist revolution. Working-class French were a small minority in the league.[49]

As 1933 came to an end, and the Stavisky Affair gathered momentum, it seemed as if the Croix de Feu's chance might just have arrived. However, while the Affair provided the league's propagandists with apparent proof of the corrupt and decrepit nature of the parliamentary regime, few observers would have predicted the rapid expansion of the movement that occurred in the wake of the February crisis. From an estimated membership of 35,000 on the eve of the *six février*, the Croix de Feu grew to a size of half a million members within 2 years, with 213 sections in Paris and 301 in the provinces by June 1936.[50] Such growth was astonishing; immediately prior to the March on Rome, the 200,000-strong membership of the Italian Blackshirts stood at less than half that of the Croix de Feu in 1936.[51] La Rocque had expanded the elitist veterans' association into a national movement. The expansion of the membership had consequences for the associational culture of the league and by 1935 its martial and masculine culture was weakening, with only one in three members now a veteran. Practising a 'national' politics and seeking to guarantee the fruits of the victory in the face of the challenge from the left and the incompetence and corruption of the Republican regime, the lieutenant colonel sought to build a movement open to all 'true' French men and women, defined according to La Rocque's own terms.[52]

1934: Development into a mass movement

La Rocque persistently denounced the decadence of the scandal-hit regime throughout the winter of 1934. He even issued an open letter to President Albert Lebrun in which he advised that power be handed over to 'a small number of resolute personalities', who would put matters right.[53] Meanwhile, Croix de Feu leaguers were placed in a state of alert in the days prior to the planned 6 February demonstration. In a communication to local leaders, La Rocque instructed: 'The goal that we pursue is to put an end to the dictatorship of socialist influence and to call to power a clean team, rid of politicians whoever they may be and targeting only the reestablishment of national order in external security.'[54] In spite of his threatening rhetoric, privately La Rocque seemed reluctant to commit the Croix de Feu to action; the moment was inopportune for an attempt on power.[55]

In the wake of the *six février*, La Rocque's tone was at once threatening, arrogant and dismissive. He told the magazine *Les Annales* in March: 'The 6 February? My men [fought] at the Chemin-des-Dames and Verdun. For them, that business at the Palais-Bourbon was nothing.' He stressed the order and discipline of his leaguers yet he underlined, too, the fact that it was *his* followers who had come closest to the gates of the Chamber. They had not taken parliament because, according to La Rocque, there was nothing to take: What, in the end, would he have done with these 'public monuments'?[56] It is thus difficult to discern the actual intentions of La Rocque during the crisis days of February. He had perhaps been keen to maintain the independent and ecumenical image of his league, reluctant to be drawn into an attempt on power that was not on his terms.[57] Soon after the riot, the lieutenant colonel's desire to preserve the apolitical patina of his movement saw him decline an invitation from Marshal Hubert Lyautey to march on parliament and seize power.[58]

La Rocque seemed satisfied with the resignation of Daladier and the installation of former president Gaston Doumergue as the head of a so-called 'truce' government. Such an attitude can be inferred from La Rocque's infamous communication to Croix de Feu section leaders on 7 February 1934: 'Government resigned. First objective obtained. Suspend actions until further notice. Maintain alert. Instructions to follow.' This statement was nevertheless ambiguous and suggested further action would be taken should the Doumergue administration fail to live up to his expectations.[59] Whatever the lieutenant colonel's plan, the league's actions on the night catapulted the movement to national attention. Its apparent dynamism, combined with its disciplined and orderly image, was to the liking of many French, and thousands of new memberships were announced in the weeks that followed.[60]

Nonetheless, the importance of the *six février* to the growth of the league should not be exaggerated. Certainly, the riot brought the Croix de Feu much publicity yet the development of provincial sections depended much on local factors, too. In Lorraine, the league gained momentum only during 1935. The crisis of February 1934 renewed the interest of some long-standing members in the league and attendances at meetings grew. However, by the end of the year only two new subsections had emerged in Pont-à-Mousson and Joeuf, and they were too small to operate independently. Twelve months later, thanks to the hard work of local propagandists and a visit by La Rocque to Metz in June 1935, the Croix de Feu counted ten new sections and subsections. The prefect of the Meurthe-et-Moselle suggested that the league had grown in reaction to the activities of the 'extreme left groups' in his department during 1935. If the *six février* was a landmark in the expansion of the Croix de Feu throughout France, it did not automatically prompt an explosion in membership. The decision to join the league still depended much on local circumstances, the work of activists and the cycle of interaction with opponents.[61]

The decline of the Croix de Feu's extreme right-wing rivals doubtless helped its growth. Unlike the other leagues, La Rocque's group took the decision to act independently while its competitors looked to form a National Front.[62] The Solidarité Française – the most dynamic of the leagues on the eve of the *six février* – suffered a protracted period of decline thanks largely to the death of Coty in July 1934 and bitter disagreements at the summit of the organization.[63] The Croix de Feu's image was aided further by the fact that the communist and socialist press designated it as the most threatening force on the extreme right, giving it much publicity in the process. Violent left-wing counter-demonstrations to Croix de Feu meetings – and the aggressive response that they provoked from leaguers – continued to ensure that the attention of the national press was firmly fixed on La Rocque. The lieutenant colonel seemed to offer embattled right-wingers the most credible chance of defeating the left.

New recruits were typically young (born after 1890) men and women, right-wing, and from middle-class occupations such as the professions, the world of business, retail and white-collar work. Industrial workers, public sector employees, artisans, shopkeepers and (until 1935) peasants were a minority in the movement.[64] Members generally hailed from the industrial and urban regions of France, where social antagonisms were worst. Paris and its suburbs counted over 100,000 members by mid-1936, but the league was successful, too, in traditionally Catholic and conservative regions such as Normandy, the Nord, the Pas-de-Calais, Alsace, Lorraine and the Basque country. Southern regions sympathetic to the left and rural departments proved more difficult to crack.[65] The reasons for joining the movement were diverse: a desire to protect one's status and property from the perceived threat of communist revolution; a feeling of marginalization and a frustration with the apparent impotence of the established parties of the right; a sympathy with the hard-line Catholic values that inspired parts of the league's programme; a longing to relive, or experience for the first time, a feeling of comradeship. Some members found their way to the movement through other extreme right-wing formations: in Vittel (Vosges), the Croix de Feu section absorbed the existing Jeunesses Patriotes group. In the Meurthe-et-Moselle, new sections were founded in areas where the Jeunesses Patriotes was relatively strong, suggesting that leaguers held double memberships.[66] Whatever the motivations for joining, a liking for democracy was unlikely to have inspired many.[67]

Women made up a substantial portion of the new membership. By June 1936, there were 315 female sections throughout France and North Africa. Each section had at least fifty members, with many counting over a hundred women leaguers. In some parts of France, new women's sections were founded at a faster rate than those of their male counterparts.[68] Only in North Africa did the league's female sections meet with relative failure. Their lethargy was in part due to the priority that section leaders gave to the political aims of the Croix de Feu, and their unwillingness to subordinate, in their eyes, the struggle against the Republic to women's social work.[69] Across the movement as a whole, by 1936 perhaps one in ten members was a woman. Female involvement in the Croix de Feu dwarfed not only the other extreme right-wing leagues but also of the Communist and Socialist parties.[70] Women – especially Catholic women – who joined the movement may have been inspired by the same concerns as their male counterparts, yet they were attracted, too, by the opportunities for social and charity work that the league offered.[71] Female members were responsible for the league's soup kitchens – 5,500 meals per day were served during winter 1934 – summer camps and clothing drives for the needy.[72] They organized events for the children of leaguers. A typical Christmas gala included a circus show, children dressed in the style of French provinces and the singing of a song entitled *We Want France to be French* (*Nous voulons la France française*). La Rocque's address asked the children to 'love all the other little children of France' as much as their country (described as 'your second mother') while leaving the important work of national reconciliation to 'us your fathers'. Consequently, the league's social work mixed charity and leisure pursuits with a 'dose of politics' and the lieutenant colonel's gendered vision of the Croix de Feu's mission.[73]

Men and women were not equals in the movement. La Rocque subscribed to the contemporary view that women and men had different 'natural' abilities. Women's natural abilities related to 'spiritual' and 'nurturing' tasks and would be best put to use looking after the family in the home. Yet he simultaneously envisaged a central role for women in French society, in which inherent feminine attributes would help to combat national decadence.[74] Women in the movement were thus in a position of *relative*, rather than *absolute*, powerlessness. The ambiguities of La Rocque's position gave them a room to manoeuvre of which they could take advantage.[75]

In late 1935, the movement unveiled a new slogan: 'Social First!' This marked a significant change in Croix de Feu strategy. Where once the league, like its rivals on the extreme right, had based its appeals on hyper-masculine and exclusionary appeals to the veterans' elite, its 'Social First!' strategy expanded the scope for action throughout French social and cultural life. Women were central to this reorientation. We should not be under the illusion, however, that the league had become a charitable organization. Social work provided a very effective means to spread not only the league's doctrine of ultra-nationalism but also its hard-line Catholicism and ethnoreligious vision of Frenchness. Croix de Feu social activists 'expanded the meaning of the social and … redefined the political', blurring the boundaries between the two at a time when women were denied the vote.[76] In fact, La Rocque believed that social reconciliation would precede political conquest.[77]

Under the guidance of Antoinette de Préval, Marie-Claire de Gérus and Germaine Féraud, women members played a 'determinate role', in the Croix de Feu's quest for political power.[78] They revealed themselves to be outstanding organizers, recruiters, propagandists and 'elite nationalists'.[79] Through their social work, women helped to bring the league's message of social and national unity – not to mention its authoritarianism – to thousands of French, and often to those living in key battleground territories where the left was strong.[80] Termed the 'penetration of the working class' (*la pénétration ouvrière*), women were tasked with reaching working-class families in a 'soft-power' strategy that complemented – and ultimately superseded – the male paramilitary politics of the street.[81]

The progressive reorientation towards social action and the effectiveness of the league's women's sections served to undermine the masculine culture that had characterized the league in its early years. Yet there was no softening of the Croix de Feu's exclusionary vision of a future France, a vision to which female members subscribed along with their male counterparts. Furthermore, women members did not act as a moderating influence on the league's violent veterans and young toughs. Women could also take part in Croix de Feu violence: they were in fact essential to the disruption of the Trocadéro meeting in November 1931 when the wives of leaguers in the auditorium held seats for their husbands who arrived at the last minute and proceeded to disrupt proceedings. By the mid-1930s, La Rocque's plan to use social and cultural action in the battle for the moral regeneration of France saw women on the front lines.[82]

The Croix de Feu and the Republic

La Rocque expressed little sentiment for the institutions of the Third Republic. Recalling a visit to the Chamber of Deputies in 1926, he recounted his 'disgust' at witnessing such a 'tragic farce'. He condemned the 'mediocrity', of the parliamentarians of 1926 and the cohort of 1934, who lacked creativity and vitality.[83] La Rocque made little distinction between parliamentarians and the institution in which they sat. He pointed to the 'gangrene' and 'rottenness' in the Republic and condemned, 'The decadence of our institutions and the treachery of those in charge of them', along with 'the administrative bodies of the State … [that] are riddled with dark forces, limited in number, but virulent'.[84]

La Rocque simultaneously scorned the practice of running for election. The very mediocrity of the candidates, not to mention their alleged corruption, repulsed him. Rather than serve the nation, pernicious politicians frequently lied to win votes to satisfy their own vainglorious careers. The problem lay in the system itself, due to, 'the far too widespread misconception that the people's verdict, whether the vote be limited or universal, serves some higher end. "Good election results" are desired as though they meant salvation'.[85] The Croix de Feu did not oppose elections entirely for it advocated both the family vote – according to which the fathers of large families would cast more than one ballot – and, within this, the enfranchisement of women. Still, the lieutenant colonel evidently did not place a high value on suffrage, stating in January 1936 that 'the mere idea of wanting to become elected makes me nauseous'.[86] On the other hand, La Rocque was open to cooperation with the successive governments of Doumerge, Pierre-Etienne Flandin (November 1934–May 1935) and Pierre Laval (June 1935–January 1936). He even scaled back the league's paramilitary activity when the latter first took office. Though relations with each prime minister deteriorated, the Croix de Feu's response to each right-wing government demonstrated once again the porous boundary between conservatism and extremism on the right.[87]

A number of conservative deputies joined the movement. The lieutenant colonel had in 1931 envisaged possible 'coordinations' – tactical political alliances – with parliamentarians that would be decided on a case-by-case basis.[88] Deputies were not excluded from the movement. For men of the Fédération Républicaine like Jean Ybarnégaray, the Croix de Feu perhaps offered a means to mobilize popular support, as the Jeunesses Patriotes had done the previous decade. (Ybarnégaray was in fact a member of both groups as was Désiré Ferry.) A state official in Lorraine noted that in areas where the left was well organized, the league brought 'a little novelty and an appearance of youth to the political struggle waged by conservative personalities'.[89]

Men such as Jacques Poitou-Duplessy, Croix de Feu member and vice president of the Fédération Républicaine, disapproved of league violence not on principle but because it was disconnected from electoral politics; Hitler and Mussolini had not made this error. Yet the Croix de Feu was not prepared to serve solely as the vanguard of a conservative party. In fact, the league had the potential to steal a march on the Fédération Républicaine: Alexander Werth noted in April 1936 in the Pas-de-Calais, 'Curious how in these parts everybody speaks of Socialists, Communists and Croix de Feu – as if all the parties of the Right and Centre were identified with the Croix de Feu.'[90] Nevertheless, it is likely that Croix de Feu members did not oppose wholesale Fédération Républicaine candidates during the elections of 1936.[91]

The Croix de Feu envisaged sweeping changes to the form and practice of government in France, specified in 1931 (in typically ambiguous fashion) as 'changes to the constitution, and not a change of constitution'.[92] La Rocque set out his plans in his 1934 book *Service Public*. In contrast to the unstable coalition governments of the Third Republic, the watchword for the future regime would be 'permanence'. As the head of the government, the leader would serve for at least two successive terms; only a vote by two-thirds of members of a National Assembly would be able to remove him before this time. The leader would appoint a team of six or seven ministers.[93] These ministers would be 'the men of Victory', that is, veterans ready to save France once more.[94]

It was not clear how this small team of veterans would come to power. La Rocque argued that while it was inevitable that a future government would turn to the Croix de Feu for salvation, his league was not prepared to act in merely an advisory role. Instead, the league's 'men of probity' would assume their place 'at the head of the great wheels of state'; La Rocque did not specify how this would happen yet one can assume it would not have been a democratically elected administration. Once in place, the cabinet would 'cleanse' the institutions of government and 'eradicate parliamentary interference from the apparatus of public service'.[95] So-called disorderly elements and obscure forces – presumably the anti-national enemies of France, such as the communists – would be eradicated.[96] Yet this would be a temporary dictatorship only. Once discipline had been restored, the institutions of government and the constitution would be amended to best accommodate the new national circumstance; La Rocque was no more specific than that on this point, yet his plans seem to bear little resemblance to the parliamentary democracy of the Third Republic.

Displays of mass strength were essential to the Croix de Feu's propaganda: they projected an image of force that was huge and disciplined and designed in part to impress sympathetic opinion. They were intended, too, to intimidate the enemy with an impressive display of numbers. Likewise, the league's parades – meticulously planned down to the exact distance between each marcher – were vaunted as the model of ordered and disciplined might.[97] La Rocque told an interviewer in March 1934 that the Croix de Feu demonstrated its strength to avoid having to use it; the movement would simply be a rallying point for those of 'good will, in case of danger'.[98] He argued that observers would see in the discipline and order of the Croix de Feu's public displays the 'will to succeed'.[99] Yet the league's mobilizations were particularly threatening when accompanied by menacing statements from La Rocque. The lieutenant colonel did little to defuse tensions between himself and the left when, for example, he boasted, 'From now on we are able to affirm that thirty-six hours would suffice to muzzle the red suburbs and to take power if necessary.'[100] La Rocque and his commanders repeatedly informed their troops that the moment of action – termed 'H-Hour' and 'D-Day' – was at hand and military metaphors filled the league's propaganda, bringing 'the apocalyptic language of war to domestic politics.'[101] Members, too, believed themselves to be 'soldiers' fighting the enemies of France, whether in the street violence of men or in the social work of women.[102]

The left believed that La Rocque was bent on an armed attempt on power, after which both democracy and the working class would be crushed.[103] Lending apparent credence to such fears, the league held mass meetings – organized in secret and involving thousands of leaguers and their motor vehicles – in locations across France.[104] Aerial flybys by light aircraft – with the movement's death's head insignia emblazoned upon them – accompanied these mobilizations, and served to amplify their impact.[105] For the commemoration of the Marne in September 1935, for example, the Croix de Feu convened 80,000 members within in 24 hours.[106] The sight of 16,000 motor vehicles travelling in convoy to the ceremony must have been a fearful spectacle indeed.[107] The socialists condemned the Marne mobilization, calling it an 'exercise in civil war', 'an army', with lookouts at crossroads to direct the mass of cars.[108] For socialist journalist Jean-Maurice Hermann, the similarity with Nazi mass meetings was plain; he saw in Laval's seeming connivance with the league an echo of Bruning.[109]

The lieutenant colonel did make episodic expressions of his commitment to Republicanism. Should we dismiss these as the sly double-speak of a canny political player? No! When the lieutenant colonel expressed loyalty to the 1875 constitution of the Third Republic, this did not preclude a desire to change this constitution. Likewise, his loyalty to Republican governments was predicated on the grounds that they reject 'intrigue' and embrace 'union and patriotism'.[110] The league's predominantly bourgeois membership did not neuter its threat to the regime. Bourgeois French could subscribe to the league's revolt against conservatives and feel a sense of marginalization, too.[111] For them, as for La Rocque, the interest of the nation trumped all other considerations, even that of the form that the regime should take: 'A "regime" is a means. The men who serve it are but instruments. Before we begin to cry "Long Live the Republic", or "Long Live the King", we demand that the cry be "Long Live France!"'[112] La Rocque's conception of the Republic differed from that of democratic Republicans.

Anti-Semitism and race

During the 1930s, a climate of xenophobia beset France. As the global economic crisis made itself felt from 1931, immigrant workers – who were tolerated during the labour shortages of the 1920s – came under attack. Political and social groups, from the Action Française to medical students, denounced foreign workers as freeloaders, parasites, stealers of jobs and terrorists. Xenophobia and racism worsened when refugees fleeing persecution in Nazi Germany and Eastern Europe crossed the border into France. Jewish refugees were rarely welcomed and old anti-Semitic stereotypes were revived: the Jew was the dark power behind international finance, and he worked to bring about war for his own profit.[113]

Anti-Semitism was not central to the political programme of the Croix de Feu. La Rocque stated that his movement welcomed 'good' French of all faiths, whether Catholic, Protestant or Jewish.[114] Some Jews held prominent positions in the league, such as Parisian section leaders Léon Koscziusko, André Lévy and Jacques Marx; Dr Raymond Benda was in the lieutenant colonel's personal entourage.[115] La Rocque's welcoming of the Jewish community into the movement rested much on the idea of the Union sacrée of wartime. In his 1934 book, *Service Public*, he wrote, 'Our dead would protest from the bottom of their heroic graves if governments afflicted with madness dared to tear from the French Community those men who, having shed their blood for it, were at the same time incorporated into its "substance"'.[116] La Rocque rejected, therefore, calls to deprive Jews en masse of French citizenship, and he condemned the excesses of Nazi anti-Semitism.[117] The league thus distinguished itself from other formations on the extreme right, such as Action Française, which indulged in daily anti-Semitic diatribes in the pages of its eponymous newspaper; the lieutenant colonel's right-wing rivals even accused him of being philo-Semitic.

La Rocque indulged in an anti-Semitism of a different kind. The lieutenant colonel made a distinction between 'good' Jews and their more undesirable counterparts. A 'good' Jew was one who had fought for France during the First World War, and, in doing so, had 'proved' both his commitment to the nation and his desire to assimilate into French Christian civilisation. A 'bad' Jew was usually a foreigner and probably a socialist, whose refusal to integrate was evident from his traditional style of dress or his preference for Yiddish over French.[118] While La Rocque expressed disdain for Hitlerian racism, he bemoaned its consequences not for Germany but for France, which was seemingly unable to stem the 'swarming, virulent crowd of outlaws', flooding across the country's eastern border.[119]

The rank-and-file membership was more prone to expressions of racial anti-Semitism than the Parisian leadership.[120] In Alsace – the first port of call for many German Jews – a Croix de Feu poster proclaimed, 'The Jew Kills Your Parents'.[121] Some provincial leaguers refused to see a distinction between the 'good' and the 'bad' Jew, and they trotted out age-old anti-Semitic stereotypes: the Jew was a greedy money grubber; a puppet master who controlled the government; a left-wing traitor and so on.[122] Such expressions of anti-Semitism from Croix de Feu leaguers were rarely based on racial science. Rather, cultural and political concerns marked members' attitudes to Jewish immigrants, and these attitudes bore the hallmark of an anti-liberal and reactionary stance that would harden after the dissolution of the league in 1936. The league therefore found itself under frequent attack from the LICA, and there were even scuffles between LICA members and Croix de Feu leaguers at a synagogue in Paris in June 1936.[123]

If La Rocque attempted to quell the more violent expressions of anti-Semitism in the league, he was more prepared to endorse xenophobia. The Croix de Feu viewed foreigners with suspicion, and the lieutenant colonel himself attacked immigrants for taking French jobs and refusing to assimilate into the nation's culture. In 1931, he wrote personally to the Minister for Labour, Adolphe Landry, to demand that bosses lay off foreigners before getting rid of Frenchmen.[124] In 1932, *Le Flambeau* noted, 'We must, above all, put an end to this striking paradox where foreigners work here while Frenchmen are unemployed; undesirables here, who escape military service, enjoy scandalous commercial privileges, taking the place of those who have paid dearly for their status of 100% French.'[125] The following year, immigrants in France were described as 'an immense danger' and an 'invasion'.[126] If La Rocque's xenophobia was based on cultural and 'spiritual' distinctions between peoples, other voices in the league preferred the language of race, arguing that the immigrant population threatened the biological purity of the French.[127] Whatever the reasons for their xenophobia, leadership and membership alike agreed upon the solution to the immigrant problem: denaturalization and expulsion.

Racism was most violent in the Croix de Feu's Algerian sections. Racist sentiment in Algerian society was generally sharper than on the mainland. Besides the inherent racism of the colonial enterprise, tensions between the Jewish, European and Maghrebin community were high. Not least among the list of flashpoints was the Crémieux decree of 1870 which had granted Algerian Jews the full rights of French citizenship. The Jewish community subsequently found itself caught between the racism of European settlers who feared their allegedly pernicious influence in the colony and the desires of the Arab community for equal rights.[128] There was thus fertile ground for anti-Semitism in the French territories of North Africa and people spoke openly of their admiration for Hitler while cheering the appearance of the Führer on cinema newsreels.[129]

The Croix de Feu had made inroads into North African territory since 1934. La Rocque's visit to Algeria in June 1935 attracted a crowd of at least 10,000 people to the Oued-Samar plain, in southern Alger. The lieutenant colonel's speech – in which he promised to take the offensive in the name of a 'French France' – was followed by a parade and a fly-past of twenty-eight planes.[130] The group was careful to tailor its strategy to the peculiarities of each department. In Alger, the sections made appeals to residents' nationalism and anti-communism, while proposing an alliance with the Muslim population. In Oran, the league took up the ferociously anti-Semitic line that had proved so useful to Jules Molle's Union Latines during the 1920s. The league was most successful in Constantine where it spoke both to the settlers' desire to break free of the Republic and their fear of the indigenous population.[131] By mid-1936, the league counted between 15,000 and 30,000 members in Algeria; four of the ten deputies elected in Algeria that year benefited from Croix de Feu support.[132] Activists courted the indigenous population to some extent but most members belonged to the traditionally right-wing European settler community.[133] Many were attracted to the anti-Semitic rabble-rousing of the league's speakers and press. Tal Buttmann and Laurent Joly go as far as to argue that 'to be a Croix de Feu in Algeria [was] to be anti-Semitic'.[134] Publicly, the Croix de Feu accepted all 'good' French regardless of race or religion.[135] At times, actions spoke louder than words: in August 1934, the left claimed that Croix de Feu members had incited the crowd during a pogrom that saw 25 people killed and 200 shops ransacked.[136] Anti-Semitism was weaker in the more moderate Alger, while in Oran, members engaged in violent anti-Semitism against the large Jewish community.[137] Such anti-Semitism was so attractive to the settlers because they identified Jews with the Republic and perceived in the Croix de Feu as a means to combat both.[138]

The question of Islam was particularly pertinent to the Croix de Feu and its North African sections. La Rocque's understanding of Islam as a force that could threaten Christian civilization was based on his appreciation of the awakening of indigenous nationalism in the colonies during the early 1930s.[139] Until 1936, the Croix de Feu attempted to attract indigenous Muslims to the organization. Anti-Semitism went hand-in-hand with this policy: settler activists looked to encourage hostility between the Jewish and Muslim populations.[140] Algerian Muslims accounted for approximately 10 per cent of the league's membership in the territory.[141] However, the requirements for membership were prohibitive: one had to prove one's 'Frenchness' to the central administration in Paris.[142] Some locals from the évolués community – the educated indigenous peoples who generally worked with the colonial administration – did rise to posts of leadership in the league, such as Augustin Iba-Zizen of the Tizi-Ouzou section.[143] However, Iba-Zizen's conversion to Catholicism meant that he was uncharacteristic of the average indigenous Algerian. The league generally enjoyed little success in recruiting such people: when La Rocque gave a conference in Constantine on 28 October 1934, only 20 members of the 1,300-strong audience were Muslims.[144] Similar failure was encountered in Tunisia and Morocco, due to both the reluctance of section leaders to admit local peoples and the suspicion with which these peoples regarded the league.[145] Efforts to recruit Arab members were eventually abandoned, something which allowed recruiters to play on fears of Muslim rebellion among the white settler.[146] The league did not consider black Africans and North African Muslims to be French subjects, even if they had fought for France during the First World War.[147]

The Croix de Feu's xenophobia was not unique, and a range of movements from the leagues to the centrist Radical Party indulged their political, cultural and racial prejudices against foreigners.[148] We can thus perceive the spirit of the times in the Croix de Feu's rhetoric.[149] However, racism and xenophobia were important components of the league's propaganda, and we should not ignore the disdain with which high-profile Jewish figures in the lieutenant colonel's circle of acquaintances were treated by the mainstream Jewish community. The Croix de Feu's conception of race and ethnic identity came to bear on the future French society that La Rocque envisaged. In ethnic terms, the future France would be exclusionary. The league espoused an ethnoreligious nationalism, in which racialist hierarchies informed much of its sociocultural action, as well as that of its successor party. For La Rocque, neither Muslims nor Jews could be French *and* maintain their ethnic specificity. The Croix de Feu was a principal component in the historical hinterland of Vichy's brutally repressive policies.[150]

Fascism and violence

La Rocque rejected all comparisons between the Croix de Feu and foreign fascism. In an interview with *L'Oeuvre* in April 1934, he stated thus: 'I stress always … the differences that exist between the situation in France and that in Italy and Germany; I am neither Mussolini nor Hitler.'[151] Recognizing that his movement was 'part of a broader trend for national renewal within Europe', and that there were lessons to be learned from foreign fascism, La Rocque stressed that Mussolini and Hitler's projects spoke to the particular circumstances of their own nations. To transpose either dictator's system directly would not suit France for they were incompatible with the French nature.[152] The Croix de Feu, on the other hand, would apply only 'French solutions'.[153] As the Croix de Feu manifesto stated in 1936, 'Fascist or Nazi imitation, by imposing upon France a regime contrary to her aspirations and genius, contrary to a respect for [her] personality, would inevitably drive her to the horrors of red revolution.'[154]

La Rocque was a 'cast-iron Germanophobe'. He condemned Nazi barbarism and the threat it posed to France.[155] The Croix de Feu refused to send delegates to the international meetings of French and German veterans. La Rocque disassociated himself from the attempts of French veterans' leaders to parlay with the Führer, notably Jean Goy's meeting with Hitler in November 1934.[156] This hostile attitude persisted beyond the dissolution of the Croix de Feu: in December 1936, the PSF's Jean Ybarnégaray condemned Germany for having 'one by one broken the chains of the Treaty of Versailles', and would soon be ready for war.[157] The lieutenant colonel's appreciation of Germany did not differ from that of his extreme right-wing competitors. From monarchist reactionaries such as Maurras to admirers of Hitler like Brasillach, all regarded Germany as a threat to France.[158] On the other hand he praised certain German accomplishments and wrote that there were certainly lessons to be learned from Hitler's example: 'Hitlerism became a preponderant political force only on the day when … it had 107 of its members enter the Reichstag.'[159] This observation prompted the Croix de Feu leadership to consider entering the league into electoral competition itself.

The Croix de Feu's belief in the deficiencies of the French regime weighed upon its appreciation of Germany. La Rocque recognized that a dialogue with Hitler was preferable to war, which, given the weakness of France, was to be avoided at all costs. A war in the west was part of a Soviet plan to launch revolutions throughout Europe. When Germany reoccupied the Rhineland in March 1936, *Le Flambeau* attacked the weakness of successive French administrations, arguing that Germany could only be dealt with from a position of strength once the French regime had undergone a thorough overhaul.[160]

As for Italy, La Rocque was more complimentary, referring to 'deserved admiration' for what Mussolini had done to unite the country. He considered the country to be a natural Latin ally of France and a necessary counterweight to Hitler. Still, the lieutenant colonel neither visited Rome nor sent an official delegation across the Alps.[161] He did not shrink from criticizing Mussolini's friendly relationship with Nazi Germany and Italy's support for Hitler's revisions of the Treaty of Versailles.[162] Fascism was a divisive force and contrary to the goal of national reconciliation towards which he was working.[163] Ultimately, one can find words of approbation and reprobation regarding the two foremost fascist regimes in interwar Europe. Certainly, for the left, such words demonstrated further the Croix de Feu's ideological affinity with fascism or Nazism. For La Rocque and his followers, they could be interpreted in a variety of ways.[164]

For antifascists, the paramilitarism of the Croix de Feu was the starkest indicator of its fascism. This fact stemmed from the view that fascism was a transnational phenomenon. Cachin warned that the leagues worked towards establishing the 'bloody regime of a Hitler and a Mussolini in France'. He noted that, in no matter which country, fascists employed '[the] same methods everywhere! [The] same politics!'[165] The leagues thus mirrored the organization of foreign fascism. In 1934, antifascists perceived the tactics of Mussolini in the Croix de Feu's practice of staging meetings in working-class districts. At the same time, they claimed that these meetings constituted a 'Hitler-style provocation'.[166] In January 1935, L'Humanité reported that a contingent of Croix de Feu leaguers had 'invaded' the town of Amiens in what amounted to a 'genuine rehearsal for a punitive expedition [and] a planned occupation'. The report continued: 'Cars full of Croix de Feu paraded ... like the vans of Mussolini's black shirts did not long ago across the Italian countryside and like those of Hitler's assault squads.'[167] That same month, Cachin warned that the leagues were preparing assault sections in the style of the squadristi and the SA: leaguers 'burn with the desire to imitate the glorious exploits of the Reich's brown shirts'.[168] The word 'Hitlerian' or 'Hitlerian-fascist' was used to describe league shock squads while Le Populaire claimed that the Dispos were the 'exact equivalent' of the SS'.[169]

The left's belief that Mussolini and Hitler achieved power through a violent coup informed its understanding of La Rocque's strategy. Documents reportedly discovered on an arrested Croix de Feu leaguer revealed, according to communist Paul Vaillant-Couturier, that La Rocque's league was 'organised militarily, with an intelligence service, secret codes, meeting plans, motorised division, vans, cars, motorbikes, plans, etc ... they imitate very faithfully – almost to the uniform – Italian and German fascists, their instigators and accomplices. They are armed. They fire. They wound and they kill.'[170] He later wrote that 'a blatant coup, in the Italian or German style' was prepared. This coup would be a violent assault on the Republic: a new six février.[171] Indeed, the belief that French fascists had tried to seize power violently in February 1934 provided further apparent evidence for the left's theory.

To combat the violence of the leagues, the antifascist allies advocated large counter-demonstrations to right-wing meetings. The Communist Party warned against individual acts of violence against leaguers. Vaillant-Couturier stated that the fascists wanted to spark off a 'guerrilla' campaign involving 'reprisal after reprisal, to create a state of endemic civil war similar to that which reigned in Germany'.[172] Such small-scale warfare would detract from the broader goal of the communist movement: the destruction of the capitalist system.[173] Nevertheless, antifascist counter-demonstrations frequently led to violence in which the activists of the extreme right were the victims, though they often responded to their attackers in kind. Left-wing attacks on league meetings were of high propaganda value to the leagues, whose leaders used the violence to underscore their own credentials as defenders of the Republican freedoms of free speech and the right to meet. Pierre Taittinger thus demanded that the government safeguard basic Republican liberties in the face of the 'bloodthirsty horde of bandits [and] foreign agitators' on the left.[174] The extreme right-wing newspaper *Je suis partout* alleged that the left used the word 'fascism' as a 'scarecrow' to whip the masses into hysteria. It was thus that 'hundreds of thousands of people – perhaps even millions – now believe that fascism means the destruction of all freedoms, the enslavement of all workers, [and] the massacre of every Republican'.[175]

The violence between Croix de Feu leaguers and antifascists came to a head in autumn 1935. In September, a convoy of Croix de Feu members was ambushed at Mondeville near Caen. Several leaguers were injured when stones – and, some said, bullets – rained down on their cars as they drove home from a gathering.[176] In October, a Croix de Feu meeting at Villepinte in the suburbs of Paris saw left-wing counter-demonstrators fight with leaguers and police in front of the venue. Several people and policemen were injured.[177] The following month, another of the league's meeting in Limoges witnessed scenes of serious violence as antifascists attempted to break into the riding school where leaguers had convened. In the ensuing melee, men on both sides suffered gunshot wounds.[178] These incidents fed left-wing fears that the much-talked-about D-Day was finally approaching.[179] The prefect of the Moselle reported that in June 1935, La Rocque had told supporters, 'the end of the parliamentary regime is in sight, probably in October or November when parliament will be unable to balance the budget. That's when the hour of the Croix de Feu will sound and our Association with its ideas in power will go into action to reorganize the country'.[180]

The left's campaign against league meetings in late 1935 saw serious violence erupt outside several Croix de Feu gatherings. Speaking to the extreme right-wing *Gringoire* after violence at Villepinte in October 1935, La Rocque assured readers that the Croix de Feu would maintain its sangfroid in the face of the left's provocation.[181] He promised to counter-attack when necessary but to remain, above all, in control of the movement's destiny, believing that public opinion would judge ill the Popular Front's criminality.[182] However, the lieutenant colonel's cautious response caused frustration on the right. *Gringoire* bemoaned La Rocque's desire to avoid confrontation with the left. The lieutenant colonel had failed to understand that Mussolini and Hitler had stood up to their opponents from the beginning. The Francistes, the Solidarité Française and the Action Française had all shown guts in taking the fight to the left. La Rocque's strategy had failed.[183]

The lieutenant colonel was in the difficult position of trying to maintain the image of a powerful, disciplined and orderly movement, while appearing able to confront the left effectively. He counselled against a direct assault on the Popular Front, yet he combined this with the promise of action should the coalition threaten revolution.[184] Certainly, the lieutenant colonel was cautious when it came to confrontation with the enemy, wary of the so-called provocations of antifascists that could prompt rash actions from leaguers and lead to a propaganda disaster.[185] Instead of violence, La Rocque advised that the demonstration of the size and discipline of the league would alone defeat its opponents.

However, the lieutenant colonel's rejection of violence was ambiguous. For one thing, displays of intimidation could be interpreted as symbolic violence in themselves. Intimidation was multifaceted, ranging from the mere presence of Croix de Feu leaguers in the street (as Caroline Campbell notes, they were stationed at 'metro entrances, parks, busy streets, café entrances') to the staging of meetings in areas deemed politically hostile, both of which were intended to bully the adversary.[186] La Rocque did not discount entirely the use of violence against his political enemies. In June 1933, he informed his followers that 'we hate violence', yet he went on to reassure them that 'violence [against us] will be broken on our inflexible energies'.[187] The following year, the lieutenant colonel wrote in *Service Public*, 'Rejecting violence is not the same as fearing it. Opposing its use does not mean excluding the possibility of using it.'[188] At a meeting in Algeria on 10 June 1935, the lieutenant colonel reportedly threatened that if Daladier had been appointed prime minister in the latest cabinet reshuffle, 'il y aura du sport'.[189] The seeming rejection of violence was thus accompanied by an apparent promise to commit violence, if an attack was deemed to have taken place. This attitude was broadly consonant with understandings of the use of violence on left and right during the interwar years. In practice, the boundary between symbolic violence and actual violence was blurred. Encounters between activists were unpredictable, with displays of symbolic violence (singing or shouting, for example) as likely to satisfy the apparent desire for confrontation as to spark a physical fight.

The defensive footing of the group came as a surprise to some members, giving the lie to the assertion that mass mobilizations kept the violent impulses of leaguers in check.[190] In October 1935, for example, police reported that some leaguers were surprised at La Rocque's recent announcement that the Croix de Feu was not an 'attack group', but rather one of defence. The lieutenant colonel gave precise instructions: absolute discipline and obedience were a necessity; the carrying of arms was forbidden; the police were not to be opposed but rather aided. Members themselves doubted La Rocque's sincerity in making such a statement and some leaguers continued to arm themselves in preparation for fighting with antifascists. From this point of view, the Croix de Feu's violence was a significant element of its political strategy. La Rocque was clearly willing to tolerate a certain level of violence, as long as it did not get out of hand and damage the image of the movement.[191]

The preparedness of antifascists to engage in violence against the Croix de Feu rendered La Rocque's position evermore precarious. The lieutenant colonel's pleas for calm hardly satisfied restless leaguers, some of whom took action into their own hands, exposing the contradiction in the league's image as a force for both order and revolution.[192] The fighting at Limoges in November 1935 shocked the political establishment, and pressure came to bear on Prime Minister Laval to deal firmly with the leagues despite the fact that Croix de Feu leaguers were often the victims, rather than the perpetrators, of offensive violence. On 30 November 1935, the popular picture magazine *Vu* asked on its front page, 'If the French fought each other, who would win?' Civil war – 'National Front versus Popular Front' – seemed a real prospect.[193]

1936: Dissolution

From his wartime prison cell, Edouard Daladier recalled his first and only encounter with François de La Rocque:

> I saw La Rocque only once, very early one October morning in 1936, in the passageway of the train that was carrying me back from Biarritz. A short, pale, rather flabby fellow, he was standing outside the door of his sleeping compartment, between two bodyguards, watching the sun come up. After that, he came to the dining car to have his café au lait and smoke a pipe. I concluded that he was not a threat to the Republic.[194]

Daladier sang a different tune in 1935. He was one of a number of Radical Party members who, increasingly wary of the Croix de Feu and 'the importation to France of the methods of Hitlerism', actively campaigned in the corridors of the Palais-Bourbon to have the league dissolved.[195]

The attitude of Radicals like Daladier was crucial to the ultimate demise of the Croix de Feu. La Rocque had always shunned electoral politics, refusing to countenance the putting up of candidates for election (including himself). Consequently, the lieutenant colonel could call upon only sympathizers in the Chamber of Deputies rather than Croix de Feu deputies. The Radicals held a quarter of the seats in the Chamber, making them the largest party in a deeply factionalized parliament. As the embodiment of the Republic itself, Radical deputies had long been the subject of verbal diatribes from La Rocque and other league leaders. They had, in recent years, become a target of physical attack, too. In March 1935, Radical deputy for the Vosges Paul Elbel lost an eye following an attack at a political meeting. Two months later, Action Française leaguers threw acid in the face of Radical Pierre Cot.[196] The Radical Party had no paramilitary arm to protect itself in the streets and meeting halls of France. It could, however, wield its power in parliament. During 1935, Radical deputies had put pressure on Laval to deal with the leagues. The violence of autumn that year hardened their resolve.

It was thus greeted with some surprise on the left-wing benches when, on 6 December 1935, Jean Ybarnégaray, nationalist deputy for the Basses-Pyrénées – and a member of the Croix de Feu – agreed to a mutual disarmament pact with the left. The acceptance caused anger among the other leagues and within the Croix de Feu, too.[197] La Rocque, however, endorsed Ybarnégaray's move. The lieutenant colonel had founded the Mouvement Social Français des Croix de Feu in autumn 1935, perhaps in an attempt to soften the image of the league and head off attempts to repress it. This umbrella group emphasized the social aspect of the organization in a self-conscious effort to move away from its image as a paramilitary force. Paramilitarism was becoming less and less compatible with La Rocque's plan to use social and cultural action to spread his political message.[198] The lieutenant colonel was further considering entry into electoral politics; this seemed like a credible tactic to adopt in light of Hitler and Mussolini's successful combination of street action and electoral politics. This reconsideration was likely prompted, too, by the threat of dissolution.[199]

Legislation was subsequently passed that went far beyond the terms of La Rocque and Ybarnégaray's understanding of the disarmament agreement. The government was soon empowered to dissolve any movement deemed a threat to public order.[200] The offer of mutual disarmament may have derived from a misjudged political calculation, but it was also a response to the political circumstances of the moment and the shifting priorities of the league. France had changed since 1934, and the Croix de Feu had to respond to this.

When in June 1936 the antifascist Popular Front coalition was elected to government, the writing was on the wall for the leagues of the extreme right. On 18 June 1936 the leagues were dissolved. The act of dissolution was expected; the foundations of the left-wing coalition were built upon the struggle against fascism and the promise to outlaw the leagues. Furthermore, in February 1936 parliament had voted to shut down the Action Française following the near-lynching of socialist leader Léon Blum by a group of dissident *camelots du roi*.[201] Following the order of dissolution in June, the smaller leagues abandoned paramilitarism and rebranded themselves. Taittinger – whose Jeunesses Patriotes had suffered in the shadow of the Croix de Feu – revived the Parti Républicain National et Social (PRNS), a group he had founded at the turn of the decade. Bucard transformed his league into both the Amis du Francisme and the Parti Unitaire Français d'Action Socialiste et Nationale. Beyond its symbolic importance, the disbandment of the smaller groups had little real impact upon French politics.

The dissolution of the Croix de Feu had significant ramifications. Supporters of the Popular Front hoped that its disappearance would spell the end for fascism in the country. The lieutenant colonel had in fact foreseen the dissolution of his movement, and the conversion of the league into a political party proceeded smoothly. If the Popular Front had hoped to put a stop to La Rocque's political project, it was to be proved sorely wrong. By 1940, the party had as many as 2 million members across 7,600 sections; La Rocque was at that time the leader of the largest political movement in French history.[202]

The contested meaning of 'Republicanism' and 'fascism' renders attempts to label the Croix de Feu perilous. La Rocque's attitude to the Third Republic was unambiguous: the regime as it functioned fell short of what he expected of a strong French state. Whether his plan to revise the constitution of the regime rendered him anti-Republican depends on one's understanding of the term and, not least, the extent to which one is willing to allow for the existence of an authoritarian Republicanism. Ambiguity likewise characterized the lieutenant colonel's stance on fascism. Elements of the ideology were evidently to his liking, and his rejection of the label seems not to have been predicated on any political or moral objections but rather on an appreciation of the foreignness of fascism and the presumed specificity of national contexts, both of which convinced him that such a political project was not suitable for France.

On the other hand, the left's belief that the decree of dissolution would destroy 'fascism' in France stemmed from its opinion that the leagues were simply French sections of an international fascist movement. Antifascists understood the fascist seizure of power by a violent coup to be a uniform process, independent of national context. The *six février* – or the 'failed fascist coup' as it was reported in the socialist press – reinforced this conviction. However, paramilitarism had represented only one strand of Hitler and Mussolini's strategy for the conquest of power. The same was true of La Rocque. By summer 1936 he had already begun to move his movement towards social action, which he perceived to be the necessary path to power. It is small wonder that the outlawing of paramilitaries did little to harm La Rocque's movement. In attempting to kill the fascist dragon, French antifascists had merely slain a scarecrow.

CHAPTER 4
FASCISM DEFEATED? THE PARTI SOCIAL FRANÇAIS AND THE PARTI POPULAIRE FRANÇAIS

On 9 November 1936, the stage was set at the Grand Theatre in Saint-Denis for the first national congress of the Parti Populaire Français (PPF). A large tricolour banner framed the platform. A red cloth, upon which was inscribed the party's initials, adorned the rostrum. On each side of the hall stood flags and standards from provincial sections. Red, white and blue drapes hung from the sealing. Looking down from the front of the room was a huge portrait of Jacques Doriot, the party's leader and mayor of Saint-Denis. The first session commenced with speakers from the Algerian sections, with one addressing the audience in Arabic. Next to take to the floor were representatives of the working-class members. They reported proudly that loyal workers had broken communist-led strikes in the factories of Peugeot, Sauter-Harlé and the Compagnie Française des Métaux. The audience – a mixed bunch of ex-communists, former leaguers, royalists and political novices – clapped enthusiastically.[1]

Finally, Doriot took to the stage to thunderous applause interspersed with cries of 'Doriot in power!' He recounted the founding of the party on 28 June 1936 in the wake of the Popular Front's electoral victory and the huge strike wave that followed. '[Our enemies] predicted a crushing failure', he crowed, 'but we are a force of 100,000 men. ... The PPF is born; it is in rude health. Nothing will stop it in its mission to renovate France, nothing will stop its march to power.' While he condemned social conservatives and Radical deputies for allowing the left into government, Doriot reserved his greatest ire for the Communist Party: 'We will not allow our sons and wives to have their throats slit [by the communists]. We will form a front of all French and we will march together with all those who fight the Communist Party. ... [If] the politicians cannot chase the communists [from power], we, by our courage, will do it ourselves.' Acclamations poured forth from the audience; many stretched out their arms in a fascist-style salute. Doriot went on to demand a 'strong State' that would return the 'soul' to France. He asked, '[Is it necessary] to change the present institutions? That's not for us to say. If Parliament, government and democracy can accomplish the mission of recovery, we must keep them; if they cannot, the people will bypass them to do it themselves.'[2]

Outside in the streets of Saint-Denis, a counter-demonstration was forming – an 'anti-Hitlerian' gathering, according to *L'Humanité*.[3] Antifascists led by communist deputy Charles Tillon gathered outside the Famille Nouvelle restaurant. The local police had organized a large security service to prevent the demonstration from reaching the theatre. About 2,000 protesters marched towards the meeting venue, but they were pushed back by police. Some demonstrators decided to return home, but the bulk of the crowd resolved to march to the town hall, the seat of Doriot's power. There were clashes between marchers and the police during which several people were injured. By midnight, calm had been restored.[4] For the left-wing supporters of the Popular Front, such scenes were gallingly familiar. The dissolution of the leagues in June 1936 had not dealt a decisive blow to those men and women whom the left identified as fascists.

The election result galvanized Doriot into founding the PPF, 'The only mass fascist organisation ever to develop on [French] soil', according to Pierre Milza.[5] The party emerged from the internecine disputes of the Communist Party. Doriot had been a leading light of the French extreme left until his expulsion from its ranks in 1934. He subsequently took a number of other communists and sympathizers with him into his new group. These 'renegades' intended to carve out their own space in the political arena at the expense of their former comrades.[6] The party initially approved of aspects of the Popular Front's social reform programme and even invited its members to join the Confédération Générale du Travail (CGT) trade union, with the intention of combating communist influence from inside the trade union itself.[7] However, it gradually moved to the extreme right, an outcome owing in part to its competition with La Rocque for the leadership of French ultra-nationalism. By the Second World War, the PPF had publicly embraced fascism, and the party became a significant collaborationist movement during the dark years of the Occupation.

For Lieutenant-Colonel François de La Rocque, the decree of dissolution was a minor setback. 'We'll have to pull on our sewer-worker boots and do politics': such was his reaction to the decree of 18 June 1936. For some of his critics, the lieutenant colonel's failure to challenge the government's decree of dissolution was a sign of weakness and compromise with the Republican system. The most intransigently antiparliamentarian of La Rocque's followers refused to join his new Parti Social Français (PSF) and a number of section presidents resigned.[8] Protests in Paris on 5 July 1936 saw crowds fight running battles with police on the Place de l'Etoile. It was estimated that 10,000 people were on the square during the violence; 107 constables were injured.[9] Despite the concerns of some members, the lieutenant colonel had not suddenly converted to the virtues of democracy. He was only prepared to wade so deep into the filth of Republican politics: 'Rest assured, my children, your father will never stand as a candidate, [he] will not solicit any post', he explained.[10] He further reassured doubters that 'we want now …, for the salvation of France, to conquer power. I am not out of the race.'[11]

The PSF was now in competition for seats in parliament, a fact that brought it into conflict with not only the Radical Party but also the right-wing Fédération Républicaine and the Alliance Démocratique. The danger that the PSF represented for the traditional parties of the right and centre was real because, for some French, La Rocque represented the only effective opposition to the left; the lieutenant colonel was still the 'boss', a providential leader who alone could reconcile the nation. At the founding meeting of the PSF on 12 July 1936, celebrated aviator Jean Mermoz told the audience at the Salle Wagram in Paris:

I know only the Leader. The captain on board [the plane] is the master after God. … The colonel, my leader, the one to whom I have devoted the best of myself, I put him on the same level as my profession, and that, for me, is the maximum that I can do. … I will always follow the leader, who will wait until the time is right. I have found this leader [and] I'm sticking with him.[12]

In addition to the reinvigorated challenge from the extreme right, socialist Léon Blum's new government faced severe challenges, domestically and abroad. Workers throughout the country celebrated the victory with a strike wave of unprecedented size. In June alone, there were 12,142 strikes involving 1,830,938 strikers.[13] The practice of occupying factories terrified some conservative onlookers who believed that social revolution was in the offing.

Beyond France's borders, within days of the new French government assuming power, the Spanish Popular Front government confronted an army rebellion that would lead to civil war. On the morning of 20 July 1936, three days after the insurrection of several Spanish garrisons in Morocco, a telegram landed on the desk of Léon Blum from his counterpart in Spain: 'Taken by surprise by dangerous military coup, ask for immediate agreement to supply weapons and planes.' After a period of agonizing deliberation, Blum agreed, to the dismay of several non-interventionist members of his government. By 2 August, France had supplied fifty-five planes to the Spanish Republicans.[14] The right-wing press was vociferous in its denunciation of the Popular Front's intervention in Spain yet French nationalists crossed the Pyrenees to join the Caudillo's crusade. In Algeria, the right-wing mayors of Oran and Sidi-Bel-Abbès, Gabriel Lambert and Lucien Bellat, travelled to Spain to offer their support to Franco in broadcasts on Radio Seville.[15] Subsequently, Blum reluctantly committed France to a policy of non-intervention though a trickle of military materiel did cross the Pyrenees to Spanish Republicans. As the Spanish rebels gained the upper hand, up to 500,000 Spanish crossed the border into France. Many of them were herded into concentration camps. The right depicted these men and women as wild revolutionaries ready to foment conflict on French soil.[16] The violence in Spain now coloured reports of violence between 'fascists' and antifascists in France as partisan newspapers associated the deeds of their opponents with those of either the Spanish nationalists or the Spanish Republicans.[17] At home and abroad, 1936 was a time of rising tension in a burgeoning international clash between fascism and its opponents.

'[The] PSF is the CF plus electoral politics'

Following the dissolution of the leagues, most members of the Croix de Feu migrated to the PSF. The new party relied greatly on the grass-roots organization of the defunct league, and it was most successful where there had been a strong Croix de Feu implantation, especially in the urban centres of traditionally right-wing departments. Support remained weak in rural areas and socialist-controlled Southern towns and cities.[18] Veterans likely continued to make up a significant proportion of the membership, especially those from the UNC.[19] La Rocque's popularity persisted in the Maghreb, and a number of North African immigrants belonged to the mainland party.[20] The social composition of the party's membership echoed that of the Croix de Feu, too. The urban lower and middle classes made up the largest proportion of members, perhaps attracted by the party's promise to defend the *classes moyennes* from both the exploitation of the bosses and the agitation of the proletariat.[21]

While to some extent the PSF's membership reflected that of the Croix de Feu, the June 1936 election result increased the attractiveness of the new party to a broader range of constituencies. With a socialist prime minister installed in the Hôtel Matignon, all those who feared the left in government, from leaguers to conservatives and moderates, became potential recruits and voters.[22] Tensions arose between La Rocque and Fédération Républicane boss Louis Marin. Marin objected to the PSF's electoral challenge to the Fédération, which he claimed was responsible for division and discord in the nationalist camp. Without naming the PSF, he wrote: '[They call for] the reconciliation of all French, apart from, in fact, the other nationalists; they shower them with insults in public and in private; they divide their constituencies.'[23] Relations between the parties were sundered in April 1937 when PSF and Fédération candidates ran against each other during a by-election in Mortain. The PSF demanded that its right-wing rival desist in the first round in order to present a single national nominee to voters. The Fédération entered two members into the contest, and their campaign included a call for La Rocque to be arrested. The second-round run-off saw the Popular Front's Mallon triumph over the PSF's Gauthier.[24]

The PSF attempted to encroach onto the electoral terrain of the Radical Party. The Radicals' traditional constituency of owners of small- and medium-size businesses found the PSF's combative attitude to big capital attractive while its trade union organization – the Syndicat Professionel Français (SPF) – offered a means by which to combat the spiralling wave of strikes.[25] Edmond Barrachin, director of the PSF's political bureau, stated in June 1937: 'The Radical-Socialist party has abandoned the defence of the middle classes, the PSF will now take them in hand.'[26] In Algeria, too, the party left the Rassemblement National d'Action Social (a coalition of anti-Popular Front parties) to better pose itself as an independent alternative to the Radical Party.[27] The PSF sought not only to attract the traditional constituency of the centre party but also to tempt Radical deputies into defecting, in an effort to split the Popular Front. To this end, La Rocque backed the successful election campaign of anti-Popular Front Radical Lucien Lamoureux in the January 1937 by-election in Lapalisse. The PSF's plan was not, however, to move towards the centre of politics but to tempt these Radicals further to the right.[28]

Working-class support for the party was relatively significant. PSF workers were likely drawn from the ranks of the unemployed, for whom the party's employment services offered the promise of a job. The PSF offered a refuge, too, to the many non-unionized labourers who found themselves victims of discrimination by left-wing union foremen, violence from strikers or in competition for jobs with immigrants.[29] In some proletarian districts of Paris, evidence shows that at least one PSF member lived at virtually every residence. The SPF was therefore comparatively successful even if its claims of a membership of 1.4 million by April 1938 seem inflated.[30]

With as many as two million members by 1940, the party's astonishing growth owed something to its propaganda efforts. La Rocque undertook gruelling speaking tours, taking planes, trains and cars, to reach as many French as possible. On 27 December 1938, for example, he spoke in Lyon at 1.00 pm and then again almost 150 miles away in Avignon that evening. On 28 December, La Rocque attended a meeting of section presidents in the Ile-de-France, while the next day he spoke successively in Angers and Bordeaux. The lieutenant colonel finished the week with a meeting in Nancy. Grass-roots activism further bolstered recruitment efforts. Members operated throughout the territory, with many taking advantage of party-sponsored courses in public speaking for budding propagandists, both male and female. In Paris, PSF speakers reached radio listeners through a weekly slot on Radio-Cité. In rural areas, Sunday mornings saw members drive to villages and hamlets to hold impromptu meetings. While the speaker set up the meeting venue – decorating it with tricolour flags and a portrait of the lieutenant colonel – members of the party's Propaganda Flying Squads (*Équipes volantes de propagande* or EVP) drummed up an audience and a newspaper seller sold the party's publications. The process would be repeated in the afternoon. Even when audiences were small, the acquisition of a few new memberships was regarded as a success.[31] New subscriptions to the party reinforced its finances, and in 1938 La Rocque acquired *Le Petit Journal*, one of the five largest morning newspapers with a daily circulation of 300,000. The newspaper of the former Croix de Feu, *Le Flambeau*, continued to sell well, printing almost one million copies each week.[32]

It is likely that new members viewed La Rocque's movement as the most robust defence of their interests against communist-led social revolution. Indeed, the turbulent months that followed the election of the Popular Front saw the PSF ramp up its rhetoric against the left: La Rocque claimed that a Soviet overthrow of the Republic was imminent now that Moscow was in control of Paris.[33] The denunciations of the left reached fever pitch in October 1936 following violence with police outside the Parc des Princes.[34]

To assuage the fears of long-standing members that the lieutenant colonel was now 'doing' politics, the PSF was at pains to stress continuity between itself and its predecessor: '[The] PSF is the CF plus electoral politics', ran the slogan.[35] Certainly, beyond the make-up of its membership, the new party resembled the former league in important ways. The PSF retained the Croix de Feu's paramilitary structures at least until 1937. The *Dispos* were disbanded in 1936 only to be replaced by the Propaganda Flying Squads.[36] Under the leadership of Varin, the Flying Squads took part in the organization and stewarding of meetings. Guards drawn from the Squads protected La Rocque's home and mounted covert surveillance operations at train stations when the lieutenant colonel was on the move. La Rocque himself joked that he could not even buy a packet of cigarettes without the accompaniment of his Flying Squad heavies.[37] Doubtless some members were attracted to the Squads for their sense of community and comradeship. Informality was the watchword, and comrades usually ended a day's propaganda activities with the sharing of a beer in a nearby bar. On the feast day of Saint Casimir, they partook of a banquet in honour of the venerable lieutenant colonel.[38] The existence of the Squads and the centralized structure of the PSF led to accusations from the left that the new party was merely a rebranded Croix de Feu and the government prosecuted La Rocque for just this reason.

The PSF gradually abandoned the parades and motorized mobilizations of the Croix de Feu era that had so impressed right-wing opinion and terrified the left. To some extent, political realities in 1936 forced the lieutenant colonel's hand on the issue of paramilitarism; with the left in command of the government and the police, paramilitary action was risky.[39] Still, while La Rocque spoke of his Squads in the same combative tone as the *Dispos*, they were fewer in number and deployed less aggressively. Furthermore, whereas the latter were intended to facilitate the collapse of the Republic, the lieutenant colonel claimed that the Squads would, in the event of revolution, fight *with* the army and the Mobile Guard to defeat the revolutionaries. La Rocque thus attempted to distance the party from its paramilitary past; in doing so, he jettisoned a key element of the Croix de Feu's populism.[40]

The PSF's rejection of paramilitarism was ambiguous. A 1937 police report noted that party members claimed to be 'partisans of order, but [were] ready to defend themselves vigorously if attacked'. The report continued: 'It is doubtless that they are individually armed like … their political opponents.'[41] Squad thugs were deployed from time to time to rough up antifascist opponents and scuffles in the street occurred regularly.[42] Paramilitary operations were still undertaken, as Philippe Rudaux (historian and former member) describes:

> The movements [of antifascists] in the red suburbs [of Paris] were put under surveillance. The green belt [around the capital] was loyal to the PSF. Three quarters of the market gardeners in the south of Paris were members. In the middle of the night they went to the market squares in long convoys and reported suspect gatherings. Their reports were collected together in a neighbouring restaurant.[43]

Meanwhile, antifascists continued to perceive the PSF as the greatest threat to the Republic. La Rocque's lawyers recorded over 200 attacks on PSF activists between June 1935 and August 1937, including 4 fatalities.[44]

In October 1936, La Rocque employed a new tactic against his antifascist opponents: the counter-demonstration. This was the form of action long familiar to left-wing street politics. When the government banned a PSF meeting in Paris only to subsequently approve a large communist rally at the Parc des Princes, La Rocque condemned the government's hypocrisy and a 'provocation directed at the Parti social Français'.[45] In a deliberate imitation of the left-wing tactic of counter-demonstrating, the lieutenant colonel organized a PSF march to the sports stadium on the day of the meeting.[46] Fighting between PSF counter-demonstrators and the police saw 1,249 arrests made.[47] Right-wingers expressed satisfaction at having seen off the challenge of the left in a predominantly bourgeois district of Paris.

The party continued to take provocative action against the left, staging meetings in working-class districts throughout France. Two incidents are worthy of mention.

On 27 February 1937, antifascists in the working-class town of Vrignes-aux-Bois (Ardennes) staged a counter-demonstration to a PSF meeting at a factory in the area. PSF members were pelted with bricks and bottles as they left the venue. When one of them – a young man named Jean Créton – lifted open a barrier to allow his comrades to exit, he was shot fatally at point-blank range. The murderer was never identified.[48] The following month, left-wingers targeted a PSF social gathering at the Olympia cinema in the Parisian suburb of Clichy. The left-wing mayor, Charles Auffray, and communist deputy Maurice Honel organized a counter-demonstration to the party's presence in an ostensibly left-wing district. Confrontations between activists and the police soon turned ugly, and the night resulted in the deaths of five demonstrators and a police officer.[49] The right cited the violence as evidence that the Popular Front could not control its fanatical followers. The communists were dismayed that a left-wing government had murdered workers, and they raised the fear that the police were still Chiappists at heart.

The lieutenant colonel's reluctance to prioritize paramilitary action did not stem from his conversion to democratic competition. Outbreaks of violence in early 1937 had once again illustrated the perils of paramilitarism. At Clichy, PSF members were largely bystanders to the clashes between demonstrators and the police; officers had in fact evacuated most of the meeting's attendees from the cinema earlier in the evening. Furthermore, official investigations into the presence of PSF agents provocateurs in the crowd proved inconclusive.[50] However, the left cited the violence as evidence of the continued threat from the fascist La Rocque as well as from extreme right-wing elements in the police. To some on the right, it seemed as if the lieutenant colonel was once again playing into the hands of his enemies. Soon after the Clichy riot, the right-wing deputy the Abbé Desgranges spoke to leading communist Jacques Duclos in the corridors of the Chamber. 'What favours this colonel does for you! He allowed you to attack the government at Clichy, and today to patch up the [parliamentary] majority. What would you do without him?' Desgranges remarked. 'Indeed, God [must have] sent him to us', Duclos replied acerbically.[51]

The PSF continued to devote much energy to social work, building upon the activities that developed under its predecessor. In an era when leisure time was expanding, thanks to the Popular Front's introduction of the forty-hour working week and paid holiday allowance, the PSF offered a huge variety of services and leisure activities, all of which amounted to a rich associational life for activists to enjoy. Holiday camps, social and community centres, charitable bazaars, study groups, children's sections, student societies, a sports club, even an aviation society: all were available to members.[52] In the words of William D. Irvine, a PSF activist

> could belong to a PSF orchestra, a PSF jazz club, or PSF glee club. … After work he could drop into the local PSF social club, play bridge or ping pong, read newspapers and have a drink. He and his family could attend any number of village fairs organized by the PSF, complete with sporting events, races for the children, dances, and fireworks displays.[53]

A range of auxiliaries were established from the Centres Universitaires for students to the Société de Préparation et d'Education Sportive and Travail et Loisir groups for sporting and leisure activities.[54]

Women remained central to the party's social strategy. Female membership of the party reached between 200,000 and 300,000 members. In some areas, women accounted for a significant proportion of activists: in Paris, 38 per cent of members were female.[55] The party divided the former women's sections of the Croix de Feu into two groups: 'Civic Action', in which women engaged in recruitment and propaganda – Charles Vallin considered women the 'best propagandists' – and 'Social Action', which was responsible for social services.[56] These responsibilities were not separated from the party's sections into a distinct women's organization. Rather, each section of the party was delegated a female Social and Civic Action representative. Women were thus fully integrated into the life of the PSF.[57]

The party's most senior woman, Antoinette de Préval, headed the 'Work and Leisure' group, which organized activities for working-class youths.[58] Meanwhile, Jeanne Garrigoux directed the Social Studies Bureau, which was responsible for the formulation of the party's social policy. La Rocque's appreciation of the Bureau – 'the organiser and controller of the sum of our action' – demonstrated the centrality of social work to the lieutenant colonel's thinking as well as the importance of women in shaping the party's political course.[59] Women were increasingly successful in making the case for the validity of social action to male members to whom the outlet of paramilitarism was gradually closed down. As more men became involved in the party's social projects, the boundaries between the political and the social continued to blur.[60]

The party's motive behind its social activities was by no means altruistic. For its leaders, the Croix de Feu's foray into social work had demonstrated the potential of this strategy to facilitate the national reconciliation that La Rocque believed was a prerequisite for power. Women were integral to the PSF's plan to remake French society from the bottom up. Social work was not merely a means by which to 'occupy activists outside electoral periods [and] to avoid their loss of enthusiasm'; to write off the party's female membership as political novices is a mistake.[61] At social events, female members schooled comrades and potential recruits in the group's romantic vision of a future France: 'A world free from class and political conflict and where happiness and security were once again possible.'[62] Meanwhile, women taught the children of party members to sing songs that celebrated the lieutenant colonel.[63] Beyond the immediate membership, social work targeted working-class communities. The aim was to 'pacify' and 'colonise' such communities, in the hope of loosening the grip of the left on the proletariat.[64] In spreading the 'spirit' of the party, social workers would help to integrate the working class into the national community, such as the PSF conceived of it.

Encroachment into the private lives of the French was an integral part of a plan to rebuild the 'true' France, an ethnically homogeneous nation, in opposition to the Republic.[65] Social and leisure services offered a conduit through which to transmit the PSF's political philosophy throughout family, social, cultural and work life; the women of the PSF considered themselves to be soldiers in a battle against the left for the soul of a new France.[66] This new France would be rooted in Catholic values and exclusionary ideas of 'Frenchness'; social workers employed an ethnic hierarchy according to which poor French received aid before their immigrant neighbours.[67]

The PSF's emphasis on the primacy of France's Christian tradition strengthened in tandem with its hostile attitude to foreigners. Refugees fleeing persecution in central and Eastern Europe continued to arrive in France during the late 1930s. Concerns about their alleged connections to international crime and terrorism were voiced in numerous quarters, and the Popular Front government established a commission to examine a 'Foreigners' Statute' to control the inflow of immigrants.[68] The PSF deemed immigration a mortal threat to the French nation, and it demanded harsh measures be taken against foreigners. Among its proposals were the complete review of all naturalizations since 1927 and the immediate expulsion of undesirable immigrants. Foreigners considered worthy enough to remain in France would be forced to pay a heavy tax for the privilege. The PSF thus hoped to coerce as many foreign residents as possible to leave the country.[69] Its pronouncements spread throughout its hundreds of thousands of members and beyond and helped to swell the tide of xenophobia.

The installation of Léon Blum as premier in June 1936 reinvigorated French anti-Semites. On 6 June 1936, the new parliament welcomed Blum and his government for the first time. Blum opened proceedings with a promise to implement the Popular Front's programme and defend democratic freedoms from violence. Fédération Républicaine deputy Xavier Vallat rose to speak following Blum.[70] Vallat's observation that, 'for the first time, this ancient Gallo-Roman country will be governed by a Jew' caused a scandal in parliament and the press. L'Action Française congratulated Vallat for having the courage to denounce the 'Yid' in charge of France. Conservative publications noted that Vallat had simply made a statement of fact.[71] Traditional anti-Semitic tropes about the 'international Jewish conspiracy' against France were applied to the new government. Blum was characterized as an unFrench agent of a Semitic conspiracy.[72]

La Rocque continued to practice an ambiguous anti-Semitism based on his distinction between 'good' and 'bad' Jews. He warned members against irresponsible attacks against patriotic Jewish French while railing against immigrants, Freemasons and Marxists, whom many members perceived to be Jewish. Consequently, provincial activists found it difficult to distinguish between the party's apparently more tolerant attitude to Jews and its broader xenophobia: as a PSF author in Le Flambeau de l'Est surmised, 'In the PSF, we are not "against the Jews" but [we are against] the "dirty Jews".'[73] PSF sections on France's eastern border attacked immigrants (mainly Jews) arriving in the country, yet French Jews came in for criticism, too.[74] Anti-Semitism was expressed in PSF sections in areas as diverse as Lyon, the Midi, Marseille, the Nord, the Haute Vienne, Brittany and the South West. Propaganda depicted Blum with deformed racial features while articles and speeches connected 'the Jew Blum' with communism, international finance and Freemasonry. Anti-Semitism was particularly virulent in the region of Alsace-Lorraine where in October 1938, members' objections to La Rocque's alleged philo-Semitism threatened to split the party.[75] It continued to be strong, too, in Algeria where members indulged in verbal and physical violence against Jews and expressed frequent admiration for foreign fascism.[76] PSF leaders in the territory thus adapted their rhetoric to suit the proclivities of their audience. Charles Vallin, speaking in Alger in 1936, claimed that France would only see justice done once Blum had been sent back to Mount Sinai.[77] PSF deputy in Constantine and editor of the party's *La Flamme* Stanislas Devaud called for settlers to 'unite against Jewry [and] against the Jew Blum'.[78] The party deployed more fully anti-Semitism as a political strategy than its predecessor, in part due to the success of the anti-Semitic PPF in the territory.[79] It could not prevent the ill-considered words of every activist and La Rocque forbade anti-Semitic insults against the socialist leader.[80] Yet even the lieutenant colonel could be tempted into addressing the Jewish 'problem'.[81] In October 1938 La Rocque declared a boycott of Jewish-owned shops in Constantine in response to the demands of his followers in the department.[82] Whether La Rocque desired the action to be temporary and limited or not, his words could only have pleased anti-Semites in the party.[83] Devaud stated: 'The Jews lack individual feelings, they have only collective goals, gregarious instincts, and they vote like sheep. It is therefore they who are racist toward us [and we] are resolutely hostile toward them.'[84]

As for the Islamic population of Algeria, the party soon abandoned attempts to recruit Muslims based on the idea of 'reconciliation'. The lieutenant colonel's understanding of French colonialism rested on the theories of 'adaptation' – defined as the improvement of the level of 'civilisation' of indigenous subjects – and 'assimilation' – that is, the acceptance of French civic rights and duties by North African subjects.[85] Consequently, La Rocque opposed plans to enfranchise a portion of the Algerian Muslim community under the Blum-Violette reforms, which would have removed the requirement for indigenous subjects to renounce Koranic law in order to attain French citizenship.[86] Concomitantly, the PSF helped to shore up settler identity and intransigence in the face of growing demands for representation from the Maghrebin population.[87] It turned subsequently to the view that all indigenous inhabitants were potential insurgents and ruled out any notion of equality in the name of defending *Algérie française*.[88]

La Rocque liked to stress the continuity between the Croix de Feu and the PSF. Indeed, the party remained attractive to the constituency that had supported the league while it simultaneously broadened its appeal through a number of auxiliary groups, the associational life on offer to members and the range of social services it operated. Doubtless some members perceived the two organizations to be the same. Dependent on circumstance, La Rocque and PSF activists were able to pick and choose which elements of the former league's politics to emphasize. The 'mystique Croix de Feu', which was said to animate the PSF, was understood in different ways; it could just as easily have been understood as a commitment to the Republic (or La Rocque's vision of the regime) as a statement of the lieutenant colonel's continued distaste for democracy.[89]

However, the PSF was not simply the Croix de Feu by another name. Certainly, the values bound up in paramilitarism – such as hierarchy, action, will, discipline and obedience – continued to dominate PSF discourse on the future of the French state.[90] It is also true that the structure of the Propaganda Flying Squads resembled that of the *Dispos*. However, one is hard pressed to find evidence that paramilitarism was as central to the PSF as it was to its predecessor.[91] In fact, the PSF's political pronouncements were much less 'apocalyptic' than those of its predecessor while the Flying Squads were smaller and less important within the organization than their forerunner. La Rocque had recognized that the road to power lay in social action, rather than presenting an image of muscular strength and physical threat.[92]

The PSF and the Republic

The Croix de Feu sought to build a veteran's state; the PSF formulated plans for the creation of what it called the French Social State (*Etat Social Français*).[93] The central pillars of this state would be 'Work', 'Family' and 'Fatherland' (*Travail, Famille, Patrie*, the slogan later appropriated by the Vichy regime). This state would remould the decadent nation into a paternalist and familialist society based on peasant and middle-class support, and build on the principles of national unity, class collaboration and corporatism.[94] Conservative Catholic values informed a great deal of the party's plans for France. Indeed, Social Catholicism – a doctrine that encouraged reconciliation and class collaboration while it opposed the elitism and Catholic nationalism of the traditional right – ran throughout the party's activities. This is unsurprising given that the majority of members came from the Catholic right. Social Catholicism also provided a useful means by which to broaden the party's appeal beyond the narrow veterans' community.[95]

When viewed in combination with its rejection of violence, the party's Catholicism might be perceived as revelatory of an unmistakably conservative character.[96] However, the PSF contrasted the virtue of its hard-line Catholic values with the decadence of democratic liberalism, individualism and godless socialism, just as the Croix de Feu had juxtaposed the selflessness of the *esprit combattant* to the narrow self-interest of the Republic.[97] Furthermore, the Catholicism inherent to the party's programme left it better placed to underscore its credentials as the vanguard of French and Christian civilization, something useful both for the elaboration of its exclusionary vision of national identity and in its attacks on the Popular Front.[98] The PSF thus presented 'an authoritarian and populist version of Social Catholicism', which placed elitism, nationalism and hierarchy at the centre of its vision of a future French State.[99]

La Rocque continued to stress his loyalty to Republican institutions. Indeed, the party's programme at the 1936 national congress affirmed its commitment to 'Republican freedoms' while rejecting fascist and communist dictatorship out of hand.[100] Expressions of loyalty to the Third Republic must be set within the context of his party's plan to transform the Third Republic into a new kind of state.[101] The PSF's agenda for institutional reform resembled closely that of the Croix de Feu: once in power, a temporary regime of 'designated men' would deal with the country's enemies and restore order to the regime.[102] The practical acceptance of the electoral route to power should not blind us to the fact that the PSF would profoundly alter Republican institutions.[103]

It is tempting to conclude that the PSF's critique of the regime, and its plans for reform, merely responded to real problems in the functioning of the regime. From this point of view, the PSF's reform programme emerged from a broader analysis of the deficiencies of the parliamentary institution and sought to render the Republic more efficient in its government of France.[104] Ostensibly one might perceive little that was undemocratic in La Rocque's desire to build 'a new Republic, according to a military vision, that is to say hierarchical, with a strengthened executive', based on broad middle-class support.[105] Indeed, it could be argued that this vision was realized with the foundation of the Fifth Republic, a regime that was very different to the previous iterations of the parliamentary Republic.[106] However, this line of argument posits the Fifth Republic as the outcome of a particular historical process towards which certain foresighted men from the past – La Rocque, for example – were working.[107] Such teleology foregrounds aspects of the past that have persisted into, or come to fruition in, the present while ignoring those elements that 'failed'. For one thing, it is unlikely that the PSF would have tolerated political pluralism in a future France of its making. The left would have been destroyed and the unions neutered; this has not happened under the Fifth Republic.[108]

The left continued to consider the PSF as the French expression of a transnational fascist movement. The Communist Party alleged that La Rocque was playing a double game. On the one hand, he posed himself as the friend of the workers; on the other hand, as a Nazi imitator, he planned their destruction.[109] Following the violence at the Parc des Princes in October 1936, *Le Populaire* drew a comparison between the PSF's demonstration and the rioting witnessed during the 'Battle of Cable Street' in London: 'The fascists are the same everywhere. Wherever they may be, they use the same violent methods.' The newspaper suggested that the violence involving the British Union of Fascists on 4 October had in part informed the French government's decision to ban the PSF in Paris.[110]

The lieutenant colonel persistently denied the accusations of the left that he was a fascist, throwing the label back in the face of the 'red fascism' of communism.[111] La Rocque's appreciation of foreign fascism changed as the geopolitics of Europe evolved. The lieutenant colonel's hopes for an alliance with Fascist Italy diminished. Mussolini had begun to move closer to Hitler at the time of the Italian invasion of Abyssinia in October 1935, and a year later the two dictatorships agreed the Rome-Berlin Axis. As the Duce's claims on French colonial territories grew more strident, the PSF became critical of his 'demagogy', 'paganism' and 'excesses'.[112] The mantle of totalitarianism now came to colour the lieutenant colonel's opinion of Rome and its German ally.[113] The cooling of La Rocque's attitude to Italy was not replicated across the board. French veterans continued to maintain relations with their Italian comrades until 1938. In February that year, the Union Fédérale's André Gervais praised the Fascists' 'Believe, Obey, Fight' mantra at the last meeting of the Union d'Anciens Combattants France-Italie. The committee was dissolved in December 1938.[114]

The PSF looked for other 'Latin' allies in Spain and Portugal. In the former, the party offered its support to the Francoist rebels, seeing in these nationalists a means to safeguard Christian civilization from Bolshevism. La Rocque demanded that the French government avoid intervention in the conflict though some PSF members in Algeria were sympathetic to the Spanish insurgents.[115] As for Portugal, the authoritarian regime of António de Oliveira Salazar offered an alternative to the fascist model. Salazar emerged as the dominant political force in Portugal following his appointment as Minister of Finance in 1928. The military dictatorship installed two years ago had fallen into financial difficulties and the regime thus turned to Salazar, a professor of economics at the elite Coimbra University, to rescue the situation. Salazar agreed, on the condition that he assume control of all government expenditure. Holding the purse strings of the state, he gradually accumulated more power until he was appointed prime minister – and de facto dictator – in 1932. A new constitution the following year cemented his position.[116] Salazar promptly embarked on his project for the Estado Novo, a Catholic and corporatist state, grounded in severe financial austerity and a celebration of Portugal's historic and colonial culture. Simultaneously, he cultivated for himself a monkish image of a man disdainful of petty politics and personally incorruptible.[117]

French interest in Salazar and the Estado Novo was considerable.[118] A great number of published works and interviews appeared in France as part of a propaganda charm offensive conducted by António Ferro, head of Portugal's Secretariado da Propaganda Nacional. These publications presented Salazar as a 'moral' and benign dictator – 'as humane and as tolerant as possible' – and a man whose austere style and deep commitment to Catholicism contrasted sharply with the ostentatious theatre and choreography of Italian Fascism and German Nazism.[119] Ferro was even invited to write an entry on Salazar in the prestigious *Encylcopédie Française*. He used the opportunity to further distance the Estado Novo from fascism.[120] Consequently, in contrast to Mussolini (away from whom the French right began to turn after 1935), Salazar was a 'hardworking' dictator who had restored order to his country, and he could thus step into the space vacated by the *Duce*.[121] For those on the right of French politics looking for an alternative to Mussolini and Hitler, Salazar presented an ideal comparison; author Emile Schreiber described Salazar as a Poincaré, with Portuguese president Carmona a Pétain.[122]

A number of other factors increased the attractiveness of the Portuguese regime for the French extreme right. First, Salazar recognized his intellectual debt to French thinkers such as Maurice Barrès, Gustave Le Bon and, in particular, Charles Maurras. Indeed, according to the Portuguese's biographer, Filipe Ribeiro de Meneses, Maurras was one of Salazar's 'usual political references'.[123] The influence of Maurrassian thought in Portugal was considerable. A long-time historic and cultural connection between France and Portugal ensured that Paris was a favourite destination for Portuguese exiles, travellers and students both before and after the First World War. Portuguese nationalists encountered the ideas of the Action Française in the French capital and took them back to Portugal where they had a formative impact on the country's own integralist nationalist movement, the Integralismo Lusitano.[124] If fascism appeared irreconcilable with French mentalities, Salazarism was perhaps better suited to the French nature.

Second, in line with French extreme right-wingers like La Rocque, Salazar considered fascism and totalitarianism incompatible with his indigenous culture. In the 1934 French translation of Ferro's *Salazar, O homem e a sua obra* (*Salazar, le Portugal et son Chef*), Salazar admitted that fascism shared several common features with his Portuguese project, notably a taste for authority, an opposition to democracy, a nationalist character and a concern with the social order. However, he rejected the revolutionary aspects of fascism and Mussolini's attitude to violence, which 'clashes with our race and our customs'.[125] He likewise viewed with disdain the all-powerfulness of the fascist state. In a 1934 speech at the Sala Portugal of the Geographical Society of Portugal, he rejected the totalitarian state as, 'an omnipotent being, the principle and end in itself'. Portugal could not submit to such absolutism because 'such a state would be essentially pagan, incompatible by its nature with the character of our Christian civilization'.[126] La Rocque's own rejection of fascism was phrased in similar terms: 'The French state, guide and protector of the Nation … could never be for us the object of a semi-religious worship, such as characterizes contemporary Italy'.[127] Historians, too, have identified the essence of the Portuguese regime as a counterpoint to the fascist dictatorships elsewhere in Europe. Rémond labelled Salazar's government 'conservative and clerical' in contrast to fascism.[128] Kéchichian argued that though Salazar employed the trappings of fascism, the nature of his regime lay in authoritarian and Catholic traditionalism. As such, the Estado Novo presented the 'closest foreign model' to what La Rocque planned for the future of France.[129]

However, a comparison between La Rocque's French Social State and Salazar's Estado Novo, by which one identifies the essence of each, brings with it certain problems. To identify certain features to be of primary significance renders others secondary. Take, for example, the veterans' mystique of the First World War. La Rocque built the Croix de Feu upon the myth of the noble veteran and, while the PSF sought to expand its appeal beyond the ranks of the ex-servicemen's community, a significant proportion of PSF members were veterans. The Portuguese veterans' movement was considerably smaller than its French counterpart, and Salazar himself did not serve during the war. Furthermore, as prime minister, he worked to marginalize the official veterans' association, the Liga dos Combatentes da Grande Guerra, for he considered it to be a haven of recalcitrant Republican officers. As Minister of War after 1936, he did not attend a single veterans' ceremony.[130] Consequently, La Rocque's politics matched those of Salazar only if we consider the lieutenant colonel's appeal to veterans to be of secondary importance.

We must also qualify Salazar's 1934 renunciation of totalitarianism. An appreciation of the domestic political context that provided the backdrop to the speech at the Sala Portugal is important to an understanding of Salazar's position. The speech, made two days prior to the eighth anniversary celebrations of the military coup, was part of the dictator's offensive against a threat from domestic fascism. In late 1933, Francisco Rolão Preto, a war veteran and co-founder of Integralismo Lusitano, founded the National Syndicalist movement. Preto sought to move the regime in a more radical – and fascist – direction. Like the prime minister, he drew inspiration from the Action Française. However, if Salazar borrowed the reactionary ideas of a Maurras, Preto preferred the revolutionary 'left' fascism of a Valois (his National Syndicalism in fact aped the structure of the Faisceau). To shore up his own position, Salazar took every opportunity to distance himself from Preto's fascism despite the fact that there were shared points of doctrine between Salazarism and National Syndicalism.[131] Consequently, while we may understand Salazar's public rejection of totalitarianism as a response to foreign fascism, it must be read, too, in the context of his own struggle to position himself in relation to the domestic challenge from National Syndicalism.[132]

There were indeed aspects of Salazar's regime that mirrored the fascist states.[133] The Legião Portuguesa (Portuguese Legion), founded in 1936, wore green-shirted uniforms and used the Roman salute. The Legionnaires took part in carefully-choreographed parades intended to impress the onlooker and intimidate dissenters.[134] That same year, the regime launched a paramilitary patriotic youth organization, the Mocidade Portuguesa (Portuguese Youth). Membership was compulsory for children under seventeen years of age.[135] Totalitarian tendencies were evident in the regime's national celebrations, too. Salazar's head of propaganda, António Ferro, was an admirer of Mussolini, and in 1936 he modelled the celebration of the tenth anniversary of the 28 May 1926 revolution on Italy's commemoration of the March on Rome.[136] The 1940 Mundo Português exhibition likewise borrowed the symbolism and theatricality of fascist propaganda and rituals in its celebration of *portugalidade* ('Portugueseness'). In fact, such events were part of raft of educative and propaganda initiatives to ground Portuguese identity in the values of the Estado Novo.[137]

Some French considered the Estado Novo to be fascist. Robert Brasillach included the regime among a list of fascist governments in his 1939 novel *Les Sept Couleurs* and his 1941 memoir *Notre Avant Guerre*.[138] Jean Renaud, head of the Solidarité Française, praised Salazar in 1935 as a model for a future French dictator. It is worth noting that Rémond described the Solidarité Française as an organization 'of the very purest fascism'.[139] PSF journalist Octave Aubry perceived in Salazar's Estado Novo project a 'Christian and humane tradition' consonant with that of the PSF; the party's newspaper, *Le Petit Journal*, regularly praised the Portuguese regime.[140] For the lieutenant colonel, the project of Salazar was analogous to his own while fascism remained incompatible with 'the French temperament'.[141] Neither Salazar's statements on totalitarianism nor La Rocque's admiration for the Estado Novo revealed the essence of their politics. Movements borrowed and adapted features from foreign doctrines while ignoring and rejecting others; boundaries were permeable and fluid, and much of this interchange and exchange depended on domestic and international political relations.

The Parti Populaire Français

It is impossible to separate the PPF from the figure of its founder and leader Jacques Doriot. The son of a former blacksmith and factory worker, Doriot arrived in the Parisian suburb of Saint-Denis – 'where the tombs of French kings are surrounded by some of the grimiest slums of the industrial *banlieue*' – in 1915, aged seventeen, to work as a metalworker.[142] Mobilized to the Western Front in April 1917, he distinguished himself when he carried an injured comrade over a mile to safety, a deed for which he was mentioned in dispatches.[143] Such daring characterized Doriot's early political career in the Communist Party after the war. In the meeting hall, he developed into an accomplished orator, 'unbeatable on the stage' with a 'powerful and consummate oratorical style'.[144] In the street, he could mobilize men against the police, using his imposing physique – Doriot liked boxing – to lead his followers into action.[145] His physical attributes were described in gendered terms; in 1924, *L'Humanité* had described the young activist: 'A big, strong, brown-haired boy, with a male face, honest eyes. … Energy and willpower seeps out of him.'[146] This emphasis on Doriot's masculinity would later form his personality cult in the PPF. By the time he was twenty-three years old, Doriot had become secretary general of the Jeunesses Communistes and occupied a seat on the praesidium of the Executive Committee of the new Communist International.[147]

Doriot was elected to parliament in 1924. On his first appearance in the Chamber in August 1924, he caused an uproar when he proclaimed, 'I am a soldier of the Red Army and I am proud of being such; if I have to take up arms for the Revolution, I will do so.'[148] His quality as a deputy did not prevent him from engaging in the street brawls to which he had become accustomed. On 12 October 1925, Doriot fought with police officers at the rue Mathurin-Moreau during a protest against the Rif War in Morocco. PPF intellectual Drieu La Rochelle later eulogized the incident in heavily gendered terms: 'Doriot, alone, [stood] up to 200 police officers, [dived] right in, [spun] a café table above his head, [raising] clusters [of people] on his powerful shoulders.'[149] His support for colonial rebel Abd el-Krim in the street and in the Chamber cemented his reputation as the *enfant terrible* of the left.

Doriot was re-elected to parliament in 1932; that same year he took up the mayoralty of Saint-Denis.[150] Although touted as a potential leader of the national party, his persistent opposition to the policy of class warfare with the Socialist Party brought him into conflict with Secretary General Maurice Thorez and the directors of the Comintern. The crisis of the *six février* sharpened Doriot's sense that the success of an antifascist strategy lay in unity on the left, but the party leadership refused to budge on the issue. Worse still from Doriot's point of view, his comrades at the head of the party were not present at the communist demonstration on 9 February, when several workers were killed in fighting with the police. The mayor of Saint-Denis, on the other hand, had been in the thick of the fight near the Gare de l'Est.[151] In the following days, Doriot worked to build an alliance with socialists in his constituency. With the Saint-Denis section of the Socialist Party and the CGT, he founded the Comité de Vigilance, which he subsequently refused to dissolve on the orders of the Communist Party.[152]

In April 1934, Doriot resigned as mayor and made public his disagreement with the leadership in *Emancipation*, the newspaper of his Communist Party section. Re-elected the following month with a huge proportion of the vote (75.9 per cent), he was emboldened to refuse an invitation to Moscow on 10 May. Doriot's days in the party were now numbered. A week later, *L'Humanité* published a resolution that accused him of attempting to split the communist movement. Thorez would brook no challenge from Doriot the 'opportunist' and 'renegade'; the latter was expelled in June 1934.[153]

Doriot's branch of the Communist Party continued to exist in an independent form, as the so-called majority section (*rayon majoritaire*), in contrast to the official Communist Party branch in Saint-Denis. The section posed as a third force on the left, continuing to celebrate days of revolutionary significance, saluting with the antifascist clenched fist, and adopting a similar style of organization to Communist Party branches.[154] Doriot's hatred of his former comrades was plain. During a speech to the Chamber of Deputies in February 1936, 'He accused them of taking money from Moscow and of wishing to drag France into a war against Germany for the benefit of the Soviet Union', with a Bolshevik revolution in France as the ultimate objective. These were the traditional anti-communist allegations of the right, and he was cheered throughout from the right-wing benches.[155] Doriot's desire to compete with the Communist Party saw him depict the USSR as the ultimate threat to peace in Europe, more serious even than that posed by Hitler. This policy did not imply any sympathy with the Nazi regime. Rather, Doriot considered a French agreement with Hitler as an obstacle to the spread of communism.[156]

The PPF was founded soon after the election of the Popular Front. Doriot was joined on the party's leadership committee by other former leading communists, such as Henri Barbé, who had previously led the Jeunesses Communistes. Indeed, upon its founding, six out of the seven party executives were former communists.[157] The PPF's opposition to the new government was not immediately clear.[158] Doriot's position on the extreme right was likewise uncertain, too; he condemned the fascism of the leagues and voted for their dissolution.[159] In fact, Doriot promoted the PPF as 'fascist' only after mid-1937 when conflict with the party's rivals on left and right prompted a change in strategy.

Nonetheless, the PPF was ultranationalist and stridently anti-communist. It desired an end to class conflict through corporatism, which would bring workers 'social peace, higher productivity, and an increase in real wages'. Thus the worker would see the uselessness of strikes and embrace class solidarity in the name of 'the common good of the enterprise', as Doriot put it in his *Refaire la France*.[160] The party's intellectual supporters, Drieu La Rochelle and Bertrand de Jouvenel, made no attempt to hide their hatred of democracy and their disgust at the spectacle of parliamentary politics, the former calling the Chamber of Deputies 'a miserable sham, unbelievably pathetic and abject, [and] of a moral and intellectual baseness beyond words'.[161]

Political violence was a routine activity for the PPF for the Popular Front parties targeted party meetings with counter-demonstrations.[162] In December 1936, for example, an antifascist demonstration outside a PPF meeting in Clermont-Ferrand saw clashes between protesters and the Mobile Guard riot police. Six guards were seriously injured while a dozen police constables were also hurt.[163] Such incidents allowed PPF propaganda to hail the masculine muscularity of its street fighters. While Doriot's party enlisted young French men into its security service, the PPF also sought to enrol North Africans into its fighting units.[164] The party was not alone in its appreciation of the alleged fighting abilities of the Maghrebis: the left nicknamed the Solidarité Française the 'Sidilarité Française', for the number of 'sidis' in its ranks.[165] The PPF's brigades could be mobilized at a moment's notice; they were deployed to particularly good effect in Simon Sabiani's Marseille, and under Joseph Darnand in the Alpes-Maritimes.[166] These men were more willing to resort to firearms – and celebrate this fact – than their right-wing counterparts.

From the outset, the PPF was well subsidized by banking and industrial interests who were keen to undermine the Popular Front's support among workers. Significant financial backers included Gabriel Leroy-Ladurie, the head of the Banque Worms, and Pierre Pucheu who had connections to the Comité des Forges.[167] Such was the importance of Pucheu's access to funds – he provided 350,000 France per month in funds from the Comptoir sidérurgique – that when he quit the party in autumn 1938, the PPF was plunged into financial crisis.[168] Mussolini's government also provided as much as nine million francs, between April 1937 and October 1938. It was with this money that the party could buy the newspaper *La Liberté* and its headquarters on the rue des Pyramides.[169]

The membership of the PPF numbered between 50,000 and 100,000 active members with a broader base of perhaps 300,000 sympathizers.[170] In mainland France, the party was strongest in the Paris region, the Rhône valley and towns such as Bordeaux, Reims, Rouen and Clermont-Ferrand. While this information suggests that the PPF had a national reach, its implantation throughout France was patchy.[171] Local personalities were significant to the PPF's success especially in the Mediterranean departments. In Marseille, for example, political boss and gangster Sabiani ran the section, taking the fascist salute from his followers and popularizing the slogan, 'Neither right nor left: France first!'[172] The PPF enjoyed a great deal of success in Algeria where its exploitation of patriotism and ethnic divisions found favour among white European settlers and members who were drawn from a variety of racist extreme right-wing groups.[173] Doubtless it benefited too from the relative lethargy with which the PSF established a presence in the country following the 1936 decree of dissolution; the PPF began operating in Algeria in autumn 1936 while the PSF emerged there only in February 1937.[174]

The social and professional backgrounds of delegates to the first congress in 1936 suggest that the majority came from the middle classes, while the ordinary members were more likely to be drawn from the working class, broadly defined.[175] Workers may have joined the PPF because of the party's offers of employment and its claim to represent the proletariat, yet it promised to protect middle-class interests primarily.[176] The social work of women members was aimed at nurturing working-class support. The party shared the view of many groups on the right and extreme right that women's role in society was limited to being a loyal wife to her activist husband and a doting mother to future generations of French. Yet like the PSF, Doriot's movement offered an opportunity for activism outside the home even if the ultimate goal was to spread a conservative and familialist message. Women's 'feminine qualities' were believed best suited to social work, framed as an important contribution to resolving class differences in France.[177] However, appeals to the working class were largely unsuccessful. Paul Jankowski's study of 408 members in Marseille found that only 7 per cent were from a working-class occupation. Unsurprisingly, therefore, the PPF's attempts to establish its own trade union failed.[178] By the second national congress in March 1938, the membership was more solidly petit bourgeois, reflecting that of other radical right movements.[179] By that time, the party itself had undergone a transformation, self-consciously adopting the fascist label as a means to distinguish itself from its opponents. To understand this move, we must look to Doriot's failed attempt to build an alliance with the PSF.

The PPF, the Freedom Front and Fascism

On 27 March 1937, Doriot launched the 'Freedom Front against Communism' (*Front de la liberté contre le communisme*). The Front's mission statement called for the defence of a number of freedoms, including those of meeting, work and the press. It expressed a desire, too, to defend 'Republican institutions', which, moreover, would not be 'called into question'. Finally, partners in the alliance would cease attacks upon each other.[180] Doriot's plan was to construct a broad anti-communist coalition from the extreme right to the anti-communist left; his appeal for support thus included not only parties such as the PSF and the conservative Fédération Républicaine but the Radical Party too. However, his attempt to build a non-partisan force soon collapsed when the Radicals refused to participate; from that moment the Freedom Front was based squarely on the right. The nascent movement was hindered, too, by the fact that only the Fédération Républicaine and Taittinger's PRNS were prepared to back it; indeed, fifty-seven of the fifty-nine Freedom Front deputies came from the former. Far from Doriot's original aspiration that the alliance represents neither the right nor the left, the Freedom Front soon became a reactionary coalition.[181]

La Rocque rejected membership of the Freedom Front. The lieutenant colonel understood that to enter an agreement with Doriot would compromise his independence of action as well as his claim to the leadership of the largest constituency on the right not to mention his attempts to attract the support of right-wing Radicals. He was likely wary, too, of Doriot's designs on attracting the PSF members to his own movement. Doriot's offer to the PSF placed La Rocque in a difficult situation. How could the leader of the PSF refuse to participate in a grand coalition of the right, a *rassemblement* of national forces for which he had long called?[182] To escape this predicament and thwart Doriot's plan, the lieutenant colonel requested that the alliance declare its respect for the Republic, in full knowledge that such a declaration would be anathema to the extra-parliamentary members of the Front. Doriot called La Rocque's bluff and duly obliged on 23 May 1937.

In the end, the lieutenant colonel was saved by the narrowness of the range of parties that supported the Front. When the Alliance Démocratique and the Parti Démocrate Populaire refused Doriot's invitation, La Rocque declined, too, claiming that the Front did not represent all the forces necessary for a national reconciliation. The failure of the Freedom Front to attract broad-based support condemned the coalition to obscurity; the press soon lost interest in the initiative. Indeed, one could argue that media interest in the proposed nationalist Front lasted only as long as the prospect of Lieutenant-Colonel de La Rocque joining.[183]

The PSF's rejection of the Freedom Front rested on a hard-nosed appreciation of the political dangers of membership.[184] La Rocque feared a loss of members to Doriot's party and warned his followers about attempts to infiltrate the PSF.[185] There were few differences between its politics and that of the PPF, especially in the areas of state reform, corporatism, the ostensible rejection of left and right and its attitude to foreigners and Jews.[186] La Rocque and Doriot had, in fact, held discussions about some form of collaboration during 1936. However, from December of that year, the establishment of the PSF's parliamentary group brought the two men into competition with each other for votes. Yet evidence suggests that members did not perceive any great difference between the parties. In November 1936, men belonging to the PSF and the PPF worked together to occupy several factories in Troyes between 9.00 pm and 3.00 am, in the apparent belief that a communist coup was imminent.[187] There were defections from one party to the other, too; an estimated 5,000 PSF members in the Paris area joined the PPF between March and June 1937.[188]

The failure of the Freedom Front marked a turning point for the PPF. Following the coalition's still-birth, the party faced marginalization. Doriot searched for a means to reinvigorate the party and mark it out from its rivals; an embrace of 'fascism' offered just such an opportunity.[189] 'Fascist' was a label that the Communist Party had long applied to him: 'A vote for Doriot is a vote for Hitler', stated communist Fernand Grenier in April 1936, before even the founding of the PPF.[190] The right, on the other hand, was less sure. When right-wing newssheets deigned to mention him at all, they branded him a dissident Bolshevik.[191] Doriot himself initially rejected the fascist label. Indeed, he claimed in his 1936 *La France ne sera un pays d'esclaves* that the PPF belonged to the antifascist front.[192] In the 10 October 1936 edition of *L'Emancipation nationale* (the PPF's national newspaper) Robert Loustau professed the democratic credentials of the party.[193]

Further difficulties in spring 1937 pushed Doriot towards adopting the term as his own. On 25 May, Minister of the Interior Marx Dormoy removed Doriot from his post of mayor of Saint-Denis following an investigation into 'abuses and irregularities' at the town hall. Doriot resigned immediately from the town council, too. His plan was to win back his seat with a large majority and thus demonstrate to Paris that he enjoyed popular legitimacy in the suburb. The plan did not work. On 20 June, Doriot was defeated in the municipal by-election, winning only 37.9 per cent of the vote. He resigned as a deputy the same day; his seat would be taken by Grenier later that year, thus delivering a further blow to the PPF.[194] Doriot could now no longer claim with any credibility that he was attracting working-class voters from the Communist Party. As the PSF rapidly grew into the most promising formation on the right – or the most threatening in the eyes of antifascists – the PPF gradually disappeared from public view.[195] Werth remarked that it was curious that 'after a few weeks of sympathetic interest in Doriot, whom they proclaimed (usually with a question mark) "the man of to-morrow", the Press of the Right dropped him'.[196]

In the wake of the PPF's poor showing in the 1937 cantonal elections, Doriot came to see Algeria as a possible means by which to revive his political fortunes. For one thing, the party's anti-communism played well to the political constituencies in the territory. In 1926, Radical parliamentarian Albert Sarraut had chosen Alger to sound his famous battle cry, 'The enemy is communism!'; the strike wave of 1936–7 had once again stoked hostility to the left.[197] Where he had previously considered anti-Semitism too narrow a programme upon which to base the party, he now gave himself over to the racism that was so popular among the PPF's constituency in Oran with a view to winning the department's parliamentary seat.[198] Articles attacking Jews appeared now in the PPF's mainstream press.[199] In July 1938, Drieu La Rochelle called both for the abrogation of the 1927 law on citizenship and the creation of a Jewish Statute that would constrain the professional and political rights of Jews.[200] By the time of the second congress of the North African sections in November 1938, Victor Arrighi could confidently assert, 'We have had enough of those who, without being from our nation, from our soil, from our blood, without being able to lay claim to our history, want to govern and subjugate our country.' The congress proceeded to demand the abrogation of the Crémieux decree, the revision of all naturalizations granted after 1918, and promised to evict the Jews from the North African colonies.[201] As for Algeria's Muslim population, the PPF courted their support more vigorously than the PSF. It proposed a Muslim-only electoral body as an alternative to the Blum-Violette decree while promising to raise the living standards of indigenous workers. It appointed Djilali Bentami (formerly a member of the Croix de Feu) to a decision-making committee in the territory. Of course, the settler community would remain dominant in any future imperial arrangement. Nevertheless, approximately 20 per cent of members in Algeria were Muslims.[202]

The PPF's anti-Semitism developed concurrently with its adoption of the fascist label. Members were required to take an oath in which they swore 'fealty and devotion to the Parti Populaire Français, to its ideal, [and] to its leader', as well as, 'to serve until the ultimate sacrifice the cause of national and popular revolution from which will emerge a new, free, and independent France'.[203] The party also adopted other features understood at the time to be part of the iconography and liturgy of fascist parties: a salute modelled on that of the Italian fascists; a song ('France, free yourself!') and a martyrology that commemorated the 'fallen' of the party.[204] The seed of a leadership cult was present upon the PPF's founding. In November 1936, Jean-Pierre Luce reported to the readers of *L'Emancipation Nationale* the proceedings of the party's first national congress in Saint-Denis. Doriot had held the audience transfixed with his oratory and ideas. Luce stated that those in attendance may have come from different political backgrounds with an ex-communist here, and a former Croix de Feu there, but Doriot had reshaped them into a uniform mass. They might be renegades but they were renegades only from dead ideas, 'and Doriot gives us life from his powerful arms'.[205] By 1938, the cult of personality was fully formed. Eric Labat, a young member of the PPF's security service in 1938, wrote that seeing and hearing Doriot speak gave one 'the impression of witnessing an enormous collective rape by a power of elemental virility'.[206] Such things gave the PPF a self-consciously fascist patina that spoke to Doriot's plan to remodel the image of the party.

The party's new programme called for the revalorization of the French peasantry, the placing of family at the centre of national life, corporatism and ultra-nationalism. The composition of the leadership committee had moved to the extreme right, now including men such as de Jouvenel, Drieu La Rochelle and Pucheu.[207] However, even in March 1938, Doriot claimed that the party was Republican. The content of his Republicanism, like that of La Rocque's, was decidedly different from the incumbent regime's parliamentarianism. In the PPF's vision of France, parliament would be subjugated to the executive, in a bid to put an end to what Doriot termed 'the era of omnipotent and incompetent antiparliamentarianism'. The 'French Popular State' would remake the institutions of the Republic into three corporative assemblies, representing the provinces, corporations and the empire.[208] At the party's second national congress in March 1938, Paul Marion claimed that the PPF would 'remake the body and spirit of France', with the party being the image in microcosm of what France would later become. Calling on the imagery of a violent hypermasculinity, Marion argued that the nation needed a 'new man' with a 'taste for danger, confidence in himself, the sense of the group, the taste for collective impulses and the memory of unanimous faiths which gave rise to [ont permis] the cathedrals and French miracles'. The congress came to a close with the warning that 'the Bolshevised Popular Front has drained France of its blood, its race, its virtues. It has crushed the French worker between plutocracy and the wog.'[209] Doriot publicly advocated the strengthening of the executive branch of the Republic with the granting of full powers to bring an end to ministerial crisis and parliamentary dithering. Parliament would act as an 'overseer' while the executive ran the country in cooperation with a corporatist assembly gifted with legislative powers. Military values such as discipline, order and hierarchy would inform the new regime.[210] State intervention in social works would produce a 'stronger, healthier race'.[211] This combination of rhetoric reminiscent of foreign fascism with a reactionary, even Catholic, traditionalism characterized the party until the outbreak of the war, described by Philippe Burrin as a proto-Vichy discourse.[212]

The party's 1938 congress took place at the moment when Germany incorporated Austria into the Third Reich. Doriot railed against the French diplomatic weakness that had led to this point and argued in favour of rapprochement with Mussolini's Italy, Franco in Spain and the conclusion of a non-aggression pact with Hitler.[213] The Sudeten crisis later that year severely tested the PPF because a certain ambiguity reigned in the movement. Doriot appeared to accept German claims on the Sudeten region of Czechoslovakia, yet he demanded that this be the last concession granted to Hitler and called for war should the German chancellor continue to act in such a way.[214]

In November 1938, when Doriot responded to Italy's claims on French colonies with the suggestion that some concessions be made to the *Duce*, a crisis within the party broke out.[215] Executive members and prominent collaborators lined up to attack Doriot. De Jouvenel, Pucheu, Loustau, Paringuaux, Arrighi, Marion, Jean Fontenoy, Barbé, Fabre-Luce, Drieu La Rochelle: all resigned from the PPF in apparent protest at the direction of the party's foreign policy. However, problems within the party exerted a greater influence than exterior events, and the rebels had simply been waiting for an opportunity to make their move. Mismanagement of party funds had led to a decline in the PPF's national and regional press. Furthermore, the failure of the Freedom Front brought to the surface personal antagonisms – not least based on social class – that had been buried while the party had been on an upward trajectory.[216] Not a few criticized Doriot's taste for fine dining, wine and prostitutes, too. Doriot was no longer the ascetic 'fanatical Bolshevik monk' of the 1920s, as described by Barbé. He had taken up smoking, drinking and living the high life.[217]

The PSF and the PPF at the end of the 1930s

It is unlikely that the PSF's huge support would have translated into parliamentary dominance should the elections of 1940 have been staged. The succession of Radical-led administrations that followed the fall of Blum's government in 1937 had reassured the conservative right. Daladier, installed as prime minister in April 1938, effectively brought an end to the Popular Front alliance. The PSF could no longer pose as the only real opposition to the socialist and communist left.[218] The party had performed well in several by-elections – counting ten deputies by 1940 – yet in terms of an electoral strategy it was effectively trying to make up lost ground.[219] At the same time it faced significant obstacles to electoral success, including persistent and ferocious attacks of the left, the dominance and hostility of candidates from established conservative parties and the well-oiled electoral machine of the Radical Party. Had the elections gone ahead in 1940 (Daladier suspended the vote until June 1942), the party would likely have won no more than 70 of the 610 seats in the Chamber.[220] Nevertheless, the PSF's huge growth demonstrated that there was a large constituency in France that was receptive to its plans for an authoritarian reform of the regime in line with Catholic and xenophobic values. The necessity of winning votes saw La Rocque set out his vision for an authoritarian and exclusionary regime that would cleanse the country of anti-French elements. All of this could be carried out within a 'Republican' system – but not a democratic one.

La Rocque took great pains to soften his movement's image in 1936 and 1937. In 1938, the PSF gave its qualified backing to aspects of the Daladier government's policy; the party's eight deputies, for example, voted to grant the government decree powers in April 1938. Feelers were put out to anti-Popular Front Radical deputies, perhaps looking to form a tentative alliance with the right of the centrist party.[221] However, rather than understanding the PSF's success in terms of a move to the centre, we should rather acknowledge the rightward shift of French politics more generally. The PSF's rhetoric in defence of the Republic sought to position the movement as the defender of France and the regime against the threat from the revolutionary left. For those French who did not identify with the politics of the Popular Front government, 'Republicanism' was interpreted through the prism of right-wing values.[222] The PSF's overtures to Radical deputies were made in order to split and destroy the party, not to form a centrist alliance.[223] The party's strategy of shifting the centre ground towards authoritarianism moved the meaning of Republicanism to the right.[224]

As for the PPF, the spate of resignations in 1938 did little to worry the mass of PPF members, and the party predicted that it would win between fifty and sixty seats in the general election of 1940.[225] Doriot's Republicanism was conceived as one in which a strengthened executive and providential leader would bring parliamentary factions to heel in the name of national unity. His vision of a 'fascist' state developed slowly. Only by 1938 had the PPF embraced what it considered to be fascism in a bid to carve out a niche for itself on the right-wing of the political spectrum. The PPF's remodelling as a 'fascist' party' was by no means predetermined. On the one hand, it resulted in part from the concerted campaign of the left against the party. Doriot could not counter effectively the accusation that he was a French fascist. On the other hand, political competition within the right saw the PPF attempt to distinguish itself from its competitors through the adoption of the fascist label and the stylistic devices associated with it.[226] We must thus understand the party's evolution as a 'complex process – [the] product of adjustments between very heterogeneous social trajectories, differentiated political courses, political skills and sometimes contradictory intellectual know-how – that led to the invention of the post of the leader of the PPF and to the transformation of the PPF into a fascist-type party'.[227] Consequently, for both the PSF and the PPF, political relationships and tactical considerations came to condition each movement's politics.

CHAPTER 5
BOMBS, BULLETS AND BLOODY MURDER: THE CAGOULE

On 20 January 1938, thirty-three-year-old businessman André Lebis made a statement to detective chief inspector Jean Quilici in Nice. It pertained to his membership in a group known as the Knights of the Claymore (*Chevaliers du Glaive*). In particular, Quilici quizzed Lebis on the manner in which he had come to join the Knights. Lebis recounted that a former comrade in the Action Française – Maurice – had invited him to a secret meeting of the group in the basement of a shoe shop on the Boulevard Carnot. What happened is best recounted in Lebis's words:

> Upon my arrival I noticed that the room was dark, lit only by two wax candles. At the doorway two strangers put a great black hood over me which covered my face and body. About ten other people also wearing hoods surrounded a table. The 'master' in a red hood gave orders to smash all the windows of Jewish shops, and to throw tar on their fronts. I objected to such a thing and immediately, I was told to be quiet, to check my 'fanciful notions', for if I committed an indiscretion, the Association had powerful means at its disposal to silence me. Thus the 'master' informed me that the organisation had Doctors and Chemists, and that it would not hesitate to use biological weapons (*bacille*) to get rid of me. … As I protested, they made me pull back my hood, so that all the people around the table could get a good look at me … they made me swear an oath on a claymore, resting on a table in the meeting room. I had to promise not to betray the secret of the claymore, and to keep the organisation secret. … All the members of this association were clearly enemies of the State authorities, but they wanted by new and more direct means to achieve their goals.[1]

The Knights of the Claymore were part of the Organisation Secrète d'Action Révolutionnaire Nationale (OSARN), an extreme right-wing organization with truly terrifying means at its disposal.[2] The OSARN was best known by its soubriquet, the 'Cagoule' or hood. From its founding in the wake of the Popular Front's electoral victory in summer 1936, the Cagoule plotted to unseat the Republic and replace it with a dictatorship in the mould of Mussolini's Fascist regime. During 1937, OSARN operatives (or 'Cagoulards') committed a series of bombings and murders designed to exacerbate feelings of insecurity in French public opinion and stoke fears of communist revolution. Most notable among their crimes were the June 1937 murders of noted Italian antifascists Carlo and Nello Roselli and the bombings of two buildings in Paris on 11 September 1937 that killed two police constables.

The group's most audacious act – and the one that led to its exposure – was launched on 15 November 1937. On this night, the OSARN leadership alerted its troops and their contacts in the army to an imminent (and illusory) communist uprising. They hoped that the military would take the bait and, with the help of Cagoulard guerrillas, put down violently the Communist Party in a pre-emptive strike. In the aftermath of this repression, with Cagoulards and army officers in possession of the reins of the state, the democratic regime would be destroyed and a right-wing dictatorship installed in its place.[3] The plan failed. The OSARN's friends in the army failed to take seriously the warnings about communist insurrection, and the Cagoulards stood down as dawn broke on 16 November. At this moment, the police – who had kept an eye on the organization for some time – decided to act. The OSARN leadership was arrested while raids throughout France saw dozens of suspected supporters taken into custody. The press subsequently regaled readers with sensational stories about secret meetings of hooded acolytes, loyalty oaths broken on pain of death and bloody assassinations.

The OSARN

The OSARN was deadly serious about its plan to destroy the Republic. During his interrogation by police in 1938, Cagoule leader Eugène Deloncle claimed that the French Communist Party was preparing to mobilize 18,000 armed followers (the majority of whom would be foreign and Moroccan shock troops) along with 65,000 French communists. He believed that the names of between 300 and 400 leading nationalist political personalities figured on a communist assassination list; these men would be eliminated before the party occupied strategically important locations throughout Paris.[4] To forestall communist plans, the Cagoule planned to act as a counter-revolutionary force in support of the army. At the grass-roots level, troops were organized into paramilitary formations from divisions and brigades to units and cells. Each cell had rifles and automatic weapons at its disposal.[5] In fact, OSARN arms dumps housed a frighteningly large stockpile of weapons, including 250 machine guns, and automatic firearms, up to 400 rifles, 300,000 cartridges and 7,000 grenades, not to mention rudimentary biological weapons.[6] At the group's largest arms stockpile in Annet-sur-Marne, police even discovered a cache of fifty German-made fountain pens containing an acidic chemical that could be sprayed into the eyes to render a victim blind.[7]

Information was collated on both the whereabouts of ministers and how to gain access to ministerial properties. Plans were made to seize and likely execute leading left-wing politicians including Blum, Chautemps, Paul Faure, Marx Dormoy and Roger Salengro.[8] According to historian J.-R. Tournoux, following the removal of these men, a number of leading nationalists were slated for execution, too, including La Rocque, Taittinger, Doriot and Chiappe, in an attempt to further terrify public opinion.[9] Maps of the capital's sewers, subterranean catacombs and public utilities systems were acquired. Command posts in and around Paris were built along with underground prison cells destined to hold political prisoners. According to Deloncle,

> Certain specially chosen groups were to go into the taxi garages, in order to quickly transform some cars … into automated weapons. These transformations would turn the cars into patrol vehicles, armed with machine guns and machine-rifles. The goal of other groups was to occupy the telephone and telegram exchanges, perhaps to destroy them. … Finally, a general transport strike was envisaged for 16 [November] and all the main roads leading to Paris were to be cut off by solidly established sentries each armed with four machine guns.[10]

In putting its plan to topple the Republic into action, the Cagoule was unique among the extreme right-wing organizations of late Third Republican France.[11] It was not, however, estranged from the leagues. The OSARN emerged from the fertile soil of the anti-Republican right. The hard core of activists at the heart of its leadership were veterans of the street politics of the era having belonged to the Action Française and its *camelots du roi* street fighters. Following the *six février* crisis, a group of these men, many of whom were based in Paris's affluent sixteenth arrondissement, became frustrated with the monarchist league's apparent lack of energy. For these young street brawlers, their own dynamism contrasted starkly with the apparent preference for words over action of the gerontocracy that directed the sclerotic league. Both Maurras and his lieutenant Daudet were in their late sixties by 1935, and it seemed unlikely that they would ever initiate a monarchist counter-revolution. Ninety-seven leaguers put their name to a manifesto – the 'Mémoire sur l'immobilisme' – that denounced the league's lethargy in its campaign against the Republic. These men counted themselves among the 'awakened of 1934'.[12] They looked to 1917 and 1923, 1929 and 1933 as the dates in their 'mythological calendar'; the elder monarchists preferred 1789 and 1815, 1871 and 1914.[13] The dissidents – including Cagoulard leader Deloncle and his henchmen Jean Filliol and Aristide Corre – resigned, or were expelled, from the Action Française during December 1935 and January 1936.[14]

The OSARN came into being at some point during the summer of 1936. The group operated under the cover of a front organization, the Union des Comités d'Action Défensive (UCAD). Led by retired air force general Edouard Duseigneur and former Croix de Feu luminary Duke Joseph Pozzo di Borgo, the UCAD functioned as an umbrella organization for a number of anti-communist groups. Duseigneur and di Borgo worked energetically to create a network of armed extreme right-wing groups; the Cagoule took advantage of this network to extend its tentacles across the territory.[15] It established connections with other right-wing groups such as the Chevaliers du Glaive in Nice, the Union des Patriotes d'Auvergne and the Enfants de l'Auvergne in Clermont-Ferrand, the fourth section of the PPF and a group known as L'Algérie Française. These connections provided the OSARN with a useful foothold in towns such as Toulouse through which the group could import weapons.

It is difficult to estimate the size of the Cagoule's membership. Usually, the leaders of each provincial group were wittingly members of the Cagoule, while their followers were kept in the dark about the connection to the secret organization. When the time for action came, these men would follow the orders of the *chef*, who alone would know the true goal of their mission: revolution.[16] Even committed Cagoulards denied the existence of the group, unprepared to break their oaths of secrecy.[17] Ultimately, while Deloncle spoke of around 130,000 men upon whom he could call, there were in fact as few as 2,000 avowed Cagoulards. When police began to make arrests in autumn 1937, they turned up only 102 suspects.[18]

Aside from cultivating grass-roots activists throughout France, Deloncle and his cronies courted support among the French officer corps. The results were mixed. During 1936, the retired Marshal Louis Franchet d'Esperey, a member of the Conseil Supérieur de la Guerre and a former Croix de Feu, took a keen interest in the group.[19] Franchet had established a reputation as a tough commander in putting down strikes in the Nord and the Pas-de-Calais during 1906. He ultimately refused to commit to the Cagoule, yet he provided letters of recommendation that ensured industrialists and businessmen made large donations.[20] Better luck was to be had with Major Georges Loustaunau-Lacau, a member of Marshal Philippe Pétain's staff. Loustaunau-Lacau was himself the leader of a right-wing group within the army, the Corvignolles, whose aim it was to weed out communist subversives in the ranks.[21] Loustaunau-Lacau stated at the post-war trial of Pétain that the marshal had asked him to 'go and have a little look at what's happening [with the Cagoule]'. The Major declined to join the group following a meeting with Deloncle, but he provided the Cagoule with access to the army's intelligence branch, the Deuxième Bureau.[22] Beyond a small group of reactionaries, the army seemed lukewarm to the approaches of the Cagoulards. In fact, the cautious attitude of the army conspirators seems to have staved off timely intervention from the government. So long as groups like the Corvignolles aimed solely to break up communist cells within the army, ministers and the police authorities were prepared to leave them alone.[23]

Better luck was to be had with French business. French business interests, including Byrrh, Michelin, Renault and Taittinger – all of whom had an interest in the destruction of communism and unionized labour – donated millions of francs to the OSARN. Wealthy individuals made substantial contributions, too: Jacques Lemaigre-Dubreuil, boss of the Huiles Lesieur company and leader of the Fédération des Contribuables, contributed one million francs. In total, police estimated that the group held between forty million and eighty million francs in funds.[24] The monies were used to purchase arms from abroad – gunrunner Gabriel Jeantet acquired large amounts of weapons from Switzerland and Belgium – and to rent properties for use as headquarters and prisons. The cash was also used to finance the luxurious lifestyle of prominent men in the group.[25] The sizeable funds upon which the Cagoule could draw were testament to the seriousness with which conservative interests in industry and business treated it.

Resources, financial and material, flowed into the OSARN from beyond France's borders, too. The spider's web of fascism that had spread across Europe by 1937 provided significant opportunities. The Cagoule established contact with the upper echelon of the

Spanish rebels. Arms were smuggled into France from Nationalist Spain, following a visit by Deloncle and General Duseigneur in January 1937. In return, OSARN operatives sabotaged aircraft on French soil destined for the Spanish Republic. Several planes were destroyed at the Toussus-le-Noble airfield on 29 July 1937. A succession of bombings was perpetrated in Perpignan where Republican refugees increasingly were housed. Meanwhile, Cagoulard operatives facilitated Spanish Nationalist missions, in particular an attack by a Francoist commando on a Republican submarine docked in Brest in September 1937.[26]

Fascist Italy provided succour, money and weapons. During late 1936, Maurice Juif and Léon Jean-Baptiste made a trip to Italy on the Cagoule's behalf to acquire firearms. Cagoulards made contact, too, with the Servizio Informazione Militare (SIM, the Italian army's intelligence section) and Mussolini's secret service, the OVRA. OVRA chief Filippo Anfuso met several times with OSARN representatives including François Méténier and Joseph Darnand. It was likely the OVRA that ordered the Roselli killings, in exchange for 100 semiautomatic Beretta rifles and the promise of future shipments.[27] The Cagoulards' cultivation of warm relations with Italy is unsurprising. According to the overseer of Italy's counter-espionage operations, Colonel Emanuele Santo, OSARN operative François Méténier informed him that

> Your Duce … is and will be our model, and we agree with him completely in considering fascism as the norm of political life on a European scale; France must, according to us, draw inspiration from the Italian fascist regime, and apply it on its own account … it would be difficult for us to understand your remaining insensitive to the fight that our movement undertakes, a fight which asks only to be the extension of yours, of which the goal is to destroy bolshevism.[28]

Few Cagoulards, despite their approval of Nazi anti-communism, envisaged an agreement with Hitler. Many of the OSARN's troops – veterans of the First World War – would not swallow a collaboration with the old enemy. Deloncle envisaged a future France as a link in the fascist alliance developing among the Latin countries of southern Europe.[29]

Who were the Cagoulards?

A closer examination of the Cagoulards reveals its important connections to the violent political subculture of interwar France.[30] At the head of the Cagoule was Eugène Deloncle, a former member of the Action Française. He was also in charge of the group's 'First Bureau', which focused its efforts on recruitment. Deloncle was a forty-seven-year-old native of Brest and a decorated veteran of the First World War. Highly intelligent – a 'man with two brains', according to a contemporary – Deloncle pursued a career after the war as a naval engineer. Married to General Duseigneur's daughter, Mercédès, he was a wealthy man by the 1930s with a house in the plush sixteenth arrondissement of Paris and several country properties. Like many Cagoulards, Deloncle was a lover of 'secret agents, mysteries, [and] complicated intrigues'. His past activity in the Action Française indicated, too, that he was partial to, 'firearms, fights, and fighters'.[31]

Deloncle brought with him into the Cagoule his former Action Française comrade Jean Filliol. A devout Catholic, Filliol sold *L'Action Française* at the doors of the Notre-Dame d'Auteuil church every Sunday. Tall, robust and muscular, he was always ready for a fight, rarely leaving home without a pistol and a bayonet (his preferred weapon), which he handled 'with the dexterity of a juggler'.[32] According to his childhood friend Henry Charbonneau, Filliol was the 'model *camelot*'. He was involved in a series of street fights during 1934–6, most notably on 9 June 1936 when he and a gang of fellow brawlers beat striking workers with truncheons at the Compagnie d'Assurances l'Abeille in Paris. The brawl spilled out onto the street and several policemen were injured too.[33] With Deloncle and Méténier, Filliol was in charge of the Cagoule's 'Section Terroriste', a role to which he seemed perfectly suited.[34]

The ties of kinship cemented bonds in the upper echelons of the group. Eugène Deloncle was joined in the leadership of the Cagoule by his elder brother, Henri, a war veteran and successful jeweller with properties in Cannes and Paris. Long-standing friendships were significant, too: Aristide Corre and Deloncle had been childhood friends, while Jacques Corrèze was a 'putative son' to the Cagoule's leader. Jean Bouvyer and Jacques Fauran, both of whom took part in the Roselli murders, were old school friends.[35]

Beyond the OSARN's leadership it is possible to piece together the profiles of rank-and-file members.[36] The seventy-nine suspects who faced trial in 1948 were drawn mainly from the professions (doctors, insurers, architects) while few came from a working-class background.[37] War veterans were common among those men investigated: police detective Jean Belin claimed that there were 'a great many Cagoulards' in the France-Germany Committee, a body founded by France's leading veterans' associations.[38] Of course, millions of men had served in the French armed forces during the First World War, and the fact that a number of Cagoulards were veterans does not indicate the susceptibility of a veteran 'mentality' to political violence. Yet the fact that the extreme right-wing leagues lionized the veteran and his noble sacrifice for France renders veteran membership of the Cagoule unsurprising.

The importance of the extreme right-wing political milieu to the OSARN's recruitment was further revealed in the police interviews conducted with suspects following the group's exposure in late 1937. Many had belonged to a paramilitary league, especially the Action Française: 'Those men who had waited impatiently for years that [the league] take action', according to Charbonneau.[39] Some belonged to an existing extreme right-wing party such as PPF and the PSF. A number of interviewees held, or had held, multiple memberships. Philippe Fournier was arrested in Nice in winter 1937 for smuggling arms; he was a member of the PPF who had formerly belonged to the Croix de Feu.[40] Yet several of the men interviewed had connections with more moderate political parties of the left and right. Interviewed in July 1939, Roger Parlange stated that he had been a member of the Republican Radical Federation of the Seine since 1936. He had come to the Radical Party by way of the leagues, having acted as a former section leader in the Solidarité Française and been a member of the Front Paysan.[41] Louis Mallet, who was suspected of having close links with the Cagoule leadership in Marseille, had links to both the Socialist Party and the PPF.[42] Meanwhile, Philippe Ciarlet, whom police described as an 'old activist' in the Croix de Feu, was also a member of the conservative Fédération Républicaine.[43] The porous boundaries between the conservative right and the extreme right resulted once again in the cross-fertilization of movements.

Acquaintances and contacts in the leagues and parties of the extreme right acted as a conduit into the group. Eugène Bancharral was inducted into what he called a 'Self-Defence Group' by his former comrades in the Croix de Feu. He understood that the aim of the group would be to fight a 'communist surprise attack', and that in this eventuality he would be given a group of women and children whom he would take to a predetermined place of safety.[44] Likewise, a former Croix de Feu comrade introduced Maurice Léopold Thomas to the Cagoule, while Olivier de Bermond claimed his superior in the PSF presented him to the group.[45] Michel-François Marie Bernollin was a personal acquaintance of Jean Filliol in the sixteenth arrondissement. He joined the OSARN when approached by Filliol who told him he was looking for 'sure men' to fight a coming communist revolution. Bernollin worked with other Cagoule members in the construction of a secret cellar. While doing so, he rented a room in Paris from a former Jeunesses Patriotes comrade.[46]

In Algeria, in March 1938 the governor general addressed a report to the minister of the interior concerning seventeen men who lived in the territory and whose name had figured on a list found by police in the Paris apartment of Corre. All but two of the men lived in Oran, the department in which extreme right-wing anti-Semitic politics thrived. The governor in fact noted that a good many of the men were known anti-Semites. Several had been active members of Jules Molle's Union Latines, yet the majority of these men had belonged to the Croix de Feu and now belonged to the PSF, often in positions of authority within local sections. Recruitment efforts targeted at the indigenous population exploited the anti-Semitism to enlist 300 men under the leadership of 'a native "führer" named El Maadi'.[47]

League violence seems to have nurtured in some of the Cagoulards a desire for an extreme form of action. Deloncle himself subscribed to a conception of violent political action as an expression of masculinity evident in aspects of the leagues' discourse on confrontation. For him, it was time to put words to one side and undertake 'virile actions'.[48] Some Cagoulard activists had experience of the street politics of the era. Charles Albert Damiani joined the Jeunesses Patriotes upon leaving the army in the late 1920s. He left Taittinger's league in January 1936 to join the Action Française where he distinguished himself as one of its most violent leaguers. Police noted that while Damiani was highly regarded for his probity and morality, in political matters he was prone to losing his head and had twice assaulted opponents.[49] Jules Servent, a dissident member of the Action Française, was the former head of the *camelots* in Marseille and thought by police to be the founder of the Cagoule group in the city.[50] One unnamed interviewee had been a member of the Croix de Feu's youth auxiliary, the Volontaires Nationaux and head of the *Dispos* combat units in the thirteenth arrondissement of Paris.[51] Meanwhile, André Roger Mandereau was an 'activist and one of the most fervent' in the PSF. He was formerly a local leader in the Croix de Feu and a current head of a section of the PSF's EVP security force.[52]

Experience of clandestine operations in the leagues further prepared Cagoulard recruits for the secrecy of the group. The organization had a penchant for codenames, secret language and signs, especially within the leadership: Deloncle went by the name 'Marie', while Filliol was 'Fifi'.[53] Meanwhile, the group possessed a number of CGT identity cards and armbands, as well as policemen's hats and batons, designed to allow members to infiltrate left-wing demonstrations and cause trouble.[54] The leagues had long used such ruses to try and enter left-wing meetings. The Action Française used coloured invitations to convey secret messages when convening its troops to a meeting: blue paper required members to bring a cane with them, while white paper and red paper signalled the need for a truncheon and a revolver respectively.[55] The Jeunesses Patriotes used coded practices to convene its members, too.[56] The Croix de Feu acted in a similar manner: following the violence outside its meetings in Limoges in November 1935, police believed that the 'pocket torches' that members had been asked to bring referred in fact to truncheons.[57] Leaguer street politics thus initiated men into a semi-clandestine behaviour that would later serve them well in the OSARN.

The importance to the OSARN of the male world of interwar street violence did not preclude female membership of the group. While it is true that many Cagoulards in the leadership were misogynists, using women members and sympathizers for sex alone, female operatives were vital also to the group's functioning. Female members accompanied their male comrades on operations: Alice Lamy was present when the Rossellis were murdered. Usually, they conducted surveillance work, in some cases tracking Cagoule targets for days before the group's hit squad struck. Women 'delivered messages, followed suspects, acted as go-betweens, and recruited members'.[58] Without members such as Hélène d'Alton (a relative of La Rocque), Thérèse Harispe and Marie de Massolles, the Cagoule may not have been able to advance its plans as far as it did.

The rich mosaic of social networks on the anti-Republican extreme right, cultivated through years of comradeship and common struggle, allowed the Cagoule to recruit throughout France. The fact that Cagoulard suspects came from a variety of leagues and parties demonstrated both the broad appeal of the OSARN and the degree to which political loyalties, especially those on the extreme right, were interchangeable.[59] Some activists on the extreme right belonged to many of its principle formations: Emile Jaillon belonged to the Faisceau, the Jeunesses Patriotes, the Solidarité Francaise, the Croix de Feu, the PSF and, during the war years, the PPF. Jaillon's trajectory was not unique.[60] As for the Cagoule, members could remain within their original organization; this was in fact essential to Deloncle's plan to further extend the reach of the OSARN.[61] The complex dynamic of interaction and confrontation between left and right not only provided political activists with the skills for perpetrating violence and operating in secrecy but also informed their view of politics as a violent struggle against an intractable enemy and an illegitimate regime. Some leaguers, with their means of political expression shut down following the dissolution of the leagues in June 1936, turned to violent extremism.

Exposure

During 1937, the Cagoule cut a bloody swathe across France. Its agents committed a series of murders and bombings in a campaign of terror that was designed to stoke fears of communist revolution. On 25 January, Filliol murdered the left-wing Russian economist Dimitri Navachine in broad daylight in the Bois de Boulogne. Using his trademark bayonet – which left tell-tale triangular stab wounds – Filliol calmly approached Navachine and stabbed him to death, shooting the Russian's dog midway through the attack.[62] According to Pierre Villemarest (son-in-law of Cagoulard Dr Félix Henri Martin), the leadership had decided to murder a prominent left-winger in order to 'convince the bourgeoisie to help a paramilitary organisation like ours', and to show that the Cagoule was 'formidable'.[63] Navachine's name had featured on a Cagoule hit list of left-wingers, and it seems that the economist was marked for death at random.

In spring 1937, another mysterious murder captured the imagination of the press and public. On 17 May, an unknown assassin killed Laetitia Toureaux in a Parisian metro carriage. The circumstances of the crime – the killer had had barely seconds to commit the act and escape unseen – and the background of the victim – the beautiful Toureaux seemingly lived beyond her means and had connections to the police as well as the louche Parisian underworld – made for a sensational story. Press and public obsessed about the 'metro enigma' for months. The police's inability to apprehend the perpetrator only heightened interest in the affair. Unbeknownst to the public, Toureaux also had information on the Cagoule and had enjoyed a love affair with prominent Cagoulard Gabriel Jeantet. It is likely that she was murdered before she could reveal any information to police.[64]

The following month, on 9 June, an assassination team led by Filliol murdered Carlo and Nello Roselli on a quiet country lane in Bagnoles-de-l'Orne. The Roselli brothers were prominent Italian antifascists living in exile in France. Police immediately suspected the crime to be the work of Mussolini's agents. Only in January 1938 did Jean Bouvyer reveal to police the details of the crime. Having kept the Rosellis under surveillance during the afternoon of 9 June, a team of Cagoulards – including Bouvyer, Jacques Fauran, Filliol, Robert Puireux and Fernand Jakubiez – followed the brothers in two cars as they drove from Bagnoles-de-l'Orne to Alençon and back again. Approximately one mile from Bagnoles-de-l'Orne, one of the cars pulled across the road to block the way. When the Rosellis got out of their car to investigate, they were brutally stabbed and shot. The murders, probably perpetrated on the orders of the Italian government, were rewarded with a modest arms shipment to the Cagoule. The crime was a gesture of goodwill, too, for a future collaboration with Mussolini once the Republic was out of the way.[65]

The OSARN's most audacious attack occurred on the evening of 11 September 1937 when agent René Locuty – dressed as a worker in a flat cap – delivered two bombs to buildings in the Etoile district of Paris: the headquarters of the Confédération Générale du Patronat Français and the Groupe des Industries Métallurgiques de la Région Parisienne. Each body represented employers in their respective industries. The bombs exploded within minutes of each other. The buildings were empty at the time except for the concierges who had taken delivery of the explosives. Two policemen were killed in the blasts, buried in the rubble.[66] To attack employers' groups suggested a communist act, as Deloncle desired. This tactic was consonant with the OSARN's Machiavellian strategy for stoking fears of communist revolution. For Deloncle, it was paramount that when the time came the OSARN's uprising be conceived as a defensive act in the name of France. 'If we are the first to take to the street', he told Filliol, 'no one will follow; yet if we [take to the street] to defend ourselves, everyone will march [behind us]'.[67]

The bombings sparked a campaign in newspapers across the political spectrum against foreign interference in French politics; left and right both believed that agents of a hostile government had planted the explosives. Such concerns were exacerbated when on 20 September a Francoist commando attacked a Spanish Republican submarine docked in Brest. Furthermore, on 24 September, White Russian General Yevgeny Miller was abducted from Paris by Soviet agents; Miller was not seen alive again. These events, coming soon after the Etoile bombings, further served to underscore the apparent foreign interference in French domestic politics. The perceived connection between the bombings of 11 September 1937 and immigrant undesirables ensured that when a number of Cagoulard members, including Deloncle, were arrested within days of the attacks, no one made the connection between the extreme right-wingers and the destruction in the Etoile district.[68]

Investigators were nevertheless on the trail of the group. The organization had first come to the attention of the authorities in February 1937 when an unclaimed trunk belonging Juif was opened at Lille railway station. During 1936, Juif and his friend Léon Jean-Baptiste had acted as the OSARN's principal gunrunners. Jean-Baptiste was murdered in October that year after falling foul of the group's leadership; taken to an isolated location outside Paris, he was dispatched by Filliol.[69] Juif feared that the same fate awaited him. He packed a trunk with incriminating material and addressed it to the late Jean-Baptiste, hoping that this would arouse the suspicions of the police.[70] Juif's fears were well founded: he was killed in February 1937, the distinctive marks of Filliol's bayonet found on his body.[71] The trunk – Juif's insurance policy – was opened by railway staff in Lille who promptly contacted the authorities. Detectives discovered documents concerning arms deals and trafficking along with information about several activists.[72] The trunk was not the only clue to fall fortuitously into the hands of the police. In June, Jakubiez was apprehended crossing the Swiss border; he subsequently furnished much information to the police.[73] Meanwhile, in September 1937, a police raid on Corre's apartment uncovered an un-encoded list of operatives, carelessly kept among other documents about the secret organization.[74]

With the police net closing in, the OSARN risked exposure if it waited much longer. Members were growing impatient for action.[75] Deloncle decided to launch his attempt on power in mid-November. The ground was carefully prepared for the night of 15 November when a communist coup would be stage-managed by the Cagoulards. In the preceding weeks, operatives mounted a misinformation campaign to strengthen the credibility of the revolutionary threat. Deloncle fed information to generals Gamelin,

Duffieux, George and Prételat that French and Russian communists were preparing for imminent action.[76] Rumours abounded in the press that the Communist Party was preparing for revolutionary action. As sun set on 15 November, the OSARN alerted its troops to be ready for action.

When H-Hour sounded, the result was a damp squib. Sympathizers in the army refused to take the bait and Deloncle's order to move against the Communist Party never came. Charbonneau recounted his experience of the mobilization, which he spent with ten students in an apartment in the sixth arrondissement:

> [There were] knocks at the door as per the rules, two long, two short, the password. … They told us that throughout the district our friends were in position. The only thing now was to wait. To wait! We waited like soldiers, smoking, chatting, snacking. And, little by little, we became concerned: what if nothing happened? Postpone it until later. … Again! After a mobilisation like this, is there the risk of everything being uncovered? At five in the morning, a last liaison agent came to give us a final order: Go back to your homes![77]

Cagoulard André Rabut recounted a similar experience: 'We waited weapon in hand … but nothing happened.'[78] With the OSARN unable to convince its powerful friends that a communist revolution was in the offing, the mobilization had been pointless. Filliol was reportedly furious: 'You are still too timid to act. You'd wait until they came to your house to cut your throat! It's now or never', he raged at Deloncle.[79]

At this moment, the authorities decided to act. Gayle K. Brunelle and Annette Finley-Croswhite believe that the police were content throughout 1937 for the Cagoule to continue to operate, even turning a blind eye to the murders of 'inconvenient émigrés'. Belin suspected that some high-ranking member of the police knew about the group; he suggested, too, that Chiappe had links to the Cagoulard leadership.[80] Yet once the Cagoulards had turned their attention to the establishment (with the bombs of September 1937 and the abortive coup attempt two months later) the police swung into action.[81] On 23 November, Minister of the Interior Dormoy revealed the nature of what he termed 'a true plot against Republican institutions'.[82] Most of the OSARN's leadership was arrested soon thereafter; Filliol, Jeantet, Corrèze and Martin managed to escape.

The press was replete with stories of arrests and discoveries of arms dumps and underground prisons.[83] The affair seemed 'too sensational to be true'.[84] The French of 1937 could hardly find more entertainment at the movies as they could in reading the latest revelations in the daily newspapers and true crime journals like *Détetcive* magazine. The affair took hold of the popular imagination: 'The fashion in the *salons* was for Cagoulard parties [with people] decked out in masks and robes. The *catherinettes*[85] donned a hood as their symbol. Cabaret artists and cartoonists took great pleasure in it.'[86]

It was difficult to know what to make of the group's plans as information trickled out. During November 1937, *L'Oeuvre*'s appreciation of the OSARN changed from scoffing at the group's 'stupidity' and 'naiveté' to reporting the 'gigantic proportions' of the plot, which had 'financial means of an exceptional power'.[87] The left situated the OSARN's plan within the long tradition of the extreme right in France as well as the threat from international fascism. In the wake of a new discovery of arms – 'supplied almost exclusively by Mussolini and Hitler', according to Lucien Sampaix – *L'Humanité* warned against the 'danger that the secret association called the Cagoule represented and STILL REPRESENTS'.[88] The newspaper referred, too, to the 'international Cagoule', of Hitler, Mussolini and Franco.[89] Fernand Fontenay, communist author of *La Cagoule contre la France* (1938), described the affair as 'the most extraordinary of political affairs that we have seen under the Republic, an affair of blood, of ruin, of treason, in comparison with which the far-off memories of Carbonarism, [and] the anarchist attacks of before the war, pale'.[90] Fontenay wrote that Deloncle, di Borgo and Duseigneur were surely just 'the tools of the conspiracy and not … the supreme leaders'. He alleged that men in the government knew who was behind the plot but would not unmask them. He was sure that 'whole sections of the conspiracy remained in the shadows', which the enquiry has been reluctant to uncover.[91]

Voices on the right were more indulgent to the group, arguing that its role was primarily defensive as a response to the 'pre-revolutionary Popular Front'.[92] Many were thoroughly dismissive of the seriousness of the Cagoule's supposed revolution, preferring to see in it a patriotic venture.[93] The arrest of veterans irked nationalists as did the conditions in which these men were held. La Rocque wrote, 'Will this scandal last for long? They apply haphazardly, with brutality, unjustly, the common law scheme to veterans; they search after anonymous denunciations and with neither rhyme nor reason.'[94] Most of the suspects were taken into custody under article 265 of the 1810 Penal Code that pertained to members of a criminal organization (*association de malfaiteurs*). The charge carried a penalty of between five and ten years' detention and forced labour.[95] The Cagoulards demanded to be incarcerated as political rather than common law offenders; conditions of prison life were much more comfortable for men who had committed a crime for a political cause. However, speaking in the Chamber of Deputies, Minister of Justice Vincent Auriol explained, 'Who can deny that these were acts of terrorism, prepared in secret, with a perverse refinement of the imagination and with cruelty until this day unknown in our country, where even the plots against state security had, in times past, an otherwise chivalrous character.' It was this that determined the common criminal charge.[96]

The OSARN's project for the authoritarian renovation of France drew on many themes familiar to the milieu of French extreme right-wing politics. The group had, after all, been forged in the political fires of the 1920s and 1930s. For DLL Parry, 'The general political beliefs of the Cagoulards were little different for the rest of the far right of the 1930s. They were nationalists, nominally Catholic without being deeply religious, who desired a strong, authoritarian government.'[97] Deloncle declared to Franchet, 'We want to bring down the State because there is no other option. We want to do it by all means necessary, including by force. We cannot live with the Republic. … We must bring back the King.'[98] The Cagoule was thus congruent with the contemporary context of French politics, even if it adopted different tactics to the dissolved paramilitary organizations.

Anticipating Vichy?

None of the Cagoulards faced trial before the Second World War. Their ability to escape prosecution rested in part on the support that they received from influential sections of the French right. The right-wing press campaign for the release of the 'terrorists' intensified as war loomed in autumn 1939, and demands were made that all experienced men be freed to join the army. However, the sheer size of the task facing prosecutors meant that work was slow. The volume of this work increased as French men and women supplied denunciation after denunciation, many of which, in an unedifying harbinger of the Occupation, stemmed from personal enmities and petty grievances, and thus led police down blind alleys.[99] Investigating magistrate Pierre Béteille's 600-page report was ready only in 1939, by which time most OSARN suspects had been released.[100]

Following the defeat, on 20 July 1940, Vichy Minister of Justice Raphaël Alibert ordered the liberation of all men held in relation to the case. Alibert was himself a former Cagoulard, and he was not the only one to rise to prominence during the war years. Jean Bassompière and Joseph Darnand, for example, would later head the Vichy regime's paramilitary Milice. However, the Vichy regime was not a natural home for all Cagoulards. Maurice Duclos, for example, worked during the war for the Gaullist Bureau Central de Renseignements et d'Action and the Free French.[101] Deloncle continued his career as a terrorist: his ultra-collaborationist Mouvement Social Révolutionnaire (MSR) murdered former Minister of the Interior Marx Dormoy – the man responsible for exposing the Cagoule – in July 1941, and bombed several Parisian synagogues the following October.[102]

In the aftermath of the Liberation it was tempting to consider the OSARN as another piece in the jigsaw of a plot that had long sort to bring down French democracy. Belin claimed that Cagoulards had plotted against the Republic with Laval and Pétain at least since November 1936. Once Pétain had buried the Republic and installed the Vichy regime, the Cagoule became 'all-powerful' in France.[103] On the other hand, former police chief Ducloux called the Cagoulards 'simple beyond belief, spellbound, confused and mentally poisoned', for thinking that their conspiracy could work.[104] One need not subscribe to such fantastical conspiracy theories to recognize that the OSARN presented a real danger to the existence of the Third Republic. As Parry writes, 'Few underground or terrorist organizations would not envy [its] arsenals, the financial resources they imply, the number of men mobilized by the Cagoule, the links to senior army officers and the aid the Cagoule received from sympathetic foreign governments.'[105] The men at the upper levels of the movement were highly educated and experienced political activists who encountered little difficulty in making contact with, and securing the support of, senior military and political figures at home and abroad. To recruit rank-and-file troops, the OSARN exploited social networks that had been formed during the era of league politics. In fact, we cannot understand the emergence of the Cagoule without an appreciation of the richer environment of violent extreme right-wing politics in interwar France. The Action Française in particular perceived itself to be the victim of state repression both in the form of mass and preventive arrests and lethal police violence. On 6 February 1934 the league suffered the highest number of fatalities of all the organizations present. There thus developed a cycle of violent interaction between the right, the left and the police, which heightened the sense of urgency among some leaguers. Ultimately, in re-contextualizing the Cagoule in the politics of the mid-1930s, we must attribute its violence not to the frustration of individuals and hotheads but to the complex web of political relationships in which activists were implicated.

CHAPTER 6
NATIONAL REVOLUTION, 1940-4

During winter 1941, Hungarian-Jewish writer Arthur Koestler wrote of his experience in France at the outbreak of the Second World War. His account, published later that year as *Scum of the Earth*, looked back to September 1939, when he perceived 'that France had morally lost the war long before the actual military collapse.[1] He cited a 'cross-section' of French society, 'three specimen examples of French people … fairly typical of the social strata they represented' in his analysis.[2] The first was Henri de Vautrange, a thirty-two-year-old car salesman who had attempted to sell Koestler a Citroën. The second was Marcel, Koestler's twenty-eight-year-old mechanic. The third example was Madame Suchet, manager of the dairy where Koestler bought his cheese. Koestler perceived in the political attitudes of Vautrange (the right-winger), Marcel (the socialist) and Madame Suchet (the apathetic) the explanation for the French collapse of 1940.

It is Koestler's analysis of Vautrange that interests us. In conversation with Koestler, Vautrange railed against the corruption and decay of France. He accused the Popular Front government and its Jewish and Masonic masters of undermining the nation. The Third Reich, according to Vautrange, showed what could be achieved with neither deputies nor parties. It was a society in which everyone knew their place. Koestler believed that Vautrange and the millions of French like him had been prepared to leave their country undefended when Germany invaded in May 1940. For these men and women their 'morale was bound to break down with the first defeat'. Supporters of the PSF, the PPF or the Action Française were thus 'the unconscious reservoir of the Fifth Column … scared by the bogy of a social revolution, they regarded Hitler as their saviour.[3] Yet prominent men and women on the extreme right wing of politics answered the call to arms. Doriot served with distinction at the front, winning the Croix de Guerre for acts of bravery and earning himself a mention in dispatches.[4] A number of Cagoulards including Jeantet, Corrèze and Darnand likewise fought bravely, the latter receiving the Legion of Honour for his service.[5] Meanwhile, La Rocque briefly considered resuming his military service before deciding that he could better serve France on the home front. His eldest son, Jean-François, was killed during the French campaign.[6] Women were caught up in the invasion, too: PSF leader Jeanne Garrigoux was killed during the exodus of French civilians moving south.[7]

The politics of these men and women did not explain the defeat of France. The defeat resulted from a failure of military tactics on behalf of the Allies rather than the politics of the interwar years. Within days of the invasion on 10 May 1940, with the bulk of the Allied force in Belgium and the Netherlands, far from the German advance further south, the government recognized that the battle was lost. Defeatists gradually gained the upper hand in the cabinet. On 16 June, deputy Prime Minister Marshal Philippe Pétain spoke out in favour of seeking peace terms with Germany. Unable to counter the challenge from France's most respected military leader, Prime Minister Paul Reynaud resigned. Pétain took over the premiership and on 17 June announced to the nation that France would sue for peace.[8] An armistice was signed on 22 June. The agreement carved France into a Northern Occupied Zone – covering approximately three-fifths of the country, including Paris and the Atlantic coastline – and a Southern Free Zone.[9]

The political conflict of the interwar years influenced the decisions taken in the wake of the armistice. On 9 July, the French parliament convened at the casino in Vichy, a spa town in the southern zone. Deputy Prime Minister Pierre Laval presented the assembled members with a motion to revise the constitution of the Republic. Parliament approved by a vote of 624 to 4. The following day, deputies approved the granting of full powers to Pétain, by 569 votes to 80.[10] On 11 and 12 July 1940, Pétain destroyed the Third Republic. He appointed himself the head of state and concentrated all powers to appoint ministers and pass laws in his hands. Parliament was put on an indefinite hiatus.[11] The *Etat Français*, more commonly known as Vichy France, was founded.

Vichy sought to undo what it perceived to be the damage wrought throughout France during decades of Republican government. The regime ascribed the defeat of 1940 to a Republican moral disorder born of effeminate men, androgynous women and a declining birth-rate. Its project to regenerate France – the 'National Revolution' – centred on a number of so-called natural communities, of which the family was the most important.[12] Propaganda for the National Revolution was thus replete with gendered imagery of women as fertile childbearers and men as virile heads of family.[13] Concomitantly, Pétain and his ministers celebrated the virtues of duty, discipline, hierarchy and obedience. The marshal was depicted as a providential man, the *Chef*, the Guide and the Saviour (there was even a prayer dedicated to him.)[14] Persecution and repression accompanied a dramatic curtailment of liberties. Communists, Freemasons, gypsies, homosexuals and anyone else deemed part of the 'Anti-France' faced discrimination and imprisonment.[15] A raft of anti-Semitic decrees and laws – including the infamous Jewish Statutes of October 1940 and June 1941 – saw thousands of mainly foreign Jews interned while their French counterparts became second-class citizens. From July 1942, Vichy helped to deport approximately 80,000 Jews to the death camps of Eastern Europe.[16]

In its relations with Germany, Vichy pursued a policy of collaboration. The marshal himself declared in late October 1940 that, after a meeting with Hitler at Montoire near Tours, France was 'entering onto the path of collaboration' with the Third Reich.[17] Some form of cooperation was unavoidable: the armistice required that all French authorities and administrative bodies in the Northern Zone 'work together' with the German military authorities in a 'correct manner'.[18] But the term 'collaboration' implied more than a mere working relationship between the Occupier and the French. Vichy viewed the policy as a means to win concessions from the Occupier, and the regime was prepared to go far to achieve such a goal.

While collaboration led to servitude and servility, Vichy did not embrace National Socialism. Certainly, there were men and women in France who desired a close ideological relationship. Such ideologues were termed 'collaborationists', and they included figures from interwar politics such as Doriot and Darnand.[19] They desired to go far beyond what they perceived to be the lukewarm relationship between the *Etat Français* and the Third Reich.[20] On the other hand, like the majority of the interwar leagues, the Vichy regime kept a cautious distance from both National Socialism and fascism, eager to present itself as of solely French inspiration. Consequently, collaborationists derided Vichy's National Revolution as '[amounting] to no more than a backward-looking restoration of past values', in comparison with their own radical project for national regeneration.[21] In turn, the Vichy leadership took advantage of popular enmity towards the collaborationists, using them when necessary as a scapegoat to hide its own shortcomings.[22] Bertram M. Gordon thus claims that the 'Vichy government opposed ideological collaboration' unlike its Paris-based (collaborationist) counterparts.[23]

There were nevertheless entanglements between Vichy and the collaborationists. The latter venerated the marshal. Doriot in fact authored the book *Je suis un homme du Maréchal* (*I am the Marshal's man*) in 1941. Pétain's often-vague statements on the Franco–German relationship allowed collaborationists to use him and his words to their own ends.[24] They reserved their vitriol instead for the men of the Vichy government. Yet their objections stemmed less from a doctrinal divergence than their frustration with the perceived slow pace of the regime's reforms. Even once Germany occupied France in its entirety in November 1942, and the collaborationists threw in their lot wholesale with the Third Reich, the worlds of Paris and Vichy remained connected. As late as August 1944, Pétain gave his approval to the Milice, Darnand's paramilitary force that collaborationist journalist Lucien Rebatet described as 'the union of French national-socialists'.[25] By that time, collaborationists occupied a number of key posts in the French government, a fact that has prompted historians to conclude that Vichy evolved from a reactionary, counter-revolutionary regime into a semi-fascist state.[26] Ultimately, factions defined themselves in relation to their rivals in order to better distinguish themselves in the competition for the leadership of France.

The single party project

In the feverish atmosphere of summer 1940, a number of extreme right-wing political players vied for influence in the fledgling regime. Lieutenant-Colonel de La Rocque's chances looked better than most: during the election campaign of 1936, Pétain had endorsed the Croix de Feu as 'one of the healthiest elements in the country' for its defence, in particular, of the French family.[27] Yet relations between La Rocque and the marshal were at times strained. In any case, the PSF was subject to Vichy's ban on political parties, and La Rocque was once again forced to transform his movement, this time into the Progrès Social Français. The large number of women among the lieutenant colonel's faithful, at a time when many men were held as prisoners of war in Germany, ensured that the transition to the new PSF was smooth.[28] The lieutenant colonel threw his support behind Pétain's vision of a future France. The marshal's exclusionary nationalism, heavily invested with Catholic moral values, chimed with La Rocque's own preferences; Vichy had even appropriated the PSF's 'Travail, Famille, Patrie' slogan.[29] Following in the footsteps of the PSF, the new movement used its social work to spread the gospel of the National Revolution, and the lieutenant colonel aimed to mould the group into the central support of the new regime.[30] Yet he desired, too, to stress the continuity between the new PSF and its predecessors. Its propaganda stated, '[The] Progrès Social Français equals the Parti Social Francais minus electoral politics. While the Parti Social Français equals the Croix de Feu plus electoral politics. The Progrès Social Français equals therefore the Croix de Feu plus the mass of good-willed [people] who have come to La Rocque [between 1936 and 1940]:[31]

La Rocque was not the only man determined to monopolize the new political arena. Within weeks of the armistice, Marcel Déat attempted to lead a move to establish a single party akin to those found in neighbouring fascist regimes.[32] Déat was a decorated veteran of the First World War and a graduate of the prestigious Ecole Normale Supérieure. During the 1920s, he rose to the upper reaches of the Socialist Party. However, he diverged increasingly from mainstream party thinking, notably recommending at the socialist national congress in July 1933 that the party should seek to mobilize the masses on a platform of order, authority and the nation; 'revisionist, authoritarian and national [socialist]', according to Pascal Ory.[33] Déat was subsequently expelled from the party with a handful of fellow dissidents. Together they founded the Parti Socialiste de France-Union Jean Jaurès, and adopted the moniker 'neo-socialists'. The neo-socialists advocated economic planning and technocratic leadership on behalf of an authoritarian state within a new European economic order.[34] They adopted a pacifist line in their relations with Germany.[35] Déat became a figurehead for left-wing pacifists when in May 1939 he wrote in the pages of *L'Oeuvre* that given the risk of a general conflagration with Germany, the French should not 'die for Danzig'.[36] In July 1940, Déat's project for a single party was already taking shape. He considered the party a means to invest the regime with some much-needed radicalism (he had condemned the first Vichy government as a sclerotic coterie of old duffers).[37] The initial signs from Vichy's leadership were encouraging: Laval named Déat the secretary general of the future single party, and Pétain designated a committee to examine the issue.[38]

Meanwhile, Doriot looked to seize the initiative. His movement emerged as one of the most significant formations in the aftermath of the defeat, benefitting from the apparent support of Goebbels's Propaganda-Abteilung in Paris and the approval of the marshal in the Southern Zone.[39] The marshal could not afford to neglect Doriot's popular following. Former PPFs had shown themselves particularly active in the weeks after the armistice in demonstrations against Jews, communists and Freemasons in several southern towns. Blum even suggested that deputies voted full powers to Pétain because of their fear of the PPF's street gangs.[40] Doriot had in fact announced in July 1940 that the PPF would 'transform the resolutions of Vichy into reality', and bring to the country 'its new structure, its modern form, its new power'.[41] He envisaged a palace coup, in which the party would assume power under the aegis of the marshal.[42] The PPF's Algerian sections figured prominently in Doriot's plan. Under the leadership of Jean Fossati, the party relaunched its newspaper, *Le Pionnier*, and overcame a period of financial difficulty to undertake social work such as a soup kitchen in Alger called 'Le Plat Unique'. Doriot's party doubtless took advantage of the decline of the PSF in Algeria. Still, the PPF was small, with fewer than 3 per cent of the adult male European population a member in Sidi-Bel-Abbès – and it was in this area that the party was relatively successful.[43]

Déat, Doriot and La Rocque all participated in discussions over the foundation of a single party, the latter two through the medium of representatives.[44] Old rivalries persisted: the lieutenant colonel bristled at Doriot's involvement in the project, and he helped to spread rumours that the leader of the PPF was in the pay of the Nazis.[45] He was perhaps spooked, too, by defections from his movement to the PPF. At any rate, the idea for a single party clearly stood in the way of La Rocque's ambition to position the PSF as the regime's cornerstone, and he withdrew from the committee on 11 August.[46] Doriot remained for a short while longer, hoping to turn the initiative to his advantage.[47]

Pétain and Laval outmanoeuvred all three men. The project for the single party was in fact doomed from the beginning. Quite aside from the fact that members of the committee could agree on few matters of practical importance, Pétain considered all forms of political party to be divisive.[48] He pulled the rug from under the feet of the proponents of the single party when he announced the founding of the Légion Française des Combattants at the end of August 1940, an amalgamation of France's numerous ex-servicemen's associations. A furious Déat stormed off to Paris from where he attacked Vichy's allegedly reactionary stance. In November 1940, he proudly declared himself a 'collaborationist', founding the Rassemblement National Populaire (RNP) the following month. Still, Déat harboured hopes of being appointed a minister, at least until Laval was removed from government in December 1940.[49]

La Rocque continued with his efforts to pose the PSF as a de facto single party. His advice to members that they should observe a 'formal discipline behind Marshal Pétain' while remaining cautious with regard to his government caused confusion and gave the impression that the lieutenant colonel was practising a 'sulking abstention' that benefited the Légion.[50] As time wore on, La Rocque became disenchanted with the regime. His frustration, however, did not stem from a divergence between his politics and that Vichy. The situation was quite the reverse in fact: La Rocque endorsed Pétain's political agenda (including discriminatory policies against Jews in France prior to summer 1942), and as late as November 1942, the lieutenant colonel offered to form a government. Yet from that point, having grown irritated with the glacial pace of reform and convinced that Vichy could not protect French sovereignty, he gravitated towards resistance.[51]

Doriot returned to Paris with the blessing of Pétain, seeing an opportunity to pose himself as a Vichy loyalist in comparison with Déat and La Rocque.[52] The marshal's goodwill translated into cold hard cash, too: Vichy funded the PPF's newspapers, *Le Cri du Peuple* in the north and *L'Emancipation Nationale* in the south.[53] In return, the PPF publicly supported Vichy. For now Doriot's collaborationism was thus tempered compared with what it would later become. Initially, his cool attitude to Germany stemmed both from a desire to remain on good terms with the *Etat Français* and the Third Reich's pact of non-aggression with the Soviet Union.[54] The war of words with

La Rocque continued as both men sought to win favour with Pétain while vying for political space on the extreme right. Typical of the PPF's propaganda was the slogan of the Marseille section: 'La Rocque + Jews + Freemasons + The English = Mers el Kébir. Long Live Pétain and Doriot.'[55] The party's support for Vichy brought it into conflict with Déat, too. The latter's close relationship with German Ambassador Otto Abetz stung Doriot. Only in April 1941 did Abetz permit the operation of the PPF in the north. By that time, the RNP had stolen a march on Doriot's movement.[56]

Historians have interpreted the failure of the single party project as evidence of the non-fascist nature of the Vichy regime; James G. Shields determines that a single party constituted the essential 'infrastructure of fascism' that Vichy lacked.[57] From this standpoint, advocates of the project appear to be 'fascists'. Déat – who made the issue his hobby horse until the Liberation – intended a single party to facilitate the fight against communism, the punishment of those to blame for France's defeat, and an effect a corporative reform of the economy. While he expressed admiration for fascist single parties, in 1940, he had not yet thrown his lot in with National Socialism.[58] Yet support for the project did not render one 'fascist'; Pétain's Maurassian confidante Henri du Moulin de Labarthète was known to be in favour of the idea.[59] On the other hand, a man such as La Rocque could evidently brook no challenge to his desire to position the PSF as the central pillar of the National Revolution. His rejection of the single party project tells us more about the continued competition on the French extreme right than about his fascist credentials.

The National Revolution

What did Vichy stand for? At first glance, the regime's programme for the political, economic, social and cultural reform of France – the National Revolution – appears confusing.[60] Its aims seem obscure – Richard Vinen comments that Pétain's agenda was 'open to an almost infinite variety of interpretations' – while its inspiration and heritage were ambiguous – Nicolas Atkin recognizes the complexities, of 'a seemingly self-contradictory project, which incorporated an eclectic mix of ideological impulses'.[61] The regime used the term most frequently during summer–autumn 1941 at a time when the first murmurings of opposition required the marshal to re-enthuse the ranks. It fell increasingly out of use thereafter, and Pétain last uttered the words on 5 January 1943.[62] As for Laval, he admitted at his post-war trial: 'I never knew what the National Revolution was, it was never defined and it was an expression that personally I never used. … Everyone put his own desire, ideal and the regime that he saw into these words, but the National Revolution was never defined in any form at any time.'[63]

The ostensible eclecticism of Vichy's political agenda is strange only if one assumes that all governments adopt a unitary and easily identifiable position. The National Revolution was 'relatively structured'.[64] In a speech on 20 June 1941, the marshal spoke of 'moral and intellectual recovery (*redressement*)', and his plans for a 'cultural revolution' in France, one defined as 'national, authoritarian, hierarchical and social'.[65] The National Revolution was presented in gendered terms. The regime did not miss an opportunity to condemn the Republic's emasculation of France and celebrate its own project to return the nation to virility. As Catholic intellectual Jean de Fabrègues wrote, 'The National Revolution is a very manly human reaction to a feminized Republic, a Republic of women or homosexuals.'[66] Vichy thus attempted to control and reshape French men and women through policies intended to encourage childbirth. With women directed back into the home to rear children, men were framed as fathers, heads of the household and warriors of the National Revolution, heavily imbued with notions of manliness.[67] As Joan Tumblety writes, 'An "appeal to virility" was part of everyday life during the Occupation years.'[68][69] Vichy's programme thus rejected individualism, and embraced gendered conceptions of order and authority. French society would be reorganized and reborn, rooted in natural communities of family, commune and profession.[70]

At the same time, the National Revolution was 'vague and malleable'; Vichy allowed a certain degree of autonomy to groups whose aims it deemed consonant with its own but which nevertheless remained beyond its control. Ministers, functionaries and third parties could therefore, to some extent, invest their own meaning in the programme.[71] This was particularly the case beyond the borders of France where Vichy's functionaries adapted the regime's dictates to local circumstance. In North Africa, the regime's representatives exploited the racist and military culture of the settler community. However, in Morocco Resident General Charles Noguès was reluctant to upset the delicate religious and ethnic relations in the country, and he stepped up police measures against right-wing extremists to prevent trouble with the Jewish population.[72] In Tunisia, Vichy's racial decrees were not applied to their fullest extent for fear that the persecution of Jewish Italians in the territory would prompt intervention from Rome.[73] In Madagascar, the government set up youth camps to indoctrinate settlers and indigenous peoples with the values of the National Revolution. The programme for Malagasy locals centred less on the values of Pétainism than on the practice of physical education and manual work, a decision that rested on racialist assumptions about the laziness of the islanders. The camps were thus intended to educate them in the value of hard work and to prepare them for service in settler-owned farms and factories.[74]

Historians have generally perceived two strands to the National Revolution: the 'traditional' and 'conservative', on the one hand, and the 'modern' on the other hand. The 'traditionalist' elements of the programme are usually attributed to the influence of Maurrasianism.[75] Charles Maurras welcomed the coming to power of Pétain as a national saviour (a 'divine surprise', as he put it), though he held no official post at Vichy and continued to advocate a restoration of the monarchy.[76] The Action Française moved its operational base to Lyon and persisted in its attacks on the Anti-France of Jews, Communists and Freemasons, with Gaullists and resisters now included in the conspiracy.[77] Vichy's rejection of individualism in favour of order and hierarchy, and its persecution of the Anti-France chimed with the Action Française's own agenda. Pétain's utterances could betray a Maurrassian influence, too, such as in 1941: 'Nature does not create societies from individuals, it creates individuals from societies'.[78] But the regime did not seek to restore the Pretender to the throne and its programme cannot be reduced to Maurassianism alone.[79]

The 'modern' aspects of the National Revolution are usually perceived in the work of the 'technocrats' under the government of Admiral François Darlan (February 1941–April 1942).[80] Darlan himself posed the technocrats as something different to the conservatives who had, up to that point, reigned at Vichy, describing them to du Moulin de Labarthète as 'better than the vestry virgins that surround you; no generals, no seminarians, young types, worldly, who will get along with Fritz'.[81] A number of the technocrats had a background in extreme right-wing politics. Pucheu, Marion, Robert Loustau, Yves Paringaux, Claude Popelin and Maurice Touzé were all former members of the PPF. If several of them had resigned their memberships in the aftermath of Munich, they had done so because of their dislike of Doriot and not their rejection of fascism.[82] These 'modernisers' were responsible for the organization of industrial production, youth and education.[83] In particular, the ministry for industrial production strove for efficiency and rationalization in factories and farming.[84]

To perceive a division between the traditional and the modern at Vichy is problematic. Much depended upon how protagonists positioned themselves in relation to their opponents. In some cases 'traditionalists' and 'modernisers' shared a common political heritage in Maurrasianism, even if some of the latter group had come to reject the staidness of the Action Française.[85] Likewise, to perceive an 'antagonism' between 'fascists' and Vichyites is to assume the strict separation of both spheres.[86] A variety of groups and men from different political heritage thus worked towards 'National Revolution' throughout successive Vichy governments from Maurrassians like du Moulin de la Barthète and Alibert to technocrats such as Pucheu and François Lehideux. Cagoulard Jeantet served as secretary general of the Amicale de France, whose network of propaganda centres promoted the National Revolution.[87] Certain themes cut across divisions: the rejection of individualism and egalitarianism in favour of a hierarchy of natural elites, in particular the family; a xenophobic and anti-Semitic nationalism; a plan for national rallying; distrust of industrialism to the benefit of rural France and the peasant; anti-intellectualism and a refusal of cultural liberalism in favour of a re-establishment of conservative morality.[88] For all, the future lay in a strong state, elitism and authority, all incarnated in the marshal.[89] Of course, certain men may have identified more with tradition (as they understood the word) than with fascism (as they understood the word), but neither position was fixed and self-contained.

The National Revolution drew inspiration from abroad, too. In particular, Vichy admired the authoritarian regime of Salazar in Portugal.[90] Salazar was a Catholic ultra-conservative, whose vision of an organic society based on nationalism, corporatism and a rejection of democracy provided the programme for his Estado Novo.[91] Vichy looked to Salazarism for inspiration and support. Pétain exchanged warm words with the Portuguese dictator, recognizing that each proposed a third way between liberalism and communism without resorting to fascist totalitarianism. Vichy's self-proclaimed affinity with Salazar thus stemmed in part from a concern to set itself apart from fascist regimes.[92] A neutral Latin bloc – including Spain – seemed possible.[93]

In seeking to determine the nature of Vichy, Milza argues that the 'first Vichy' (July 1940–April 1942) 'most closely resembled the paternalist regime of Dr Salazar'.[94] The Légion, for example, was a 'government party' rather than a fascist single party, and it was therefore much like Salazar's National Union.[95] There were differences: in contrast to Portugal, for example, Vichy's regressive ideal was more difficult to implement in an industrialized country like France.[96] Milza's approach involves determining which aspects of each regime were revelatory of its nature and relegating other features to secondary status. In doing so, it seems that Milza does not consider Vichy's anti-Semitism to be an essential feature of its project; Salazar did not pursue an anti-Semitic agenda.[97] Furthermore, to determine the essence of Vichy as something different to fascism and Nazism ignores the cross-fertilization and transnational appropriations and adaptations that the regime engaged in. Maurrassian thought, for example, lent itself as much to Vichy as it did to Mussolini's fascism and Salazar's reaction.[98] To assimilate Vichy into a Portuguese-style authoritarianism (and therefore different to fascism) ignores common features between the regimes of Salazar, Hitler and Mussolini, as well as shared elements between Vichy and the fascist regimes.[99]

Attempts to classify Vichy therefore run into difficulties. Robert Paxton at once claimed that the National Revolution occupied a place on 'a spectrum of radical right regimes', but 'nearer the conservative than the fascist end'. He further insisted that fascism played a 'relatively restricted role' at Vichy. However, if one defines fascism as 'hard measures by a frightened middle class … [then] Vichy was fascist'.[100] On the 'nature' of Vichy and the National Revolution, we prefer Kevin Passmore's conclusion:

> Vichy was a complex patchwork of shifting interests and ideologies. … Categorization obscures the diverse reasons for which people embraced Vichy, their different degrees of commitment, their various appreciations of what it stood for, not to mention their understandings and misunderstandings of foreign ideologies. It also masks the shifting and contested ways in which contemporaries conceived and used political labels, combined them with others and manoeuvred them for advantage.[101]

From the Légion to the Milice

The Légion Française des Combattants was formed from an amalgamation of France's nebula of First World War veterans' associations. The *anciens combattants* had long held Marshal Pétain in high regard, in contrast to the self-serving politicians of the Third Republic. It was these men, rather than the veterans of 1939–40, who came to dominate the Légion.[102]

Legionaries acted as the apostles of the National Revolution. The organization was a quasi-chivalric order in which all were united in their loyalty to the marshal.[103] The regime's political agenda spread through the Légion; members promoted, for example, Vichy's familialist message that condemned abortion and emphasized the woman's place in the homestead as wife and mother.[104] Large-scale propaganda displays were intended to impress public opinion and engender loyalty to the regime. On 31 August 1941, a procession of 50,000 members marched along Nice's avenue de la Victoire, after having sworn an oath to the marshal.[105]

Social work provided a further means by which to spread Pétain's gospel. In autumn 1942, the Légion founded the Dames des Services Médicaux Sociaux (Dames SMS), a 'sort of social action feminine section', to expand the local implantation and influence of the group. The uniformed women of the Dames SMS provided childcare and health care services, and offered support to the wives of prisoners of war and war widows. Strict moral and ethnic criteria were applied to recruitment. Members with a past in communist politics and Freemasonry were excluded as were divorcees. Jews – even those of French nationality – were likewise barred from membership.[106] Given the exclusionary bent of its social work, it is unsurprising that the Légion attracted PSF members to its ranks.[107]

Aside from its propaganda function, the Légion operated as a tool of surveillance. According to Roger Bourderon, legionaries were 'militants, propagandists, and informers, ready to fill the prisons'.[108] Veterans of the interwar extreme right dominated the Departmental Unions, the upper echelon of the provincial leadership structure.[109] Grass-roots members rooted out dissenters in local government, reported people who listened to the BBC, and bullied and intimidated anyone whose support for the regime seemed suspect. Violence between legionaries and recalcitrant French was not uncommon; Légion secretary in Nice Noël de Tissot warned dissenters, 'We can "make" understand those people who do not want to [do so]'.[110] Consequently, if the provincial character of the group appeared to mark it out as less extreme than its paramilitary successors, we must recognize that the Légion was 'an active agent of the politics of exclusion and repression that characterised the regime, anti-Semitism included'.[111] Vichy wanted to be feared and loved, and the Légion worked to both ends.[112]

The Légion established sections in France's overseas territories. The Algerian sections, for example, proved themselves wholly committed to the National Revolution. In the departments of Alger and Oran, 38 per cent and 42 per cent of adult men, respectively, were members (the national average for mainland France was 25 per cent).[113] In their political and social work, Algerian legionnaires were 'more virulent' than their metropolitan counterparts in their attacks on the regime's enemies and in their advocacy of the marshal's political programme. Likewise, their support for collaboration was wholehearted.[114]

For contemporaries who wished to see Vichy equipped with a single party, the Légion fell short. However, there was no single character to the group: in some areas the Légion took on a folkloric aspect while in others it was a proactive and malicious proponent of Pétainism. The activities of the Légion were tailored to local circumstance. In Montpellier, some legionaries expressed admiration for Hitler, while others preferred Mussolini and Salazar.[115] In Martinique, the group's 3,000 members acted as partisans of 'moral order', combating establishments of ill repute.[116] In French West Africa – a territory threatened by Gaullist dissidence – the Légion sought to repress dissent.[117]

The Légion is usually dismissed as a pale imitation of a fascist-style party.[118] Contemporary Jean Guéhnno in fact described the group as operating in a 'rotten world' where the 'basest idiocy is king'.[119] But the purpose and aims of the group were contested, and its strength varied throughout France. The group's potential to become a single party remained. In November 1941, Marion and Pucheu (secretary general for information and propaganda and minister of the interior respectively) opened the ranks of the movement to non-veteran members; the Légion now became the Légion des Combattants et des Volontaires de la Révolution Nationale. Their aim was to move the group in a more radical direction, through the opening of the ranks to women, non-combatants and younger French.[120] By the end of the year, there were up to 1.5 million members with roughly 220,000 members hailing from North Africa.[121] Marion and Pucheu's initiative amounted to little, yet it demonstrated both the contested nature of aspects of the regime and the persistent entanglements between men of the extreme right and apparently conservative institutions.

By late 1941, moves were underway to radicalize the Légion's provincial sections. In December, Darnand founded the Service d'Ordre Légionnaire (SOL). Darnand was a veteran of both wars and had been very active in interwar extreme right-wing politics, notably the Action Française and the Cagoule.[122] The SOL grew out of his frustration with the lethargic and 'lousy' Légion (as he put it), and he intended the new group to act as a shock squad in the style of the Cagoulards.[123] Like Darnand, SOL leaders were convinced Pétainists who believed in a German victory.[124] The new group combined a martial masculinity with a predilection for violence. New recruits, fitted out in the uniform of a khaki shirt, blue beret, black tie and insignia, were admitted upon taking an oath of allegiance: 'I swear to fight against the democrat, Jewish leprosy and Gaullist dissidence.' The title of its newspaper – La Trique (The Cudgel) – left few in doubt about its function as a gang of heavies.[125] The SOL was particularly active in North Africa where SOL and PPF activists collaborated. This is unsurprising given that the PPF's national council in the free zone had encouraged activists to join the Légion from as early as December 1940, facilitating the formation of 'Doriotist enclaves' in the group.[126] In Tunisia, SOL members invaded Jewish districts, robbed Jewish businesses and expelled Jewish families from their homes. In Morocco, they assaulted Jews and vandalized synagogues in Casablanca. The SOL's collaboration extended to military cooperation with the Germans, and its legionaries fought the Allied invasion of November 1942.[127]

The founding of a paramilitary police force – the Milice Française – in January 1943 was indicative of the regime's extremist trajectory.[128] The Milice originated in the context of the growing tide of unrest that developed in the wake of the introduction of the Service du Travail Obligatoire (STO), a scheme to conscript young French men into German factories.[129] On 5 January 1943, Pétain informed the leaders of the Légion of his intention to detach the SOL from its parent association. He believed that move would free up the SOL to better work to maintain order with the French police. The Milice proved useful for Laval, too, in the face of the increasingly strident challenges from the Paris collaborationists.[130] With a paramilitary structure and an emphasis of manly violence reminiscent of the interwar leagues, the group was intended to be a 'knighthood for modern times'.[131] At its centre was a hard core of ultra-collaborationists, many of whom had enjoyed a long history with the extreme right.[132] For the group's leader, Darnand, the Milice was a 'heroic elite that would push through the National Revolution'.[133] Burrin thus perceives in the Milice evidence of the regime's 'evolution towards radicalisation'. This evolution owed much to the worsening of Germany's position following the reversals in the East. In France, the growing organization and confidence of Charles de Gaulle's Free French and the resistance movements saw the exacerbation of a repressive tendency at Vichy evident from the early days of the regime.[134]

The Milice attracted 30,000 members, with approximately one-third of this number on active duty. Members lived mainly in the south of France for the group was authorized in the north only in April 1944.[135] The average recruit was between sixteen and twenty-five years old, from a modest social and economic background, and with less political experience than the group's leaders. Political conviction cannot be discounted as a motive for enlistment. Some members were extreme right-wingers and dedicated Pétainists (the marshal publicly supported the group until 6 August 1944.) Others joined to escape labour service in Germany: of the 1,000 *miliciens* in Marseille, up to one-third of members were fugitives from the STO. The Milice promised a steady income, too. *Miliciens* could earn as much as 4,500 francs, along with bed and board, as a member of the group's elite Franc-Garde.[136]

Repression was but one function of the Milice. Members engaged in social work such as the organization and operation of soup kitchens and rationing, as well as aid work in the wake of Allied bombing. Up to one-quarter of *miliciens* were involved in such social work.[137] Still, the repressive function of the Milice sharpened throughout 1943. On 30 December 1943, Laval invited Darnand into government as secretary of state for the maintenance of order. In January 1944, Darnand assumed control of the French police, a move that placed 76,000 officers under his command.[138] Milicien Philippe Henriot was appointed secretary of state for information and propaganda in January 1944. The Milice now sat at the head of Vichy's repressive and propaganda functions.[139] The group worked increasingly with German forces to fight the resistance. It received its first arms shipment in October 1943, courtesy of the SS who began to train the group's shock troops.[140] During 1944, an atmosphere of terror reigned in parts of the south as *miliciens* and resisters fought each other with assassinations and reprisals.[141] Radio-Londres broadcast the slogan, 'Miliciens assassins, fusillés de demain' (*Miliciens* murderers, shot tomorrow).[142] Resisters executed Philippe Henriot on 28 June 1944, in response to which Milice thugs killed Georges Mandel.[143] For their part, *miliciens* took part in German operations against the resistance, notably during the siege of the Glières plateau in March 1944.

The failure to 'fascistise' the regime through the foundation of a single party tells us much about the reactionary essence of the 'first Vichy' (as Milza terms it) only if one believes that such an essence can be identified.[144] The content of the regime and its institutions remained contested. On the one hand, the Légion's recruitment of veterans (a constituency once understood to be inherently Republican) and its propaganda and social work appeared to render it a benign political force, which it doubtless was in some parts of the southern zone. When one takes into account its support for the regime's repression, the political content of its social action and the radical agendas of some provincial leaders, the Légion's character looks more ambiguous. Likewise, men at Vichy such as Marion and Pucheu believed in authoritarian government based on modern elites and a single party; they represented a collaborationist tendency in the early years of the regime.[145] This tendency grew as the war progressed. As the German war effort faltered during 1943, Vichy's grip on the country weakened in the face of growing opposition. The Milice represented the ultimate outcome of the repressive tendency evident at the outset of the regime. It was the ultimate expression of collaborationism in government as evermore proponents of ideological collaboration gained positions of power.[146]

Collaborationism in Paris

The collaborationists chose Paris as their base. The capital represented the best location from which to win the ear of the Occupier because of the numerous German agencies and institutions based there, from the Germany Embassy, the Abwehr (German army intelligence) and the security services (the Sicherheitsdienst or SD) to the German military administration (the Militärbefehlshaber in Frankreich). A nebula of collaborationist formations emerged. Some of these groups had a long history of engagement with fascism – Bucard, for example, reconstituted the Francistes – while others, such as Pierre Constantini's Ligue Française, were founded following the armistice.[147] The most significant collaborationist movements in terms of the size of their membership and their political influence were Déat's RNP and Doriot's PPF. The collaborationist newspaper, *Je suis partout*, enjoyed a circulation of almost 300,000 in 1943. Men such as Brasillach (the newspaper's editor until 1943) and Lucien Rebatet declared themselves fascists of the first hour; they saw in fascism a means by which to rescue a feminized France. By 1944, the newspaper's commitment to Nazism was plain, with Rebatet thundering: 'Death to Jews! Long live the National-Socialist Revolution! Long live France!'[148] In total, the collaborationist groups represented up to 200,000 French men and women but sympathy for collaborationism extended beyond the immediate membership of the parties.[149]

Déat was the first to declare himself a collaborationist, and he soon developed a good relationship with the German embassy. Ambassador Abetz assumed France would be merely a satellite state, yet he saw in left-wingers such as Déat the best means to mobilize popular support for the policy of collaboration.[150] With the approval of Abetz, Déat launched the RNP in January 1941. The group sought to unite a number of collaborationist strands: anti-communist and pacifist left-wingers, right-wing veterans (especially those of the UNC), Eugène Deloncle's MSR and a number of minnows of the pro-Nazi world.[151] Laval, estranged from Vichy since his sacking in December 1940, was also represented on the leadership committee. Déat's aim was to unify left- and right-wing collaborationism into a totalitarian-style single party. The RNP's eclecticism was reflected in its array of auxiliary groups from its labour section aimed at industrial workers to its paramilitary Légion National Populaire, under Deloncle's leadership.[152] In fact, by 1944 Gordon claims that the party had developed the structures of a totalitarian organization, reaching into many aspects of French society.[153]

In mid-1941, tensions developed between factions within the RNP. Deloncle wanted to turn the group to violent activism. His Légion, which drew heavily on the MSR for recruits, confiscated and ransacked Jewish properties. The MSR was implicated, too, in the bombings of Parisian synagogues on 2 October 1941.[154] Left-wingers and former parliamentarians in the RNP baulked at working with the former Cagoulard leader. Relations between Déat and Deloncle fell apart when in August 1941 the former was injured during an attempt on Laval's life at Versailles. Déat and Laval suspected Deloncle of plotting the act and Deloncle was swiftly ejected from the RNP.[155]

Déat envisaged a future France as an authoritarian and corporatist regime within a German economic bloc under the tutelage of the Third Reich. With *L'Oeuvre* as his mouthpiece, he did not cease to represent the Fuhrer as a 'socialist, aiming to organise Europe on economic lines, in brief to project his own image onto [Hitler]'.[156] The single party would connect the masses with the regime. This was Déat's personal hobby horse: he wrote thirty articles on the subject between 18 July 1942 and 4 September 1942, which he believed would bring pressure to bear on Vichy to reconsider the issue.[157] Neo-socialists and anti-communist trade unionists came to dominate the leadership, and the party took an increasing interest in labour matters (Déat was later appointed to Vichy as minister for labour.)[158]

At its highpoint in mid-1941, Déat's movement had as many as 20,000 members though it is likely that many were inactive. The size of the membership hardly grew once Laval authorized the RNP to operate in the southern zone after April 1942. The party's focus on labour issues seems to have attracted higher working-class support than its rivals.[159] Similarly, women were more prominent in the ranks of the RNP than in other collaborationist formations. In Dijon, 55 per cent of the RNP branch members were women; in the departments of the Indre-et-Loir and the Loiret, women made up 25 per cent and 27 per cent of the party's membership respectively. Gordon suggests a variety of reasons for women joining the movement including peer pressure, the opportunity to socialize and the mistaken belief that the commitment might secure the release of a prisoner of war.[160] While Gordon does not suggest that sympathy for the RNP's collaborationism motivated women members, this should not be discounted given the long history of female involvement with the extreme right in France.

Doriot did not fare as well as Déat upon his arrival in Paris in late 1940. Abetz was less well disposed to the PPF (the personal enmity between Doriot and Déat probably exacerbated things),[161] and the party was authorized to operate in the north only in April 1941, mainly thanks to Doriot's politicking with various rival German authorities in the zone. Doriot's programme was little changed from that of 1938; with anti-communism and anti-Semitism to the fore, it was compatible with Vichy's goals.[162] The party envisaged a revolutionary reconstruction of France within the new Europe. Its uniformed young men and women embodied this vision of a revitalized nation. Doriot framed the task as one for real men and honest women. Speaking in August 1940, he informed his faithful that 'the task that we have undertaken is not one for weaklings. France has no need for saviours in slippers. … It needs honest men and women who speak the no-nonsense language of popular France, who speak the truth fraternally to their opponents, and who, having spoken [the truth] are prepared to die [for it].'[163] Images of uniformed young PPF toughs standing in ranks beneath slogans such as 'Unity, Strength, Honour' and 'Believe, Desire, Act' reinforced the party's outward preparedness for manly action and violence.[164] The party took advantage of its existing apparatus, not to mention generous subsidies from Vichy and the Germans, to mobilize support. By September 1943, the PPF had 30,000 members; a year later the party's paper in the north had up to 115,000 readers.[165] The party maintained its regional power bases in Nice, Marseille, Lyon, Corsica, and North Africa.[166] Its constituency, too, reflected that of the pre-war years, based in the lower middle class.[167]

Doriot's struggle for official recognition pushed him closer to collaborationism, and in May 1941 he announced his adhesion to the Nazi racial new order in Europe and demanded the leadership of France.[168] The following month, the invasion of the Soviet Union saw Doriot proclaim: 'The crusade against Bolshevism gives the present war its true meaning', he said.[169] PPF members took part in the arrests of Jews, the capture of young men fleeing labour service in Germany and the fight against the resistance (the party claimed 600 PPFs died in violence with resisters.)[170] Doriot's persistent claims on the leadership of France hobbled the movement in the south; Pucheu banned the PPF in the Free Zone as its attacks on the regime grew and the party gradually broke with Vichy.[171] A planned seizure of power in November 1942 turned into a damp squib when Hitler made it known that he would not allow a French Fuhrer to assume control of the country. The PPF subsequently declined as members grew increasingly frustrated and the likelihood of a German victory diminished.[172]

Unity proved elusive for the collaborationists. The only tangible agreement between collaborationist groups was the 2 September 1941 pact between Doriot and Constantini's Ligue Française d'Epuration, d'Entraide Social et de Collaboration Européenne.[173] The Nazi sought to sew division between the collaborationists. In August 1940, Abetz made it clear to his subordinates that France was to be 'kept in a condition of internal weakness … [and] estranged from foreign powers hostile to the Reich. … Everything must be done on the German side to promote the weakness and internal disunity of France … only those forces likely to create discord should be supported; sometimes these will be elements of the Left, sometimes of the Right.'[174] The totalitarian reshaping of France likewise held little interest for Hitler.[175]

Nevertheless, all collaborationists were united in the sense that, in condemning the French divisions of the 1930s and hailing the success of fascism elsewhere in Europe, in the aftermath of the defeat they looked to secure a place for France in Hitler's new European order.[176] In this respect, their vision of a constructive collaboration did not differ drastically from that of Vichy. Indeed, the relationship between the collaborationists and Vichy was complex. Marshal Pétain was held in high regard, and few dared to attack him directly. Similarly, the National Revolution was heralded as the root-and-branch renovation necessary to secure France's survival. The collaborationists instead attacked Pétain's advisers and ministers for the failings of the regime and the obstruction of a more radical reform agenda. A poster for Déat's RNP thundered, 'Vichy plots with Jews and international freemasons, with financiers and American arms dealers who are laying down the law.'[177] Déat blamed the 'anonymous clique' and 'intriguers without mandate', around Pétain.[178] Likewise Doriot celebrated Pétain while he railed against the 'gangsters' and 'pimps' in government.[179] He feared for the National Revolution under the influence of parliamentarians, Action Française reactionaries and PSF conservatives. In the south, collaborationists likewise bemoaned the regime's immobilism. In Marseille, PPF boss Simon Sabiani attacked 'those who only conserve' at Vichy, when it seemed that the revolutionary side of the National Revolution was faltering at the turn of 1941.[180] Collaborationists thus hoped to use their influence with the Germans to bring pressure to bear on Vichy.

Collaborationism reached its zenith with the founding of the Légion des Volontaires Français contre le Bolchevisme (LVF) in July 1941.[181] The group sought to recruit volunteers to fight alongside Germany and its Allies on the Eastern Front. The brainchild of Doriot ('From now on this war is our war. It is the logical outcome of the fight we began in Saint-Denis, almost five years ago to the day', he is reported to have said upon the news of the invasion of the Soviet Union'),[182] the LVF received endorsement from a number of leading collaborationists, including Constantini, Deloncle and Déat, who declared at an LVF rally in Paris in February 1942: 'This war is Europe's war. Europe is forging its unity and conquering its independence on the battle fields. France is still wretchedly hesitant and divided, still unable to break with the past. Fortunately, an elite of men answered history's call and threw themselves into battle in the name of France.'[183] M. Reboulleau, one of the LVF's regional representatives, claimed that military collaboration offered the only true means to seal a 'Total Entente' with Germany and a national, socialist and racist revolution in France.[184] Doriot was the LVF's most famous recruit, serving at the front a number of times, notably during March 1943 and January 1944.[185] Military service offered the perfect opportunity for the PPF leader to realize his long-held hatred of communism: 'We are engaged in a battle that we cannot afford to lose. We must win or be destroyed,' he told his compatriots.[186] Doriot's intentions were not solely idealistic: he hoped that his willingness to serve would win him favour with the Germans and gift him the upper hand over his rival collaborationists.

The mission of the LVF was couched in the gendered terms familiar to the tradition of extreme right-wing paramilitarism in France: that of a muscular and elitist masculinity prepared to deploy violence against the enemy. Propaganda called on young French men to follow the example of the LVF's soldiers: 'Young French, attracted by the unprecedented sacrifice of a handful of heroes who did not want to despair of the destiny of France and Europe, find again the path of greatness and the taste for heroic combat through joining the Legion.'[187] These brave men offered 'the rampart of their chests' in the defence of Western civilization against Muscovite barbarism.[188] Mixing gendered imagery, the organization's leadership considered the LVF the nucleus of a future French army and the 'mother cell' that would give life to the new Europe.[189]

Women were encouraged to support the LVF through a variety of social works. They became *marraines de guerre* to volunteers fighting on the Eastern Front. The *marraines* and their soldier pen pals exchanged letters and parcels.[190] The leadership called on the ideal of motherhood in its appeal to French women. Deloncle spoke to the 'maternal thoughtfulness' and the 'heart of woman' in a request for Christmas gifts for the children of volunteers.[191] From May 1942, women were employed in the LVF's holiday camps for children. These camps were no small matter for the LVF. Between 1 July and 31 December 1943, the LVF spent 822,000 francs on bed, board and travel for 300 children.[192] The group also welcomed children whose parents were unable to look after them into its boarding house on the rue des Belles Feuilles.[193] Children's services were just one area of activity for the LVF's Social Services division. Legionnaires could apply for financial and legal aid and health care in the Villers-le-Lac sanatorium or the group's convalescence homes for injured combatants.[194]

The public response to the LVF was disappointing. The initial influx of recruits from the LVF's collaborationist supporters soon dried up.[195] Abetz had hoped to attract immediately 15,000 volunteers, and the LVF had opened eighty recruitment offices in the capital. In fact, it took two years to enlist 12,000 men, and Abetz's target was never reached. Worse still, only 5,800 were accepted as physically fit for service. Many were rejected for spurious reasons, and it is possible that Hitler intervened to keep membership low. Beside the fact that the Fuhrer had a low opinion of French soldiery, he did not wish to see an armed group develop in an occupied territory.[196] The first transports of volunteers arrived at Camp Deba, south of Warsaw, on 8 October 1941. They were placed under the command of Colonel Roger Henri Labonne, the former French military attaché to Turkey. Legionaries under Labonne's command were deployed mainly in a policing capacity, fighting partisans in Belorussia.[197] From November 1944, all French volunteers – some 12,000 men – were incorporated into the 33rd SS Charlemagne division.[198] Ninety of these men would take part voluntarily in the defence of Berlin, some, according to Ory, 'fighting still in the cellars and sewers of the capital of the Greater German Reich', days after Hitler's suicide

What motivated the men who signed up to fight for the Third Reich? Supporters of the LVF framed the group as a virile and chivalric warrior order. Catholic Cardinal Baudrillart (a member of the LVF's 'Committee of Honour') claimed that the legionnaires were 'the Crusaders of the twentieth century', who were 'helping to prepare the great French renaissance'.[199] Some volunteers perhaps subscribed to this view: their memoirs attest to a belief in the eagerness of women to satisfy the sexual needs of the courageous French soldiers.[200] For other recruits, unemployment and difficult personal circumstances motivated their membership.[201] A member of the LVF, if he were unmarried, could earn 1,800 francs each month. Married men were paid 2,400 francs plus a premium of 360 francs for each child. Volunteering for the LVF was thus more lucrative than working in a German factory.[202]

Vichy and fascism

It is generally understood that if, in its final months, Vichy displayed extremist tendencies, it fell short of full-blown fascism. For Julian Jackson Vichy became 'a police state, [but] not a fascist State', and Jean-Pierre Azéma agrees.[203] Milza perceives a 'fascistisation' of the leadership and the apparatus of state from January 1943 (the founding date of the Milice) as collaborationists 'colonised' the regime at several levels.[204] However, Vichy never took the 'decisive step' towards fascism.[205] Gordon, on the other hand, considers the appointment of Déat, Henriot and Darnand to government in the final months of the Occupation as evidence of Vichy's transformation into a 'thoroughgoing fascist state'.[206] Few historians claim that Vichy was a fascist state throughout the course of the war. Communist historian Bourderon is unusual in this respect: he perceives 'some essential traits common to Fascist regimes' in Vichy along with 'all the essential themes that we find in the Fascist, Nazi, National-Syndicalist ideologies' present in the National Revolution. Vichy was 'preparing' to be fascist from the outset.[207]

Prior to the desperate twilight of the regime, the nature of Vichy is typically judged according to its structure and its ideological content. In terms of its structure, Vichy, it is argued, was not fascist for it lacked a single party. The Légion certainly sought to mobilize support for the regime and Ángele Alcalde recognizes in the group certain fascist traits modelled on the figure of the Italian fascist veteran.[208] However, the Légion was a site of contest at local and national level. As Darnand explained at his trial, 'The Légion, in certain departments, was reactionary. In other departments, it was very maréchaliste, very "National Revolution". In certain regions of the south, in certain corners of the south, the Freemasons were in full control. ... Everyone did as they wanted. I shaped the Légion to my own temperament.'[209] Within the government, extreme right-wingers likewise sought to mould the group to their own desires. Some collaborationists were, however, disappointed, and they derided the Légion; Déat dismissed it as the expression of the reactionary and Maurrassian politics of the regime.[210] Yet Déat's rejection of the group stemmed, too, from his attempts to position the RNP as a single-party-in-waiting. When considering the collaborationists' dismissal of the Légion, it is important to consider the entity as a rival to other collaborationist formations.

The content of the National Revolution's political programme is likewise considered to have fallen short of fascism. In one respect, it is deemed to have lacked certain 'essential' features of fascist doctrine. Milza, for example, argues that the National Revolution differed from fascism for it did not aim to create a 'new man'.[211] Yet the regime did seek to regenerate French masculinity, and in doing this, it drew on similar Maurrassian and Barrèsian roots that inspired the collaborationists.[212] In any case, whether one determines that this construction of a new man was an essential feature of fascism depends upon one's definition of the phenomenon. The French roots of the National Revolution are likewise cited as evidence of the non-fascist character of the programme. Paxton forcefully argues that one could look to French history to explain the origins of the Vichy regime. Yet the National Revolution drew on foreign political doctrine as much as French political heritage.[213] Ideological borrowings, appropriations and adaptations, not to mention the fact that French political thought inspired, and was inspired by, foreign ideologies, ensured that no political movement could claim a uniquely national heritage.

As for the collaborationists, Déat and Doriot's predilection for authoritarianism may have left them well disposed towards the Occupier, but there was nothing inevitable about their ultimate wholesale engagement with collaborationism. To understand their trajectory one must look to their relationships with each other, with Vichy and with the Occupier. Both men desired that Marshal Pétain's regime undertake a more radical renovation of France than the National Revolution seemed to propose. Pétain's rejection of the single party project irked Déat more than Doriot, the former lacking the popular support base and party structure enjoyed by the latter. With the door apparently closed to him at Vichy, Déat sought the ear of the Occupier. His warm relations with Abetz and his increasing estrangement from Vichy pushed him further towards collaborationism.[214]

During 1940 and 1941, Doriot cultivated an image as a man of the marshal, keeping the Germans at arm's length and hoping to influence the regime; he founded the Rassemblement pour la Révolution Nationale in Paris, before the PPF was authorized.[215] His position was perhaps not purely tactical, and his commitment to Vichy may be dismissed as such only if one accepts that Doriot was fascist and the regime's true nature was not.[216] However, there was much in the National Revolution that chimed with Doriot's own politics, not least its anti-communism and anti-Semitism. In any case, Pétainism lent itself to a variety of interpretations as evidenced by the number of political factions who subscribed to the marshal's plan. The PPF leader's frustrated ambition in the north before April 1941 worked to maintain his link with Pétain and prompted him to seek closer collaboration with Abetz's German rivals.

The invasion of the Soviet Union allowed Doriot to throw himself wholesale into collaborationism through military service in the LVF. Déat's unique position as the paragon of French collaborationism was thus threatened, and this fact spurred on his own commitment to National Socialism; in January 1942, he spoke for the first time of a 'totalitarian' regime for a future France. The following spring the RNP was transformed into a fascist-style party, and Déat was, according to Burrin, well on his way to 'Nazification' by the end of the year.[217] Whether either man understood what Nazism 'really was' is beside the point.[218] Déat sought to achieve class collaboration in a corporatist economy. Doriot wanted the tools to eliminate communism and establish popular and authoritarian government. Nazism seemed to represent the means for both men to achieve their goals.[219] Their realization of this arrived as the result of a complex interaction of frustrated ambition, tactical calculation and competition.[220]

CHAPTER 7
THE FRONT NATIONAL

In March 2018, Marine Le Pen, president of the Front National (FN, the National Front),[1] France's largest and most successful post-war extreme right-wing party, announced that she would soon be consulting members about changing the name of the movement to the 'Rassemblement National' (National Rally). In addition to the desire to form a more inclusive coalition of nationalists, the move was the latest step in a strategy to detoxify the party's image since Le Pen took over its presidency from her father, Jean-Marie.[2] Doubtless, she hoped that the rebranding exercise would attract the support of French who had previously baulked at voting for a party regularly accused of racism and anti-Semitism. Yet critics were quick to point to the historical precedent of the new name: Déat's RNP, the collaborationist organization of the Vichy years.[3]

Marine Le Pen has found it difficult to cast aside the 'ideological baggage' of fascism, and the Rassemblement National controversy was not the first time that Le Pen had come unstuck with regard to her party's relationship to the past.[4] Barely a year previous, on 9 April 2017, Le Pen had, in the words of Henry Rousso, 'reopened the file on Vichy', with a statement about French responsibility in the round up of thousands of Jews in Paris during the infamous Vél d'Hiv raids of July 1942. During a television interview, she stated:

> I think that France was not responsible for the Vél d'Hiv [round up]. If anyone is guilty it is those who were in power at the time, it is not France. Really, we have taught our children that they have many reasons to criticise [France], to see in it perhaps only the darkest parts of its history. I want them to be proud once again to be French.[5]

In uttering these words, Le Pen was taking aim at former president Jacques Chirac's admission in 1995 that France, not simply Vichy, was responsible for the arrests. Her statement recalled the frequent controversies that her father courted. Most infamously, in 1987 Le Pen senior described the Holocaust as a mere 'detail' in the history of the period, a view for which he was punished in the French courts and, over a decade later, in Germany, where he had repeated the statement.

Marine Le Pen's statements on the past are consonant with her party's double game in matters of recent French history. The party has sought to distance itself from the fascist excesses of the mid-twentieth century while attempting to rehabilitate Pétain's regime (and thus restoring to respectability the political tradition that it incarnated) and exonerate collaborators in the name of national reconciliation. It strives simultaneously to discourage what it perceives to be a sort of self-flagellation with regard to the nation's past, from Vichy to the crimes of the French imperial state.[6] At the same time, anti-FN campaigns mobilize around the theme of antifascism, and the party is usually framed as the last bastion of collaborationism.[7] Ambiguity thus characterizes the FN's relationship to France's historical extreme right for its supporters and its opponents.

Fascism often provides the starting point for scholars of the FN. The usual approach to the subject involves the definition of the essential features of the ideology against which the Le Pens' party is subsequently measured.[8] It is relatively simple to find similarities between the FN's politics and those of historical French 'fascist' movements: a belief in 'natural communities' as a basis for the organization of politics and society; a rejection of egalitarianism; a preference for a strong state and an emphasis on law and order; a discourse of decline and decadence attributed to democratic politics and an attendant designation of scapegoats; and traditionalism in family and gender policy.[9] The party's populism builds on that of Boulangism and Drumont in its opposition to a Republican 'Establishment' and its preference for direct democracy.[10] In line with Barrèsian and Maurrasian thought, the FN prioritizes emotion and action while denouncing external and internal enemies (often characterized in racial terms), and appealing to the 'real' people.[11] The nation is at the root of all things, an organic entity into which one may enter only after a long period of acculturation, if ever.[12] Such comparisons have drawn the charge of fascism levelled at the party by its opponents. Yet like their pre-war counterparts, few groups on the post-war extreme right have claimed the fascist label. Those that have openly celebrated the doctrine, especially its original Italian version, could claim only a handful of members.[13]

A number of historians consider the party to be a manifestation of France's extreme right-wing tradition. Brian Jenkins has noted that the FN's traditionalist values are the same as those that informed the ideology of the Vichy regime.[14] Milza perceives a 'distant relationship' between the FN and Vichy, yet he identifies, too, Boulangism's brand of nationalist populism in the party.[15] Peter Davies sees aspects of Barrèsian, Maurrassian and Pétainist politics in the movement while admitting that the influences upon its programme are diverse.[16] Finally, Shields notes traces of Pierre Poujade's post-war populism in Marine Le Pen's left-leaning economic policy.[17]

While we may identify elements of the historical extreme right in the party's programme, from its Boulangist-style populism to its Vichyite traditionalism, the FN cannot be understood solely as the modern expression of a historical authoritarian nationalism born in the late nineteenth century. Jacques Tarnero argues that though the FN may appear to be 'one of the last avatars of a [French] fascism (*un fascisme hexagonal*)', to understand the party simply as the latest manifestation of the Vichy tradition is to fail to account for the contemporary influences on the party, its membership and the French who vote for it.[18] The legacy of the Algerian War, the experience of the Cold War, the civil and political unrest of the 1960s and the long march of globalization have all influenced the FN's programme, too.[19]

Accusations of fascism levelled at the party have not deterred millions of French from casting their vote for the Le Pens. The FN has broadened its appeal beyond the handful of former Vichyites, colonialists and thugs of its early days. Its greatest successes came during the presidential elections of 2002 and 2017. In the former, Jean-Marie Le Pen for the first time advanced to the second-round run-off against conservative candidate Jacques Chirac. While Chirac scored a thumping victory with 82 per cent of the vote, Le Pen improved upon his performance in the first round in all but two departments, winning approximately 5.5 million votes.[20] The party succeeded in forcing its policy programme into mainstream politics, prompting a rightward shift in discourse, especially with regard to immigration, that influenced the political debate in subsequent elections.[21] In 2017, Marine Le Pen contested the second round of the presidential election with the centrist Emmanuel Macron. She was, like her father, defeated. Nevertheless, 10.6 million French (almost 33 per cent of the election turnout) cast their vote for the FN candidate.[22] When one considers that during the late 1960s, the groups of the extreme right could muster barely 100,000 votes at the ballot box, the progress of the FN has been considerable.[23]

The wilderness years: 1944–81

In the immediate post-war years, the crimes of the Vichy regime and the Nazi Occupier, the purges that followed the Liberation and the foundation of the Fourth Republic condemned the extreme right to the margins of politics. Only a handful of intractable extremists strove to keep the flame of a French fascism alive. Men nostalgic for Hitler's New Order such as Maurice Bardèche – a veteran of the interwar extreme right who styled himself as the principle defender of the 'purged' (*épurés*) – worked to rehabilitate Vichy in their writing and political action. Bardèche's Mouvement Social Européen, founded in 1951, counted in its ranks neo-fascists and negationists from across Europe.[24] In France, he and his comrades were isolated figures, thanks both to the wave of Republicanism that swept the country and the strength of the Communist Party. While the onset of the Cold War (with its attendant anti-communism) and the instability of Republican governments provided some hope for a resurgence, the French extreme right was largely confined to the work of intellectuals and tiny political formations.

A breakthrough came in the mid-1950s. In November 1953, Pierre Poujade launched the Union de Défense des Commercants et Artisans (UDCA). Poujade was a shopkeeper and Gaullist councillor from Saint-Céré (Lot). He came from a reactionary and Catholic background – his architect father was a member of the Action Française – and as a teenager Poujade had been close to the PPF. During the war, he led a section of Vichy's Compagnons de France youth group. The UDCA spoke to the concerns of shopkeepers, small businessmen and craft workers who were struggling to survive in difficult post-war economic conditions prompted largely by a political drive to modernize – or 'Americanise', as Poujade put it – the economy of the Fourth Republic.[25] True, the French economy was expanding considerably, yet the boom in the main benefited industrial and service sector workers. Farmers and small shopkeepers meanwhile found themselves squeezed, a result of a flight of French from the countryside and the growth of large supermarkets and retail chains. Concomitantly, the government's heavy-handed approach to the tax inspections of small businesses raised tensions as property was seized and offenders were imprisoned.[26] These groups were attracted to Poujade's demand for a fair deal for the overlooked and overtaxed 'honest toilers' of France from the politicians, capitalists and bureaucrats of the Republican elite. The UDCA spread throughout France and Algeria via chambers of commerce and local sections, growing to a size of over 350,000 members.[27]

In January 1956, Poujadist candidates contested the legislative elections as the Union et Fraternité Française party. The ballot came at a time of crisis in France with the Algerian conflict gaining momentum, and the cry of 'Algérie française' found support in Poujade's movement.[28] Poujade's campaign echoed the antiparliamentarianism of the 1930s with a propaganda that denounced the political elite as a 'gang of vultures' and called on voters to 'kick out' the established parties; it thus spoke to extreme rightists who looked to use the movement as a Trojan horse against the Republic. Poujade was a popular orator who spoke a 'simple and popular language', and loved 'fighting talk'. He had 'the gift of the gab' according to Milza.[29] Meanwhile, Poujadist activists trashed the political meetings of their left-wing opponents.[30] On 2 January 1956, the UFF polled 2.48 million votes and won 52 seats in the National Assembly, one of which went to a twenty-seven-year-old Jean-Marie Le Pen.[31]

The parliamentary experience of the new Poujadist deputies was an unhappy one. These political amateurs had little of substance to offer in terms of policy, and they found themselves out of their depth in the institutional world of the Fourth Republic. Poujade himself had not run for election for he preferred to manage the UCDA outside the party system and thus maintain his ostensible apoliticism. This was a tactical error for it allowed newly elected deputies, not least Le Pen, to exert an influence over the political direction of Poujadism. Le Pen's ultranationalist interventions in the assembly, not to mention the fistfights between Poujadists and left-wingers on the floor of parliament, saw the UFF and the UCDA labelled fascists by their opponents, much to Poujade's consternation. Le Pen defended French intervention in Algeria and demanded that captured nationalists face summary execution. He referred frequently to his experience fighting communist rebels in Indochina in his attacks on the extreme left in the Chamber. In his later political career, Le Pen liked to be pictured in uniform, wearing his red paratrooper beret to underscore his credentials as a (virile) patriot.[32] Poujade could not tolerate such a challenge to his position as leader, and Le Pen was excluded in May 1957. A little over a year later, Poujadism disintegrated in the context of General Charles de Gaulle's assumption of power and the founding of the Fifth Republic in 1958, something that Poujade opposed, in contrast to the majority of his followers. The lower-middle-class discontent upon which Poujadism fed was unable to provide a solid basis for a new political party.[33]

There were elements to Poujadism that certainly recalled those of interwar fascism not to mention the radical right-wing thinking of Barrès and the integral nationalism of Maurras: '[Poujadism's] leadership cult, its antiparliamentarism, its increasing nationalism and xenophobia, [and] its periodic recourse to violence and intimidation.'[34] Poujade and his supporters likewise made use of anti-Semitic tropes in their attacks on the Fourth Republic (a regime allegedly in thrall to 'stateless financial powers') and on Prime Minister Pierre Mendès-France, a man who lacked 'a drop of Gallic blood' and was not 'the son of an ancient land like France'. Poujadist anti-Semitism echoed the familiar themes of Drumont, Barrès and the 1930s attacks on Blum, in its allegations that Jews lacked rootedness in French soil, culture and history.[35]

Poujade himself claimed that his eclectic politics, which drew on left- and right-wing currents in its opposition to socialism and conservatism, was 'unclassifiable'. At times he posed himself as simply the interpreter of the public mood: 'I was only a reflection of opinion, a loudspeaker, a flag-carrier'. This supposed deep connection to popular sentiment, linked to an appropriation of a revolutionary heritage and grounded in a desire for direct democracy, was framed according to Republican rhetoric. His movement campaigned for a new sitting of the estates general to air the grievances of ordinary French. Shields claims that such discourse complicates the accusation of fascism against the movement. Extreme right-wingers were unable to direct Poujadism against the Republic thanks largely to Poujade's refusal to be drawn into political factions and the mainly socio-economic concerns of his base. Ultimately, for Shields, the Poujadist project confirmed the 'continued marginality' of the extreme right in post-war France.[36]

In the wake of Poujadism, several small groups took up the cause of Algérie française such as Robert Martel's 'MP13', Colonel Château-Jobert's Mouvement de Combat Contre-Révolutionnaire and Jean-Claude Perez's Front National Français. Their campaigns spoke to the desires of the European settler population of Algeria for an authoritarian regime to better wage war in the territory and safeguard the French presence there. Yet they attracted a diverse range of supporters among those people who, according to Milza, 'desired revenge on 1945' such as former Vichyites and collaborationists who couched the defence of French Algeria in the vocabulary of anti-communism and the defence of Western civilization.[37] De Gaulle's withdrawal of France from Algeria in 1962 undercut the principal arm of the extreme right and groups were reduced to denouncing de Gaulle's supposed pro-communist foreign policy and the immigration of North Africans to France.

The presidential elections of 1965 – the first held under the new regime – presented an opportunity to run a 'national' candidate against de Gaulle. This candidate was Jean-Louis Tixier-Vignancour. Tixier had served as a deputy between 1936 and 1940 and worked for Vichy's information ministry during 1940–1. He was a fervent supporter of Algérie francaise, having co-founded the Front National pour l'Algérie Française and acted as a lawyer for several members of the violent Organisation de l'Armée Secrète that had waged a guerrilla war on Algerian and French soil. With Le Pen as his campaign manager Tixier made appeals to a number of right-wing constituencies in an attempt to federate the movements of the extreme right. The results were disappointing. Tixier won 5.27 per cent of the ballot and approximately 1.25 million votes; he was eliminated in the first round.[38] Subsequently, the parliamentary elections of June 1968 saw extreme right-wing parties secure a mere 0.1 per cent of the vote as electors once again put their faith in de Gaulle's Republic.[39]

By the close of the 1960s, the French extreme right was in the doldrums. Rousso concluded that at that moment, the appeal of the extreme right was limited to 'a few old men nostalgic for the brown-shirted rallies of another era and to a few young firebrands with shaved heads'.[40] Nevertheless, something was afoot within the intellectual circles of the extreme right. For a decade, activists such as François Gaucher and Dominique Venner and reviews such as Bardèche's negationist *Défense de l'Occident* and Venner's own *Europe-Action* had embarked on the wholesale reinvention of extreme right-wing doctrine that could bring together conservative nationalists and extremists.[41] The political divisions and setbacks of the 1960s did little to retard this drive for programmatic revision.[42]

The Groupe de Recherche et d'Etude pour la Civilisation Européenne (GRECE), founded in 1969 by former Fédération des Etudiants Nationalistes leader Alain de Benoist, played a leading role in the development of the so-called 'Nouvelle Droite' (New Right). This New Right project entailed no less than the creation of an intellectual counterculture founded on a 'plentiful doctrinal corpus'.[43] To this end, a range of political, social, economic and cultural subjects came under scrutiny in the reviews and journals of the New Right, many of which were previously unaddressed by right-wing thinkers. Concomitantly, the Nouvelle Droite drew on the radical right-wing racist thought of the late nineteenth and early twentieth centuries, notably in its belief in a natural inequality of races. 'A modern, intellectual and highly sophisticated lobby', the writers and intellectuals of the GRECE and its collaborators aimed to penetrate mainstream political thinking with their ideas and prepare the ground for future electoral conquest.[44]

A revision of political strategy accompanied this right-wing intellectual revolution. The new strategy emerged from within the ranks of Ordre Nouveau. Ordre Nouveau was perhaps the most important group on the extreme right to that point. Its influence was far greater than its membership of 5,000 activists; Jean-Yves Camus and René Monzat described it as a 'management school' (*école des cadres*) not only for future extreme right-wing personalities but also for several members of the parliamentary right.[45] Founded in 1969, Ordre Nouveau brought together the most influential political activists of the French extreme right, including Bardèche, former Cagoulard Jeantet, former *milicien* Charbonneau and a number of veteran Poujadistes and Tixieristes.[46] The group's most influential strategists, François Duprat and François Brigneau,[47] targeted a breakthrough into mainstream politics, rejecting illegal street violence in favour of political engagement with the institutions and conservative parties of the Fifth Republic. The strategy retained the goal of destroying the democratic regime, yet this would be accomplished from within the system itself.[48] Plans were initiated to establish a federation – or front – of extreme right-wing associations that could both unite the fascists and nationalists of the extreme right and appeal to conservatives disappointed with the presidency of Georges Pompidou.[49]

Ordre Nouveau's plan took shape when, on 5 October 1972, the FN was established with a view to contesting the municipal elections of March 1973. Le Pen was appointed leader of the new formation. The choice of Le Pen as president of the FN served to emphasize the legalist bent of the new formation, but members of Ordre Nouveau who advocated direct action occupied key positions in the party: Brigneau was vice president while his comrade Alain Robert was appointed secretary general.[50] Le Pen's own commitment to electoralism was itself ambiguous: during the party's 1982 congress, he told activists: 'We must be respectful of legality while it exists.'[51]

The membership of the party during the 1970s bore the marks of the historical battles of the extreme right. The legacy of Vichy certainly loomed large. At the FN's first public meeting, banners erected on stage proclaimed, 'Stop the Popular Front', and 'Chase the Thieves from Power' next to Vichy's 'Work, Family, Fatherland' slogan.[52] A survey of delegates to the FN congress in 1978 showed that approximately one-third had belonged to one of the interwar leagues or parties of the extreme right, such as the PSF.[53] However, the FN was not simply a haven for old guard Vichyites. Roughly half of the delegates to the congress were born during the war, and the party claimed an above-average number of students in its ranks.[54] Furthermore, a generation that had come of age during the Algerian conflict formed a significant caucus within the party.[55] The diverse provenance of members gave rise to tensions within the FN. Followers of Ordre Nouveau attempted to steer the party into violent street politics contrary to the desires of the legalist faction. Robert and Brigneau subsequently left the movement. The government's dissolution of Ordre Nouveau in 1973 allowed the FN's more moderate section to consolidate its position. The party developed an apparatus oriented towards populist electoral politics and engagement with Republican plural democracy.[56]

The FN's first electoral programme – *Défendre les Français*, produced for the 1973 parliamentary elections – prioritized the fight against communism and Moscow's interference in French domestic affairs (a hangover from Ordre Nouveau's own 1970 anti-communist manifesto). The issue that would become the FN's hobby horse – immigration – featured little in the programme. Likewise, Le Pen's campaign during the 1974 presidential election focused little on immigration. Only after the disappointment of 1974 – Le Pen won a meagre 0.74 per cent of the vote – did the party make immigration a central policy issue. With unemployment creeping up, the party declared: 'One million unemployed is one million immigrants too many! France and the French first!'[57] The national congress in November 1978 developed further the presumed relationship between unemployment and immigration. Moreover, it framed the presence of foreigners in the country in neo-Darwinian terms, an existential threat to French (and Western) cultural and biological identity. Interracial births, for example, were depicted as a side effect of globalization that undermined the quality of the French race.[58] The party's xenophobia thus betrayed a number of influences from the biological racism of Duprat and Venner to the Maurassianism of former PPF and FN activist Plonchard d'Assac.[59]

The party's political strategy failed to resonate with voters. FN candidates won a paltry 0.29 per cent of the vote in the 1978 parliamentary elections. Worse was in store. In preparation for the 1981 presidential election, Le Pen failed to secure the backing of the 500 sponsors necessary to stand as a candidate. The party's vote share in the subsequent legislative elections fell even further than that of 1978 to a derisory 0.18 per cent. Successive disasters at the polls suggested that the FN's plan to conquer power looked hopelessly optimistic.[60]

Breakthrough: The 1980s

Within two years of the disappointments of 1981, the FN made a breakthrough in the municipal elections of March 1983. Le Pen stood as a candidate for the twentieth arrondissement of Paris, a working-class district with a significant immigrant community. He exploited locals' fear of unemployment and hostility to foreign 'job-stealers', posing as a man-of-the-people unafraid to address issues ignored by the mainstream parties, in terms that echoed those of Poujade: 'I [say] out loud what people here think inside'. The strategy brought some success: with 11.3 per cent of the vote, the FN's leader took a seat on the capital's council. The result was a surprise given that over half of voters in the district had supported socialist President François Mitterrand in the election two years previous.[61] Leftist publications such as *Rouge* cast an eye back to the 1930s, assimilating the FN into historic fascism. Outgoing socialist Mayor Françoise Gaspard described Le Pen's election as evidence of the 'rise of fascism', reminding people that it was not simply the bourgeoisie that carried Hitler to power.[62] Still, left-wing journalists noted with some surprise that Le Pen voters in the area included dyed-in-the-wool socialist voters.[63]

Further improvements in the party's electoral fortunes followed. In September 1983, FN candidate Jean-Pierre Stirbois won 16.7 per cent of the first-round vote in the municipal by-election at Dreux (Eure-et-Loir).[64] In the second round, an alliance was agreed with the two parties of the conservative mainstream, the Gaullist Rassemblement pour la République (RPR) and the centre-right Union pour la Démocratie Française (UDF). The RPR-UDF-FN list won 55 per cent.[65] This was not the first time that the FN had come to a political arrangement with conservative candidates. Alliances had been concluded during the municipal elections of 1977 in Courbevoie, Mérignac, Toulouse and Villefranche-sur-mer.[66] The importance of conservative-FN alliances was exposed several weeks after the Dreux election when the party polled 9.3 per cent in the Parisian suburb of Aulnay-sous-Bois. In this instance, the RPR refused to cooperate in the second round, and the FN was eliminated.[67] The disappointment at Aulnay did not hamper the party's progress for long and improving local results hinted at a burgeoning national support. In the 1984 elections to the European parliament, more than two million French cast their vote for the party, rewarding the FN with a 12 per cent share.[68]

The FN's electoral breakthroughs of the early 1980s, not to mention Le Pen's frequent media appearances, exposed evermore French to the party's programme. Le Pen waxed lyrical about the virtues of Franco, Salazar and Pinochet, promising to reinforce French law and order. He spoke out against the permissiveness (*laxisme*) of a society in thrall to decadence, which he alleged was epitomized in the availability of abortion and the practice of homosexuality. He took aim at the Communist Party and promised to defend French and Western civilization against Moscow.[69] Yet it was the FN's stance on immigration that trumped all other matters for both the party's supporters and its opponents. The issue assumed central importance in the FN's 1986 parliamentary election manifesto.[70] Under the influence of GRECE thinking on the subject, the party's strategy aimed to ostracize the immigrant in political, cultural and economic, rather than racial, terms. FN candidates blamed foreigners for a growing sense of *insécurité*, a nebulous term that came to encompass concerns over crime, drugs, gang warfare, urban violence, civil disorder and the threat of civil war.[71] The focus of FN rhetoric shifted from skin colour to matters of historical and cultural differences.[72] In this vein, Le Pen rejected the notions of integration and assimilation not simply on the grounds of racial hierarchies and alleged ethnic aptitudes but on deeply rooted cultural and historical differences.

Le Pen publicly rejected all forms of racism. He instructed activists to avoid the use of inflammatory language in favour of a more technical vocabulary. An internal party document advised members against demanding to '[dump the] wogs in the sea', in favour of stressing the necessity of '[organising] the repatriation of Third World immigrants'.[73] The party spoke of an 'anti-French racism' inherent to government policies that allegedly favoured immigrants over indigenous inhabitants in a number of sectors, not least the labour market. The FN thus advocated the policy of 'national preference' that would grant native French preferential access to jobs, housing and social security.[74] The party simultaneously proposed the mass expulsion of illegal immigrants, restrictions on foreigners' rights and a tightening up of laws on citizenship and naturalization.[75]

Le Pen singled out the North African community for special opprobrium. He cast the arrival of nationals from France's former overseas territories as akin to the barbarian invasion of Rome and the German invasion of France in 1940. Party spokespersons warned of the 'Islamization' and 'Lebanonization' of France. They drew on long-held beliefs in the incompatibility of the French Christian and Muslim civilizations citing everything from the Medieval Crusades to the war in Algeria. Young Muslim men in particular were depicted as the enemy within, blamed for crime, terrorism and welfare fraud. According to Le Pen, such people were 'French only on paper' (*Français de papier*) and could never be considered on the same terms as those of 'French stock' (*Français de souche*).[76] Campaigning principally on an anti-immigration ticket, the FN won over 2.7 million votes during the parliamentary elections of 1986. This success, in an election held under a proportional voting system, saw thirty-five FN deputies take their seats in the National Assembly. This was an unprecedented success for the party.[77]

Analysis of FN voters during Mitterand's first term (1981–8) showed that they were most receptive to the party's attacks on immigrants and its emphasis on law and order (*insécurité*). Such voters were likely to live in areas on the periphery of towns and cities with high immigrant populations and heightened levels of crime.[78] Journalist Anne Tristan, who published her account of infiltrating the FN in Marseille during 1987, noted that the conversations of party activists returned frequently to the 'problem' with immigrants in France: 'Vandalised bus shelters, broken call boxes, stuck bus doors, all these things destroyed, damaged, it's the Arabs' fault'; Arabs were 'vandals', 'yobs' and 'scum'.[79] Even socialist supporters could sympathize with the FN's hard line on immigration, as Tristan found: her landlady, a supporter of the Socialist Party who had been an activist during the late 1940s, hated Le Pen and the FN but desired to see the Arabs leave France.[80] Yet the party found support too in districts where indigenous French made up the majority of the community. Such areas were most receptive to the FN where poverty and job insecurity were high; the policy of national preference played particularly well in these constituencies. In this respect, social factors trumped traditional political allegiances in the decision to vote for the FN.[81]

The apparent success of the FN in exploiting immigration as a political issue caught the attention of the mainstream political parties because a high proportion of votes came from radicalized supporters of the conservative parties in France. These people were anxious about the perceived breakdown of society and the disappearance of traditional values, subjects to which the traditional right-wing parties seemed unable to speak.[82] Conservative politicians from the RPR and UDF increasingly spoke out against multiculturalism while advocating assimilation in a political strategy that sought to both damage the left and move onto the terrain of the extreme right.[83] Leading right-wingers had flirted with xenophobia in the past. As mayor of Paris during the 1970s, Jacques Chirac had connected unemployment with immigration; he would in the 1990s bemoan not only the French 'overdose' on immigration but also the 'noise' and 'smell' of immigrant families living in social housing.[84] Meanwhile, the municipal elections of 1983 saw both the RPR and the UDF include immigration and *insécurité* in their manifestoes, and it has proved fertile ground for electoral alliances between the three parties.[85] We must recognize that the conservative parties' stance on immigration was less radical than that of the FN. Le Pen's de facto deputy, Bruno Mégret, for example, proposed the revision of all naturalizations granted since 1974, framing his views on immigrants in the language of identity, blood and national community.[86] Yet the collaboration of the RPR and the UDF with the FN – an extremist party bent on closing the borders and 'taking down' the Fifth Republic – helped to consolidate support for Le Pen in his heartlands, launch the party into new territories and normalize FN rhetoric.[87]

By the mid-1980s, the FN claimed to have as many as 65,000 members. The true number was likely significantly lower than this figure. Still, at a time when the membership of political parties was stagnating, the FN was growing.[88] Members of the FN – like its voters – were predominantly male. The party framed feminism as a Marxist conspiracy, citing the movement as further evidence of the decadence of modern France. In this vein, the party's affiliate, the Cercle National des Femmes d'Europe, led by Martine Lehideux, promoted a conservative conception of womanhood that prioritized family life.[89] Le Pen envisaged a future France as one with a strict hierarchical sexual order, with men responsible for work and women at home to raise the family.[90] The party proposed preferential treatment for families (conceived in party discourse as the basic unit of society) with measures such as a guaranteed 'maternal income', tax concessions to parents and a family vote. It sought to curb perceived threats to French family life such as divorce, homosexuality, abortion and contraception.[91]

The party did not discourage female activism. Lehideux, for example, urged women to take part in politics but in the name of the family.[92] As Tristan discovered, the FN's youth group, the Front National de la Jeunesse (FNJ), offered opportunities for activism consonant with the party's ideas on female capabilities (she was appointed to the post of administrative secretary for her typing skills.)[93] Women could, however, assume positions of responsibility. Valérie Lafont's interviews with FNJ members revealed that the group's counter-society provided marginalized women with an opportunity for independence. One activist, 'Blanche', told Lafont that she had found employment, sociability and a place in the world through the FNJ. In a position of leadership in her section – and the only girl – Blanche stated proudly, 'I'm the boss, I rely on myself alone, I can be a rebel if I want, it's great!'[94] Even street violence was not off limits. Prior to a march at a Le Pen rally in Marseilles, Tristan's friend Véronique had expressed a desire to see a fight between FN members and counter-demonstrators from SOS-Racisme; she later took part in scuffles with North African men during the event.[95]

Given that Le Pen had been unable to run in the 1981 presidential election, his performance in 1988 could only be regarded as a success. His score of 14.4 per cent of the ballot – 4,300,000 votes and a record score for an extreme right-wing candidate – suggested that his programme appealed to French beyond his base. The party polled well in traditional areas of support and made breakthroughs among white- and blue-collar workers who were concerned with *insécurité*.[96] Of course, we cannot discount the fact that a vote for the FN may be understood as a protest. Some FN voters were not interested in Le Pen becoming president; they wanted the party to win enough votes simply to 'scare' the mainstream.[97] Yet the peculiar political situation at the time – the 'cohabitation' of conservative Chirac as the prime minister and socialist Mitterrand as the president – allowed Le Pen to present the FN as the only genuine alternative to the parties of government.[98] Speaking at Reims in February 1988, the FN president claimed,

> The common trait of these past fourteen years of French decadence, is socialism, and socialism, it's a sort of political AIDS, of mental AIDS. … In this type of disease, there is a deadly phase close to agony, the one of the 'socialiques' and of the 'socialpositifs' that are the RPR and the UDF, each one having the same illness.[99]

Despite the fact that the return of the majority voting system in the subsequent parliamentary elections saw the party lose all but one of its deputies, the fortunes of the FN during the 1980s suggested it could become a force to be reckoned with in French politics.[100]

Consolidation and division: The 1990s

Efforts to establish the FN as a mainstay of the political landscape suffered several setbacks during the late 1980s, thanks in no small part to the president of the party itself. Most infamously, during a television interview in September 1987 Le Pen described the Nazi gas chambers as merely a 'detail' (*point de détail*) in the history of the Second World War and questioned the significance of their role in the massacre of European Jews. He was later fined under the Gayssot law of July 1990 pertaining to Holocaust denial. Further anti-Semitic barbs saw Le Pen widely accused of inciting racial hatred. When a Jewish cemetery was desecrated at Carpentras in May 1990, the FN's opponents blamed the party for reviving anti-Semitism in France, though no FN members were involved in the crime.[101] Le Pen's anti-Semitic provocations not only stemmed from his attitude to Jews in France but also looked to grab media attention at a time when the party's influence in parliament was slight. They chimed, too, with the beliefs of a significant proportion of the FN's membership. In an April 1990 poll by SOFRES[102] of the FN cadres found that 88 per cent of respondents believed that Jews had too much power in Europe.[103]

In preparation for the 1995 presidential elections, the party renewed its attacks on the French 'banana' republic. Constitutional revision was the centrepiece of Le Pen's manifesto.[104] Such a stance threatened to harm the party's electoral prospects: prior to the 1995 presidential election, opinion polls found that 86 per cent of French believed that Le Pen was incapable of running the country. Seventy-three per cent of those questioned considered his party a danger to French democracy.[105] In the event, Le Pen won 15 per cent of votes cast in the first round. This score saw him eliminated, yet he had succeeded in attracting 200,000 more votes than in the first round of the 1988 election.[106] The party subsequently secured municipal election wins in Toulon, Orange and Marignane, and its share of the vote held up in the parliamentary elections of 1997 and the regional ballots of 1998.[107]

The 1990s witnessed perceptible changes in both the party's membership and its voting base. First, the passage of time reduced the number of members who were veterans of the interwar extreme right. Now, almost two-thirds of members had been politicized in the nationalist groups and networks of the years after 1945. Second, the party's breakthrough during the 1980s had prompted a growing number of young people to join the movement. Indeed, in 1987 Tristan was surprised to find that her new comrades were not all 'embittered old men'.[108] The majority of these new members had little previous political experience.[109] Finally, after 1986 the FN became increasingly attractive to conservatives who were disappointed with the perceived moderation of the RPR and the UDF. The FN attacked both parties as the 'false right', in thrall to 'globalised values' and in the pay of 'ethnic lobby groups'.[110]

Beyond the ranks of the movement, the FN strove to convince voters that Le Pen and his followers were bona fide candidates for election. The party developed a sophisticated propaganda machine, producing FN-branded merchandise from key rings and badges to bow ties and perfume. The party was the first in France to operate an internet site.[111] Advances were made into new constituencies, notably finding success among French who identified strongly with neither the right nor the left (Nonna Mayer's so-called ninistes, for their 'ni droite, ni gauche' politics). FN voters in this constituency, like the party's loyalists, were shown to be most concerned with unemployment, insécurité and immigration.[112]

The most commented-upon change in the FN electorate during Mitterand's second term as president (1988–95) was the apparent defection of a proportion of left-wing voters to Le Pen, a phenomenon termed gaucho-lepénisme.[113] Thirty per cent of working- and lower-class French who voted in 1995 cast a vote for Le Pen.[114] While this switch of allegiance may be attributed to the decline of the Communist Party, disaffected socialist voters were also likely to vote for the FN in the mid-1990s.[115] The trend was not general, and voting preference depended a great deal on local issues. In Vitrolle (Bouches-du-Rhône), for example, where Mégret's wife Catherine was elected the mayor in 1997, gaucho-lepénisme owed more to specific local circumstances than an automatic preference of former left-wing voters for the FN.[116] Furthermore, given the FN's influence on the national political agenda, left-wing parties were forced to engage with Le Pen's agenda, blurring the distinction between left- and right-wing positions on some issues. The majority of FN voters still hailed from the right-wing of politics.[117]

At the close of the twentieth century, the FN entered a period of difficulty. On the one hand, the party's electoral prospects were improving markedly: the 1997 parliamentary elections saw its share of the vote stabilize at around 15 per cent, securing its position as the second most powerful force on the right. Yet internal divisions worked to undermine this ostensible strength. Mégret split from the party in early 1999 to found the Front National-Mouvement National (later renamed the Mouvement National Républicain [MNR]). Mégret's decision to leave came when, in preparation for the European elections of 1999, Le Pen appointed his wife Jany to lead the list of party candidates rather than Mégret. In truth, Mégret's star was in the ascendancy in the party, and Le Pen had looked to counter the potential threat to his leadership that his deputy represented.[118] Half of the FN's elected representatives defected to the MNR as did nearly two-thirds of the party's departmental secretaries. The FN's membership shrank to around 25,000 members from a figure previously twice that number.[119] Few commentators therefore predicted the political earthquake of the 2002 presidential election.

2002–11: At the gates of power

In the first round on 21 April 2002, Le Pen won 16.9 per cent of the vote, placing him second behind incumbent Jacques Chirac on 19.9 per cent. With 16.1 per cent, socialist candidate and Prime Minister Lionel Jospin was beaten into third place and eliminated. The profile of Le Pen's vote in 2002 showed that he had topped polls in over one-third of departments, performing well in rural communities and 'peri-urban' areas on the outskirts of large towns and cities.[120] He found support from a range of constituencies, including workers, young French, the unemployed, farmers and the professions.[121] Worryingly for Republicans of all colours, a breakdown of the first-round result showed significant support for anti-Republican candidates across the board. The largest parties of the left were soundly beaten: more voters cast their ballot for the extreme right-wing candidates Le Pen and Mégret (standing for his MNR) than for the communist and socialist candidates combined.

What explained Le Pen's first-round success? Prior to the election, Le Pen had moderated his rhetoric somewhat, dropping some of his more extreme proposals while characterizing Mégret as the extremists' choice.[122] The party reinforced its appeals to those French who felt marginalized and excluded from mainstream politics. Le Pen claimed that he was on the side of the 'little people' against the corruption and power of the Establishment (*l'établissement*).[123] Immigration policy remained central to the FN's campaign, and the post-9/11 international political context amplified Le Pen's warnings about Islamic extremism.[124] He made appeals to the 'true French', while presenting the country as under siege from North African invasion, Islamification and terrorism.[125] The FN's strategy succeeded in placing *insécurité* at the top of the political agenda, and all parties spoke to this as a prime concern of French voters.[126] The media took up the matter, too, and the daily news carried numerous reports of violent crime in the weeks and days prior to the first-round vote. These stories allowed Le Pen and Chirac to portray the socialist Prime Minister Jospin as soft on crime and weak on terrorism.[127]

Mass protests between rounds one and two saw over a million French demonstrate their dismay and anger at the success of the FN.[128] Jospin advised left-wingers to vote for Chirac in the run-off in the name of defending the Republic. The conservative candidate won comfortably, with 82 per cent of the vote. Nevertheless, Le Pen's share of the vote increased in all but two departments.[129] This result was notable given the strength of the political and media campaign against the FN before the second ballot on 5 May.[130] Despite the fears of Republicans, there was no notable swing to the extreme right. In fact, Le Pen's percentage of the vote in 2002 represented an increase of only 2.5 per cent since 1988. While this increase was sufficient to get him over the first-round hurdle in 2002, it was small. Moreover, fewer than half of Le Pen voters questioned in 2002 actually wanted him to be elected president while over a quarter of them believed that his progression to the second round was a danger to democracy. For many, a vote for the FN was still a protest vote against the political mainstream or a 'negative mobilization', in Shields's terms.[131]

The shock of 2002 was not repeated in the presidential election five years later.[132] In fact, if in 2002 pollsters had underestimated Le Pen's chances, in 2007 they overestimated them. The FN president came in a poor fourth in the first round, his worst performance since 1974. There were several explanations for the disappointment of 2007. First, voter turnout in the first round was high. In 2002, record abstention rates, especially among socialist voters, had allowed Le Pen to advance. Perhaps with this in mind, 83.77 per cent of registered voters turned out in 2007, compared with 71.6 per cent five years ago.[133]

Second, the right-wing candidate, Nicolas Sarkozy, succeeded in appropriating a number of the FN's policy points in his own campaign. As Chirac's minister of the interior, Sarkozy had cultivated an image as a combative character with a tough stance of crime. In 2005, when riots broke out across France in areas with high immigrant populations, Sarkozy promised to end the violence by removing the 'scum' from the streets.[134] His 2007 presidential campaign focused on immigration and national identity. He posed immigration and Islam as dual threats to indigenous French culture and domestic law and order, declaring his intention to open a Ministry for Immigration and National Identity should he be elected. Sarkozy openly courted FN voters with his robust rhetoric and his 'Love France or leave it' position (a phrase that he denied uttering but which stuck to his campaign).[135]

Finally, Le Pen once again attenuated the more extreme points of his programme, depicting himself as 'a man of the centre right' and lauding Republican values. The FN retained key aspects of its immigration agenda (such as the policy of national preference) yet the so-called foreign invasion accounted for only two of the sixty-eight pages in the party's 'Programme de Gouvernement de Jean-Marie Le Pen 2007' manifesto.[136] Consequently, some traditional FN voters and radicalized conservatives turned to Sarkozy as the candidate who seemed best placed to enact policies to their liking.[137]

The immense disappointment of the 2007 presidential election, followed by paltry results (4.3 per cent of the vote) in parliamentary elections that year, signalled to some that the FN was in terminal decline.[138] Shields points out that the FN's decline was a long-term phenomenon. Aside from the unexpected result of the 2002 presidential election and a strong showing in the 2004 regional ballot, the period between 1999 and 2009 was characterized by 'declining electoral performance'. For this reason, the party experienced severe financial difficulties.[139] Nevertheless, Le Pen continued to drive a rightward shift of the political centre that saw parties of the mainstream left and right brought onto FN terrain. The party continued to set the political agenda on immigration, national identity and Europe.[140]

2011–18: A *Bleu Marine* Revolution?

In April 2010, Le Pen announced his decision to retire from the party's leadership. FN members subsequently elected his youngest daughter, Marine Le Pen, to the presidency. Le Pen wasted little time in her campaign to reorient the party's image, a process known as *dédiabolisation*, or detoxification. To dispel the concerns of democrats, she used her inaugural speech at the party conference in 2011 to pose the FN as 'a great Republican political party'. She laid claim to the regime's *Liberté, Egalité, Fraternité* motto and described FN members as 'the true defenders of the Republic'.[141] In an attempt to cast off its image as a single-issue party, Le Pen has developed a number of new policies in areas relatively untouched during her father's tenure. The FN has devoted more serious attention to complex political and economic issues. It has, for example, mounted a sustained quasi-Poujadiste critique of economic globalization, intended to appeal to the victims of the 2008 financial crisis.[142]

Le Pen has deployed the party's newfound Republicanism in her campaign against immigration. In the name of secularism (*laïcité*), she has condemned the Islamization of France, evidence of which she has cited in the alleged banning of pork from school canteens and the French's apparently unwitting consumption of halal meat. Both stories have been shown to have little basis in fact. The FN's embrace of *laïcité* – described as 'this good and great principle of the French Republic' – thus smacks of dog-whistle politics and a '[repackaging of] a discriminatory policy agenda as a defence of liberal values and personal rights'.[143]

The party's reinvigorated opposition to globalization is part of a reorientation away from explicit ethno-nationalism and towards economic protectionism based on the defence of indigenous French.[144] Le Pen herself has condemned 'identity-massacring globalisation (*mondialisation identicide*)', describing its effects as 'an economic nightmare, a social tsunami, [and] a moral Chernobyl'.[145] The FN subsequently sought to defend French national identity from organizations such as the European Union, which, it alleges, looks to subsume and efface national cultures.[146] It is in the realms of economic policy that the real innovation in Marine Le Pen's renewal of the party lies, amounting to a 'left-leaning agenda of anti-capitalism and social welfare provision in response to a growing public demand for social and economic protection'.[147] In this area, Shields perceives a radicalization in the extension of demands for the policy of national preference from the domains of jobs, housing and social security to public sector employment, and family allowances.[148]

In tandem with programmatic revisions, the party has undergone significant structural changes since 2011. A new generation of activists and party leaders has come to the fore, untainted by connections with Vichy and France's colonial wars while less under the influence of the New Right of the 1960s and 1970s. These men and women have backed the campaign to transform the FN from an anti-system protest group into a party of government.[149] Meanwhile, Le Pen has strived to nurture both a mass base of support and a pool of potential electoral candidates.[150] At the grass-roots level the party provides social services in communities where state provision has been cut or removed entirely. Activists are able to respond in material terms to local hardship while communicating the party's agenda on national issues.[151] Electoral candidates are selected from within their native constituencies, their social and economic backgrounds matching those of their target audience.[152] In this way, the party aims to strengthen its local implantation and to reshape cultural and community identities in its own image, sensitizing communities to national political issues in a way not dissimilar to the PSF's social work agenda of the 1930s.[153]

Le Pen's performance in the 2012 presidential election hinted at the relative success of her political strategy. The FN candidate came third, with 17.9 per cent and 6,421,426 votes. The party achieved its best ever scores across all age groups and socio-economic categories and continued to close the gender gap that traditionally defined its electorate. The party made further breakthroughs in rural and peri-urban territories. In these areas, distant from urban centres and inhabited by those most exposed to the globalized economy and its perceived harm – working- and lower-class French – economic hardship is rife and social mobility is low. Unemployment, fear of *insécurité* and resentment of foreigners make these areas fertile ground for the FN's protectionist message.[154]

Did these voters consider the FN a respectable Republican party like any other? During the election campaign, President Sarkozy himself described the FN as a 'democratic party ... compatible with the Republic'. Furthermore, his continued appropriation of the FN's rhetoric on immigration, Islam, secularism and national identity lent legitimacy to Le Pen's programme.[155] However, Sarkozy found that he could not as easily siphon votes from the FN as he had done in 2007. Traditional FN voters were disappointed with the president's record in government, and they remained loyal to their party.[156] Le Pen's announcement that she would spoil her ballot in the second round dissuaded many of her followers from voting for Sarkozy and socialist François Hollande carried the day.[157] In fact, up to 1.3 million French may have transferred their vote from Le Pen to Hollande between the first and second rounds.[158] Such a figure indicates that Le Pen had not been entirely successful in transforming the FN into a party of government. In fact, in April 2012, 44 per cent of voters surveyed after the first-round ballot stated that they had cast a vote for Le Pen as an expression of opposition to the mainstream candidates rather than as a positive vote for the FN.[159]

The parliamentary elections of 2012 returned two FN deputies to the National Assembly, the party's first elected representatives in the legislature since the 1980s.[160]

In 2014, FN candidates won 11 mayoralties in cities over 10,000 people, besting 1995's previous high of three. The party further secured 1,498 seats on municipal councils, bettering 2008's score of just 59. More success came with the 2014 elections to the European parliament where the FN won the largest share of France's seats (twenty-four out of seventy-four).[161] It thus appears that the FN's strategic shift – 'recasting itself as a mainstream formation that seeks to exercise political power' – has borne fruit.[162] The party has consolidated its support in rural communities and those on the margins of metropolitan areas. Its programme, based on tough measures against 'job-stealing' immigrants and the undermining of traditional French values, plays well in such areas where citizens feel marginalized and ignored by mainstream political parties in a globalizing environment centred on cultural diversity.[163] However, if the elections of 2002 and 2017 have given rise to the belief that the FN is an irresistible force in French politics, its results in all elections since the early 1980s suggest 'a very modest creeping, ineffectual advance over a quarter-century of electioneering' rather than a rising tide.[164] The FN's isolation in the political arena continues to hamper its chance of success. Still, the party has confounded repeated predictions of its demise and did so once again in 2017 when Marine Le Pen, like her father fifteen years ago, advanced to the second round of the presidential election with barely one million votes fewer than the eventual victor, Emmanuel Macron.[165]

CONCLUSION

The array of leagues and parties examined in this book illustrates the diversity of French 'fascism' since the First World War. Historical political groups have contributed to this picture of diversity in their own emphases on the uniqueness of their doctrine, their methods and their goals. Activists laid claim to a variety of labels: monarchist, nationalist, Republican, fascist. They argued forcefully in favour of their own projects to renovate France from the return of the king or an authoritarian renovation of the Republic to a National Revolution and the installation of a full-blown fascist dictatorship. Each claimed that their plan represented the only chance of success. Rivals were treated as misguided fellow travellers, and divisions between movements could prompt both verbal and physical attack. Leaders guarded their followers jealously and discouraged them from dividing their loyalties.

Nevertheless, we may perceive a similarity of attitude on a number of issues that cut across the carefully constructed boundaries between the groups of the 'fascist' right. Differences were surmountable and alliances were concluded both between leaders and activists in the street. Jenkins is quite correct to claim that 'these movements were all fishing in the same pool of ideas', and it was common for activists to hold memberships to a multitude of groups.[1] Finally, the passage of time did not obstruct partisans of the extreme right from migrating to new groups: former members of the 1920s Faiseau joined the Croix de Feu during the 1930s while ex-PPFs were present at the founding of the FN during the 1970s.

A promise to profoundly alter the democratic political institutions of France lay at the heart of all groups' political programmes. The means proposed to enact this change varied. The Faisceau envisaged a violent seizure of power by its paramilitary shock squads. The Croix de Feu believed that the Republic would soon collapse under the weight of its own contradictions. During the Occupation, collaborationist groups worked to guarantee a national and socialist future for France in the Nazi New Order. More recently, the FN has developed a sophisticated electoral machine to conquer power at the polls. In peacetime, few leaders explicitly expressed their desire to overthrow the democratic regime. Rather, ambiguity characterized their pronouncements on this matter: Le Pen's 1982 statement on his respect for legality 'while it exists' recalled La Rocque's commitment of loyalty to the 'presently existing constitution' in 1934. Yet their political programmes made clear that the instruments of democratic government and the values at the heart of the Republican project would be reconfigured beyond recognition or simply erased.

For the interwar leagues, the task of governing would generally be entrusted to a group of men noted for their military service or patriotic character. Parliament – a body deemed responsible for the national chaos that allegedly reigned – would be curtailed if not closed down. Political pluralism would cease to exist once the left was destroyed.

The alleged enemies of France – Freemasons, communists, pacifists, the childless – would suffer persecution and criminalization. Minorities – Jews, Muslims, foreigners – deemed 'unassimilable' into the new national community would face discrimination, denaturalization and expulsion. A version of this plan was installed after the defeat of 1940, and the project to render the country politically and racially homogeneous was implemented. This vision of France lingers on today in the programme of the FN and its attacks on a Republican establishment that has allegedly undermined French national identity.

Central to the 'fascist' right's project was a violent hypermasculinity expressed in paramilitary hierarchies, the hard bodies of uniformed street fighters and the celebration of virile icons from the providential leader to the First World War veteran. Propaganda was replete with vocabulary coded as masculine: courage, willpower, self-sacrifice and discipline were the order of the day. Young men were trained for combat in the street, a theatre in which they could test their mettle. From the Jeunesses Patriotes' centuries to the skinheads of the late twentieth century, via the Croix de Feu *Dispos* and the young volunteers in the LVF, violence offered a means to demonstrate both one's commitment to the cause and one's masculinity in contrast to the anti-national effeminacy of the enemy. Parades of young men and women presented an image of orderly and controlled strength, ready to be unleashed at a moment's notice against the emasculated and chaotic Republic.

Women have played a central role in the ostensibly male world of the French extreme right. With the family placed at the heart of political programmes as the essential cell of society, women were celebrated as loving mothers in whose womb lay the future of France. All groups sought to return women to the home, and Vichy pursued this idea with vigour. However, the social work of several parties and leagues afforded female activists a gateway into the public sphere otherwise denied to them, at least before their enfranchisement in 1945. Women were employed in medical centres, soup kitchens, charity sales and holiday camps, all of which gave free rein (or so it was thought) to their natural caregiving qualities. This social work was not incompatible with politics. The Croix de Feu-PSF in particular viewed the 'social' as inherently political. La Rocque predicated his vision of a future France on a basis of national reconciliation and harmony that he believed social action could bring about. Female social workers spread the lieutenant colonel's gospel as they served meals to the needy, provided medical treatment to the sick and dished out Christmas presents to the young. They were able to access areas – notably working-class districts – that were generally closed off to their male comrades; in this way, women ensured a deep penetration of society for the Croix de Feu-PSF's ideas. La Rocque's movement was the largest group to engage women in politicized social work, but it was not the only one; the Jeunesses Patriotes, the Légion, the LVF and the FN all afforded women an opportunity for action.

Hostility to foreigners, Jews and Muslims runs throughout the leagues and parties examined in this book. During the interwar years, foreigners bore the blame for the many social and economic problems suffered after the Crash of 1929. Groups on left and right offered solutions to the so-called immigrant problem, and there were frequent calls for the revision of naturalizations and the expulsion of foreign undesirables. In the wake of successive refugee crises during the 1930s, hostility to foreigners often shaded into hostility to Jews. Some leagues and parties had long been explicit in their anti-Semitism: the Action Française, the Solidarité Française and the PPF (after 1937) relentlessly attacked the Jewish community in France. Their anti-Semitism drew in large part on long-held hostilities to a people believed to be 'rootless'. The line between cultural expressions of anti-Semitism and biological racism was blurred, and some activists on the extreme right subscribed to a conception of race familiar to Nazism. The Croix de Feu-PSF was more prudent with its anti-Semitism than some of its competitors. It distinguished between 'good' or patriotic Jews and 'bad' or anti-national Jews. This position was nonetheless discriminatory, and it mirrored that of the Vichy regime whose Jewish statutes exempted certain categories of 'worthy' citizens. Like its historical predecessors, the FN has long campaigned on an anti-immigrant ticket. Its differentiation between naturalized immigrants and citizens 'of French stock' recalls the attitudes of the 1930s and 1940s. The party has come to eschew the explicit anti-Semitism of its first president in favour of a thinly veiled Islamophobia epitomized in its emphasis on secularism. Ultimately, the drive to establish a national community that, if not entirely ethnically homogeneous, favours those French with deep roots in the 'blood and soil' of the *patrie*, is a key tenet of the French extreme right.

Collaboration with the mainstream right has helped to spread 'fascist' politics and normalize extremist discourse. The rejection of party politics, mainstream electioneering and the political establishment is a mainstay of French extreme right-wing discourse. During the interwar years, as today, it was an important means by which to distinguish the 'real country' from the 'legal country', in the words of the Action Française. Republican politicians were routinely pilloried for their alleged corruption and self-interest. Nevertheless, deputies belonged to the interwar leagues and parties, and in some cases they endorsed their policies and rhetoric. Conservative parliamentarians and parties made local alliances with extremist groups when it served their own ends. The FN concluded several alliances with the conservative mainstream parties at the turn of the 1980s in an attempt to breakthrough into national politics. Cooperation between the extreme and the conservative right has helped to normalize the discourse of extremism. Consequently, in the 1930s the 'fascist' campaign against the Republic prompted more moderate heads to contemplate state reform projects. In the early twenty-first century, right-wing candidates appropriated the FN's hard-line language on immigration to steal a march on the far right. Such cross-fertilization renders the 'fascist'-moderate dichotomy problematic.

Finally, few groups in this book readily claimed the label 'fascist'. During the interwar and war years, the word was associated with a foreign ideology unsuited to the French genius. Even those men who readily deployed the term stressed that the doctrine would need to be adapted to suit French mores. The collaborationist groups of the war years likewise called for a national and socialist revolution in France while remaining aware that such an experiment would need to be rendered fit for the French context. After 1945, the French extreme right had to contend with the toxic legacy of fascism, the Occupation and the Holocaust. The complexities of the memory of the Vichy years and the ambiguity with which some viewed the regime doubtless aided the FN's argument that its roots – and those of the *Etat Français* – lay in a French tradition that had little to do with fascism. Even after the political establishment acknowledged French participation in the Holocaust in the mid-1990s, both Jean-Marie and Marine Le Pen questioned the notion of national culpability and criticized French self-flagellation for the crimes of the past. 'Fascism' remains a malleable concept, a label deployed and understood in the context of political competition. The leagues and parties who publicly distanced themselves from the ideology often held idiosyncratic understandings of its content and character, and they were prepared to adopt, imitate and adapt aspects of this to serve their own ends.

APPENDIX: THE FRENCH ALLERGY TO FASCISM

René Rémond's founding work and the 'orthodox' school

René Rémond's 1954 book *La Droite en France* is the foundation work for all analysis of fascism in France. Rémond, who died in 2007, was a towering figure in French academia. The author of numerous works, he founded the Institut d'histoire du temps présent in 1979 and was president of the prestigious Fondation nationale des sciences politiques between 1981 and 2007. In 1998, Rémond was elected to the Académie Française, a select body of just forty members chosen for their services to the French language.

Rémond experienced first-hand some of the most momentous and turbulent episodes in the history of twentieth-century France. As an army reservist, he saw the exodus of refugees fleeing the Nazi invader in 1940. He subsequently returned to Paris to complete his studies, where he also worked for the resistance, providing information about Wehrmacht positions during the liberation of Paris in August 1944. After the war, Rémond continued to find himself at the epicentre of significant political moments: he was at the protest march against the coup in Algeria on 28 May 1958 that heralded the beginning of the end of the Fourth Republic; as an academic he taught at the Nanterre campus during the 1968 student revolt and that same year he was an observer at the triumphant parade of Gaullists down the avenue des Champs-Elysées in central Paris.[1]

La Droite en France argued that since the final defeat of Napoleon Bonaparte, three political traditions had dominated the French right: a counter-revolutionary and aristocratic 'ultraism' or ultra-royalism (later called legitimism) that sought to reverse the changes that followed the 1789 revolution; the moderately conservative Orleanism, which spoke to the concerns of bourgeois French, and Bonapartism, which mixed nationalism and populism. Rémond claimed that these three right-wing traditions had shown a remarkable resilience during the nineteenth and twentieth centuries. They had mutated according to circumstance yet remained essentially the same, dominating the right wing of French politics and leaving little room for anything else.[2]

What about fascism? Where did this twentieth-century political ideology fit into the story of the French right? Rémond's answer was that it did not fit very well at all. He rejected the accusations of fascism made by the left against the large interwar leagues such as the Croix de Feu as little more than a catch-all insult aimed at any movement that was not self-consciously socialist. Rémond continued that if one moved beyond the slander of the left, one saw the paramilitary leagues for what they really were: hollow imitations of Italian Fascism that were, in reality, too conservative to be truly fascist. For Rémond, fascism's appeal to the sovereign will of the people was anathema to conservatives. He admitted that there were energetic young men and war veterans who liked to dress up in uniforms, march in the street and greet each other with the straight-armed salute. But their 'fascism' was merely skin deep – a 'Roman whitewash', in Rémond's words. Rather, the leagues belonged to the longer history of the indigenous right, the latest manifestation of the Bonapartist tradition.[3]

Rémond did not argue that fascism was *entirely* absent from France. He did allow for the fact that some smaller leagues and parties – the Francistes, the PPF and the Solidarité Française – were authentically fascist. However, the smallness of their memberships (fanatics, hotheads and mercenaries in the main) and their short lifespans were revelatory of the failure of fascism's appeal in France: 'What are twenty thousand recruits, even devoted ones, in a nation of forty million!' he asked.[4] As for the Croix de Feu and its successor the PSF, Rémond did not discern fascism in Lieutenant-Colonel François de La Rocque's movement. Rather, he saw in it an 'irreproachable Republican loyalism', dismissing its large paramilitary mobilizations as boy scout-style exercises for adults. The PSF's astonishing growth after 1936 in the wake of La Rocque's apparent conversion to democratic politics simply served to underscore the public's attachment to parliamentarianism.[5]

Why did fascism fail to take root in France? Rémond suggested several contextual factors. The country was – at least in comparison with its eastern neighbour – largely unaffected by the upheavals felt elsewhere in the aftermath of the First World War and the financial crisis of the 1930s. This meant that the 'usual' fascist constituency – those who had experienced a decline in social status (the *déclassés*), disgruntled war veterans and general malcontents – simply did not exist to a large enough extent in France. In any case, the leagues expressed only a 'rudimentary' politics unsuited to effecting real change in a democratic system.[6] Beyond the immediate circumstances of the interwar years, Rémond cited a much deeper – and highly significant – explanation for the French resistance to fascism; the 'wisdom of the French people' and their 'political maturity' ensured that the fascist seed fell on stoney ground.[7] France's long history of democracy ensured that fascism did not succeed – *could not succeed* – in the country.

As a work of academic history, there are problems with Rémond's 1954 edition. At the time of writing, the apparent paucity of research into the nature of the Croix de Feu prompted Rémond to look to the PSF to determine the essence of the league in a feat of astonishing retrospective extrapolation. Rémond made no allowance for the fact that the two organizations – one a paramilitary league, the other a bona fide political party – were very different, as were the political contexts in which each one operated. Rather, he determined that given the conservatism of the PSF, the Croix de Feu must have been relatively harmless. It would be churlish to take Rémond to task for not having available to him the sources that we have today; he was writing within only fifteen years of the end of the Third Republic after all. However, among the handful of sources on the Croix de Feu cited in the bibliography of the 1954 edition, one finds *Six ans chez les Croix de Feu* (1935), a warts-and-all exposé written by disgruntled former member Paul Chopine. Chopine had been head of the Croix de Feu's paramilitary squads. Rémond describes Chopine as 'a bad-tempered but *well-informed* witness'.[8] Given that Chopine's book contained information on La Rocque's alleged plans for a paramilitary seizure of Paris and other large cities in the event of communist insurrection, it is odd that Rémond was so dismissive of the Croix de Feu's paramilitarism as 'boy scouting for grown ups'.[9] Chopine's book does not appear in the bibliography of the 1982 re-edition of Rémond's text. In its place is the 1962 work by La Rocque's wife Edith and his son Gilles, *La Rocque tel qu'il était.* A note accompanies the bibliographic entry: 'Rectifies errors and … received ideas'.[10] If Chopine's book should be treated with a healthy scepticism, we must treat the La Rocques' evident attempt to rehabilitate the lieutenant colonel with a critical eye, too.

To understand Rémond's thesis fully, we must take into account the context in which it was proposed and the author's aim in doing so. Passmore has pointed out that, in 1954, *La Droite en France* was not only a historical work but also a political intervention.[11] Rémond was a conservative, raised in a Catholic household by parents who read the *Echo de Paris* (described by Rémond himself as a newspaper that appealed to 'right-minded people … a Catholic audience attached to moral values, [and] to the fatherland').[12] He displayed an occasional antipathy for the interwar left: Rémond sympathized with the right-wing demonstrators on 6 February 1934, and he was 'joyous' at the failure of the general strike on 30 November 1938.[13] However, Rémond's Catholic conservatism was far from that of extreme right-wing groups such as the anti-Republican Action Française. On the contrary, his love of France was deeply infused with Republicanism and a desire to defend its values: 'My attachment to my country, to its history was inseparable from the attachment to the universal values the conception, proclamation and service of which I knew [France] had more than any other [country] contributed to.'[14] Thus in June 1940, at twenty-one, he and his army comrades listened, 'heart filled with rage', to Marshal Philippe Pétain's announcement of the cessation of hostilities with Germany.[15]

Writing barely a decade after the difficult experience of Vichy, Rémond sought to detoxify the right wing of French politics by making a distinction between, on the one hand, the Republican and parliamentary right, and, on the other hand, the authoritarian variant that surfaced during the dark years. In doing so, he foregrounded the Republicanism of French conservatives and marginalized the extremism of the interwar and war years.[16] In the four pages devoted to Vichy in the 1954 edition, Rémond claimed that, if in the last years of its existence Pétain's regime flirted with fascism, at its core the *Etat Français* was conservative, based on the traditional elites, and 'the very opposite of fascism'.[17] The book thus served to reinforce the comforting idea that the wartime regime was an abhorrent anomaly in French history. It spoke, too, to the mood of the times and the rehabilitation of the right in the new Cold War climate of anti-communism.[18]

The 1960s and 1970s saw Rémond's central thesis adopted widely. Philippe Machefer's 1974 history of the interwar leagues used numerous vague and somewhat enigmatic phrases to skirt round the issue of fascism in France. He described the Jeunesses Patriotes as 'Bonapartist, coloured with the taste of the times'; the Faisceau was 'a moderate avatar of fascism, adapted to the French national temperament'; the Solidarité Française was 'of Bonapartist inspiration dressed up in fascist rags'. Machefer was comfortable only with classifying the Francistes as truly fascist but while their fascism was 'virulent', it remained 'without troops'.[19] In a similar vein, Antoine Prost's magisterial 1977 *Les anciens combattants et la société francaise, 1914-1939*, a three-volume history of the interwar French veterans' movement, concluded that while a handful of *anciens combattants* were attracted to the siren call of the extreme right, the three-million-strong veterans' movement constituted 'one of the major obstacles to the development of fascism in France'.[20]

Challengers to Rémond's thesis remained marginal and disparate.[21] Several English-language works raised the spectre of a French fascism but they focused mainly on groups that, though influential, were small (see, for example, George Mosse's work on the right-wing 'Yellow' trade unions and Ernst Nolte's examination of the Action Française).[22] Such was the influence of Rémond that later critics of his thesis – for example, Brian Jenkins – would fail to contest the central argument in their earlier works.[23] Ultimately, *La Droite en France* had an immeasurable impact on modern French political historiography. Revised, updated and translated several times over, it has helped to shape academic discourse, research agendas and university curricula for decades.[24]

The 1980s I: The Sternhell controversy

At the turn of the 1980s, Israeli historian Zeev Sternhell launched the most significant attack to date on the Rémondian thesis. Like Rémond, Sternhell was personally implicated in his object of study. Born in 1935, he grew up in Poland during the Second World War, experiencing both Soviet and Nazi occupations, and losing several members of his family in the Holocaust. In 1951 Sternhell moved to Israel where, besides serving as a soldier in several conflicts, he graduated from the Hebrew University of Jerusalem with a degree in history and political science. He received his doctorate in 1969 from Sciences Po in Paris. According to Serge Berstein, Sternhell's experience of fascism and anti-Semitism inspired his work, leading him to conceive of his scholarship as 'a fight that he must wage against the adversary (fascism) in the name of his convictions (progress)'.[25]

In two important books Sternhell attempted to overturn the Rémondian orthodoxy. His first intervention came in the 1978 *La Droite révolutionnaire*, a book that took as its focus the French political and intellectual climate between 1885 and 1914. Subtitled 'The French origins of Fascism', the work claimed that fascism's synthesis of nationalism and socialism was first articulated by French intellectuals at the turn of the nineteenth century. Far from being an alien concept, fascism in its purest intellectual form *came from France*.[26]

Sternhell followed up this work in 1983 with a book that proved explosive. In *Ni droite, ni gauche*, the focus shifted to the crucial years of the 1930s. Relying on the writings of interwar intellectuals, Sternhell argued that, far from being averse to the ideology, France was in fact 'impregnated' with fascism.[27] French historian Raoul Girardet had made a similar claim in 1955, but Sternhell now made the case more forcefully. He set out the reach of fascism throughout French politics and society, including the so-called third way between Bolshevism and capitalism of the young nonconformists of the 1930s whose writing conformed to Sternhell's own definition of fascism.[28] The real threat to democracy in France lay not in the minor movements of veterans and street fighters but in these men, the 'fascists without knowing it', whose work facilitated the penetration of fascist ideas in France.[29] Sternhell's book was ground-breaking: in his response to *Ni droite ni gauche*, Jacques Julliard suggested that Sternhell's work would act as an 'icebreaker', in much the same way that Robert Paxton's 1972 book on Vichy France had opened up investigations into the collaboration of the war years. Once again, a foreign historian had taken the initiative in approaching a subject that French scholars seemed reluctant to tackle.[30]

The broader political context in which Sternhell's book appeared was significant. In 1983, Jean-Marie Le Pen's extreme right-wing FN made an electoral breakthrough both at the municipal elections and in the by-election at Dreux in October. The spectre of a revived French extreme right – and the desire to combat it – served to maximize the impact of Sternhell's work and was evidently at the forefront of some French academic minds. Indeed, Pierre Milza began his 1987 *Fascisme français*, with the question, 'Is France becoming fascist?', before lamenting the fact that the advances of the FN made a 'remake' of the 1930s seem possible.[31]

A number of French academics launched a multi-fronted assault on Sternhell's thesis. In a series of publications, they took the Israeli to task over the quality of his research and his approach to both the sources and the period.[32] Sternhell stood accused of crowbarring a multitude of ideas espoused by a diverse array of thinkers into an artificial framework. Where Sternhell perceived the development and realization of a coherent fascist ideology, his critics saw a hotchpotch of confused and conflicting pronouncements by myriad intellectuals, politicians and activists from the left and right, some well-known, others less so.[33] Philippe Burrin claimed that Sternhell had used his knowledge of the interwar years to read history backwards, producing a synthesis that had not existed at the time.[34] His formulation of a French fascism was therefore an artificial amalgamation of disparate elements, the importance of which he had exaggerated.[35] The groups in which Sternhell perceived a French fascism were unrepresentative of mainstream political currents and had a miniscule impact on real politics. In Bertsein's words, Sternhell's construction of France existed in a universe 'detached from reality', a 'strange vision of history, reduced to the world of pure ideas.'[36]

The most forceful attack on Sternhell came from Berstein, who attempted to demolish Sternhell's thesis through the diagnosis of a French 'allergy' to fascism.[37] Berstein agreed with Rémond that the French leagues were conservative rather than fascist, despite their paramilitary styling and intemperate language.[38] He argued that France was 'impermeable' to fascism because of its long experience of democracy, a fact that rendered the French allergic to the ideology.[39] Berstein would later reinforce his position in a 2001 article in which he cited a French democratic consensus that rested both upon 'commonly accepted values' and a belief in the Republican institutions that marginalized anti-democratic groups.[40] It is somewhat ironic that Berstein accused Sternhell of ignoring the 'complexity of human behaviours' in the analysis of fascism, when he himself favoured an argument in which a democratic political culture somehow rendered the French *a priori* 'allergic' to fascism.

Rémond did not respond directly to Sternhell. Rather, he updated his argument in the 1988 book *Notre Siècle de 1918 à 1988*. Citing the long implantation of democracy in the country, consolidated by the people's experience of universal suffrage, a free press, a Republican school system and military service, Rémond permitted himself no small amount of speculation: 'Who knows if the most decisive causes of the weak impact of fascism in France should not be found in a collection of older customs and which history has transformed into second nature?'[41] One wonders about the amount of research upon which this assertion was based.

Sternhell responded to the criticisms of *Ni droite ni gauche* in 2000 with the allegation that the 'consensus' among his critics was based on the academic chauvinism of historians who were either unable or unwilling to read the work of foreign historians, all in an effort to preserve the exceptionalism of France and its history.[42] With the political agenda behind *La Droite en France* in mind, Marc Angenot is probably correct in his assertion that Rémond's defence of France derived from more than simply the obstinate attitude of the academic. It is less certain, however, that Rémond acted as an 'all-powerful mandarin', who 'reigned over the discipline through two generations of respectful pupils ([who were] cautious in their criticism of his ideas)'.[43] Passmore's opinion on the matter is more even-handed, yet even he makes the observation that 'those [historians] who criticise the Rémondian thesis hold hardly any strategic posts in the discipline of history [in France]'.[44] Milza, while not subscribing to such a conspiracy theory, has noted the influence of the 'nebula [of academics] essentially grouped around René Rémond ... at the university of Paris X-Nanterre and Sciences Po'.[45] It may be striking that French political historians of the twentieth century have largely followed Rémond's line, yet to speak of a 'French orthodoxy' is inaccurate. Passmore has demonstrated the debate in the historiography cannot be easily split along French/non-French lines.[46] This does not mean that a 'Rémondian' school of thought does not exist; the evidence proves the contrary. This body of work probably developed, as Jean-Noël Jeanneney has claimed, through the proximity in which scholars were educated, trained, researched and published.[47] Rémond's supporters vigorously deny the charge of conspiracy.[48]

The 1980s II: Battle lines are drawn

In 1985, as the Sternhell controversy rumbled on, Robert Soucy, an American historian working at Oberlin College in Ohio, published *French Fascism: The First Wave*. It was not Soucy's first work on the French extreme right: he had produced two previous books on the intellectuals Maurice Barrès and Pierre Drieu La Rochelle, in 1972 and 1979 respectively, along with several articles in a diverse selection of academic journals.[49] *The First Wave* examined the extreme right-wing groups of the 1920s: the Légion, the Jeunesses Patriotes and the Faisceau. Soucy's express aim was to correct several 'misconceptions' about fascism in France, notably Rémond's thesis that fascism was an ideology that was both alien to French political tradition and unpopular with the public at large. Defining the objects of his study as fascist, Soucy claimed that support for the ideology in France was 'hardly negligible': approximately 370,000 French men and women belonged to a fascist group by 1934.[50]

Soucy further sought to challenge the argument that fascism had little in common with conservatism. Rather, he situated fascism squarely on the right of politics, different from conservatism only in degree. Notably, this brought him into disagreement not only with the French historians, who considered fascism as too much of a revolutionary force to be located comfortably on the right, but also with Sternhell, who argued that fascism borrowed elements from both right and left.[51] It is here that we begin to perceive the problems with defining fascism: Rémond judged the leagues to be too conservative to be fascist, while Soucy considered the leagues to be fascist *because* they were conservative.

Soucy's *The First Wave* appeared in French translation in 1989.[52] The book did not receive the same attention from French academics as Sternhell's publications. One can hazard only a guess at the reasons for this. Perhaps it was because Soucy had focused on relatively minor movements such as the Faisceau and the Jeunesses Patriotes. While French historians could not deny that the former was avowedly fascist, the latter, in their opinion, was closer to Bonapartism. In any case, both were small enough to be dismissed as short-lived experiments. Soucy had not, in this first book, addressed the most contentious issue of the fascism of the Croix de Feu and the PSF. He had hinted at his attitude to these groups in the preface to *The First Wave*, describing the latter as one of the four major fascist movements in 1930s France, while including La Rocque in a rogue's gallery of fascist leaders along with Franciste chief Bucard and PPF head Doriot.[53] However, with the Sternhell controversy in full swing, French historians had bigger fish to fry.

Two other books of note appeared on the subject during the 1980s. In *La Dérive fasciste* (1986), Swiss historian Philippe Burrin outlined three zones of fascism in France's 'fascistoid nebula', from the hard core (the PPF and the RNP), through a zone of 'fascistisation' (encompassing some elements of the leagues), to the outer zone of 'fascination and magnetisation', or 'magnetic field', of those French who were attracted to fascism, but who did not call themselves fascist.[54] He argued that if one discounted the leagues and the Croix de Feu then fascism in interwar France was insignificant.[55] Meanwhile, Milza's *Fascisme français. Passé et present* (1987) surveyed the subject from the leagues of the 1920s through to the rise of the FN in the 1980s. Milza subscribed to the idea of a fascist impregnation of society, yet he concluded that the failure of the ideology in France was due to 'the resistance offered to its enterprises by a political culture deeply rooted in the republican model … [and] … the adhesion of a very large majority of the nation to a system of values and to institutions that they wished to render more efficient but that few French wished to destroy'.[56]

In 1989 French political scientist Michel Dobry made an intervention that proposed a new approach to the study of fascism in France. In an article on the riots of February 1934, Dobry sought to break free from the interminable to-ing and fro-ing between historians on both sides of the debate.[57] He railed against the obsession with the finding of an ahistorical definition of fascism and the search for the ideology's essential nature. He criticized historians' attempts to fit movements in the past into their own definition of fascism, a process that he termed the 'classificatory logic'.[58] Dobry was not the first to perceive a problem in the endless search for a workable definition of fascism. In 1976, Klaus-Jürgen Müller had pointed out that the 'mechanical' application of a definition of fascism to history, which resulted only in a futile re-categorization of movements and political ideologies, was an exercise that had little explanatory value. If Müller did not, like Dobry, reject the project of defining fascism altogether, some of his criticisms harbingered those of Dobry.[59]

Dobry was most critical of the Rémondian position, attacking the idea of a specifically French 'political culture' that apparently rendered France impermeable to fascism.[60] He called this the 'immunity thesis', that is, the school of thought that sought to 'prove that French society rejected fascism'.[61] Historians of this persuasion had too often looked to the 'outcome' of history and then used it to explain retrospectively the period in question. In the case of the Third Republic, the fact that the regime survived the fascist challenge until the military defeat of 1940 demonstrated that it could *never* have fallen to fascism. Dobry's landmark article and the points raised within made little immediate impact and the fixation with definitions persisted. By the end of the 1980s, the battle lines that would divide the historiography for the following twenty years were drawn.

The 1990s: Obsession

In the historiography of French fascism, the 1990s were characterized by an obsession with two political movements: the Croix de Feu and its successor, the PSF. Since Rémond's conclusion in 1954 that the Croix de Feu-PSF was not fascist, to think otherwise was framed as a naive acceptance of the slanderous accusations of La Rocque's opponents. Rémond restated this argument in his 1988 *Notre Siècle de 1918 à 1988*. La Rocque was a 'legalist' and a 'nationalist', who desired only 'strong government'; he thus helped to 'prepare the ground' for de Gaulle and his Rassemblement du Peuple Français (RPF).[62]

The most strident challenge to this interpretation was raised in 1991 in the work of Soucy and Canadian historian William Irvine.[63] In a pair of articles, Irvine and Soucy took aim at the 'consensus' founded on Rémond's work. Irvine engaged with contemporary French scholarship on the movement, arguing that while it was more difficult to decide upon the precise nature of the PSF, its forerunner was 'more fascist than any other formation of the Third Republic'.[64] Soucy's own 'dissenting interpretation' was unequivocal: the Croix de Feu-PSF was fascist and La Rocque deserved to be mentioned in the same breath as Hitler and Mussolini.[65] Soucy developed his attack further in his 1995 *French Fascism: The Second Wave, 1933-1939*. This book surveyed the extreme right-wing political movements, large and small, of the 1930s, with a particular focus on the Croix de Feu-PSF and the PPF.[66]

Irvine and Soucy disagreed fundamentally with Rémond's definition of fascism; they both proposed a definition that located the phenomenon squarely on the spectrum of conservatism. Irvine dismissed the Croix de Feu-PSF's anti-capitalist attacks on business and its appeals to the working class as little more than 'rhetorical froth'.[67] He perceived behind this pseudo-revolutionary language a conservatism, which, when combined with La Rocque's desire to mobilize the masses, distinguished the Croix de Feu-PSF from the traditional right and brought it closer to fascism.[68] Likewise, Soucy counselled against confusing fascism's 'anti-bourgeois *rhetoric*' with its 'pro-bourgeois *reality*'; the 'socialism' of France's largest fascist movements was 'spiritual' rather than 'material'.[69] Soucy understood fascism to be a 'new variety of authoritarian conservatism and right-wing nationalism' that shared a conservative social and economic outlook with the more traditional right.[70] At the heart of the matter lay the contention that a definition of fascism could help one to determine the 'real' intentions and the 'true' nature of La Rocque's movement. In this respect, Irvine and Soucy's approach echoed that of Rémond.

In 1995, Passmore offered a different perspective on the Croix de Feu-PSF. Rather than dismiss the radical aspects of the movement, Passmore proposed a definition of fascism that demonstrated it was 'both reactionary in its opposition to the Left and radical in its opposition to the old Right and the state'.[71] This definition of fascism as a form of radical-populism that synthesized reaction and radicalism did not require Passmore to explain away inconvenient aspects of the Croix de Feu-PSF. It also led Passmore to conclude that if the Croix de Feu had been fascist, its successor was not; the difference lay in the former's desire to mobilize the masses through paramilitarism, something that was less prominent once the movement became the PSF.[72] Passmore's contribution to the debate about the definition of fascism was doubtless important, yet by the end of the 1990s he had begun to examine other aspects of the Croix de Feu-PSF, specifically its women's sections, a subject into which the debate over issues of definition had up to that point obscured.[73]

The challenges to the Rémondian thesis did not go unanswered. Michel Winock's 1992 book on French nationalism, anti-Semitism and fascism was the most significant French-language work on the subject during the 1990s.[74] Winock surveyed the history of these three elements of right-wing politics from the end of the nineteenth century. His chapter on the interwar leagues took up some familiar arguments: groups such as the Faisceau were fascist but insignificant; the riot of 6 February 1934 had not been an attempted coup but rather a display designed to intimidate the government.[75] Winock admitted that, along with the usual array of small fascist groups – the Solidarité Française, Francisme, the PPF and the Cagoule – a 'fascist state of mind' affected the French right from time to time. This mindset was evident in the writing of right-wing intellectuals in newspapers such as *Gringoire* and *Candide*.[76] In the Croix de Feu-PSF, Winock perceived a conservative, Christian and legalist essence. In fact, La Rocque had helped to block fascism's route to power in France.[77] As for the failure of French fascism, Winock cited the fact that the 'usual clientele of fascism' remained loyal to Republican groups such as the Radical Party. The explanation for this lay in the apparent Republican reflex of the party's middle-class constituency. This reflex, which did not exist in Germany under the short-lived Weimar democracy, derived from the 'legacies and … cultural habits' of the French: 'It is unquestionable that in France one-hundred-and-fifty years of "esprit républicain" and of periodic resistance to counter-revolutionary attempts [on power] have mithridatised the social body to a great extent.[78] The argument was clear: France's experiences with the sporadic attempts on power of the extreme right had immunized it against fascism.

Several shorter works further rebuffed the revisionists' challenge. In his entry on 'French fascism' in Jean-François Sirinelli's historical dictionary of twentieth-century French politics, Milza asserted that though the work of 'foreign' historians and political scientists had prompted a reconsideration of the subject, the 'propositions' made in Rémond's work were still 'generally valid'.[79] Jean-Paul Thomas's examination of new sources concerning the membership of the PSF suggested that a good proportion of its activists later joined de Gaulle's RPF. Thomas's work was Rémondian in the sense that it rejected the notion of a strong French fascism while looking to longer term attitudes and patterns of behaviour on the right. It also served to bring an aura of retrospective legitimacy to the PSF through linking it with de Gaulle's post-war party.[80]

If the debate about the fascism of the Croix de Feu-PSF apparently made the divisions between the two schools of thought in the historiography clearer, there were disagreements *within* each school. Burrin's 1992 essay on French fascism, for example, was Rémondian for it attributed the fact that fascism remained a marginal political force thanks to France's deep democratic roots, the durability of right-wing traditions and a 'collective mentality' informed by conservatism and pacifism.[81] Yet he modified the Rémondian understanding of Bonapartism, allowing for two variants – national-Caesarism and national-populism – the latter of which shared certain affinities with fascism, notably a violently racist and anti-Semitic political discourse of decadence.[82] Such a modification illustrated a further criticism of Rémond's work in Burrin's essay: the model of the 'three rights' seemed fitting for history writ large, yet it was not sufficiently refined for understandings of discrete periods.[83] It is worth noting, too, that until the turn of the twenty-first century, Sternhell did not consider the Croix de Feu to have been fascist. In a 1980 essay, he regarded the movement as the shock troops of the bourgeoisie, 'the praetorian guard of the traditional right' that sought, along with its middle-class paymasters, to preserve the status quo.[84] Only in Sternhell's later work did he determine that La Rocque was a genuine fascist, a conclusion that Sternhell's opponents considered to be an expedient reversal under the influence of Soucy's work.[85]

The obsession with defining fascism and classifying the Croix de Feu-PSF as either fascist or Republican obstructed investigation into important aspects of the movement, and the right more broadly. Irvine made just such an observation in 1977 when he bemoaned the paucity of research into significant movements of the French right, apparently because they were not deemed fascist and, by extension, not interesting enough.[86] In 1994, Canadian historian John Bingham articulated more fully the problems in the field. He suggested that historians move beyond the fruitless exercise of defining fascism – which produced definitions that were little more than 'rigidified … static, emotion-laden, black-and-white categories of moral judgement after the fact', and which beyond 'making it easier to pin neat labels' on people in the past, achieved little.[87] Bingham suggested an approach based on in-depth archival research that took account of the pressures on, and motivations of, political actors about whom the 'fascist' label seemed to explain little.[88] The scholarship of the 1990s was ground-breaking for what it had revealed about one of the most important political movements in French history. Yet research was focused very much on the search for the 'correct' definition of fascism, and there was still much left to discover about the extreme right-wing politics of the interwar years.

The twenty-first century: Directions both old and new

In the early years of the twenty-first century, two significant works from the revisionist school were published.[89] The first collection, entitled *Le mythe de l'allergie française au fascisme* (2003), brought together historians, political scientists and sociologists from a number of countries to examine aspects of the French extreme right between the wars. Dobry – the collection's editor – developed further his critique of the immunity thesis. He suggested that political movements should be studied in their environment, that is, in the interactions with their allies and enemies, in the negotiations and adaptations made with stakeholders within and without and, according to which, groups constantly attempted to redefine and reposition themselves in relation to political conjuncture. In taking this 'relational perspective', Dobry continued, it was possible to gain a better understanding of the behaviour of groups in the past, a behaviour that was not dictated by an 'essence', 'nature' or classification imposed upon them by historians in the present.[90] Concomitantly, he took aim at the 'obstinacy, occasional aggressiveness, and not a little blindness' of those scholars who had, since the 1950s, defended the exceptional nature of French society and its 'allergy', 'impermeability' and 'immunity' to fascism. Dobry admitted that the immunity thesis school had adapted itself to Sternhell's challenges and that its arguments were no longer identical to that of Rémond. Yet these adaptations were merely 'tactical retreats', and the Rémondians' belief in French society's immunity to fascism remained at the heart of their work.[91]

Dobry's appeal was brought to an English-language audience in the 2005 collection of essays, *France in the Era of Fascism*, under the editorship of Jenkins. The authors, among whom were Dobry, Passmore, Soucy and Sternhell, made further attacks on the immunity thesis. In his conclusion, Jenkins surmised that, despite the immunity thesis historians having their differences, their denial of the existence of a significant French fascist force essentially relied on the dubious idea of a 'democratic political culture'.[92] The collection underscored the fact that the so-called 'revisionist' historians have their differences, too, not least in their definitions of fascism. Echoing Dobry, Jenkins recommended that scholars might expend their energies more fruitfully if they moved away from the issue of defining fascism and the classificatory logic to examine the 'fluidity and dynamism of political processes' in interwar France that helped to shape the 'interactive environment in which political movements [operated]'.[93]

In the wake of Dobry and Jenkins's call to rescue the field from the sclerosis into which it was descending, Soucy's second volume appeared in translation as *Fascisme français? 1933-1939*. Its publication came nine years after the book's English-language editions, and this delay ensured that Soucy's arguments – untouched by those scholars who had published on the subject since 1995 – reached some in France for the first time. The effect was to reinvigorate the increasingly tired debate over the definition of fascism and the classification of the Croix de Feu-PSF. In the pages of French history journal *Vingtième Siècle*, Winock deconstructed Soucy's thesis point-by-point. Some of his criticisms were valid: he questioned Soucy's willingness to dismiss both La Rocque's more moderate proclamations as legalist pretence and anything that did not conform to his own definition of fascism as 'artificial'.[94] Winock concluded that La Rocque simply perceived evident faults in the system that were corrected and realized in the constitution of the Fifth.[95]

Soucy was afforded the right to reply in the pages of *Vingtième Siècle* the following year. His response was structured around differences between his definition of fascism and that of Winock.[96] Winock's response was withering, and his criticisms echoed those made against Sternhell twenty years ago: Soucy had been selective in his use of sources; he had ignored the idiosyncrasies of individuals' trajectories; he had deformed the evidence.[97] Winock left it to Berstein to draw a close to the argument. Berstein was right to point out the 'impasse' that had been reached in the debate about the Croix de Feu-PSF, which he termed a 'dialogue of the deaf'. Rather more contentious was the claim that those historians who conducted 'serious' research were unanimous on the marginal nature of fascism in interwar France.[98] Berstein attacked Dobry's 2003 collection of essays as 'unworthy of a response', comparing its 'aggression' and 'insinuations' – termed 'intellectual terrorism' – to that of Stalinism. He dismissed the contributions of 'Anglo-Saxon' historians to the debate. Berstein claimed that whereas French historians of fascism began with the scientific approach of defining their object of study, their 'Anglo-Saxon' opponents rejected this 'essentialism' and 'classificatory obsession'. Here, he attempted to apply Dobry's conception to all opponents, neglecting the fact that some 'Anglo-Saxon' historians engaged just as much in the game of definitions as their Gallic opponents.[99] According to Berstein, unlike their opponents, French historians did not base their work on 'approximation, makeshift, and prejudice'.[100]

Specialists in the field continued to mine the archives of the Croix de Feu-PSF. Their work brought fresh approaches to this movement, and while these works did not leave behind the matter of definition altogether, it was not the principal lens through which the movement was studied. Albert Kéchichian's 2006 history of the Croix de Feu is the most recent scholarly study of the league in French. It presented a detailed analysis of the group from its origins to the act of dissolution in 1936. Kéchichian situated the movement on the Catholic-infused conservative right. He rejected the charge that the league incarnated a French fascism for La Rocque refused to countenance the fascist idea of the 'New Man'. On the contrary, the Croix de Feu's mission was altruistic. It sought to rally all French who believed in social justice and civil peace while the lieutenant colonel's social strategy used charity to appeal to the 'lost sheep' in the communist movement.

Kéchichian nailed his colours to the Rémondian mast with the argument that France during the 1930s did not offer conditions propitious for the development of fascism. The French were deeply attached to democracy for they considered it inseparable from a love of their country.[101]

Kennedy's 2008 book is the most comprehensive history of the Croix de Feu-PSF of recent years. If Kéchichian considered La Rocque's movement to be an obstacle to the enemies of democracy in France, Kennedy situated the Croix de Feu-PSF within a broader move towards authoritarianism in France that culminated in Vichy. Kennedy's book explored in depth La Rocque's plans for a 'counter-society' built upon the PSF's precepts of *Travail, Famille, Patrie*. He shed light, too, on the trajectory of the party during the Second World War and after. Kennedy did not leave the question of fascism unaddressed. Like Kéchichian, Kennedy argued that La Rocque did not pursue the 'ongoing radicalization and the creation of a new man' that was characteristic of fascism.[102] Unlike Kéchichian, Kennedy concluded that 'arguing that the Croix de Feu is better understood as authoritarian than as fascist should not be equated with implying that it was somehow moderate'; its proposed reforms to the Republic were 'hardly of a democratic nature'.[103] Consequently, Kennedy's intervention tried to counter the assumption in the literature that a non-fascist Croix de Feu-PSF was automatically Republican.

Caroline Campbell's 2015 book on understandings of gender and race in La Rocque's movements represented an important shift away from matters of definition in the study of the Croix de Feu-PSF. Limited studies of gender and the French extreme right had pointed to the significance of women in the social and political strategies of a number of movements.[104] Samuel Kalman and Sean Kennedy's 2014 collection of essays on the interwar right had hinted that the study of gender and both conservatism and fascism promised to be a fruitful avenue of inquiry; five of the thirteen chapters in the book took gender as their focus. That same year, Geoff Read's analysis of gendered and racialist discourse on the left and right exposed shared attitudes across the political spectrum.[105] Campbell's was the most comprehensive study to date, demonstrating convincingly the significance of women to the Croix de Feu-PSF's move towards social action from the mid-1930s. Women's social work was far from politically neutral. Female members often operated in left-wing districts ostensibly closed to their male comrades. They had helped to spread La Rocque's brand of ethno-nationalism to the working class. Campbell demonstrated incisively that to understand the political trajectory of the Croix de Feu-PSF during the 1930s it was vital to account for the role of women in the movement.[106]

Regional studies of fascism offered further avenues of research. Samuel Huston Goodfellow's 1999 study of fascist groups in the border regions between France and Germany examined branches of national movements in the territory as well as region-specific formations such as Joseph Bilger's Bauernbund that based its appeal on a uniquely Alsatian sense of community and a focus on local rural concerns. Goodfellow presents the Bauernbund as evidence of a 'regional fascism'.[107] While Goodfellow treated some movements with a broad brush – the Croix de Feu-PSF is categorized as fascist with little distinction made between the movements – he drew attention to the diversity of fascist movements in France. The development of Alsatian regional fascism thus pointed to the 'diversity and complexity' of a '[French] fascism that was neither monolithic nor comprised of isolated strands'.[108]

Samuel Kalman's 2013 work shifted the focus of regional study to the French North African territories. Kalman exposed the 'colonial fascism' of the European settler community that was grounded in anti-Semitism, a belief in Latin racial hegemony and a desire to break free from the Republic and install an authoritarian regime to defend Algeria's economic and cultural specificity. During the 1920s, Jules Molle's Union Latines tailored their fascism to local concerns, succeeding where metropolitan movements failed. During the 1930s, the movements of the extreme right catered to the demands of their followers for an anti-Semitic and violent politics that frequently clashed with the dictates of the mainland leaderships. Party leaders were nevertheless prepared to overlook such excesses in order to ensure the support of a settler community that held sympathies for Spanish and Italian fascism. Like Goodfellow, Kalman drew out the importance of contextual factors in influencing the doctrine and behaviour of regional 'fascist' groups.[109]

New approaches to the question of fascism have suggested that historians might be ready to abandon the classificatory logic. In this respect, Laurent Kestel's 2012 study of Jacques Doriot and the PPF is one of the most significant books on French interwar politics to emerge in recent years.[110] Kestel adopted Dobry's relational approach to the movement and its fascism, bringing into focus the 'struggles over classifications' (luttes de classements) within and without the PPF over how best to understand and label the party. Kestel demonstrated that the party slowly came to adopt the fascist label, as well as the style and trappings believed to be those of fascism, following a gradual process of interaction and competition with rivals, enemies and allies. Kestel grounded his study of the party firmly within its political context, while shunning simplistic categorization and essentialism; in this way he has provided a model for the future study of historical political movements.

In 2015, Brian Jenkins and I followed Dobry's approach in our work on the riot of 6 February 1934, the first book-length scholarly study on the subject. Rather than interpreting the riot and its aftermath according to the dubious notion of a democratic political culture, we stressed the important interaction between rioters in the street and politicians at the helm of the Third Republic. As members of the leagues and veterans' associations mixed with each other and rioters and police exchanged blows, the riot took on a dynamic of its own. The statements of political groups before the night counted for little in the heat of the violence. Meanwhile, in the aftermath of the fighting, Daladier and his ministers acted according to their own assessments of what might come next, not to mention their personal self-interest. The Republic was 'saved' not by the inherent French preference for democracy but by the desire of political wheeler-dealers to save their own skin.[111]

Alongside this promising new work in the field, the debate about fascism continues to rear its head. In 2014, the La Rocque family published a collection of diverse notes and essays, discovered in 1982, and marketed as the lieutenant colonel's prison notebooks (carnets de captivité). In his preface to the work, Berstein rehearsed once again the tiresome argument that the PSF obstructed the development of fascism. In any case, the title of the book – *Pourquoi je suis républicain* – left the reader in little doubt about the lieutenant colonel's politics.[112]

In 2014, Berstein and Winock edited a collection of previously published and new essays entitled *Fascisme Français? La controverse*. The editors intended the book to be a response to Zeev Sternhell's latest publication in which the Israeli historian once again took aim at the scholars of Sciences Po. Berstein and Winock made their usual criticisms of Sternhell's work and suggested that the Israeli had fallen under the influence of Soucy in his volte-face on the Croix de Feu.[113] Thomas further criticized the work of the Sternhellians (Soucy, Passmore, Kennedy and Kestel) for their 'lack of elementary objectivity and multiple historical errors'. Thomas lamented these historians' apparent unwillingness to engage with historians on the 'other' side of the debate. It is worth stating here that Thomas's is the only chapter in Berstein and Winock's book to tackle seriously the English-language work on French fascism.[114] In the conclusion, the editors advised that, instead of spinning a 'web of errors, inaccuracies [and] counter-truths', and 'breaking … simple but necessary rules that [we] would not tolerate from any of [our] students', Sternhell should have taken into consideration the influence of a French political culture that penetrated political parties, veterans' associations, the public consciousness and the contemporary intellectual milieu. This belief in democratic Republicanism acted as a 'breakwater' to fascism.[115]

In 2016, Berstein and Thomas presided over a collection of fifteen essays on the PSF.[116] The fruit of a colloquium held two years previously, the book was the first academic work to focus solely on La Rocque's political party. Contributors examined the party and its politics from a number of angles including its foreign policy, women's membership, anti-Semitism, economic outlook and the Second World War. The collection was a welcome addition to scholarship on the PSF, bringing to the reader's attention scholars other than those generally associated with the topic and suggesting that a new generation of academics will continue to engage with France's largest ever political movement. The book bore several traces of the fascism debate; Winock, for example, reprised his rebuke of Soucy. In his concluding remarks, Gilles Richard lamented the fact that historians and political scientists from the opposing 'camp' had not been afforded the opportunity to participate in the 2014 colloquium. It is equally lamentable that the authors in the work – whom Berstein and Thomas describe as 'specialists of the period' – did not engage with the rich Anglophone scholarship on the subject: in the book's 339 pages, *only one footnote refers to an English-language source*.[117] The obtuse attitude of the editors to the work of their academic opponents is perhaps the reason for this absence. According to Berstein and Thomas, 'Anglo-Saxon historians' and 'sociologists' (a veiled reference to Dobry) have one thing in common: in arriving at their dubious conclusions they ignore the archives. The most cursory examination of the 'Anglo-Saxon' historiography reveals this assertion to be false.[118]

It is tempting but incorrect to conceive of the fascism debate as one that pitches 'Anglo-Saxon' scholars who believe in the strength of a French fascism against their French opponents who minimize its importance.[119] For one thing, one could count on the 'French' side Swiss historian Burrin, British historian Julian Jackson and American historian Bertram M. Gordon.[120] On the 'Anglo-Saxon' side, one might include French political scientist Dobry and historian Kestel, as well as the Israeli Sternhell (who was largely educated as a graduate student in France). Such catch-all terms as Anglo-Saxon, French, Rémondian and Sternhellian have distorted the positions of scholars in the debate.[121] Kennedy, for example, claims that while the PSF may have presented a threat to the Third Republic, it was not fascist. Nevertheless, Thomas dismisses Kennedy's work for falling 'in line with' Soucy.[122] Labels have further reduced the arguments of scholars to their most basic element: whether fascism *was* or *was not* a significant force in France. In doing so, they have obscured differences of approach and opinion as well as being used to imply a conspiracy on both sides. As new scholars enter the field and new avenues of investigation develop, it is to be hoped that the entrenched positions that have thus far characterized the historiography be consigned to the past.

NOTES

Introduction

1. In the text, Fascism (with an uppercase 'F') refers to Italian Fascism. The word written with a lowercase 'f' refers to the phenomenon in a universal sense.

2. René Rémond, *La Droite en France de 1815 à nos jours. Continuité et diversité d'une tradition politique* (Paris: Aubier, 1954), 215.

3. Ibid., 206–7; 215.

4. Zeev Sternhell, *La Droite révolutionnaire, 1885–1914. Les origines françaises du fascisme* (Paris: Seuil, 1978).

5. Zeev Sternhell, *Ni droite ni gauche. L'idéologie fasciste en France* (Paris: Seuil, 1983).

6. Marc Angenot, 'L'immunité de la France envers le fascisme: un demi-siecle de polémiques historiennes', *Etudes françaises* 47, no. 1 (2011): 15–42; John Bingham, 'Defining French Fascism, finding Fascists in France', *Canadian Journal of History* 29, no. 3 (1994): 525–43; Kevin Passmore, 'L'historiographie du "fascisme" en France', *French Historical Studies* 37, no. 3 (2014): 469–99.

7. Julian Jackson, *France: The Dark Years, 1940–1944* (Oxford: Oxford University Press, 2001), 1–20.

8. Robert O. Paxton, *Vichy France: Old Guard and New Order* (New York: Alfred A. Knopf, 1972).

9. Michel Dobry, 'La thèse immunitaire face aux fascismes', in *Le mythe de l'allergie française au fascisme*, ed. Michel Dobry (Paris: Albin Michel, 2003), 17–67.

10. Brian Jenkins and Chris Millington, *France and Fascism: February 1934 and the Dynamics of Political Crisis* (Abingdon: Routledge, 2015), 9.

11. A useful introduction to the topic of fascism is Roger Griffin, *The Nature of Fascism* (London; New York: Routledge, 1993).

12. William I. Shorrock, 'France and the rise of Fascism in Italy, 1919–1923', *Journal of Contemporary History* 10, no. 4 (1975): 595–7.

13. The *arditi* were an elite unit of the Italian army known for their extreme violence. See Ángel Alcalde, *War Veterans and Fascism in Interwar Europe* (Cambridge: Cambridge University Press, 2017), 25.

14. Ibid., 62; 82.

15. Piere Milza, *L'Italie fasciste devant l'opinion française* (Paris: Armand Colin, 1967), 15; Alcalde, *War Veterans and Fascism*, 82.

16. Shorrock, 'France and the rise of Fascism in Italy', 599.

17. Emile-G. Léonard, 'Qu'est-ce que le fascisme?' *La Revue hebdomadaire et son supplément illustré* 33 (19 August 1922): 284–94.

18. Pierre Dominique, 'Le rôle de Benito Mussolini', *La Revue hebdomadaire et son supplément illustré* 44 (4 November 1922): 103–14.

Notes

19. Maurice Tournier, 'Naissance du vocabulaire *fasciste* en France 1914–1945', in *Propos d'étymologie sociale. Tome II. Des mots en politique*. [online] Lyon: ENS Editions. http://books.openedition.org/enseditions/1718?lang=fr, note 5.

20. Archives Nationales, Pierrefitte-sur-Seine (hereafter referred to as AN) F7 13209, A. G., 'Chemises et faisceaux', *L'Oeuvre*, 18 November 1925.

21. On 'Boulangism' see Frederic H. Seager, *The Boulanger Affair: Political Crossroad of France, 1886–1889* (Ithaca: Cornell University Press, 1969) and James Harding, *The Astonishing Adventure of General Boulanger* (London: WH Allen, 1971). On nationalist and conservative politics in late nineteenth-century France see Bertrand Joly, *Nationalistes et conservateurs en France 1885–1902* (Paris: Indes Savantes, 2008).

22. Gilles Vergnon, *L'antifascisme en France de Mussolini à Le Pen* (Rennes: Presses Universitaires de Rennes, 2009), 21.

23. On the Ligue des Patriotes see Peter M. Rutkoff, 'The Ligue des Patriotes: The nature of the radical right and the Dreyfus Affair', *French Historical Studies* 8, no. 4 (1974): 585–603.

24. For example see AN BB18 2775, 'Le Procureur Général près la Cour d'Appel de Lyon à Monsieur le Garde des Sceaux', 28 May 1927.

25. See for example AN F7 14747, 'Le Ministre de l'Intérieur à M. le Ministre de la Défense Nationale', 28 May 1932.

26. Alcalde, *War Veterans and Fascism*, 202.

27. AN F7 13093, 'Le Commissaire Spécial de Briey à Monsieur le Contrôleur Général des Services de Police Administrative, Briey', 30 March 1926.

28. Caroline Wiegandt-Sakoun, 'Le fascisme italien en France', in *Les Italiens en France de 1914 à 1940*, ed. Pierre Milza (Rome: Ecole française de Rome, 1986), 431–69; Archives de la Préfecture de Police, Le Pré Saint-Gervais (hereafter referred to as APP) BA 1907, 'Au sujet du mouvement antifasciste', 14 September 1924; Alcalde, *War Veterans and Fascism*, 202.

29. Vergnon, *L'antifascisme en France*, 46–50. In 1933 alone, thirty books appeared in France on Nazi Germany.

30. For example: Armand Ansay, *La politique de crédit du fascisme de 1922 à 1932* (Paris: Recueil Sirey, 1935); Sotiris Agapitidès, *Le Corporatisme en Italie* (Paris: Librairie Lipschutz, 1935).

31. For example: Francesco Cambo, *Autour du fascisme italien. Réflexions et commentaires sur quelques problèmes de politique contemporaine* (Paris: Plon, 1925); H. de Vries de Heekelingen, *Le Fascisme et ses résultats* (Paris: Social Editions, 1928); Luigi Comapolonghi, *Avec l'Italie? Oui! Avec le Fascisme – Non!* (Paris: Ligue des Droits de l'Homme, 1930); Silvio Trentin, *Aux sources du fascisme* (Paris: Marcel Rivière, 1931); Henri Massis, *Chefs* (Paris: Plon, 1939).

32. Vergnon, *L'antifascisme en France*, 21.

33. Louis Latzarus, 'Le fascisme serait-il possible en France?' *La Revue hebdomadaire et son supplément illustré* 44 (4 November 1922): 115–17.

34. Daniel Hedinger, 'Universal Fascism and its global legacy: Italy's and Japan's entangled history in the early 1930s', *Fascism* 2, no. 2 (2013): 144.

35. Alcalde, *War Veterans and Fascism*, 100; 215.

36. AN F7 13209, 'La prétetnion dictatoriale des chemises bleues', *L'Homme libre*, 18 November 1925; Bernard Gervaise, 'Formez les faisceaux', *Paris-Soir*, n.d.

37. Alcalde, *War Veterans and Fascism*, 99.

38. Robert Soucy, *French Fascism: The First Wave* (New Haven; London: Yale University Press, 1986), 60–1.

39. Chris Millington, 'The shooting at Chartres: A case study in French political violence', in *France in an Era of Global War, 1914–1945*, ed. Ludivine Broch and Alison Carrol (Basingstoke: Palgrave Macmillan), 77–8.

40. Joel Blatt, 'Relatives and rivals: The response of the Action Française to Italian Fascism, 1919–1926', *European History Quarterly* 11, no. 3 (1981): 263; 'Camelots du Roi', *Time*, 11 June 1923, 11.

41. Chris Millington, *Fighting for France: Violence in Interwar French Politics* (Oxford: Oxford University Press, 2018), 30–1.

42. Eugen Weber, *Action Française: Royalism and Reaction in Twentieth-Century France* (Stanford: Stanford University Press, 1962), 130–1.

43. APP BA 1907, Ubaldo Triaca [vice-président de la Ligue Italienne des Droits de l'Homme], *Le Fascisme en Italie* (Paris, 1927).

44. Vergnon, *L'antifascisme en France*, 42.

45. Chris Millington, 'Communist veterans and paramilitarism in 1920s France: The Association républicaine des anciens combattants', *Journal of War and Culture Studies* 8, no. 4 (2015): 300–14.

46. Vergnon *L'antifascisme en France*, 21–31; 42.

47. For example see Florimond Bonté, 'Le social-fascisme et la fascisation de l'Etat bourgeois vue de Lens', *L'Humanité*, 8 April 1930, 1–2.

48. Michel Dobry, 'Février 1934 et la découverte de l'allergie de la société française à la "révolution fasciste"', *Revue Française de Sociologie* 30, no. 3–4 (1989): 511–33.

49. Alcalde, *War Veterans and Fascism*, 227–8.

50. AN F7 13210, 'Rapport, Strasbourg le 16 avril 1926'.

51. Jean Philippet, *Le temps des ligues: Pierre Taittinger et les jeunesses patriotes (1919–1944)* (Lille: Atelier nationale de reproduction des thèses, 2000), II, 857.

52. Hedinger, 'Universal Fascism and its global legacy', 145; Alcalde, *War Veterans and Fascism*, 201.

53. AN F7 14747, 'Note. Le Comité italien "Pro Patria", la "Cinquième Colonne" et le "Comité d'Action pour l'Universalité de Rome"', 4 August 1939.

54. Hedinger, 'Universal Fascism and its global legacy', 145; Philippet, *Le temps des ligues*, IV, 2156–8; Alcalde, *War Veterans and Fascism*, 234.

55. AN F7 14747, 'Note. Le Comité italien "Pro Patria", la "Cinquième Colonne" et le "Comité d'Action pour l'Universalité de Rome"', 4 August 1939.

56. Jean-Yves Boulic and Anne Lavaure, *Henri de Kerillis. L'absolu patriote* (Rennes: Presses Universitaires de Rennes, 1997), 120; 127.

57. Alcalde, *War Veterans and Fascism*, 235.

58. Ibid., 273.

59. See Wolfgang Geiger, *L'image de la France dans l'Allemagne nazie, 1933–1945* (Rennes: Presses Universitaires de Rennes, 2015).

60. Claire Aslangul, 'De la haine héréditaire à l'amitié indéfectible', *Revue historique des armées* 256 (2009): 3–13; Christian Delporte, 'Méfions-nous du sourire de Germania! L'Allemagne dans la caricature française (1919–1939)', *Mots* 48 (1996): 33–54.

Notes

61. Antonin Vitkine, *Mein Kampf. Histoire d'un livre* (Paris: Flammarion, 2009), 145–6; Bruno Goyet, *Charles Maurras* (Paris: Presses de Sciences Po, 1999), 76.

62. Philippet, *Le temps des ligues*, II, 836; 857.

63. La Rocque is routinely referred to in the literature of the period as 'Colonel' de La Rocque. However, as Gilles Richard points out, he did not achieve this rank and remained a lieutenant colonel until his death. For the sake of accuracy, I refer to La Rocque throughout the book as Lieutenant-Colonel François de La Rocque. See Gilles Richard, 'Comment définir le plus grand parti politique que la France a connu?' in *Le PSF. Un parti de masse à droite*, ed. Serge Berstein and Jean-Paul Thomas (Paris: CNRS Editions, 2016), 326.

64. Lieutenant-Colonel François de La Rocque, *Service Public* (Paris: Editions Bernard Grasset, 1934), 122.

65. Pierre Milza, *Fascisme français. Passé et présent* (Paris: Flammarion, 1987), 122. Latzarus, 'Le fascisme serait-il possible en France?' 115–7; Massis, *Chefs*, 40.

66. Jacques Bainville, *Les Dictateurs* (Pairs: Les Editions Denoël et Steele, 1935), 254.

67. Robert Soucy, *French Fascism: The Second Wave* (New Haven; London: Yale University Press, 1995), 139.

68. Albert Kéchichian, *Les Croix-de-Feu à l'âge des fascismes. Travail, famille, patrie* (Seyssel: Champ Vallon, 2006), 242–3; Massis, *Chefs*, 15.

69. Soucy, *The Second Wave*, 82; 139; Samuel Kalman, *The Extreme Right in Interwar France: The Faisceau and the Croix de Feu* (Aldershot: Ashgate, 2009), 59; Milza, *L'Italie fasciste*, 156–7.

70. Massis, *Chefs*, 6.

71. Ibid., 39.

72. Antonio Costa Pinto, 'Salazar's *Estado Novo*: The nature of a "para-fascist" regime', in *The Fascism Reader*, ed. Aristotle A. Kallis (London; New York: Routledge, 2002), 317.

73. Richard Griffiths, 'Fascist or Conservative? Portugal, Spain and the French Connection', *Portuguese Studies* 14 (1998): 148.

74. Bainville, *Les Dictateurs*, 270.

75. Specifically, the challenge to Salazar from National Syndicalists. António Costa Pinto, '"Chaos" and "Order": Preto, Salazar and charismatic appeal in inter-war Portugal', *Totalitarian Movements and Political Religions* 7, no. 2 (2006): 203–14.

76. Aslangul, 'De la haine héréditaire à l'amitié indéfectible', 3–13; Delporte, 'Méfions-nous du sourire de Germania!' 33–54.

77. 'Comme en Allemagne ... C'est une véritable expédition contre les Juifs que la 'Solidarité Française' avait organisée rue Vieille du Temple, *L'Oeuvre*, 27 September 1935.

78. APP BA 1894, 'Des "camelots" du roy provoquent une bagarre à Berck en s'opposant à une quête faite par des juifs', *Le Peuple*, 22 August 1933.

79. Léo Spitzer, 'La vie du mot "nazi" en Français', *Le français modern. Revue de synthèse et de vulgarisations linguistiques* 2, no. 1 (1934): 263–9; Bainville, *Les Dictateurs*, 278.

80. AN F7 13322, Jacques Duclos, 'Versaillais et Fascistes', *Le Combattant*, June 1926; 'Le parti socialiste avec la République des fusilleurs', *L'Humanité. Edition spéciale*, 11 February 1934, 2; APP DB 533, 'Le serment du 14 juillet renouvelé devant cinq cerceuils', *L'Humanité*, 22 March 1937; *9 février 1934. Journée rouge* (Paris: Les Publications révolutionnaires, 1934), 3; 18–23.

81. Eugène Frot, 'Assez de violence! De l'ordre pour tous!', *La République*, 22 November 1935, 1.

82. Comité de Vigilance des Intellectuels Antifascistes, *Qu'est-ce que le fascisme? Le fascisme et la France* (Paris, 1935), 5.

83. Ibid., 5; 7–9.

84. Ibid., 42; 43; 60.

85. Jacques Nobécourt, *Le Colonel de La Rocque (1885–1946). Ou les pièges du nationalisme chrétien* (Paris: Fayard, 1996), 1020n8. As Pierre Milza writes, 'Only a handful of intellectuals pondered the ideological foundations [of fascism], its universal character or on the other hand its Italian specificity, [and] the existence or not of a French matrix of fascism': Milza, *Fascisme français*, 117.

86. AN F7 13238, 'A tous les Antifascistes, Le Rayon communiste and la Section socialiste de Saint Quentin'.

87. Werner Hirsch, *Leçons de courage. Comment les révolutionnaires allemands supportent la torture et la captivité* (Paris: Défense Editions, 1935).

88. Marcel Cachin, 'Désarmement des ligues fascistes', *L'Humanité*, 10 January 1935, 1; Millington, *Fighting for France*, xxv–xxvi.

89. Vergnon, *L'antifascisme en France*, 85.

90. Gilles Vergnon, *Un enfant est lynché. L'affaire Gignoux* (Paris: Presses Universitaires de France/Humensis, 2018), 57.

91. Aumont Bernard, 'Témoignage. La chasse aux papillons à Paris en 1935', *Vingtième Siècle* 11 (1986): 38. See also Marcel Cachin, 'Ecartez la peste fasciste!', *L'Humanité*, 10 May 1935, 1; Tournier, 'Naissance du vocabulaire *fasciste* en France', paragraph 33; Gilles Morin, 'La gauche et le PSF, du Front populaire à la guerre', in *Le PSF*, 112–13.

92. Laurent Kestel, 'Were French elites allergic to fascism? A study of the reception of the 1930s dictatorships in three French periodicals', in *The French Right Between the Wars: Political and Intellectual Movements from Conservatism to Fascism*, ed. Samuel Kalman and Sean Kennedy (New York: Berghahn, 2014), 196.

93. Tournier, 'Naissance du vocabulaire *fasciste* en France'.

94. Dobry, 'La thèse immunitaire face aux fascismes', 17–67.

95. With regard to works on French fascism, it has become a meaningless ritual to lament the difficulties of arriving at a definition of the ideology before proposing one's own list of essential criteria.

96. Kevin Passmore, *The Right in France from the Third Republic to Vichy* (Oxford: Oxford University Press, 2013), 308. For a recent work that likewise eschews definitions of fascism see Alcalde, *War Veterans and Fascism*.

97. Françoise Thébaud, 'Maternité et famille entre les deux guerres: Idéologies et politique familiale', in *Femmes et Fascismes*, ed. Rita Thalmann (Paris: Editions Tierce, 1986), 85.

98. Jenkins and Millington, *France and Fascism*, 159.

Chapter 1

1. The account of the violence at the rue Damrémont in the first two paragraphs of this chapter is taken from the dossier on the incident, AN F7 13236.

2. AN F7 13236, Claire Gonon, 'On poursuit l'audition des témoins de la défense', *Le Quotidien*, 29 April 1926. See also Chris Millington, 'Getting away with murder: Political violence on trial in interwar France', *European History Quarterly* 48, no. 2 (2018): 256–82.

3. Various sources estimate the Action Française to have had 30,000–40,000 members, and the Faisceau and the Jeunesses Patriotes 60,000 each. Considering the likelihood that some members belonged to more than one group, the likelihood that the three leagues combined could call upon 100,000 followers does not seem unreasonable.

4. *L'Italie sous la terreur. A bas le fascisme assassin!* (Paris: Editions du Secours Rouge International, 1926), 6–7.

5. Marcel Cachin, 'Nous ne laisserons pas dénaturer les faits!', *L'Humanité*, 26 April 1925.

6. AN F7 13198, 'Après le guet-apens des sociétés savantes', *L'Humanité*, 16 March 1926.

7. Milza, *Fascisme français*, 120.

8. Philippet, *Le temps des ligues*, I, 243–4.

9. Tournier, 'Naissance du vocabulaire *fasciste* en France', paragraphs 35, 46, and 47.

10. Benjamin Martin, *France and the Après Guerre, 1918–1924* (Baton Rouge: Louisiana State University Press, 1999), 247.

11. AN F7 13209, Binet-Valmer, 'Le cri d'alarme', *La Liberté*, 26 November 1925.

12. Jenkins and Millington, *France and Fascism*, 28–9; Passmore, *The Right in France*, 211.

13. AN F7 14608, 'L'Union Civique: Bulletin d'Adhésion'; one's status as a veteran appeared to be the sole membership criterion; AN F7 14608, 'Le préfet de la Haute-Garonne à Monsieur le Ministre de l'Intérieur', 25 May 1920; AN F7 14608, 'Décret du 30 avril 1920'; 'Les volontaires', *Le Temps*, 14 May 1920; Jean Bastide, 'L'Union Civique Parisienne', *L'Echo de Paris*, 28 April 1920.

14. Tyler Stovall, *The Rise of the Paris Red Belt* (Berkeley: University of California Press, 1990), 2; 61.

15. Jenkins and Millington, *France and Fascism*, 31; 66.

16. Jean-Claude Delbreil, *Centrisme et démocratie chrétienne en France. Le Parti Démocrate Populaire au MRP, 1919–1944* (Paris: Publications de la Sorbonne, 1990), 156; Passmore, *The Right in France*, 235.

17. General Yves Gras, *Castelnau ou l'art de commander, 1851–1944* (Paris: Denoël, 1990), 396–99; Passmore, *The Right in France*, 234; Delbreil, *Centrisme et démocratie chrétienne en France*, 174.

18. Michel Winock, 'L'Action française', in *Histoire de l'extrême droite en France*, ed. Michel Winock (Paris: Points, 2015), 139–40.

19. 'Restaurer l'idéal républicain', *Le Radical*, 24 April 1924, 1. This newspaper article is referred to in Weber, *Action Française*, 131.

20. Passmore, *The Right in France*, 231.

21. Joan Tumblety, *Remaking the Male Body: Masculinity and the Uses of Physical Culture in Interwar and Vichy France* (Oxford: Oxford University Press, 2013), 152–3.

22. APP BA 1894, 'La Fédération nationale des camelots du roi', June 1923; untitled report, 31 December 1924.

23. On Rédier and the Légion see for example Cheryl A. Koos, 'Fascism, fatherhood, and the family in interwar France: The Case of Antoine Rédier and the Légion', *Journal of Family History* 24, no. 3 (1999): 317–29.

24. 'Les cendres de Jaurès au Panthéon', *Le Matin*, 24 November 1924.

25. Philippet, *Le temps des ligues*, I, 61; 67.

26. The Jeunesses Patriotes was established prior to the general election that year.

27. Soucy, *The First Wave*, 40–2; 51.

28. Ibid., 64–7; William D. Irvine, *French Conservatism in Crisis: The Republican Federation of France in the 1930s* (Baton Rouge: Louisiana State University Press, 1979), 105.

29. Serge Berstein, 'Une bien étrange approche de l'histoire', in *Fascisme Français? La controverse*, ed. Serge Berstein and Michel Winock (Paris: CNRS Editions, 2014), 17–33; Pierre Milza, 'L'ultra-droite des années trente', in *Histoire de l'extrême droite*, 164; Philippe Burrin, 'Le fascisme', in *Histoire des droites en France*, I, ed. Jean-François Sirinelli (Paris: Gallimard, 1992), 634.

30. AN F7 13209, 'Les jeunesses patriotes recoivent leurs drapeaux à Luna-Park', *L'Humanité*, 16 November 1925. See Philippet, *Le temps des ligues*, V, annexe III, 254–71, for a list of deputies affiliated to the league.

31. Jean-François Colas, *Les droites nationales en Lorraine dans les années 1930: Acteurs, organisations, réeseaux* (Lille: Atelier national de reproduction des thèses, 2002), 133.

32. Ibid., 137.

33. Soucy, *The First Wave*, 71–5.

34. Ibid., 53.

35. Irvine, *French Conservatism in Crisis*, 104–12; Passmore, *The Right in France*, 230; 235

36. Soucy, *The First Wave*, 44.

37. Tumblety, *Remaking the Male Body*, 153; APP BA 1942, 'Au sujet des Jeunesses Patriotes, Septembre 1936'.

38. Soucy, *The First Wave*, 49.

39. APP BA 1942, untitled report, n.d.; Soucy, *The First Wave*, 39–87. See also AN F7 13234, 'Réunion privée de propaganda organisée par les Jeunesses patriotes de Levalois-Perret, Salons Lagarde, 7 Février 1927', 8 February 1927.

40. APP BA 1942, 'Ligue des Jeunesses Patriotes'; AN F7 13234, Untitled report, 21 February 1927. See also AN F7 13232, 'Au sujet des Phalanges Universitaires', January 1929; Soucy, *The First Wave*, 205–7.

41. AN F7 13233, 'Le Préfet des Alpes-Maritimes à Monsieur le Ministre de l'Intérieur', *Nice*, 7 June 1926; 'Le Directeur de la Police d'Etat à Monsieur le Secrétaire Général du Ministère de l'Intérieur, Directeur de la Sûreté Générale, Nice', 19 June 1926; 'Constitution d'un groupe de JP: Deuxième reunion'; 'Assemblée Generale du club sportif des Jeunesses Patriotes's, 19 July 1925; APP BA 1942 Ligue des Jeunesses Patriotes, police file; on the league see also AN F7 13232, 'Jeunesses Patriotes. Armement', n.d. (probably 1926).

42. AN F7 1323, 'Réunion privée de propagande organisée par la ligue des Jeunesses Patriotes', 26 March 1926; Passmore, *The Right in France*, 249; Allen Douglas, *From Fascism to Libertarian Communism: Georges Valois against the Third Republic* (Berkeley; Oxford: University of California Press, 1992), 101.

43. AN F7 13232, 'Au sujet des Phalanges Universitaires', January 1929.

44. AN F7 13233, 'Le Commissaire Central a Monsieur le Ministre de l'Intérieur, Nantes', 25 June 1925; Soucy, *The First Wave*, 52; Philippet, *Le temps des ligues*, I, 238n96.

45. AN F7 13236, 'Chambre des députés: Compte rendu analytique officiel', Séance du vendredi 24 April 25; Philippet, *Le temps des ligues*, I, 221.

46. Philippet, *Le temps des ligues*, I, 221.

Notes

47. Soucy, *The First Wave*, 55–6.

48. APP BA 1942, letter from L. Burnouf of the JP Secteur Région Est, to M. Fouquet, Commssaire de Police, Vincennes, 9 December 1926; Le Chef du Service des Reseignements Générax et des Jeux à Monsieur le Préfet de Police, Paris, 11 December 1926.

49. Passmore, *The Right in France*, 235; Soucy, *The First Wave*, 52; Gabriel Goodliffe, *The Resurgence of the Radical Right in France: From Boulangisme to the Front National* (Cambridge: Cambridge University Press, 2012), 20.

50. Jenkins, 'The right-wing leagues and electoral politics in interwar France', *History Compass* 5, no. 4 (2007): 1370.

51. Passmore, *The Right in France*, 241–3.

52. AN F7 13232, 'Les Jeunesses Patriotes', May 1925.

53. AN F7 13233, 'Les Jeunesses Patriotes', 7 March 1925; F7 13232, 'Les Jeunesses Patriotes', May 1925; Danielle Tartakowsky, *Les manifestations de rue en France 1918–1968* (Publications de la Sorbonne: Paris, 1997), 139–40.

54. Philippet, *Le temps des ligues*, II, 885–91.

55. Soucy, *The First Wave*, 84–6.

56. Philippet, *Le temps des ligues*, II, 896–7.

57. Jacques Cantier, *L'Algérie sous le régime de Vichy* (Paris: Odile Jacob, 2002), 23.

58. Samuel Kalman, *French Colonial Fascism: The Extreme Right in Algeria, 1919–1939* (New York: Palgrave Macmillan, 2013), 24–31; Sophie B. Roberts, 'Anti-Semitism and municipal government in interwar French colonial Algeria', *Journal of North African Studies* 17, no. 5 (2012): 821–37.

59. Kalman, *French Colonial Fascism*, 31–50.

60. See Philippet, *Le temps des ligues*, I, 600–1; 616.

61. Cheryl Koos and Daniella Sarnoff, 'France', in *Women, Gender and Fascism in Europe, 1919–45*, ed. Kevin Passmore (Manchester: Manchester University Press, 2003), 168–89.

62. Magali Della Sudda, 'Gender, Fascism and the right-wing in France between the wars: The Catholic', *Politics, Religion and Ideology* 13, no. 2 (2012): 191.

63. Daniella Sarnoff, 'An overview of women and gender in French fascism', in *The French Right Between the Wars*, 146.

64. APP BA 1942, 'Ligue des Jeunesses Patriotes', n.d.

65. Koos and Sarnoff, 'France', 177; Della Sudda, 'Gender, fascism and the right-wing', 191.

66. Passmore, *The Right in France*, 244; Sarnoff, 'An overview of women and gender in French fascism', 144–7; 156; Della Sudda, 'Gender, fascism and the right-wing', 190–3.

67. Passmore, *The Right in France*, 244; Soucy, *The First Wave*, 80–1.

68. Sarnoff, 'An overview of women and gender in French fascism', 142–3. See also Cheryl Koos, 'Gender, the family, and the fascist temptation: Visions of masculinity in the natalist-familialist movement, 1922–1940', in *The French Right Between the Wars*, 112–26.

69. Daniella Sarnoff, 'Interwar fascism and the franchise: Women's suffrage and the ligues', *Historical Reflections/Réflexions Historiques* 34, no. 2 (2008): 114.

70. Sarnoff, 'An overview of women and gender in French fascism', 153–4.

71. Koos and Sarnoff, 'France', 177.

72. Sarnoff, 'Interwar fascism and the franchise', 113–4; Soucy, *The First Wave*, 81.

73. Della Sudda, 'Gender, fascism and the right-wing', 192.

74. Sarnoff, 'Interwar fascism and the franchise', 115.

75. Sarnoff, 'An overview of women and gender in French fascism', 150.

76. Soucy, *The First Wave*, 57.

77. Ibid., 57–9; 176–80; Douglas, *From Fascism to Libertarian Communism*, 101–2.

78. 'Le Faisceau de Paris est né hier', *Le Matin*, 12 November 1925, 2.

79. Ibid. Douglas (on page 89 of *From Fascism to Libertarian Communism*) notes that 4,000 men attended the meeting and 250 marched to the Arc de Triomphe afterward.

80. AN F7 13209, André Kaminker, 'Coup d'oeil sur les choses qui sont.', *Le Rappel*, 18 November 1925.

81. AN F7 13209, 'Devant le péril fasciste', *Libertaire*, 28 November 1925.

82. AN F7 13209 René Thèvenin, 'Le pays peut-il rester inactive devant le danger fasciste?' *Ere nouvelle*, 24 November 1925. Italy and Mussolini were mentioned in reports from *L'Humanité*, *La Liberté*, *L'Oeuvre*, and *L'Homme libre*.

83. On Valois's early life see Douglas, *From Fascism to Libertarian Communism*, 1–5.

84. Ibid., 8–9.

85. Ibid., 10.

86. Ibid., 19–36.

87. Ibid., 54–64.

88. Soucy, *The First Wave*, 126–73; Jules Levey, 'Georges Valois and the Faisceau: The making and breaking of a fascist', *French Historical Studies* 8, vol. 2 (1973): 279–304; Michel Winock, *Nationalisme, antisémitisme et fascisme en France*, rev. edn (Paris: Editions du Seuil, 2014), 243.

89. Zeev Sternhell, 'Strands of French fascism', in *Who were the Fascists?* ed. Stein Ugelvik Larsen, Bernt Hagtvet and Jan Petter Myklebust (Oxford; New York; Oslo: Universitetsforlaget, 1980), 484.

90. Ibid., 34–6.

91. Ibid., 73.

92. Passmore, *The Right in France*, 235; Soucy, *The First Wave*, 87; 96–7; 99; Milza, 'L'ultra-droite des années trente', 172. On the founding of the Faisceau see Milza, *L'Italie fasciste*, 131–3; Douglas, *From Fascism to Libertarian Communism*, 83; 128.

93. Levey, 'Georges Valois and the Faisceau', 292.

94. Soucy, *The First Wave*, 111; Douglas, *From Fascism to Libertarian Communism*, 94–5.

95. Soucy, *The First Wave*, 111; Goyet, 'La "Marche sur Rome": version originelle sous-titrée. La reception du fascisme en France des années 20', in *Le mythe de l'allergie française au fascisme*, 96–7.

96. Allen Douglas, 'Violence and Fascism: The Case of the Faisceau', *Journal of Contemporary History* 19, no. 4 (1984): 691; 694; Soucy, *The First Wave*, 89; AN F7 13208, 'Faisceau Notes', 13 December 1927.

97. AN F7 13208, untitled report, 9 June 1926.

98. Soucy, *The First Wave*, 89; Della Sudda, 'Gender, fascism and the right-wing', 189; Levey, 'Georges Valois and the Faisceau', 287–8; Douglas, *From Fascism to Libertarian Communism*, 115.

99. Soucy, *The First Wave*, 113–14; Goyet, 'La "Marche sur Rome"', 102; Levey, 'Georges Valois and the Faisceau', 294–5; Douglas, *From Fascism to Libertarian Communism*, 105–11.

100. Passmore, *The Right in France*, 235; Soucy, *The First Wave*, 90; 112; Sternhell, 'Strands of French fascism', 485–7; Levey, 'Georges Valois and the Faisceau', 297.

101. Kalman, *The Extreme Right in Interwar France*, 149.

102. AN F7 13210, Debû-Bridel, 'Belle réunion du Faisceau des corporations', *Nouveau Siecle*, June 1926.

103. AN F7 13208, 'Réunion organise par "les Légions"', 1 July 1926; Le Préfetf de la Meuse à Monsieur le Ministre de l'Intérieur', 29 May 1926; Soucy, *The First Wave*, 88–9.

104. F7 13006, 'Le commissaire spécial à M. Le Directeur de la Sûreté Générale', 12 November 1925; Passmore, *The Right in France*, 251; AN F7 13209, Le préfet des Basses-Pyrenees a Monsieur le Ministre de l'Intérieur', *Pau*, 22 December 1926.

105. Soucy, *The First Wave*, 87; Passmore, *The Right in France*, 253; Kalman, *The Extreme Right in Interwar France*, 5; AN, F7 13006, 'Le commissaire spécial à M. Le Directeur de la Sûreté Générale', 12 November 1925; AN, F7 13208, 'Le Commissaire Central à M. le Directeur de la Sûreté Générale', 21 November 1925; 'Faisceau Notes', 13 December 1927; 'Un grand movement national. Les Légions veulent donner à la France la politque de la victoire', *Paris-Centre*, 21 August 1925.

106. Levey, 'Georges Valois and the Faisceau', 291.

107. Soucy, *The First Wave*, 91.

108. Ibid., 91; 164.

109. Ibid., 92.

110. Kalman, *The Extreme Right in Interwar France*, 59. Klaus-Jurgen Muller, 'French fascism and modernisation', *Journal of Contemporary History* 11, no. 4 (1976): 80; Douglas, *From Fascism to Libertarian Communism*, xvi.

111. Kalman, *The Extreme Right in Interwar France*, 59; 232.

112. Ibid., 18.

113. Sternhell, 'Strands of French fascism', 488; Douglas, *From Fascism to Libertarian Communism*, 119–20.

114. Ibid., 118–19.

115. Soucy, *The First Wave*, 93; 117; 167.

116. See Millington, 'Communist veterans and paramilitarism'.

117. Sarnoff, 'An overview of women and gender in French fascism', 153.

118. Kalman, *The Extreme Right in Interwar France*, 129–34.

119. Passmore, *The Right in France*, 244; Sarnoff, 'An overview of women and gender in French fascism', 146–7.

120. Kalman, *The Extreme Right in Interwar France*, 119.

121. See chapter three in Kalman, *The Extreme Right in Interwar France*.

122. Sarnoff, 'Interwar fascism and the franchise', 124–5.

123. Della Sudda, 'Gender, fascism and the right-wing', 190.

124. Ibid., 187–8.

125. AN F7 13210, Maurice Pujo, 'L'école de la défaite', *Action Française*, 3 July 1926.

126. AN F7 13197, Untitled report, 16 November 1926; Soucy, *The First Wave*, 180; Winock, 'L'Action française', 142–3.

127. AN F7 13209 'Réunion organisée par "Le Faisceau" pour la creation du "Faisceau Universitaire"', 15 December 1925; Soucy, *The First Wave*, 182.

128. Uttered by a young man leaving the December 1925 meeting and mentioned in Tumblety, *Remaking the Male Body*, 152.

129. AN F7 13209 L'agression de l'Action française', *Nouveau Siècle*, 16 December 1925.

130. AN F7 13208, 'Georges Valois, Sur l'agression de l'Action française', *Nouveau Siècle*, 15 December 1925; 'Georges Valois chassé par les étudiants', *L'Action Française*, 15 December 1925.

131. Weber, *Action Française*, 210–11; AN F7 13197, 'Au sujet d'un coup de main du Faisceau à l'Action Française', 18 Novembre 1926; Soucy, *The First Wave*, 183–4.

132. Paul Sérant, *Les dissidents de l'Action Française* (Paris: Copernic, 1978), 29.

133. Philippet, *Le temps des ligues*, I, 264.

134. Passmore, *The Right in France*, 247.

135. Ibid., 248; Philippet, *Le temps des ligues*, II, 849.

136. Serge Berstein, 'La ligie', in *Histoire des droits en France*, vol. 2, ed. Jean-François Sirinelli (Paris: Gallimard, 1992), 90; Soucy, *The First Wave*, 39.

137. Milza, *Fascisme Français*, 112.

138. Philippet, *Le temps des ligues*, I, 243–4.

139. Milza, *L'Italie fasciste*, 57.

140. Blatt, 'Relatives and rivals', 263; Weber, *Action Française*, 142; Goyet, 'La "Marche sur Rome"', 84.

141. Milza, *L'Italie fasciste*, 20.

142. Vergnon, *L'antifascisme en France*, 38.

143. Blatt, 'Relatives and rivals', 276–80. See also Goyet, 'La "Marche sur Rome"', 84.

144. Ibid., 93.

145. Milza, *L'Italie fasciste*, 134.

146. AN F7 13210, 'Rapport, Strasbourg le 16 avril 1926'.

147. Douglas, *From Fascism to Libertarian Communism*, 125–31.

148. Ibid., 132; 136.

149. AN F7 13210, untitled report, 26 April 1926.

150. Douglas, *From Fascism to Libertarian Communism*, 131; Soucy, *The First Wave*, 184.

151. Stéphane Courtois and Marc Lazar, *Histoire du Parti communiste français* (Paris: Presses Universitaires de France, 1995), 91.

152. Edward Mortimer, *The Rise of the French Communist Party (1920–1947)* (London: Faber, 1984), 133; 144.

153. Philippet, *Le temps des ligues*, I, 299.

154. Soucy, *The First Wave*, 197.

155. Passmore, *The Right in France*, 280–2.

156. Police believed there was still a hard core of activists in Paris ready to be mobilized at a moment's notice: AN F7 13199, 'Le préfet de police à Monsieur le Ministre de l'Intérieur', 1 July 1929; Winock, 'L'Action française', 143–4.

157. Douglas, *From Fascism to Libertarian Communism*, 126.

158. Levey, 'Georges Valois and the Faisceau', 295–6.

159. Soucy, *The First Wave*, 185–95; Douglas, *From Fascism to Libertarian Communism*, 113.

160. Ibid., 132–46.

161. Blatt, 'Relatives and rivals', 267; 270; 276.

162. Milza, *L'Italie fasciste*, 133; Kalman, *The Extreme Right in Interwar France*, 18.

163. Sérant, *Les dissidents de l'Action Française*, 32; Kalman, *The Extreme Right in Interwar France*, 81–3; Goyet, 'La "Marche sur Rome"', 88–90.

164. Passmore, *The Right in France*, 232.

Chapter 2

1. Jenkins and Millington, *France and Fascism*, 179–85.

2. William L. Shirer, *The Collapse of the Third Republic: An Inquiry into the Fall of France in 1940* (London: Literary Guild, 1970), 195–6.

3. Yann Galera, *La Garde républicaine mobile à l'épreuve du 6 février 1934* (Maisons Alfort: Service historique de la Gendarmerie nationale, 2003), 26.

4. On the victims of the violence see appendix four in Jenkins and Millington, *France and Fascism*.

5. Henri Béraud in *Gringoire*, cited in Winock, *Nationalisme, antisémitisme et fascisme en France*, 401.

6. Pierre Drieu la Rochelle, 'Air de février 1934', *Nouvelle Revue Française*, March 1934, 568–9, quoted in Mary Jean Green, *Fiction in the Historical Present: French Writers and the Thirties* (Hanover, NH; London: University Press of New England, 1986), 294n46.

7. *9 février 1934*, 27.

8. 'A l'origine du déchirement de la France, il y a le 6 février', Jean Glaive, 'Xe anniversaire. 6 et 12 Février 1934', *Le Populaire*, January 1944, 3. See also: *Le Populaire: Organe du Comité d'Action socialiste*, 1 April 1943 edition, which mentions the anniversary of the *six février* on page one.

9. Eugen Weber, *The Hollow Years: France in the 1930s* (London: Sinclair-Stevenson, 1995), 26–54.

10. Ibid., 20–31.

11. Julian Jackson, *The Politics of Depression in France, 1932–1936* (Cambridge: Cambridge University Press, 1985), 25–9.

12. Weber, *The Hollow Years*, 33.

13. Jackson, *The Politics of Depression*, 57–63; Jenkins and Millington, *France and Fascism*, 50.

14. Jackson, *The Politics of Depression*, 78; Jenkins and Millington, *France and Fascism*, 38n76; Weber, *The Hollow Years*, 34; 47.

15. Weber, *The Hollow Years*, 34–9; Jackson, *The Politics of Depression*, 77–9; Jenkins and Millington, *France and Fascism*, 38.

16. Roger Austin, 'The conservative right and the far right in France: The search for power, 1934–44', in *Fascists and Conservatives: The Radical Right and the Establishment in*

Twentieth-Century Europe, ed. Martin Blinkhorn (London; Boston: Unwin Hyman, 1990), 177.

17. Jean Renaud, *La Solidarité Française attaque …* (Paris, 1935), 222.

18. The fullest examination of the Solidarité Française in English is in Soucy, *The Second Wave*, 59–103.

19. Sternhell, 'Strands of French fascism', 490.

20. Ibid., 490.

21. Soucy, *The Second Wave*, 73; Gilles Lahousse, 'De la solidarité française au parti du faisceau français: un exemple de radicalisation politique', *Vingtième Siècle* 58, no. 1 (1998), 46.

22. Renaud, *La Solidarité Française attaque…*, 44; 69.

23. Pascal Ory, *Les collaborateurs, 1940–1945* (Pairs: Editions du Seuil, 1976), 95.

24. Colas, *Les droites nationales en Lorraine*, 100–05; Soucy, *The Second Wave*, 40. See also Marcel Bucard, *Le Francisme. Paix, justice, ordre* (Paris, n.d.).

25. Ory, *Les collaborateurs*, 26; Sternhell, 'Strands of French fascism', 491. The most comprehensive examination of the Francistes is Alain Déniel, *Bucard et le francisme* (Paris: J. Picollec, 1979); the quotation from Bucard comes from pages 8 and 9 of this source.

26. See for example the violence at Basse-Yutz in 1934: AN BB18 2918, 'Le Procureur Général près la Cour d'Appel de Colmar à Monsieur le Garde des Sceaux, Ministre de la Justice', 23 July 1934.

27. Henri Noguères, *La Vie quotidienne en France au temps du Front Populaire 1935–1938* (Pairs: Hachette, 1977), 57–9. Soucy, *The Second Wave*, 38–40.

28. Nobécourt, *Le Colonel de La Rocque*, 199–201; Kéchichian, *Les Croix-de-feu*, 164; Caroline Campbell, *Political Belief in France, 1927–1945: Gender, Empire and Fascism in the Croix de Feu and Parti Social Français* (Baton Rouge: Louisiana State University Press, 2015), 35–6; Philippe Rudaux, *Les Croix de Feu et le PSF* (Paris: Editions France-Empire, 1967), 47–8.

29. Soucy, *The Second Wave*, 111; Kéchichian, *Les Croix-de-feu*, 201; Sean Kennedy, *Reconciling France against Democracy: The Croix de Feu and the Parti Social Français, 1927–1945* (Montréal; Ithaca: McGill-Queen's University Press, 2007), 88.

30. Chris Millington, *From Victory to Vichy: Veterans in Inter-war France* (Manchester: Manchester University Press, 2012), 42–3.

31. Lynette Shaw, 'The anciens combattants and the events of February 1934', *European History Quarterly* 5 (1975): 302.

32. Jenkins and Millington, *France and Fascism*, 73.

33. Weber's words, quoted in Jenkins and Millington, *France and Fascism*, 76.

34. Jenkins and Millington, *France and Fascism*, 56; 128.

35. On the details of the Affair and its aftermath see Paul Jankowski, *Stavisky: A Confidence Man in the Republic of Virtue* (Ithaca; London: Cornell University Press, 2002).

36. See Jenkins and Millington, *France and Fascism*, 63–4, notes, 10, 11 and 12; Weber, *The Hollow Years*, 32–3; William L. Shirer, *20th Century Journey: A Memoir of a Life and the Times. Volume 2: The Nightmare Years, 1930–1940* (New York: Bantam Books, 1984), 89–92.

37. Robert Brasillach, *Notre avant-guerre* (Paris: Godefroy de Bouillon, 1998), 157.

38. Jenkins and Millington, *France and Fascism*, 54.

39. Weber, *The Hollow Years*, 131; Shirer, *20th Century Journey*, 91.

Notes

40. Jean Belin, *My Work at the Sûreté* (London: George G. Harrap, 1950), 138.

41. Prince would later be found dead in mysterious circumstances: Belin, *My Work at the Sûreté*, 148–54.

42. Weber, *The Hollow Years*, 130–1.

43. Jenkins and Millington, *France and Fascism*, 51–2; Anne-Claude Ambroise-Rendu, *Crimes et délits. Une histoire de la violence de la Belle Epoque à nos jours* (Paris: Nouveau Monde, 2006), 107–15.

44. Louis Ducloux, *From Blackmail to Treason: Political Crime and Corruption in France, 1920–40* (London: André Deutsch, 1958), 139.

45. Jankowski, *Stavisky*, 194.

46. Ambroise-Rendu, *Crimes et délits*, 112.

47. Jenkins and Millington, *France and Fascism*, 55; Pierre Pellissier, *6 Février 1934. La République en flames* (Paris: Perrin, 2000), 42.

48. Jenkins and Millington, *France and Fascism*, 178; Marcel Le Clère, *Le 6 Février* (Paris, 1967), 83; Pellissier, *6 février 1934*, 39–61.

49. La Rocque, 'Vers la victoire avec l'alliance du peuple', *Le Flambeau*, 1 February 1934; Shirer, *The Collapse of the Third Republic*, 181; Brian Jenkins, 'Plots and rumors: Conspiracy theories and the *six février 1934*', *French Historical Studies* 34 (2011): 649–78.

50. Jackson, *The Politics of Depression*, 66–76.

51. Shirer, *20th Century Journey*, 95.

52. Christian Guiraud, *La Police et l'ordre public; thèse pour le doctorat présentée et soutenue le mardi 13 décembre 1938* (Bordeaux: Imprimeries Delmas, 1938), 27–8.

53. Jenkins and Millington, *France and Fascism*, p. 57.

54. 'Avant la séance d'aujourd'hui', *L'Action Française*, 6 February 1934, 1.

55. AN 451 AP/81, circular from La Rocque, 3 February 1934.

56. The appeals of the groups cited here can be found in Jenkins and Millington, *France and Fascism*, 179–86.

57. Pellissier, *6 février 1934*, 109–10.

58. Shirer, *The Collapse of the Third Republic*, 195.

59. Pellissier, *6 février 1934*, 117–19.

60. Edith and Gilles de La Rocque, *La Rocque tel qi'il était* (Paris: Fayard, 1962), 107.

61. Jenkins and Millington, *France and Fascism*, 71–2.

62. Pellissier, *6 Février 1934*, 124; Shirer, *20th Century Journey*, 97.

63. Yvan Combeau, *Paris et les élections municipales sous la Troisième République: La scéne capitale dans la vie politique française* (Paris: L'Harmattan, 1998), 335–40.

64. Ibid., 368.

65. Ibid., 347.

66. Pelissier, *6 février 1934*, 96.

67. Ibid., 135–9; Jenkins and Millington, *France and Fascism*, 88.

68. Rudaux, *Les Croix de Feu et le PSF*, 69.

69. Pelissier, *6 février 1934*, 158–9.

70. Shirer, *The Collapse of the Third Republic*, 196.

71. Pelissier *6 février 1934*, 142–50.

72. Ibid., 145.

73. Shirer, *20th Century Journey*, 98.

74. Jankowski, *Stavisky*, 219.

75. Shirer, *20th Century Journey*, 98.

76. Edith and Gilles de La Rocque, *La Rocque, tel qu'il était*, 110.

77. Shirer, *20th Century Journey*, 98.

78. APP BA 1853 Report of 7 février, in folder B1: 'Rapports d'ensemble de la journée du 6 février'.

79. Millington, *From Victory to Vichy*, 63.

80. Ibid., 63–4.

81. Ducloux, *From Blackmail to Treason*, 147.

82. Millington, *From Victory to Vichy*, 52–83; Shirer, *20th Century Journey*, 100–1; Pellissier, *6 février 1934*, 177.

83. Jenkins and Millington, *France and Fascism*, 78. See also Olivier Fillieule and Danielle Tartakowsky, *La manifestation* (Paris: Presses de la Fondation Nationale des Sciences Politiques, 2008): 'les formes prises par les interactions au cours d'un événement constituent des signaux qui contribuent à informer la perception de la situation par les adversaires', 88.

84. Jenkins and Millington, *France and Fascism*, 73–8.

85. Ibid., 69; Danielle Tartakowsky, *Le pouvoir est dans la rue. Crises politiques et manifestations en France* (Paris: Aubier: 1998), 95–7.

86. Pellissier, *6 février 1934*, 183–4; Jenkins and Millington, *France and Fascism*, 189.

87. Jenkins and Millington, *France and Fascism*, 82–6.

88. Ibid., 87.

89. Shirer, *20th Century Journey*, 105.

90. Weber, *The Hollow Years*, 137; Pellissier, *6 février 1934*, 237.

91. Jenkins and Millington, *France and Fascism*, 3.

92. *Journal Officiel du 16 février. Débats parlementaires no. 14. Chanbre des Députés*, 454.

93. Weber, *The Hollow Years*, 137

94. Jenkins and Millington, *France and Fascism*, 10.

95. Ibid., 99n91.

96. Rudaux, *Les Croix de Feu et le PSF*, 87.

97. AN 451 AP/84, *Que veulent ... Que peuvent. ... Les Croix de Feu*, June 1935, 8. See also Henry Malherbe, *La Rocque: Un chef. Des actes. Des idées* (Paris: Librarie Plon, 1934), 87–8.

98. Tartakowsky, *Les Droites et la rue*, 67.

99. Jenkins and Millington, *France and Fascism*, 91–2.

100. On this see Ibid., 126–49.

101. AN F7 12963, 'Conférence de M. Paul Reynaud', 8 March 1934.

102. Irvine, *French Conservatism in Crisis*, 116–17.

103. Pierre Pucheu, *Ma vie* (Paris: Amiot Dumont, 1948), 138.

104. Christian Bernadec, *Dagore: Les carnets secrets de la Cagoule* (Paris: France-Empire, 1977), 20.

105. Carmen Callil, *Bad Faith: A Forgotten History of Family and Fatherland* (London: Vintage, 2007), 113–14.

106. Noguères, *La Vie quotidienne en France*, 41.

107. AN F7 13306, 'Manifestation organisée à l'occasion de la Fête Nationale de Jeanne d'Arc', 13 May 1934.

108. Jenkins and Millington, *France and Fascism*, 151.

Chapter 3

1. 'Les Croix de Feu et les Volontaires Nationaux', *Le Flambeau*, 20 July 1935, 2; Rudaux, *Les Croix de Feu et le PSF*, 96.

2. '17.700 Croix de feu ont parade militairement a l'Arc de Triomphe', *L'Humanité*, 15 July 1935, 6.

3. Claude Martial, 'Le rassemblement', 4 and Y. Grosrichard, 'Au long du cortège', *L'Oeuvre*, 15 July 1935, 4.

4. Jackson, *The Politics of Depression,* 105–6; 124.

5. See Robert J. Soucy, 'French press reactions to Hitler's first two years in power', *Contemporary European History* 7, no. 1 (1998): 21–38.

6. Philippet, *Le temps des ligues*, II, 818.

7. Emmanuel Braganca, 'The curious history of "Mein Kampf" in France', *The Conversation*, 5 July 2016, https://theconversation.com/the-curious-history-of-mein-kampf-in-france-58196 (accessed 9 April 2018); Luigi Comapolonghi, *Avec l'Italie?*, 44.

8. Philippet, *Le temps des ligues*, II, 842.

9. Braganca, 'The curious history of "Mein Kampf" in France'.

10. Fernand de Brinon, 'Une conversation avec Adolf Hitler', *Le Matin*, 22 November 1933, p. 1; Vitkine, *Mein Kampf. Histoire d'un livre*, 120–2.

11. Lucien Lemas, 'Hitler nous parle des relations futures entre la France et l'Allemagne', *L'Intransigeant*, 21 September 1934, 1.

12. Jean Goy, 'Un entretien de Hitler avec MM. Jean Goy et Robert Monnier', *Le Matin*, 18 November 1934, 1. On Hitler's interviews in the French press, see Dominique Pinsolle, 'L'art d' interviewer Hitler', *Le Monde diplomatique*, August 2017, 2, https://www.monde-diplomatique.fr/2017/08/PINSOLLE/57780 (accessed 9 April 2018).

13. Colas, *Les droites nationales en Lorraine*, 602.

14. In July 1934, the Communist and Socialist parties agreed to put aside their differences and form an antifascist coalition. A year later, on 14 July 1935, the Radical Party formally joined the 'Popular Front'.

15. Michel Winock, 'Les intellectuels dans le siècle', *Vingtième Siècle* 2, no. 1 (1984): 7.

16. Paul Faure, 'Prolétaires, unissez-vous!', *L'Humanité*, 7 February 1934, 1.

17. 'Le colonel de La Rocque se déclare "républicain" et affirme que les Croix de Feu ne sont pas armés', *L'Oeuvre*, 14 April 1934, 6.

18. Richard Millman, *La question juive en France entre les deux guerres. Ligues de droite et antisémitisme en France* (Paris: Armand Colin, 1992), 102–3.

19. Nobécourt, *Le Colonel de La Rocque*, 94–7.

20. Kalman, *The Extreme Right in Interwar France*, 47–8.

21. Kennedy, *Reconciling France against Democracy*, 38.

22. Milza, *Fascisme français*, 133–42; Passmore, *The Right in France*, 311; Millington, *From Victory to Vichy*, 121–4.

23. AN 451 AP 83, 'Croix de Feu et Briscards (section du Rhône)', *La Relève*, April 1931.

24. Rudaux, *Les Croix de Feu et le PSF*, 44.

25. Millman, *La question juive en France*, 104.

26. Kéchichian, *Les Croix-de-Feu*, 29. Kalman gives June 1930 as the date of the founding of the FFCF (Kalman, *The Extreme Right in Interwar France*, 161) while Campbell states that the group was founded in 1931 (*Political Belief in France*, 31–2). See also Laura Lee Downs, '"Each and every one of you must become a *chef*": Toward a social politics of working-class childhood on the extreme right in 1930s France', *Journal of Modern History* 81, no. 1 (2009): 1–44.

27. Nobécourt, *Le Colonel de La Rocque*, 201. La Rocque had been the driving force of the league since autumn 1931.

28. Sternhell, *Ni droite, ni gauche*, 85; Rudaux, *Les Croix de Feu et le PSF*, 34; 43.

29. Edith and Gilles de La Rocque, *La Rocque tel qu'il était*, 69–70.

30. Kennedy, *Reconciling France against Democracy*, 27–9; Soucy, *The Second Wave*, 106; Milza, *Fascisme français*, 134.

31. Shirer, *20th Century Journey*, 88; AN 451 AP 83, unnamed publication, 11 November 1935. Alexander Werth thought the lieutenant colonel 'dapper' and 'personally charming' in *The Destiny of France* (London: Hamish Hamilton, 1937), 353–4.

32. Passmore, *The Right in France*, 309–10.

33. Nobécourt, *Le Colonel de La Rocque*, 106–7.

34. Kennedy, *Reconciling France against Democracy*, 30.

35. Nobécourt, *Le Colonel de La Rocque*, 199–201; Kéchichian, *Les Croix-de-Feu*, 164; Rudaux, *Les Croix de Feu et le PSF*, 47–8.

36. Kennedy, *Reconciling France against Democracy*, 31; Soucy, *The Second Wave*, 107; Kéchichian, *Les Croix-de-Feu*, 165.

37. Or July 1931, according to Nobécourt, *Le Colonel de La Rocque*, 191–2.

38. Kennedy, *Reconciling France against Democracy*, 31; Kéchichian, *Les Croix-de-Feu*, 165–6. Passmore calls the *Dispos* a 'citizens' militia' in *From Liberalism to Fascism: The Right in a French Province, 1928–1939* (Cambridge: Cambridge University Press, 1997), 229–36.

39. Milza, *Fascisme français*, 135.

40. Nobécourt, *Le Colonel de La Rocque*, 289–91.

41. Jean Vavasseur-Desperriers, 'Des Croix de Feu au PSF', in *Le PSF*, 28n20.

42. Nobécourt, *Le Colonel de La Rocque*, 192.

43. La Rocque, 'Méthodes d'action', *Le Flambeau*, 1 November 1933, 1.

Notes

44. 'Contre les objecteurs de conscience', *Le Flambeau*, 1 December 1933, 2 and 5.

45. Edith and Gilles de La Rocque, *La Rocque tel qu'il était*, 95.

46. Campbell, *Political Belief in France*, 32; 49; Kevin Passmore, '"Planting the tricolor in the citadels of communism": Women's social action in the Croix de Feu and Parti Social Français', *Journal of Modern History* 71, no. 4 (1999), 814–51; Kalman, *The Extreme Right in Interwar France*, 123–5; Kennedy, *Reconciling France against Democracy*, 36; 40; 88; Kéchichian, *Les Croix-de-Feu*, 31; Nobécourt, *Le Colonel de La Rocque*, 288–9; Koos and Sarnoff, 'France', 182–5; Sarnoff, 'Interwar fascism and the franchise', 112–33; Della Sudda, 'Gender, fascism and the right-wing', 179–95.

47. Kéchichian, *Les Croix-de-Feu*, 167; Kennedy, *Reconciling France against Democracy*, 37; Kalman, *French Colonial Fascism*, 56.

48. Michel Abitbol, *The Jews of North Africa during the Second World War* (Detroit: Wayne State University Press, 1989), 35.

49. Kéchichian, *Les Croix-de-Feu*, 32–4; Kalman, *The Extreme Right in Interwar France*, 85.

50. Nobécourt, *Le Colonel de La Rocque*, 286; Soucy, *The Second Wave*, 111; Kéchichian, *Les Croix-de-Feu*, 201; Kennedy, *Reconciling France against Democracy*, 88.

51. Sternhell, *Ni droite, ni gauche*, 87.

52. Kennedy, *Reconciling France against Democracy*, 38–9.

53. Ibid., 45.

54. AN 451 AP 81, letter from La Rocque, Paris, 5 February 1934.

55. Kennedy, *Reconciling France against Democracy*, 45–6; Milza, *Fascisme français*, 140.

56. AN 451 AP 121, Jean-Henry Morin, 'Interview du Colonel de La Rocque sur les événements du 6 février', *Les Annales*, 2 March 1934, 237–8; Kennedy, *Reconciling France against Democracy*, 49.

57. Ibid., 46–7.

58. Richard Griffiths, *Marshal Pétain* (London: Constable, 1970), 190; Rudaux, *Les Croix de Feu et le PSF*, 80; 89; Laurent Kestel, *La conversion en politique. Doriot, le PPF et la question du fascisme français* (Paris: Raisons d'agir, 2012), 120; Edith and Gilles de La Rocque, *La Rocque tel qu'il était*, 130.

59. Soucy, *The Second Wave*, 112.

60. Kennedy, *Reconciling France against Democracy*, 49; Soucy, *The Second Wave*, 111.

61. Colas, *Les droits nationales en Lorraine*, 84–96.

62. Millington, *From Victory to Vichy*, 109–10; Nobécourt, *Le colonel de La Rocque*, 278–81.

63. See Lahousse, 'De la solidarité française au parti du faisceau français', 257–8.

64. Kennedy, *Reconciling France against Democracy*, 89; Milza, *Fascisme français*, 138; Passmore, *The Right in France*, 313; Goodliffe, *The Resurgence of the Radical Right in France*, 21. In 2006, former Croix de Feu leaguer Jean Boissonnat spoke of his father's membership of the league; his father considered himself a 'right-wing worker'; 'Mon père était Croix-de-Feu', *Vingtième Siècle* 90, no. 2 (2006): 29–31.

65. Kennedy, *Reconciling France against Democracy*, 88; Kéchichian, *Les Croix-de-Feu*, 201–2; Campbell, *Political Belief in France*, 51.

66. Colas, *Les droits nationales en Lorraine*, 157.

67. Kennedy, *Reconciling France against Democracy*, 90–6.

68. Campbell, *Political Belief in France*, 60.

69. Ibid., 149–57; 160.

70. Ibid., 61; Kennedy, *Reconciling France against Democracy*, 97–8.

71. Passmore, *The Right in France*, 313; Della Sudda, 'Gender, fascism and the right-wing', 194.

72. Vavasseur-Desperriers, 'Des Croix de Feu au PSF', 29.

73. Vergnon, *Un enfant est lynché*, 144–5.

74. Campbell, *Political Belief in France*, 53–4.

75. Passmore, '"Planting the tricolor in the citadels of communism"', 825–6.

76. Ibid., 846–7; Downs, '"Each and every one of you must become a *chef*"', 17–18.

77. Passmore, '"Planting the tricolor in the citadels of communism"', 849.

78. Ibid., 831–2.

79. Campbell, *Political Belief in France*, 58–65.

80. Ibid., 62; 64; Passmore, '"Planting the tricolor in the citadels of communism"', 835.

81. Downs, '"Each and every one of you must become a *chef*"', 6; 20; Laura Lee Downs, '"Nous plantions les trois couleurs": Action sociale féminine et recomposition des politiques de la droite française. Le mouvement Croix-de-feu et le Parti social français, 1934–1947', *Revue d'histoire moderne et contemporaine* 58, no. 3 (2011), 121. Kéchichian is wrong to describe the involvement of women in the Croix de Feu as an 'apolitical mobilisation' in *Les Croix-de-Feu*, 31.

82. Campbell, *Political Belief in France*, 34–7; 65.

83. de La Rocque, *Service Public*, 71–5.

84. Ibid., 209–10 [check]; Kéchichian, *The Croix-de-Feu*, 237; Kalman, *The Extreme Right in Interwar France*, 237.

85. La Rocque, *Public Service*, 70; 78.

86. Ibid., 164–5; Kevin Passmore, 'The Croix de Feu and fascism: A foreign thesis obstinately maintained', in *The Development of the Radical Right in France from Boulanger to Le Pen*, ed. Edward J. Arnold (Basingstoke: Palgrave, 2000), 106; Kéchichian, *The Croix-de-Feu*, 235–6.

87. Kennedy, *Reconciling France against Democracy*, 54–5.

88. Vavasseur-Desperriers, 'Des Croix de Feu au PSF', 23.

89. Colas, *Les droits nationales en Lorraine*, 151.

90. Werth, *The Destiny of France*, 244.

91. Irvine, *French Conservatism in Crisis*, 112–26.

92. Vavasseur-Desperriers, 'Des Croix de Feu au PSF', 23.

93. La Rocque, *Service Public*, 214.

94. Ibid., 216. See also Kalman, *The Extreme Right in Interwar France*, 42–3.

95. La Rocque, *Service Public*, 222.

96. Passmore, *The Right in France*, 315.

97. See for example the description in, 'Les Croix de Feu et les Volontaires Nationaux', *Le Flambeau*, 20 July 1935, 2. See Passmore, *From Liberalism to Fascism*, 229–36.

98. AN 451 AP 121, Morin, 'Interview du Colonel de La Rocque sur les événements du 6 février', 237–8.

Notes

99. AN 451 AP 81, 'Note aux présidents', 13 November 1933.

100. Kevin Passmore, 'Boy-scouting for grown-ups? Paramilitarism in the Croix de Feu and the Parti Social Français', *French Historical Studies* 19, no. 2 (1995), 527–7.

101. Soucy, *The Second Wave*, 168; Passmore, *The Right in France*, 315.

102. Campbell, *Political Belief in France*, 23–4; 180.

103. Passmore, 'The Croix de Feu and fascism', 103.

104. See for example the 'expedition' from Paris to Amiens reported here: APP BA 1901, 'Le Directeur des Renseignements Généraux et des Jeux à Monsieur le Préfet de Police', 26 January 1935.

105. Sean Kennedy, 'The Croix de Feu, the Parti Social Français and the politics of aviation, 1931–1939', *French Historical Studies* 23, no. 2 (2000): 381–2.

106. This number comes from Kéchichain, *Les Croix-de-Feu*, 199. La Rocque claimed that 150,000 followers attended the meeting (see 'Vers la victoire par la victoire', *Le Flambeau*, 5 October 1935, 1).

107. Kéchichain, *Les Croix-de-Feu*, 199; Passmore, *The Right in France*, 315–6.

108. 'Le Colonel Casimir de la Rocque a fait sa rentrée', *Le Populaire*, 23 September 1935, 2.

109. J.-M. Hermann, 'Le gouvernment était au courant de la mobilisation des Croix de Feu de dimanche', *Le Populaire*, 24 September 1935, 1–2.

110. La Rocque, *Public Service*, 207.

111. Passmore, *The Right in France*, 313. In *Fascisme français*, Milza uses the bourgeois membership of the league as a factor in his argument that the Croix de Feu did not present a threat to the Republic: 138.

112. La Rocque, *Public Service*, 160; Passmore, 'The Croix de Feu and fascism', 107.

113. Kalman, *The Extreme Right in Interwar France*, 204. On the broader topic see Greg Burgess, *Refuge in the Land of Liberty: France and its Refugees from the Revolution to the End of Asylum, 1787–1939* (Basingstoke: Palgrave, 2003); Michael R. Marrus and Robert O. Paxton, *Vichy France and the Jews* (New York: Basic Books, 1981); Ralph Schor, *L'opinion française et les etrangers en France, 1919–1939* (Paris: Publications de la Sorbonne, 1985); Vicki Caron, *Uneasy Asylum: France and the Jewish Refugee Crisis, 1933–1942* (Stanford: Stanford University Press, 1999).

114. Kennedy, *Reconciling France against Democracy*, 62.

115. Millman, *La question juive en France*, 107; 220–1; Richard Millman, 'Les croix-de-feu et l'antisémitisme', *Vingtième Siècle* 38, no. 1 (1993): 50.

116. Philippe Machefer, 'La Rocque et le problème antisémite', in *La France et la question juive*, ed. Georges Wellers, André Kaspi and Serge Klarsfeld (Pairs: Editions Sylvie Messinger, 1981), 96.

117. Kalman, *The Extreme Right in Interwar France*, 209; Millman, 'Les croix-de-feu', 53–4; Millman, *La question juive en France*, 107–10.

118. Kalman, *The Extreme Right in Interwar France*, 203; Millman, 'Les croix-de-feu', 53–4.

119. Sternhell, *Ni droite, ni gauche*, 89.

120. Kéchichian, *Les Croix-de-feu*, 95.

121. Samuel Huston Goodfellow, *Between the Swastika and the Cross of Lorraine: Fascisms in Interwar Alsace* (DeKalb: Northern Illinois University Press, 1998), 146.

122. Kalman, *The Extreme Right in Interwar France*, 204–8; Kennedy, *Reconciling France against Democracy*, 152–3.

123. Millman, *La question juive en France*, 111–3; 228.

124. Kéchichian, *Les Croix-de-Feu*, 94; Millman, *La question juive en France*, 223; Soucy, *The Second Wave*, 153; Kalman, *The Extreme Right in Interwar France*, 223.

125. 'Xénophobie?', *Le Flambeau*, 1 May 1932, quoted in Millman, 'Les croix-de-feu', 53.

126. Kéchichian, *Les Croix-de-Feu*, 95.

127. Kalman, *The Extreme Right in Interwar France*, 224; Kéchichian, *Les Croix-de-Feu*, 224.

128. Millman, *La question juive en France*, 192–5.

129. Ibid., 223.

130. Cantier, *L'Algérie sous le régime de Vichy*, 25.

131. Kalman, *French Colonial Fascism*, 56–9.

132. The figure of 30,000 comes from Kennedy, *Reconciling France against Democracy*, 88. Kalman gives the figure of 10,000 in August 1935 (*The Extreme Right in Interwar France*, 211), reaching 15,000 in 1936 (Kalman, *French Colonial Fascism*, 56). On the deputies elected with Croix de Feu support see Cantier, *L'Algérie sous le régime de Vichy*, 26n24.

133. Soucy, *The Second Wave*, 133.

134. Tal Bruttmann and Laurent Joly, *La France antijuive de 1936* (Paris: Editions des Equateurs, 2006), 180.

135. Kalman, *French Colonial Fascism*, 212; Roberts, 'Anti-Semitism and municipal government in interwar French colonial Algeria', 830–1.

136. Kalman, *French Colonial Fascism*, 216. Kéchichain disputes the involvement of the Croix de Feu in this violence, stating that Croix de Feu-Muslim relations *after* the riot led the left to read events backwards (Kéchichian, *Les Croix-de-Feu*, 234). Joshua Cole's excellent chapter on the violence does not resolve the question of the Croix de Feu's involvement: 'Anti-Semitism and the colonial situation in interwar Algeria', in *The French Colonial Mind: Violence, Military Encounters, and Colonialism*, ed. Martin Thomas (Lincoln: University of Nebraska Press, 2011), 77–112.

137. Kalman, *French Colonial Fascism*, 64–5.

138. Kalman, *The Extreme Right in Interwar France*, 217; Kalman, *French Colonial Fascism*, 58–60.

139. Campbell, *Political Belief in France*, 160–1.

140. Aomar Boum, 'Partners against anti-Semitism: Muslims and Jews respond to Nazism in French North African colonies, 1936–1940', *Journal of North African Studies* 19, no. 4 (2014): 557.

141. Cantier, *L'Algérie sous the régime de Vichy*, 230.

142. Campbell, *Political Belief in France*, 157; Kéchichian, *Les Croix-de-Feu*, 232. On Croix de Feu relations with Muslims, see Samuel Kalman, 'Fascism and algérianité: The Croix de Feu and the indigenous question in 1930s Algeria', in *The French Colonial Mind: Violence, Military Encounters, and Colonialism*, 112–40.

143. Campbell, *Political Belief in France*, 12; 158–60; 167; Kalman, *French Colonial Fascism*, 65–8.

144. Kéchichian, *Les Croix-de-Feu*, 232; Campbell, *Political Belief in France*, 158–9; Kalman, *French Colonial Fascism*, 65–9.

145. Campbell, *Political Belief in France*, 157–8.

146. Kalman, *French Colonial Fascism*, 56–76; Campbell, *Political Belief in France*, 158–60.

147. Campbell, *Political Belief in France*, 55.

148. Kéchichian, *Les Croix-de-Feu*, 97.

149. Winock, *Nationalisme, antisémitisme et fascisme en France*, 295–300.

150. Kalman, *The Extreme Right in Interwar France*, 228–9.

151. 'Le colonel de La Rocque se déclare 'républicain' et affirme que les Croix de Feu ne sont pas armés', *L'Oeuvre*, 14 April 1934, 6.

152. Kennedy, *Reconciling France against Democracy*, 112; Kéchichian, *Les Croix-de-Feu*, 243; Nobécourt, *Le Colonel de La Rocque*, 205.

153. Kennedy, *Reconciling France against Democracy*, 113; Alcalde, *War Veterans and Fascism*, 223.

154. Kennedy, *Reconciling France against Democracy*, 118; Soucy, *The Second Wave*, 138; Kéchichian, *Les Croix-de-Feu*, 243.

155. Michel Winock, 'En lisant Robert Soucy: Sur La Rocque et les Croix-de-feu', *Vingtième Siècle* 95, no. 3 (2007): 238; Nobécourt, *Le Colonel de La Rocque*, 176.

156. Ibid., 314–16.

157. Anne Dulphy and Christine Manigand, 'Le PSF et les question internationales', in *Le PSF*, 123–4.

158. Emmanuel Braganca, *La crise allemande du roman français* (Oxford: Peter Lang, 2012), 3–9.

159. Kennedy, *Reconciling France against Democracy*, 75.

160. Ibid., 65; Soucy, *The Second Wave*, 141.

161. Nobécourt, *Le Colonel de La Rocque*, 317–20; Kennedy, *Reconciling France against Democracy*, 60.

162. Winock, 'En lisant Robert Soucy', 240.

163. Nobécourt, *Le Colonel de La Rocque*, 176.

164. Soucy, 'French press reactions to Hitler's first two years in power', 21–38; Kestel, 'Were French elites allergic to fascism?', 195–210.

165. Marcel Cachin, 'COMPLOT contre la sûrete du peuple', *L'Humanité*, 18 June 1935, 1.

166. See for example 'La suspension du maire de Villepinte', *Le Populaire*, 9 October 1935, 2; Marcel Cachin, 'Les mineurs d'Hénin-Liétard décident le grève générale pour lundi', *L'Humanité*, 13 April 1934, 1.

167. 'Les grandes manoeuvres de guerre civile du colonel de la Rocque', *L'Humanité*, 7 Janaury 1935, 1–2; Marcel Cachin, 'COMPLOT contre la sûreté du peuple', *L'Humanité*, 18 June 1935, 1.

168. Marcel Cachin, 'Désarmement des ligues fascistes', *L'Humanité*, 10 January 1935, 1.

169. 'La réunion des Croix de Feu à Villepinte était une démonstration d'intimidation soigneusement organisée', *Le Populaire*, 8 October 1935, 2.

170. Paul Vaillant-Couturier, 'Laissera-t-on longtemps le colonel comte de La Rocque faire tirer sur des Français?', *L'Humanité*, 8 October 1935, 1.

171. Paul Vaillant-Couturier, 'Le nouveau 6 fevrier "est fin prêt"', *L'Humanité*, 12 October 1935, 1.

172. Paul Vaillant-Couturier, 'A Ormesson, des provocateurs fascists tentent un coup de main sur la mairie rouge et, surprise, tirent', *L'Humanité*, 15 August 1935, 1.

173. 'L'auto-defense de masse contre le fascisme', *L'Humanité*, 24 October 1934, 4.

174. Pierre Taittinger, 'Guerre civile et assassinat', *Le National*, 16 June 1934, 1; Philippe Henriot, 'Le réveillon chez les francs-macons', *Je suis partout*, 23 June 1934, 1–2.

175. Dorsay, 'Où veut aller "l'homme qui sourit"', *Je suis partout*, 9 June 1934, 1.

176. See AN F7 13241 and AN BB18 2959 for the police investigation into this violence.

177. See AN F7 14795 and AN BB18 2960 for the police investigation into this violence.

178. Kéchichian, *Les Croix-de-Feu*, 217–8. See AN BB18 2959 for the police investigation into this violence.

179. Marcel Cachin, 'Les hitlériens français saccagent la Maison du Peuple d'Argenteuil et la Maison des Syndicats de Levallois', *L'Humanité*, 6 September 1935, 1.

180. Austin, 'The conservative right and the far right in France', 180.

181. On this incident see Danielle Tartakowsky, 'Les Croix de feu à Villepinte, octobre 1935', in *Banlieue rouge, 1920–1960: Années Thorez, années Gabin: archétype du populaire, banc d'essai des modernités*, ed. Annie Fourcault (Paris: Editions Autrement, 1992), 68–80.

182. 'Un interview du colonel de La Rocque', *Gringoire*, 11 October 1935, 2.

183. 'Entre eux et nous c'est une question de force', *Gringoire*, 22 November 1935, 1–2.

184. Kéchichian, *Les Croix-de-Feu*, 206–7.

185. Kennedy, *Reconciling France against Democracy*, 68–73. La Rocque, for example, advised members against taking part in any commemoration of the *six février* in 1935 lest violence from the left work to the detriment of the Croix de Feu (AN 451 AP 81, 'Note au sujet du 6 Février 1935').

186. Campbell, *Political Belief in France*, 36.

187. AN 451 AP 82, untitled letter, written by La Rocque, 10 June 1933.

188. Quoted in William D. Irvine, 'Fascism in France and the strange case of the Croix de Feu', *Journal of Modern History* 63, no. 2 (1991): 276. La Rocque made a similar point in the *Gazette de Lausanne* in 1934/35: 'We hate violence. But, when the existence of our country is at stake, we are not afraid of violent attacks: our organisation and our ardour would not fail to reduce them to nothing' (AN 451 AP 121).

189. Marcel Cachin, 'Il y aura du sport', *L'Humanité*, 17 June 1935, 1.

190. Kéchichain, *Les Croix-de-Feu*, 205.

191. Austin, 'The conservative right and the far right in France', 181.

192. Kéchichian, *Les Croix-de-Feu*, 212.

193. *Vu*, 30 November 1935.

194. Edouard Daladier, *Prison Journal, 1940–1945* (Boulder; Oxford: Westview Press, 1995), 247–8.

195. Serge Berstein, *Histoire du Parti radical. Vol. 2: Crise du radicalisme, 1926–1939* (Paris: Presses de Sciences-Po), 392–5.

196. Weber, *The Hollow Years*, 149; AN BB18 2959, 'Le Procurer Général près la Cour d'Appel de Chambéry à Monsieur le Garde des Sceaux', 5 July 1935.

197. See for example APP BA 1901, untitled report, 10 December 1935.

198. Campbell, *Political Belief in France*, 34–7.

199. Jenkins, 'The right-wing leagues', 1372–5.

200. Kennedy, *Reconciling France against Democracy*, 72; Kechichian, *Les Croix-de-Feu*, 299–303.

201. Weber, *Action Française*, 369.

202. Soucy, *The Second Wave*, 114. The PSF counted 3,000 mayors in municipalities up and down the country (Nobécourt, *Le Colonel de La Rocque*, 386) and had 17 sections abroad (Rudaux, *Les Croix de Feu et le PSF*, 222).

Chapter 4

1. Werth, *The Destiny of France*, 367.

2. Jean Delage, 'Un long exposé de M. Jacques Doriot sur la politique intérieure et extérieure', *L'Echo de Paris*, 10 November 1936, 3.

3. 'Vigoureuse manifestation antihitlérienne', *L'Humanité*, 10 November 1936, 3.

4. APP BA 1946, 'Au sujet d'incidents sur la voie publique survenus le 9.11.1936 à Saint-Denis, à l'occasion d'une réunion du PPF'.

5. Milza, *Fascisme Français*, 225.

6. Upon its founding, six out of the seven party executives were former communists. Jean-Paul Brunet, *Jacques Doriot. Du communisme au fascisme* (Balland, 1986), 224; Soucy, *The Second Wave*, 230–1.

7. Philippe Burrin, *La Dérive fasciste. Doriot, Déat, Bergery, 1933–1945* (Paris: Seuil, 1986), 280.

8. Colas, *Les droits nationales en Lorraine*, 179–80.

9. Nobécourt, *Le Colonel de La Rocque*, 442–3; Werth, *The Destiny of France*, 256–357.

10. Edith and Gilles de La Rocque, *La Rocque tel qu'il était*, 135.

11. Philippe Bourdrel, *La Cagoule. Histoire d'une société secrète du Front populaire à la Ve République* (Paris: Albin Michel, 1992), 55.

12. Edith and Gilles de La Rocque, *La Rocque tel qu'il était*, 135–7.

13. Julian Jackson, *The Popular Front in France: Defending Democracy, 1934–1938* (Cambridge: Cambridge University Press, 1990), 85.

14. Bourdrel, *La Cagoule*, 165–8.

15. Cantier, *L'Algérie sous le régime de Vichy*, 28.

16. Weber, *The Hollow Years*, 259–60.

17. Vergnon, *Un enfant est lynché*, 156.

18. Jean-Paul Thomas, 'Les effectifs du Parti social français', *Vingtième Siècle* 62, no. 1 (1999): 75; Kennedy, *Reconciling France against Democracy*, 194–7; Irvine, 'Fascism in France', 280–4; David Bensoussan, 'La structuration et la géographie d'un parti de masse de droite: le PSF (1936–1940), in *Le PSF*, 37–54.

19. Ibid., 43–4.

20. Kalman, *French Colonial Fascism*, 154; Thomas, 'Les effectifs du Parti social français', 65.

21. Kennedy, *Reconciling France against Democracy*, 194–7; Irvine, 'Fascism in France', 280–1; 284; Passmore, *From Liberalism to Fascism*, 271–2; Passmore, *The Right in France*, 332–3.

22. Kennedy, *Reconciling France against Democracy*, 130; 189.

23. Colas, *Les droites nationales en Lorraine*, 242.

24. Philippe Machefer, 'L'Union des droits, le PSF et le Front de la liberté, 1936–1937', *Revue d'histoire moderne et contemporaine* 17, no. 1 (1970): 116; 118n3 and n4.

25. Soucy, *The Second Wave*, 128–32; Nobécourt, *Le Colonel de La Rocque*, 657–8; Passmore, *From Liberalism to Fascism*, 274–87; Austin, 'The conservative right and the far right in France', 184.

26. Check source, p. 25.

27. J Cantier, *L'Algérie sous le régime de Vichy*, 29.

28. Kennedy, *Reconciling France against Democracy*, 150–1. Colas claims that the PSF's favourable attitude to some Radicals was evidence of the party's move to the centre in *Les droites nationales en Lorraine*, 539–40.

29. Kennedy, *Reconciling France against Democracy*, 189; 194–7; Soucy, *The Second Wave*, 131; 134; Passmore, *The Right in France*, 333.

30. Thomas, 'Les effectifs du Parti social français', 64–5; Nobécourt, *Le Colonel de La Rocque*, 657; Kennedy, *Reconciling France against Democracy*, 212–5.

31. Rudaux, *Les Croix de Feu et le PSF*, 188–92; 217–8.

32. Soucy, *The Second Wave*, 114; Rudaux, *Les Croix de Feu et le PSF*, 185–7.

33. Kennedy, *Reconciling France against Democracy*, 123–4.

34. See APP BA 1863 for extensive police reports on the violence.

35. Soucy, *The Second Wave*, 144.

36. Ibid., 117; Nobécourt, *Le Colonel de La Rocque*, 486–8.

37. Rudaux, *Les Croix de Feu et le PSF*, 199–200; 217–18.

38. Maurras gave La Rocque the nickname 'Casimir'. It was subsequently taken up by the communists: Rudaux, *Les Croix de Feu et le PSF*, 200.

39. Passmore, *From Liberalism to Fascism*, 295; Passmore, *The Right in France*, 329.

40. Passmore, 'Boy-scouting for grown-ups?', 540; Passmore, *From Liberalism to Fascism*, 261–3. On the EVPs see APP BA1952, 'Réunion des Equipes Volantes de Propagande de l'Ile de France du Parti Social Français', 9 July 1937.

41. AN BB18 3062, 'Le Directeur de la Police d'Etat à Monsieur le Procureur de la République', 18 March 1937.

42. For example, APP BA 1952, untitled report, twenty-two hours thirty minutes, 5 September 1936; untitled report, 12 December 1936; AN 451 AP 129, 'Les odieuses agressions de Fives', *Le Flambeau*, 8 May 1938.

43. Rudaux, *Les Croix de Feu et le PSF*, 156n1.

44. Vergnon, *Un enfant est lynché*, 234.

45. La Rocque, 'Du nouveau', *Le Flambeau*, 10 October 1936, 1.

46. AN 451 AP 107, 'Au Parti Social Français', 2 October 1936.

47. APP BA 1863, untitled report, 4 October 1936; '20.000 agents et gardes ont réussi à éviter tout incident grave au Parc des Princes', *Le Journal* , 5 October 1936; Werth, *The Destiny of France*, 361–4.

48. AN BB18 3072, 'Le Procureur de la République à Monsieur le Procureur Général près la Cour d'Appel à Nancy', 28 February 1937; AN BB18 3072, 'Le Procureur Général près la

Cour d'Appel de Nancy à Monsieur le Garde des Sceaux, Ministre de la Justice', 15 March 1937.

49. Millington, *Fighting for France*, 140–50.

50. APP BA 1866, 'Le Commissaire de Police André Roches, attaché à la Direction de la Police Judiciaire à Monsieur le Directeur de la Police Judiciaire', Paris, 3 April 1937; Nobécourt, *Le Colonel de La Rocque*, 509–14; Kennedy, *Reconciling France against Democracy*, 128–9; Général André Chérasse, *La hurle. La nuit sanglante de Clichy 16–17 mars 1937* (Editions Pygmalion/Gérard Watelet, 1983).

51. Jean-Maris Desgranges, *Journal d'un prêtre-député* (Paris: La Palatine, 1960), 106.

52. Nobécourt, *Le Colonel de La Rocque*, 656–60; Jean-Paul Thomas, 'Les jeunes dans le mouvements Croix de feu-PSF', *Recherches contemporaines* 6 (2000–2001): 189–97.

53. Irvine, 'Fascism in France', 281.

54. Vavasseur-Desperriers, 'Des Croix de Feu au PSF', 33.

55. The female membership of the PSF dwarfed that of other political parties. The communist Union des jeunes filles de France had 20,000 members in 1935. The Socialist Party had 2,800 women members, amounting to 3 per cent of the overall membership. The Radical Party had only 150 women members. Sabrina Tricaud, 'Les femmes et la famille dans la vision du PSF', in *Le PSF*, 206; 206n2.

56. Campbell, *Political Belief in France*, 75; Kennedy, *Reconciling France against Democracy*, 205–6; Tricaud, 'Les femmes et la famille dans la vision du PSF', 211.

57. Tricaud, 'Les femmes et la famille dans la vision du PSF', 207–8.

58. Campbell, *Political Belief in France*, 75.

59. Ibid., 75; Passmore, '"Planting the tricolor in the citadels of communism"', 824.

60. Campbell, *Political Belief in France*, 83; Passmore, '"Planting the tricolor in the citadels of communism"', 828; 836–8; Downs, '"Each and every one of you must become a *chef*"', 6–7.

61. Thomas, 'Les effectifs du Parti social français', 66; Thomas, 'Le Parti social français (PSF), obstacle à la radicalization des droites. Contribution historique à une réflexion sur les droites, la radicalité et les cultures politiques françaises', in *A droite de la droite. Droites radicales en France et en Grande-Bretagne au XXe siècle*, ed. Philippe Vervaecke (Lille, Presses universitaires du Septentrion, 2012), 249.

62. Passmore, *From Liberalism to Fascism*, 264–5.

63. Ibid., 288.

64. Laura Downs's terms cited in Passmore, *The Right in France*, 331.

65. Passmore, *From Liberalism to Fascism*, 264; Kennedy, *Reconciling France against Democracy*, 190; 203–22; Passmore, '"Planting the tricolor in the citadels of communism"', 838; Kennedy, *Reconciling France against Democracy*, 182; Kalman, *The Extreme Right in Interwar France*, 223; 229.

66. Passmore, *The Right in France*, 331: Campbell, *Political Belief in France*, 81; Kennedy, *Reconciling France against Democracy*, 203–12; Kalman, *The Extreme Right in Interwar France*, 162–4.

67. Campbell, *Political Belief in France*, 79.

68. Chris Millington, 'Immigrants and undesirables: "Terrorism" and the "terrorist" in 1930s France', *Critical Studies on Terrorism* 12, no. 1 (2019): 40–59.

69. Kennedy, *Reconciling France against Democracy*, 180–1; Kalman, *The Extreme Right in Interwar France*, 25; Millman, 'Les croix-de-feu et l'antisémitisme', 57.

70. Vallat was third to respond to the new Prime Minister after Fernand Laurent, Paul Reynaud and Jean La Cour Grandmaison.

71. Bruttmann and Joly, *La France antijuive de 1936*, 45–95.

72. Ibid., 127–34.

73. Emmanuel Debono and Jean-Paul Thomas, 'Le PSF et la question d'antisémitisme', in *Le PSF*, 227.

74. Millman, 'Les croix-de-feu et l'antisémitisme', 57–9.

75. Millman, *La question juive en France*, 262–3; Debono and Thomas, 'Le PSF et la question d'antisémitisme', 224–30.

76. Kalman, *French Colonial Fascism*, 157; Debono and Thomas, 'Le PSF et la question d'antisémitisme', 221–4.

77. Debono and Thomas, 'Le PSF et la question d'antisémitisme', 220.

78. Kestel, *La conversion en politique*, 183–4.

79. Dónal Hassett, 'Proud *colons*, proud Frenchmen: settler colonialism and the extreme right in interwar Algeria', *Settler Colonial Studies* 8, no. 2 (2017): 10.

80. Machefer, 'La Rocque et le problème antisémite', 291.

81. Soucy, *The Second Wave*, 156–7; Millman, 'Les croix-de-feu et l'antisémitisme', 59; Irvine, 'Fascism in France', 291–3.

82. Millman, 'Les croix-de-feu et l'antisémitisme', 59–60.

83. Debono and Thomas, 'Le PSF et la question d'antisémitisme', 223–4.

84. Abitbol, *The Jews of North Africa*, 26.

85. Philippe Machefer, 'Autour du problème algérien en 1936–38: La doctrine algérienne du PSF. Le PSF et le projet Blum-Viollette', *Revue d'histoire moderne et contemporaine* 10, no. 2 (1963): 149.

86. Kennedy, *Reconciling France against Democracy*, 153; Kalman, *French Colonial Fascism*, 168–1; Machefer, 'Autour du problème algérien', 148–9.

87. Kalman, *French Colonial Fascism*, 184–5.

88. Ibid., 166–8.

89. Irvine, 'Fascism in France', 277.

90. Kalman, *The Extreme Right in Interwar France*, 64–5.

91. Soucy cites only several instances of the colonel's strong rhetoric and the fact that several meetings during 1937 resembled those of the Croix de Feu: *The Second Wave*, 174–5.

92. See for example AN 451 AP 126, 'Les apirations de l'étudiant. L'esprit du Parti Social Français', n.d.; Passmore, 'Boy-scouting for grown-us?', 553; Kalman, *The Extreme Right in Interwar France*, 39–40; Passmore, *From Liberalism to Fascism*, 265.

93. See also *Parti Social Français. Une mystique. Un programme* (Paris, n.d.).

94. Passmore, *The Right in France*, 330–1; Kennedy, *Reconciling France against Democracy*, 172–7.

95. Campbell, *Political Belief in France*, 65; Kalman, *The Extreme Right in Interwar France*, 46; Passmore, *The Right in France*, 334; Passmore, '"Planting the tricolor in the citadels of communism"', 822.

96. Winock, *Nationalisme, antisémitisme et fascisme en France*, 255–6; 287.

97. Kalman, *The Extreme Right in Interwar France*, 49–50.

98. Kennedy, *Reconciling France against Democracy*, 152.

99. Kalman, *The Extreme Right in Interwar France*, 52–8; Passmore, *The Right in France*, 334.

100. Winock, *Nationalisme, antisémitisme et fascisme en France*, 291.

101. Kennedy, *Reconciling France against Democracy*, 223.

102. Passmore, *From Liberalism to Fascism*, 260.

103. Kennedy, *Reconciling France against Democracy*, 121; 148; Passmore, *The Right in France*, 335; Passmore, *From Liberalism to Fascism*, 260; 266.

104. Winock, *Nationalisme, antisémitisme et fascisme en France*, 291–2. Jean Félix de Bujadoux offers a relatively benign analysis of the PSF's reform programme in his essay, 'Le PSF et la réforme de l'Etat', in *Le PSF*, 87–105.

105. Winock, *Nationalisme, antisémitisme et fascisme en France*, 209.

106. Ibid., 315.

107. See for example Bujadoux, 'Le PSF et la réforme de l'Etat', 105.

108. Passmore, *The Right in France*, 335.

109. Morin, 'La gauche et le PSF, du Front populaire à la guerre', 109.

110. APP BA 186, 'Le gouvernement est décidé à mettre fin à l'agitation des factieux', *Le Populaire*, 6 October 1936; 'A Londres et à Paris', *Le Populaire*, 6 October 1936.

111. Soucy, *The Second Wave*, 138–9.

112. Kennedy, *Reconciling France against Democracy*, 187. See Yves-Marie Hilaire, '1900–1945. L'ancrage des idéologies', in *Histoire des droites en France*, I, 519–59.

113. Dulphy and Manigand, 'Le PSF et les questions internationales', in *Le PSF*, 125–6.

114. Alcalde, *War Veterans and Fascism*, 267.

115. Dulphy and Manigand, 'Le PSF et les questions internationales', in *Le PSF*, 127–8.

116. António Costa Pinto, 'Single parties and political decision-making in Fascist-era dictatorships', *Contemporary European History* 11, no. 3 (2002): 431; David Birmingham, *A Concise History of Portugal* (Cambridge: Cambridge University Press, 2007), 161–70.

117. Filipe Ribeiro de Meneses, *Salazar: A Political Biography* (New York: Enigma Books, 2009), 180.

118. On this subject Olivier Dard and Ana Isabel Sardinha-Desvignes, *Célébrer Salazar en France 1930–1974. Du philosalazarisme au salazarisme Français* (Brussels: Pete Lang, 2018).

119. Meneses, *Salazar: A Political Biography*, 175–6; quotation from Emile Schreiber, *Le Portugal de Salazar* (Paris: Editiosn Denoël, 1938), 13; Massis, *Chefs*, 84–137.

120. Dard and Sardinha-Desvignes, *Célébrer Salazar en France*, 70–2.

121. Meneses, *Salazar: A Political Biography*, 175.

122. Schreiber, *Le Portugal de Salazar*, 22; 30.

123. Meneses, *Salazar: A Political* Biography, 84.

124. Douglas L. Wheeler, *Historical Dictionary of Portugal* (Metuchen, NJ and London: The Scarecrow Press, Inc., 1993), 92–4; Weber, *L'Action Française*, 484–6; H. R. Martins, 'Portugal', in *European Fascism*, ed. SJ Woolf (London and Edinburgh: Morrison & Gibb Ltd, 1968), 302–3.

125. Antonio Ferro, *Salazar, le Portugal et son Chef* (Paris: Editions Bernard Grasset, 1934), 147–51.

126. The speech can be read in full in English here: Antonio de Oliveira Salazar, *Doctrine and Action: Internal and Foreign Policy of the New Portugal, 1928–1939*, trans. by Robert Edgar Broughton (London: Faber and Faber, 1939), 225–9. See also Ferro, *Salazar, le Portugal et son Chef*, 149.

127. La Rocque, *Public Service*, 205.

128. Rémond, *La Droite en France* [1963 edition], 214.

129. Kéchichian, *Les Croix-de-feu*, 10; 243–5.

130. Silva Barbosa Correia, 'The veterans' movement and First World War memory in Portugal (1918–33): Between the Republic and dictatorship', *European Review of History/Revue européenne d'histoire* 19, no. 4 (2012): 531–51.

131. Richard Griffiths, 'Fascist or Conservative?' 148.

132. Meneses, *Salazar: A Political Biography*, 127; António Costa Pinto, '"Chaos" and "Order": Preto, Salazar and charismatic appeal in inter-war Portugal', *Totalitarian Movements and Political Religions* 7, no. 2 (2006): 203–14; António Costa Pinto, 'The radical right and the military dictatorship in Portugal: The National May 28 League (1928–1933)', *Luso-Brazailian Review* 23, no. 1 (1986): 1–15.

133. António Costa Pinto, 'Elites, single parties and political decision-making in Fascist-era dictatorships', *Contemporary European History* 11, no. 3 (2002): 452.

134. Griffiths, 'Fascist or Conservative?', 149.

135. Pinto, 'Elites, single parties and political decision-making', 429–54; Luís Nuno Rodrigues, 'The creation of the Portuguese Legion in 1936', *Luso-Brazilian Review* 34, no. 2 (1997): 91–107; Meneses, *Salazar: A Political Biography*, 141–5; Luis Reis Torgal, 'L'Etat Nouveau portugais: esquisse d'interprétation', *Pôle Sud* 22 (2005): 39–48; Pinto, 'Salazar's *Estado Novo*', 313–19.

136. David Corkill and José Carlos Pina Almeida, 'Commemoration and propaganda in Salazar's Portugal: The *Mundo Português* exposition of 1940', *Journal of Contemporary History* 44, no. 3 (2009): 391; Léonard Yves, 'Le Portugal et ses "sentinelles de pierre". L'exposition du monde portugais en 1940', *Vingtième Siècle* 62, no. 1 (1999): 27–37.

137. Corkill and Almeida, 'Commemoration and propaganda in Salazar's Portugal', 381–99.

138. Griffiths, 'Fascist or Conservative?', 142.

139. Soucy, *The Second Wave*, 72; Rémond, *La Droite en France*, [1963 edition], 215.

140. Kennedy, *Reconciling France against Democracy*, 187 and 250; Dard and Sardinha-Desvignes, *Célébrer Salazar en France*, 146–57.

141. Soucy, *The Second Wave*, 139.

142. Werth, *The Destiny of France*, 366.

143. Brunet, *Jacques Doriot*, 17–9.

144. Georges Loustaunau-Lacau, *Mémoires d'un Français rebelle* (Paris: Laffont, 1948), 121.

145. Brunet, *Jacques Doriot*, 35. On p. 126, Brunet describes Doriot's 'magnetism' and 'dynamism'; he was a 'fighter' and a 'leader of men'.

146. Ory, *Les collaborateurs*, 102.

147. Brunet, *Jacques Doriot*, 9.

148. Ibid., 47.

149. Ibid., 65.

150. Burrin, *La Dérive fasciste*, 161; Brunet, *Jacques Doriot*, 127.

151. Brunet, *Jacques Doriot*, 150–1; Burrin, *La Dérive fasciste*, 168–9.

152. Burrin, *La Dérive fasciste*, 170.

153. Soucy, *The Second Wave*, 210–11; Brunet, *Jacques Doriot*, 14–15. Burrin gives date of dismissal as 27 July: *La Dérive fasciste*, 163–4; 174–5.

154. Burrin, *La Dérive fasciste*, 185; Milza, 'L'ultra-droite des années trente', 179.

155. Werth, *The Destiny of France*, 365.

156. Burrin, *La Dérive fasciste*, 184–6.

157. Brunet, *Jacques Doriot*, 224; Soucy, *The Second Wave*, 230–1.

158. Burrin, *La Dérive fasciste*, 280.

159. Soucy, *The Second Wave*, 211.

160. Ibid., 248–9; 252–3; 268–79.

161. Ibid., 269.

162. Ibid., 219.

163. AN F7 14817, 'Communication téléphonique reçue 10h10 de M. Delsahut, Commissaire de police mobile S/Chef à la 6e Brigade Régionale à Clermont-Ferrand, Paris', 17 December 1936.

164. Soucy, *The Second Wave*, 220.

165. Geoffrey Warner, 'France', in *European Fascism*, 264.

166. Brunet, *Jacques Doriot*, 220; Soucy, *The Second Wave*, 220; 234.

167. Soucy, *The Second Wave*, 224; Brunet, *Jacques Doriot*, 203; 235.

168. Brunet, *Jacques Doriot*, 236; Kestel, *La Conversion en politique*, 192–3.

169. Kestel, *La Conversion en politique*, 193–4.

170. Several estimates of the party's size can be found in the historiography. See Soucy, *The Second Wave*, 242; Winock, *Nationalisme, antisémitisme et fascisme en France*, 250; Milza, 'L'ultra-droite des années trente', 180; Brunet, *Jacques Doriot*, 229; Burrin, *La Dérive fasciste*, 286.

171. Milza, 'L'ultra-droite des années trente', 180; Brunet, *Jacques Doriot*, 230.

172. Brunet, *Jacques Doriot*, 214–16; 250.

173. Soucy, *The Second Wave*, 242; Kestel, *La Conversion en politique*, 184–7.

174. Cantier, *L'Algérie sous the régime de Vichy*, 230.

175. Brunet, *Jacques Doriot*, 232.

176. Soucy, *The Second Wave*, 237; Winock, *Natioanlisme, antisémitisme et fascisme en France*, 254.

177. Kevin Passmore, 'Class, gender and populism: The Parti Populaire Français in Lyon, 1936–40', in *The Right in France, 1789–1997*, ed. Nicholas Atkin and Frank Tallett (London; New York: IB Tauris, 1998), 198–202.

178. Paul Jankowski, *Communism and Collaboration: Simon Sabiani and Politics in Marseille, 1919–1944* (New Haven: Yale University Press, 1989), 60; 95; Kevin Passmore, 'The French

Third Republic: Stalemate society or the cradle of fascism?', *French History* 7, no. 4 (1993): 444; Kestel, *La Conversion en politique*, 199–200.

179. Goodliffe, *The Resurgence of the Radical Right in France*, 21.

180. Brunet, *Jacques Doriot*, 269–73.

181. Ibid., 290; Burrin, *La Dérive fasciste*, 285; Thomas, 'Le Parti social français', 261.

182. Winock, *Nationalisme, antisémitisme et fascisme en France*, 256.

183. Kestel, *La Conversion en politique*, 162–74.

184. Winock, *Nationalisme, antisémitisme et fascisme en France*, 256.

185. Colas, *Les droites nationales en Lorraine*, 247.

186. Kestel, *La Conversion en politique*, 167–8.

187. APP BA 1952, 'Le Préfet de l'Aube, à Monsieur le Ministre de l'Intérieur', Troyes, 25 November 1936.

188. Kestel, *La Conversion en politique*, 168–9.

189. Ibid., 174.

190. Ibid., 142–4.

191. Ibid., 153–5.

192. Ibid., 161.

193. Brunet, *Jacques Doriot*, 245.

194. Ibid., 275–80; Burrin, *La Dérive fasciste*, 286.

195. Kestel, *La Conversion en politique*, 160–1; 175; Vergnon, *Un enfant est lynché*, 234.

196. Werth, *The Destiny of France*, 368.

197. Cantier, *L'Algérie sous le régime de Vichy*, 29.

198. Kestel, *La Conversion en politique*, 188–9.

199. Ibid., 181; Burrin, *La Dérive fasciste*, 296.

200. Kestel, *La Conversion en politique*, 182–3.

201. Brunet, *Jacques Doriot*, 263. Kestel, *La Conversion en politique*, 183–4.

202. Hassett, 'Proud *colons*, proud Frenchmen', 13–4; Cantier, *L'Algérie sous le régime de Vichy*, 222–3.

203. Reproduced in Brunet, *Jacques Doriot*, 249.

204. Ibid., 250–2; Soucy, *The Second Wave*, 217–33; Winock, *Nationalisme, antisémitisme et fascisme en France*, 250.

205. Jean-Pierre Luce, 'Et maintenant quelque chose grandit!', *L'Emancipation nationale*, 14 November 1937, 2.

206. Brunet, *Jacques Doriot*, 208.

207. Soucy, *The Second Wave*, 232; Winock, *Nationalisme, antisémitisme et fascisme en France*, 250.

208. Brunet, *Jacques Doriot*, 258–9; Burrin, *La Dérive fasciste*, 281.

209. Ibid., 292–5.

210. Soucy, *The Second Wave*, 272–4.

211. Winock, *Nationalisme, antisémitisme et fascisme en France*, 254.

Notes

212. Burrin, *La Dérive fasciste*, 306–7.

213. Brunet, *Jacques Doriot*, 287

214. Ibid., 291–4; Kestel, *La Conversion en politique*, 300.

215. Burrin, *La Dérive fasciste*, 303.

216. Kestel, *La Conversion en politique*, 214–25.

217. Brunet, *Jacques Doriot*, 295–8; Soucy, *The Second Wave*, 242–3; Winock, *Nationalisme, antisémitisme et fascisme en France*, 401; 419.

218. Soucy, *The Second Wave*, 119.

219. Burrin, *La Dérive fasciste*, 325.

220. Kennedy, *Reconciling France against Democracy*, 168–72.

221. Ibid., 160–5.

222. Ibid., 127.

223. Ibid., 151; Passmore, *The Right in France*, 334–5.

224. Ibid., 330; 335; Kennedy, *Reconciling France against Democracy*, 200–1.

225. Brunet, *Jacques Doriot*, 299.

226. Kestel, *La Conversion en politique*, 7–10.

227. Ibid., 192.

Chapter 5

1. AN F7 14673, 'Procès-verbal. André Lebis', 20 January 1938. Jean Belin describes a similar initiation ceremony in Belin, *My Work at the Sûreté*, 196. See also Bourdrel, *La Cagoule*, 64–5; and J.-R. Tournoux, *L'Histoire secrète* (Paris: Plon, 1962), 39–43.

2. The OSARN was also known as the Comité Secrèt d'Action Révolutionnaire (CSAR).

3. AN BB18 3061/3, 'Tribunal de première instance de la Seine. Procès-verbal d'interrogatoire et de confrontation', n.d.

4. AN BB18 3061/2, 'Tribunal de Première Instance du Département de la Seine', 4 June 1938.

5. Valerie Deacon, *The Extreme Right in the French Resistance: Members of the Cagoule and the Corvignolles in the Second World War* (Baton Rouge: Louisiana State University Press, 2016), 49–50; Belin, *My Work at the Sûreté*, 199–201; Tournoux, *L'Histoire secrète*, 16.

6. DLL Parry, 'Counter-revolution by conspiracy, 1935–1937', in *The Right in France*, 162; Joel Blatt, 'The Cagoule plot', in *Crisis and Renewal in France, 1918–1962*, ed. Kenneth Mouré and Martin S. Alexander (New York: 2002), 93; Milza, *Fascisme français*, 156; Gayle K. Brunelle and Annette Finley-Croswhite, *Murder in the Metro: Laetitia Toureaux and the Cagoule in 1930s France* (Baton Rouge: Louisiana State University Press, 2010), 123–42 on the Cagoule's arms smuggling.

7. Bourdrel, *La Cagoule*, 100. There is a photo of one of these pens in Tournoux, *L'Histoire secrète*, 56–7.

8. Bourdrel, *La Cagoule*, 97.

9. Tournoux, *L'Histoire secrète*, 98.

10. Ibid., 98–9.

11. For an account of the attempted coup see Ducloux, *From Blackmail to Treason*, 159–219.

12. Blatt, 'The Cagoule plot', 88.

13. Ory, *Les collaborateurs*, 121.

14. Bourdrel, *La Cagoule*, 59.

15. Ibid., 57; Blatt, 'The Cagoule plot', 89; Nobécourt, *Le Colonel de La Rocque*, 544–6.

16. AN BB[18] 3061/2, '1ere partie: Etat actuel de l'information au regard des diverses inculpations et des différents inculpés'; Jean-Claude Valla, *La Cagoule* (Paris: Librairie Nationale, 2000), 48; Henry Charbonneau, *Les mémoires de Porthos* (Paris: Editions du Trident, 1963), 155, 158. See also Blatt, 'The Cagoule plot', 94–5; Parry, 'Counter-revolution by conspiracy', 176; Brunelle and Finley-Croswhite, *Murder in the Metro*, 147; Bourdrel, *La Cagoule*, 74–7; 94–5; Belin, *My Work at the Sûreté*, 199–200.

17. Belin, *My Work at the Sûreté*, 199.

18. Blatt, 'The Cagoule plot', 89–90; Brunelle and Finley-Croswhite, *Murder in the Metro*, 105. Parry claims that there were 2,800 members of UCAD members, of whom 1,260 featured on a Cagoule membership list that fell into police hand; Parry, 'Counter-revolution by conspiracy', 264.

19. Shirer, *The Collapse of the Third Republic*, 209; Tournoux, *L'Histoire secrète*, 307–9.

20. Tournoux, *L'Histoire secrète*, 34.

21. Deacon, *The Extreme Right in the French Resistance*, 65–85.

22. Marshal Pétain was likely aware of the group and its efforts to stockpile weapons. See Blatt, 'The Cagoule plot', 92; Parry, 'Counter-revolution by conspiracy', 167; Loustaunau-Lacau, *Mémoires d'un français rebelle*, 114–15; Tournoux, *L'Histoire secrète*, 29n2.

23. Blatt, 'The Cagoule plot', 93, Parry, 'Counter-revolution by conspiracy', 166–70; Brunelle and Finley-Croswhite, *Murder in the Metro*, 103.

24. Blatt, 'The Cagoule plot', 89; Parry, 'Counter-revolution by conspiracy', 172–3; Bourdrel, *La Cagoule*, 104–8.

25. Brunelle and Finley-Croswhite, *Murder in the Metro*, 139.

26. Parry, 'Counter-revolution by conspiracy', 165; Bourdrel, *La Cagoule*, 172–7.

27. Blatt, 'The Cagoule plot', 91; Brunelle and Finley-Croswhite, *Murder in the Metro*, 128–31; Parry, 'Counter-revolution by conspiracy', 165.

28. Bourdrel, *La Cagoule*, 146; Tournoux, *L'Histoire secrète*, 89.

29. Bourdrel, *La Cagoule*, 143.

30. See Brunelle and Finley-Croswhite, *Murder in the Metro*, 107–22 for 'Cagoulard Profiles'; and Bourdrel, *La Cagoule*, 63–8.

31. Blatt, 'The Cagoule plot', 87; Bourdrel, *La Cagoule*, 60–3; Brunelle and Finley-Croswhite, *Murder in the Metro*, 109–10; Charbonneau, *Les mémoires de Porthos*, 153–5; Tournoux, *L'Histoire secrète*, 47–8.

32. Bruenelle and Finley-Croswhite, *Murder in the Metro*, 101–2; Brigitte Delluc and Gilles Delluc, *Jean Filliol, du Périgord à la Cagoule, de la Milice à Oradour* (Périgueux: Pilote 24 édition, 2005), 19–22; Bourdrel, *La Cagoule*, 59; Charbonneau, *Les mémoires de Porthos*, 90–1.

33. Bourdrel, *La Cagoule*, 59.

34. Delluc and Delluc, *Jean Filliol*, 22; Brunelle and Finley-Croswhite, *Murder in the Metro*, 112–13.

35. Ibid., 109–15.

36. Much of what follows in the text draws on the notes compiled during the interrogation of men suspected of belonging to the group following the failed coup of November 1937. See AN F7 14673, F7 14815, F7 14816, and APP BA 1903.

37. Deacon, *The Extreme Right in the French Resistance*, 54–5; Parry, 'Counter-revolution by conspiracy', 173.

38. Belin, *My Work at the Sûreté*, 205.

39. AN BB18 3061/2, 'Réquisitoire, 2 August 1939. Cour d'appel de Paris. Chambre des Mises en accusation', n.d.; Charbonneau, *Les mémoires de Porthos*, 155.

40. AN F7 14673 'Procès Verbal', 10 February 1937.

41. AN F7 14815, 'Proces-Verbal', 10 July 1939.

42. AN F7 14673, 'Le Commissaire Divisonnaire, Chef des Services de Police Spéciale à Monsieur le Préfet des Bouches-du-Rhône', 8 February 1938.

43. AN F7 14673, 'Le Directeur de la Police d'Etat à Monsieur le Préfet des Alpes-Maritimes', 3 February 1938.

44. AN F7 14815, 'POURCHER Paul Commissaire', 31 January 1938.

45. AN F7 14815, 'André Roche', 7 January 1938; AN F7 14815, 'Le Commissaire de Police Mobile Heriot à M. Le Commissaire Divisionnaire, Chef de la 2e Section de l'Inspection Générale des Services de Police Criminelle', 28 November 1938.

46. AN F7 14817, 'Pierre Béteille. La Seine', 29 January 1938.

47. Belin, *My Work at the Sûreté*, 202; Deacon, *The Extreme Right in the French Resistance*, 54–5.

48. Bernardec, *Dagore: Les carnets secrets de la Cagoule*, 23; Parry, 'Counter-revolution by conspiracy', 163; Weber, *Action Française*, 368; AN BB 18 3061/2, 'Le Procureur de la République à Monsieur le Procureur Général', 25 September 1937.

49. AN F7 14673, 'Le Directeur de la Police d'Etat à Mosnieur l'Inspecter Général chargé des services de Police criminelle', 16 September 1937.

50. AN F7 14673, 'Le Commissaire Divisionnaire, Chef des Services de Police Spéciale e à Monsieur le Préfet des Bouches-du-Rhône', 8 February 1938.

51. AN F7 14815, 'FOURCHER Paul Commissaire', 15 January 1938.

52. AN F7 14815, 'Jean Félix Buffet Commissaire Divisionnaire', 23 November 1937.

53. Charbonneau, *Les mémoires de Porthos*, 157; Belin, *My Work at the Sûreté*, 201; Tournoux, *L'Histoire secrète*, 43–4. For an example of the code used see Bourdrel, *La Cagoule*, 355–61 (Annex 2) and 84–5 for an explanation of the code.

54. Bourdrel, *La Cagoule*, 111; Tournoux, *L'Histoire secrète*, 49.

55. AN BB18 2920, untitled report 17 February 1934.

56. Noguères, *La Vie quotidienne en France*, 54.

57. AN BB 18 2959, 'Le Procureur de la République à Limoges a Monsieur le Procureur Général', 22 March 1936.

58. Brunelle and Finley-Croswhite, *Murder in the Metro*, 120.

59. As Brian Jenkins has argued, the extreme right-wing leagues, though distinct organizations, were all 'fishing in the same pool of ideas'. See Jenkins, 'The six février 1934 and the "survival" of the French Third Republic', *French History* 20, no. 3 (2006): 333–51.

60. Colas, *Les droites nationales en Lorraine*, 156.

61. Charbonneau, *Les mémoires de Porthos*, 155.

62. Bourdrel, *La Cagoule*, 125–8.

63. Alain Decaux, *Destins Fabuleux* (Paris: Perrin, 1987), 332; Delluc and Delluc relate a similar story in *Jean Filliol*, 47.

64. Brunelle and Finley-Croswhite, *Murder in the Metro*.

65. A police resumé of the murders can be found in Bourdrel, *La Cagoule*, 150–11; 362–7.

66. Blatt, 'The Cagoule plot', 93; Brunelle and Finley-Croswhite, *Murder in the Metro*, 99–101.

67. Parry, 'Counter-revolution by conspiracy', 170.

68. Millington, 'Immigrants and undesirables'.

69. Belin, *My Work at the Sûreté*, 196–7.

70. Brunelle and Finley-Croswhite, *Murder in the Metro*, 134–5.

71. Belin, *My Work at the Sûreté*, 197.

72. AN BB18 3061/2, 'Le Procureur de la République à Monsieur le Procureur Général', 8 July 1938; 'Le Procureur Général près la Cour d'Appel de Douai à Monsieur le Garde des Sceaux, Ministre de la Justice à Paris', 5 March 1937; Ducloux, *From Blackmail to Treason*, 163–8.

73. Brunelle and Finley-Croswhite, *Murder in the Metro*, 146; Ducloux, *From Blackmail to Treason*, 172–3.

74. Brunelle and Finley-Croswhite, *Murder in the Metro*, 146; Bourdrel, *La Cagoule*, 218–19.

75. Charbonneau, *Les mémoires de Porthos*, 163.

76. Tournoux, *L'Histoire secrète*, 93–4. Gamelin was generalissimo; Duffieux was inspecteur général de l'infanterie and member of the Superior Council of War; Georges was sous-chef d'état-major général.

77. Charbonneau, *Les mémoires de Porthos*, 166.

78. Bourdrel, *La Cagoule*, 222.

79. Tournoux, *L'Histoire secrète*, 109.

80. Belin, *My Work at the Sûreté*, 198.

81. Brunelle and Finley-Croswhite, *Murder in the Metro*, 151.

82. Ibid., 154.

83. Bourdrel, *La Cagoule*, 237–9.

84. Tournoux, *L'Histoire secrète*, 110.

85. The Catherinettes were single women under the age of twenty-five who remained unmarried on 25 November (St Catherine's Day) each year. Each year the *catherinettes* would confect a headpiece to celebrate the day.

86. Bourdrel, *La Cagoule*, 242.

87. 'Le complot des "oustachis" français prend d'énormes proportions', *L'Oeuvre*, 19 November 1937, 1.

88. Lucien Sampaix, '106 caisses contenant près de 4.000 grenades que l'on croit être à gaz lacrymogène ou asphyxiant sont trouvées abandonnées dans la region parisiennce', *L'Humanité*, 3 December 1937, 1.

89. Gabriel Peri, 'Les menées de la "Cagoule" et la politique du Quai d'Orsay', *L'Humnaité*, 14 January 1938, 3.

90. Fernand Fontenay, *La Cagoule contre la France. Ses crimes. Son organisation. Ses chefs. Ses inspirateurs* (Paris: Editions sociales internationales, 1938), 11.

91. Ibid., 157.

92. Edmond Barrachin, 'Un comble', *Le Petit Journal*, 9 February 1938, 1; Charbonneau, *Les mémories de Porthos*, 168.

93. See for example Philippe Roques, 'M. Dormoy prétend avoir découvert un complot contre la République', *L'Echo de Paris*, 24 November 1937, 1.

94. La Rocque, 'Cagoules', *Le Petit Journal*, 5 December 1937, 1. See also Bourdrel, *La Cagoule*, 241; 'Le Front populaire viole la loi constitutionelle', *L'Echo de Paris*, 29 November 1937, 1–2.

95. AN BB18 3061, 'Le Procureur Général près la Cour d'Appel de Paris à Monsieur le Garde des Sceaux', 7 January 1939.

96. *Journal Officiel du 10 décembre 1937. Débats parlementaires*, 80, 9 December 1937, 2811–12.

97. Parry, 'Counter-revolution by conspiracy', 171.

98. Tournoux, *L'Histoire secrète*, 35.

99. Bourdrel, *La Cagoule*, 243.

100. Deacon, *The Extreme Right in the French Resistance*, 63.

101. Bourdrel, *La Cagoule*, 89.

102. Brunelle and Finley-Croswhite, *Murder in the Metro*, 164–7.

103. Belin, *My Work at the Sûreté*, 200–1. Bourdrel pours cold water on the Cagoule-Pétain-Laval conspiracy theories: *La Cagoule*, 205–10.

104. Ducloux, *From Blackmail to Treason*, 162.

105. Parry, 'Counter-revolution by conspiracy', 162.

Chapter 6

1. Arthuer Koestler, *Scum of the Earth* (London: Eland, 2006 [originally published London: Jonathan Cape, 1941]), 51.

2. Ibid., 51.

3. Koestler, *Scum of the Earth*, 51–2.

4. Brunet, *Jacques Doriot*, 306.

5. Brunelle and Finley-Croswhite, *Murder in the Metro*, 140–1.

6. Kennedy, *Reconciling France against Democracy*, 227; 232.

7. Campbell, *Political Belief in France*, 184–5.

8. The best account of the defeat is Julian Jackson's *The Fall of France: The Nazi Invasion of 1940* (Oxford: Oxford University Press, 2003).

9. Jackson, *France: The Dark Years*, 127.

10. There were seventeen abstentions; communists were not permitted to vote; deputies who had fled on the Massilia could not vote, see ibid., 132.

11. Ibid., 133.

12. The other 'natural communities' were the workplace or profession and the region.

13. Luc Capdevila, 'The quest for masculinity in a defeated France, 1940–1945', *Contemporary European History* 10, no. 3 (2001): 427–8.

14. Marc-Olivier Baruch, 'Charisma and hybrid legitimacy in Pétain's Etat français', *Totalitarian Movements and Political Religions* 7, no. 2 (2006): 218.

15. Shannon L. Fogg, '"They are undesirables": Local and national responses to Gypsies during World War II', *French Historical Studies* 31, no. 2 (2008): 327–58; Michael Sibalis, 'Homophobia, Vichy France, and the "crime of homosexuality": The origins of the ordinance of 6 August 1942', *GLQ: A Journal of Lesbian and Gay Studies* 8, no. 3 (2002): 301–18.

16. Paxton, *Vichy France*, 174–9; Jean-Louis Panicacci, 'Une section modèle? La Légion des Alpes-Maritimes', *Annales du Midi. Revue archéologique, historique et philologique de la France méridionale* 116, no. 245 (2014): 99; Henry Rousso, 'Vichy, le grand fossé', *Vingitème Siècle* 5, no. 1 (1985): 58.

17. Jackson, *France: The Dark Years*, 172–3.

18. Milza, *Fascisme français*, 226.

19. Historians have identified a number of different types of collaboration from collaborationism to the generally more pragmatic collaboration 'for reasons of State'. On the other hand, terms such as 'accommodation' and 'cohabitation' have been proposed both to account for the variety of ways in which the French facilitated the Occupation and to avoid the moral judgement that 'collaboration' entails. See Stanley Hoffman, 'Collaborationism in France during World War II', *Journal of Modern History* 40, no. 3 (1968): 378. Robert Gildea uses 'cohabitation' in *Marianne in Chains* (London: Macmillan, 2002). Burrin prefers 'accommodation' in *Living with Defeat: France under German Occupation, 1940–1944* (London: Arnold, 1996).

20. Bertram M. Gordon, *Collaborationism in France during the Second World War* (Ithaca: Cornell University Press, 1980), 19.

21. Ariane Chebel d'Appollonia, 'Collaborationist fascism', in *The Development of the Radical Right in France*, 173.

22. Jean-Pierre Azéma, 'Vichy', in *Histoire de l'extrême droite en France*, 208.

23. Gordon, *Collaborationism in France*, 23.

24. Hoffman, 'Collaborationism in France during World War II', 376–80; Fabian Lemmes, 'Collaboration in wartime France, 194–1944', *European Review of History/Revue européenne d'histoire* 15, no. 2 (2008): 161; Gordon, *Collaborationism in France*, 76.

25. Ory, *Les collaborateurs*, 254; Azéma, 'Vichy', 211–12.

26. Milza, *Fascisme français*, 268.

27. Francine Muel-Dreyfus, *Vichy et l'éternel féminin* (Paris: Seuil, 1996), 249.

28. Campbell, *Political Belief in France*, 185–8.

29. Kennedy, *Reconciling France against Democracy*, 233–4.

30. Burrin, *La Dérive fasciste*, 358.

31. Cantier, *L'Algérie sous the régime de Vichy*, 232.

32. Jackson, *France: The Dark Years*, 143; Brunet, *Jacques Doriot*, 319.

33. Soucy, *The Second Wave*, 55; Ory, *Les collaborateurs*, 105; Gordon, *Collaborationism in France*, 45–6.

34. Ory, *Les collaborateurs*, 28.

Notes

35. Jean-Paul Brunet, 'Déat, Marcel', in *Dictionnaire historique de la Vie Politique Française au XXe Siècle*, ed. Jean-François Sirinelli (Pars: Presses Universitaires de France, 1995), 256–8.

36. Marcel Déat, 'Mourir pour Dantzig?' *L'Oeuvre*, 4 May 1939, 1 and 4; Gordon, *Collaborationism in France*, 46; Jean-Paul Cointet, *La Légion Française des Combattants. La tentation du fascisme* (Paris: Albin Michel, 1995), 30–1.

37. Burrin, *La Dérive fasciste*, 343; 346.

38. Ibid., 332; 343; Azéma, 'Vichy', 223.

39. Brunet, *Jacques Doriot*, 314–15.

40. Burrin, *La Dérive fasciste*, 351; Gordon, *Collaborationism in France*, 74; Brunet disputes this in *Jacques Doriot*, 314.

41. Burrin, *La Dérive fasciste*, 349.

42. Brunet, *Jacques Doriot*, 313.

43. Cantier, *L'Algérie sous the régime de Vichy*, 218–32.

44. Burrin, *La Dérive fasciste*, 345; Brunet, *Jacques Doriot*, 320.

45. Burrin, *La Dérive fasciste*, 344; Cointet, *La Légion Française des Combattants*, 43.

46. Burrin, *La Dérive fasciste*, 349; Kennedy, *Reconciling France against Democracy*, 251.

47. Burrin, *La Dérive fasciste*, 349.

48. Azéma, 'Vichy', 223; Gordon, *Collaborationism in France*, 47–8; Milza, *Fascisme français*, 241–2.

49. Burrin, *La Dérive fasciste*, 386; 389.

50. Cantier, *L'Algérie sous the régime de Vichy*, 233–4.

51. Burrin, *La Dérive fasciste*, 359; Kennedy, *Reconciling France against Democracy*, 255; 260.

52. Cantier, *L'Algérie sous the régime de Vichy,* 234.

53. Burrin, *La Dérive fasciste*, 422; Ory, *Les collaborateurs*, 101; Milza, *Fascisme français*, 253; Brunet, *Jacques Doriot*, 322.

54. Burrin, *La Dérive fasciste*, 424.

55. On 3 July 1940, the British navy attached the French nave at the base of Mers el Kébir, of the coast of Algeria. Jankowski, *Communism and Collaboration*, 78.

56. On Abetz see Gordon, *Collaborationism in France*, 67.

57. Azéma, 'Vichy', 223–5; Milza, *Fascismes français*, 243; Baruch, 'Charisma and hybrid legitimacy in Pétain's Etat français', 216; J. G. Shields, *The Extreme Right in France: From Pétain to Le Pen* (Abingdon: Routledge, 2007), 42.

58. Burrin, *La Dérive fasciste*, 346.

59. Julian Jackson, 'Vichy and fascism', in *The Development of the Radical Right in France*, 169.

60. The expression was not an original one: the Jeunesses Patriotes had employed the phrase in their propaganda: Richard Vinen, *The Unfree French: Life under the Occupation* (New Haven: Allen Lane, 2006), 71.

61. Ibid., 71; Nicholas Atkin, *The French at War, 1934–1944* (Harlow: Longman, 2001), 40.

62. Philippe Burrin, 'The ideology of the National Revolution', in *The Development of the Radical Right in France*, 139–40.

63. Vinen, *The Unfree French*, 76.

64. Burrin 'The ideology of the National Revolution', 138.

65. Azéma, 'Vichy', 197.

66. Michèle Bordeaux, 'Femmes hors d'Etat français, 1940–1944', in *Femmes et Fascismes*, ed. Rita Thalmann (Paris: Editions Tierce, 1986), 138.

67. Capdevila, 'The quest for masculinity', 427–8.

68. Tumblety, *Remaking the Male Body*, 206.

69. Capdevila, 'The quest for masculinity', 429–30.

70. Jean-Pierre Azéma, 'Vichy face au modèle républicain', in *Le modèle républicain*, ed. Serge Berstein and Odile Rudelle (Paris: Presses Universitaires de France, 1992), 340–1.

71. Burrin, 'The ideology of the National Revolution', 138; Jackson, 'Vichy and fascism', 159.

72. Mohammed Kenbib, 'Moroccan Jews and the Vichy regime, 1940–1942', *Journal of North African Studies* 19, no. 4 (2014): 547.

73. Terrence Peterson, 'The "Jewish question" and the "Italian peril": Vichy, Italy and the Jews of Tunisia, 1940–1942', *Journal of Contemporary History* 50, no. 2 (2015): 234–58.

74. Eric T. Jennings, 'Vichy à Madagascar. La "Révolution nationale", l'enseignement et la jeunesse, 1940–1942', *Revue d'histoire modern et contemporarine* 46, no. 4 (1999), 742–3.

75. Milza, *Fascisme français*, 228–9.

76. Samuel M. Osgood, *French Royalism under the Third and Fourth Republics* (The Hague: Martinus Nijhoff, 1960), 163–4.

77. Ibid., 165.

78. Rousso, 'Vichy, le grand fossé', 60.

79. Azéma, 'Vichy face au modèle républicain', 348; Osgood, *French Royalism under the Third and Fourth Republics*, 164.

80. Vinen, *The Unfree French*, 75.

81. Denis Peschanski, 'Vichy au singulier, Vichy au pluriel. Une tentative avortée d'encadrement de la société (1941-1942)', *Vingtième Siècle* 43, no. 3 (1988), 640.

82. Jackson, *France: The Dark Years*, 158–9.

83. Atkin, *The French at War*, 45.

84. Paxton, *Vichy France*, 219–20.

85. Jackson, *France: The Dark Years*, 48–51.

86. D'Appollonia, 'Collaborationist fascism', 173; Burrin, 'The ideology of the National Revolution', 146–7.

87. Peschanski, 'Vichy au singulier, Vichy au pluriel', 644.

88. Azéma, 'Vichy', 199–203.

89. Burrin 'The ideology of the National Revolution', 143–5.

90. On Salazar's Portugal see António Costa Pinto, 'Le salazarisme et le fascisme européen', *Vingtième Siècle* 62, no. 1 (1999): 15–25; Dard and Sardinha-Desvignes, *Célébrer Salazar en France*, 157–64.

91. Pinto, 'Le salazarisme et le fascisme européen', 17–18; António Costa Pinto, *Salazar's Dictatorship and European Fascism: Problems of Interpretation* (Boulder: Social Science Monographs, 1995), 29.

92. Pinto, 'Le salazarisme et le fascisme européen', 24.

93. Helena Pinto Janeiro, 'Salazar et les trois France (1940–1944)', *Vingtième Siècle* 62, no. 2 (1999): 40–1; Pinto, *Salazar's Dictatorship*, 26: 'No-one looked to the Portuguese "New State" as much as sectors of the Vichy regime did'; Milza, *Fascisme français*, 230.

94. Ibid., 230.

95. On the party see António Costa Pinto, 'Le salazarisme et le fascisme européen', 17–18; Milza, *Fascisme français*, 243.

96. Ibid., 230.

97. Janeiro, 'Salazar et les trois France', 40; Irene Flunser Pimentel and Cláudia Ninhos, 'Portugal, Jewish refugees, and the Holocaust', *Dapim: Studies on the Holocaust* 29, no. 2 (2015): 101–13.

98. Roger Bourderon, 'Was the Vichy Regime fascist?' in *Contemporary France: Illusion, Conflict and Regeneration*, ed. John C. Cairns (New York: New Viewpoints, 1978), 212–20; Passmore, *The Right in France*, 363: 'Vichy appropriated and re-appropriated ideas from a multiplicity of sources'.

99. Passmore, *The Right in France*, 350–1.

100. Paxton, *Vichy France*, 231–3.

101. Passmore, *The Right in France*, 351.

102. Millington, *From Victory to Vichy*, 92; Pierre Giolitto, *Histoire de la Milice* (Paris: Perrin, 2002), 16; Cantier, *L'Algérie sous the régime de Vichy*, 204; Cointet, *La Légion Française des Combattants*, 53–61.

103. Capdevila, 'The quest for masculinity', 430.

104. Muel-Dreyfus, *Vichy et l'éternel féminin*, 134; 207–8; 322–3; Miranda Pollard, *Reign of Virtue: Mobilizing Gender in Vichy France* (Chicago; London: University of Chicago Press, 1998), 34–5.

105. Panicacci, 'Une section modèle?' 94–6.

106. Muel-Dreyfus, *Vichy et l'éternel féminin*, 215–6; 356; Panicacci, 'Une section modèle?' 94–6; Giolitto, *Histoire de la Milice*, 42–3.

107. Jean-Marie Guillon, 'La Légion française des combattants ou comment comprendre la France de Vichy', *Annales du Midi. Revue archéologique, historique et philologique de la France méridionale* 116, no. 245 (2004): 17.

108. Bourderon, 'Was the Vichy Regime fascist?' 217.

109. Panicacci, 'Une section modèle?' 102.

110. Ibid., 96; 99–100; Jankowski, *Communism and Collaboration*, 72–3.

111. Guillon, 'La Légion française des combattants', 13.

112. Paxton, *Vichy France*, 224.

113. Cantier, *L'Algérie sous le régime de Vichy*, 208.

114. Ibid., 212–15.

115. Passmore, *The Right in France*, 353.

116. Eric Jennings, 'La politique colonial de Vichy', in *L'Empire colonial sous Vichy*, ed. Jacques Cantier and Eric Jennings (Paris: Odile Jacob, 2004), 20–1.

117. Pierre Ramognino, 'L'Afrique de l'Ouest sous le proconsulat de Pierre Boisson (Juin 1940–juin 1943)', in ibid., 79–81.

118. Baruch, 'Charisma and hybrid legitimacy in Pétain's Etat français', 217.

119. Jean Guéhenno, *Diary of the Dark Years: Collaboration, Resistance and Daily Life in Occupied Paris* (Oxford: Oxford University Press, 2014), 172.

120. Jackson, 'Vichy and fascism', 164; Peschanski, 'Vichy au singulier, Vichy au pluriel', 652; Guillon, 'La Légion française des combattants', 20; Giolitto, *Histoire de la Milice*, 23; Cointet, *La Légion Française des Combattants*, 130–1; 154–60.

121. Ory, *Les collaborateurs*, 250; Martin Thomas, *The French Empire at War, 1940–45* (Manchester: Manchester University Pres, 2007), 237; Cantier, *L'Algérie sous the régime de Vichy*, 207.

122. For a biography of Darnand see Giolitto, *Histoire de la Milice*, 102–24.

123. Jean-Pierre Azéma, 'La Milice', *Vingtième Siècle* 28, no. 4 (1990): 85; Ory, *Les collaborateurs*, 248–9; Gordon, *Collaborationism in France*, 167–72; Milza, *Fascisme français*, 269–70.

124. Azéma, 'La Milice', 85–6; Ory, *Les collaborateurs*, 249.

125. Abitbol, *The Jews of North Africa*, 118; Milza, *Fascisme français*, 270; Giolitto, *Histoire de la Milice*, 65–6; Cointet, *La Légion Française des Combattants*, 188–91.

126. Cantier, *L'Algérie sous le régime de Vichy*, 236.

127. Abitbol, *The Jews of North Africa*, 53; 138; 145.

128. For a summary of the Milice see Giolitto, *Histoire de la Milice*, 125–190.

129. Jackson, Vichy and fascism', 168; Azéma, 'La Milice', 88; Cointet, *La Légion Française des Combattants*, 250–60.

130. Azéma, 'La Milice', 137–8.

131. Panicacci, 'Une section modèle?' 104; Azéma, 'La Milice', 91; Giolitto, *Histoire de la Milice*, 72–3.

132. Azéma, 'La Milice', 99.

133. Gordon, *Collaborationism in France*, 178.

134. Burrin, 'The ideology of the National Revolution', 136; Philippe Burrin, 'Vichy et les expériences étrangères', in *Le régime de Vichy et les Français*, ed. Jean-Pierre Azéma and François Bédarida (Paris: Fayard, 1992), 657. In *The French at War*, Atkin perceives a 'fascist trajectory' in the development of the regime (46); Milza, *Fascisme français*, 248.

135. Azéma, 'La Milice', 96; 98; Jackson, 'Vichy and fascism', 168; Ory, *Les collaborateurs*, 250–1; Gordon, *Collaborationism in France*, 183; 355–6.

136. Ory, *Les collaborateurs,* 251–2; Azéma, 'La Milice', 90–8; Jankowski, *Communism and Collaboration,* 122–3; Gordon, *Collaborationism in France*, 183–4.

137. Azéma, 'La Milice', 90; Jankowski, *Communism and Collaboration*, 124.

138. Azéma, 'La Milice', 95–6.

139. Ibid., 97; Capdevila, 'The quest for masculinity', 427; Milza, *Fascisme français*, 273.

140. Ory, *Les collaborateurs*, 253; Gordon, *Collaborationism in France*, 191.

141. Marcel Baudot, 'La Résistance française face aux problèmes de répression et de l'épuration', *Revue d'histoire de la Deuxième Guerre mondiale* 81 (1971): 29–31. See also Perry Biddiscombe, 'The French resistance and the Chambéry incident of June 1945', *French History* 11, no. 4 (1997): 438–60; Olivier Wieviorka, 'Guerre civile à la française? Le cas des années sombre (1940–1945)', *Vingtième Siècle* 85, no. 1 (2005): 5–19.

142. Azéma, 'La Milice', 103.

143. Ibid., 99–102; Gordon, *Collaborationism in France*, 294–6.

144. For Milza, this 'first Vichy' was essentially conservative and reactionary: 'Return to the roots, and to the farthest reaches of the national tradition. … France turned instinctively to its deepest roots, like a wounded soldier towards his childhood.' Fascist regimes, on the other hand, seek the 'construction of a new society, founded on non-traditional communities (the single party, paramilitary formations, professional and youth organisations entirely dependent on the party and the State, and enjoying a monopoly, etc) and it targets the advent of a futurist humanity having broken with the links of the past', Milza, *Fascisme français*, 227.

145. Peschanski, 'Vichy au singulier, Vichy au pluriel', 651.

146. Milza, *Fascisme français*, 271.

147. Gordon, *Collaborationism in France*, 214–29; Milza, *Fascisme français*, 250–2.

148. Ory, *Les collaborateurs*, 117; 127; Joan Tumblety, 'Revenge of the fascist knights: Masculine identities in *Je suis partout*, 1940–1944', *Modern & Contemporary France* 7, no. 11 (1999): 11–20.

149. Ory, *Les collaborateurs*, 113. Azéma estimates that up to 100,000 men and women were collaborationists: Azéma, 'Vichy', 208. Lemmes estimates that there were 250,000 collaborationists: Lemmes, 'Collaboration in wartime France', 160–1; Gordon estimates that there were between 100,000 and 200,000 collaborationists: *Collaborationism in France*, 327.

150. Burrin, *La Dérive fasciste*, 395; Ory, *Les collaborateurs*, 109–10.

151. Present at the constitutive meeting of the RNP on 31 January 1941 were: Déat, Jean Goy, Deloncle, Fontenoy, Perrot (representing the *syndicalistes*), Cathala (representing Laval) and Vanor: Burrin, *La Dérive fasciste*, 389; Ory, *Les collaborateurs*, 106; 112; Milza, *Fascisme français*, 257. On the array of smaller collaborationist groups see Gordon, *Collaborationism in France*, 357–60.

152. Gordon, *Collaborationism in France*, 100.

153. Ibid., 118. See Henri Michel, *Paris Allemand* (Paris: Albin Michel, 1981), 108–9, on the RNP's affiliates and its subsections.

154. Gordon, *Collaborationism in France*, 96; 102; 201–2; Michel, *Paris Allemand*, 100–1.

155. Burrin, *La Dérive fasciste*, 390–1; Gordon, *Collaborationism in France*, 103; 106–7.

156. Burrin, *La Dérive fasciste*, 417.

157. Ory, *Les collaborateurs*, 109; Gordon, *Collaborationism in France*, 125.

158. Ibid., 109; 114–5.

159. Ory, *Les collaborateurs*, 113; Burrin, *La Dérive fasciste*, 393; 409–13. On the RNP's estimated membership see Gordon, *Collaborationism in France*, 99; 119–21; Milza, *Fascisme français*, 259.

160. Gordon, *Collaborationism in France*, 122–3.

161. Brunet, *Jacques Doriot*, 318.

162. Jankowski, *Communism and Collaboration*, 75.

163. AN F7 14960, 'Le secretariat général au PPF aux secrétaires régionaux & fédéraux', August 1940.

164. AN F7 14960, 'IVe Congrès National du Parti Populaire Français. 4, 5, 6, 7 et 8 Novembre 1942. Paris'.

165. Burrin, *La Dérive fasciste*, 426; 440; Azéma, 'Vichy', 208. Gordon suggests that there were 20,000 members: *Collaborationism in France*, 145.

166. Milza, *Fascisme français*, 255.

167. Gordon, *Collaborationism in France*, 146–7.

168. Burrin, *La Dérive fasciste*, 428.

169. Ibid., 430.

170. Ibid., 434–1. On the PPF's wartime anti-Semitism see Brunet, *Jacques Doriot*, 341–9.

171. Milza, *Fascisme français*, 254; Brunet, *Jacques Doriot*, 359.

172. Gordon, *Collaborationism in France*, 148–53; 281–5.

173. Ory, *Les collaborateurs*, 97; Gordon, *Collaborationism in France*, 135.

174. Owen Anthony Davey, 'The origins of the Légion des Volontaires Français contre le Bolchevisme', *Journal of Contemporary History* 6, no. 4 (1971): 39–40; James G. Shields, 'Charlemagne's Crusaders: French collaboration in arms, 1941–1945', *French Cultural Studies* 18, no. 1 (2007): 86.

175. Burrin, *La Dérive fasciste*, 354–5; Gordon, *Collaborationism in France*, 25–6; Jackson, 'Vichy and fascism', 155.

176. D'Appollonia, 'Collaborationist fascism', 178; 180–1; 185–7.

177. Ibid., 182.

178. Milza, *Fascisme français*, 249; Ory, *Les collaborateurs*, 58; Brunet, *Jacques Doriot*, 323.

179. Milza, *Fascisme français*, 253; AN F7 14960, 'Le secrétariat général au PPF aux secrétaires régionaux & fédéraux', August 1940.

180. Jankowski, *Communism and Collaboration*, 76.

181. On the full extent of French military collaboration see Gordon, *Collaborationism in France*, 244–8.

182. Brunet, *Jacques Doriot*, 361.

183. '"Le bolchevisme est un ennemi qui ne pardonne pas"', *Le Matin*, 2 February 1942, 1 and 4; Burrin, *La Dérive fasciste*, 432; Gordon, *Collaborationism in France*, 248; Michel, *Paris Allemand*, 119.

184. AN F7 14956, 'Réunion des inspecteurs régionaux, jeudi 11 Mars 1943'.

185. Doriot also served with the LVF during September-November 1941, February-March 1942, and on several occasions between March 1942 and March 1943: Milza, *Fascismes français*, 256n77.

186. '"Le bolchevisme est un ennemi qui ne pardonne pas"', *Le Matin*, 2 February 1942, 1 and 4.

187. AN F7 14957, LVF magazine, 'La Légion anti-Bolchevique et l'Etat Français'.

188. AN F7 14956, letter template, signed Eugène Deloncle, undated.

189. AN F7 14956, Colonel Henriet 'Note verbale', 11 January 1943; AN F7 14956, 'Réunion des inspecteurs régionaux, jeudi 11 Mars 1943'; AN F7 14956, 'Réunion des inspecteurs régionaux, jeudi 11 Mars 1943'.

190. See AN F7 14956, letter to Pierre Lelièvre, 17 March 1943.

191. AN F7 14956, letter template, signed Eugène Deloncle, undated.

192. AN F7 14956, 'Budget de la Légion des Volontaires Français', 1943; AN F7 14956, 'Compte rendu de la séance du comité en date du 12 mai 1942'.

Notes

193. AN F7 14957, LVF magazine, 'Service social de la LVF'.

194. Ibid..

195. AN F7 14956, A. de Rose, 'Rapport', January 1942.

196. Michel, *Paris Allemand*, 118; Lemmes, 'Collaboration in wartime France', 162; Gordon, *Collaborationism in France*, 245; 250. Davey, 'The origins of the Légion des Volontaires Français contre le Bolchevisme', 32; 38; 40–1; Burrin, *La Dérive fasciste*, 431; Shields, 'Charlemagne's Crusaders', 87; 91; Vichy forbade recruitment in the south though Pétain's position on the group was ambiguous. In January 1943, Laval recognized the group and appointed de Brinon head of its central committee: Ory, *Les collaborateurs*, 242.

197. Davey, 'The origins of the Légion des Volontaires Français contre le Bolchevisme', 44; Philippe Carrard, 'From the outcasts' point of view: The memoirs of the French who fought for Hitler', *French Historical Studies* 31, no. 3 (2008): 485; 492–3; Ory, *Les collaborateurs*, 243–5. On the PPF and the LVF see Brunet, *Jacques Doriot*, 364–74.

198. Ory, *Les collaborateurs*, 267; Gordon, *Collaborationism in France*, 277–8.

199. Davey, 'The origins of the Légion des Volontaires Français contre le Bolchevisme', 34–5. The same claim was made about the men of the French Waffen-SS Charlemagne Division – see Shields, 'Charlemagne's Crusaders', 83–105; Albert Merglen, 'Soldats français sous uniformes allemands, 1941–1945: LVF et "Waffen SS" français', *Revue d'histoire de la Deuxième guerre mondiale* 108 (1977): 71–84. On the membership of the Comité d'Honneur, see Gordon, *Collaborationism in France*, 246.

200. Carrard, 'From the outcasts' point of view', 485; 492–3; Ory, *Les collaborateurs*, 136–8.

201. Lemmes, 'Collaboration in wartime France', 162–3; Davey, 'The origins of the Légion des Volontaires Français contre le Bolchevisme', 42.

202. Michel, *Paris Allemand*, 121.

203. Jackson, 'Vichy and fascism', 168; Azéma, 'Vichy', 212.

204. Milza, *Fascisme français*, 268.

205. Ibid., 238.

206. Gordon, *Collaborationism in France*, 290.

207. Bourderon, 'Was the Vichy regime fascist?' 213; 216.

208. Alcalde, *War Veterans and Fascism*, 269–70.

209. Milza, *Fascismes français*, 269. See also Cointet, *La Légion Française des Combattants*, 78.

210. Marcel Déat, *Mémoires politiques* (Paris: Denoël, 1989), 619.

211. Milza, *Fascisme français*, 239.

212. Tumblety, 'Revenge of the fascist knights', 18.

213. Bourderon, 'Was the Vichy regime fascist?' 212–20.

214. Burrin, *La Dérive fasciste*, 402.

215. Michel, *Paris Allemand*, 103.

216. Ory, *Les collaborateurs*, 102.

217. Burrin, *La Dérive fasciste*, 401–3.

218. Hoffman, 'Collaborationism in France during World War II', 376.

219. Burrin, *La Dérive fasciste*, 449.

220. Brunet, *Jacques Doriot*, 323.

Chapter 7

1. Throughout this chapter, the party now known as the Rassemblement National is referred to as the Front National.

2. Pascal Perrineau, 'LE PEN Jean-Marie', in *Dictionnaire historique de la vie politique française au XXe siècle*, 572–5.

3. Hélène Combis-Schlumberger, 'Le FN devient "Rassemblement national": un nouveau nom au lourd passé', 12 March 2018, https://www.franceculture.fr/politique/le-fn-devient-ra ssemblement-national-un-nouveau-nom-au-lourd-passe (accessed 20 June 2018).

4. Catherine Fiesch, *Fascism, Populism and the French Fifth Republic* (Manchester: Manchester University Press, 2004), 13.

5. Henry Rousso, 'Après la déclaration de Marine Le Pen sur le Vel d'Hiv, quelle responsabilité de la France et des Français sous l'Occupation', 11 April 2017, https://www.huffingtonpost.fr/ henry-rousso/le-pen-vel-dhiv-vichy_a_22034882/ (accessed 20 June 2018).

6. Peter Fysch and Jim Wolfreys, *The Politics of Racism in France* (Basingstoke: Palgrave Macmillan, 2003), 141–2; Henry Rousso, *The Vichy Syndrome: History and Memory in France since 1944* (Cambridge; London: Harvard University Press, 1996), 195; Milza, *Fascisme Français*, 709–10.

7. Rousso, *The Vichy Syndrome*, 198.

8. Fiesch, *Fascism, Populism and the French Fifth Republic*, 13. For an example of this approach see Milza, *Fascisme français*.

9. Pierre Milza, 'Le Front national crée-t-il une culture politique?' *Vingtième Siècle* 44, no. 1 (1994): 41–3; Milza, *Fascisme français*, 701–14; 721–2; Peter Davies, *The National Front in France: Ideology, Discourse and Power* (London and New York: Routledge, 1999), 120–4.

10. Milza, 'Le Front national crée-t-il une culture politique?' 42–3.

11. Fiesch, *Fascism, Populism and the French Fifth Republic*, 138–49.

12. Frédéric Boily, 'Aux sources idéologiques du Front national: le marriage du traditionalisme et du populisme', *Politique et Sociétés* 24, no. 1 (2005): 35.

13. For example the Action nationaliste of Jean-Gilles Malliarakis that was active during the late 1960s. See Jean-Yves Camus and René Monzat, *Les Droites nationales et radicales en France. Répertoire critique* (Lyon: Presses Universitaires de Lyon, 1992), 24–6; 89.

14. Brian Jenkins, *Nationalism in France: Class and Nation since 1789* (London and New York: Routledge, 1990), 182–3.

15. Milza, 'Le Front national crée-t-il une culture politique?' 41–2; Milza, *Fascisme français*, 708; 18.

16. Davies, *The National Front in France*, 221–2.

17. James Shields, 'The Front National since the 1970s: Electoral impact and party system change', in *France since the 1970s: History, Politics and Memory in an Age of Uncertainty*, ed. Emile Chabal (London and New York: Bloomsbury Academic, 2015), 55.

18. Jacques Tarnero, 'Le Pen, Vitrolles et les lois Debré. Vichy blues?' *Hommes et Migrations* 1207 (May–June 1997): 117.

19. Rousso, *The Vichy Syndrome*, 199; Tarnero, 'Le Pen, Vitrolles et les lois Debré', 115; Davies, *The National Front in France*, 225.

Notes

20. Pascal Buléon and Jérôme Fourquet, 'Vote Front National 1984–2002, géographies et interprétations sucessives: Une equation politique', *Espace, populations, sociétés* 3 (2003): 453.

21. Davies, *The National Front in France*, 1.

22. Nick Hewlett, 'The phantom revolution: The presidential and parliamentary elections of 2017', *Modern & Contemporary France* 25, no. 4 (2017): 382.

23. Bert Klandermans and Nonna Mayer, 'Links with the past', in *Extreme Right Activists in Europe*, ed. Bert Klandermans and Nonna Mayer (London and New York: Routledge, 2006), 19.

24. Milza, *Fascisme français*, 280.

25. Ibid., 298–9.

26. Harvey G. Simmons, *The French National Front: The Extremist Challenge to Democracy* (Boulder: Westview Press, 1996), 28; Milza, *Fascisme français*, 298–9.

27. Shields, *The Extreme Right in France*, 68–9; Simmons, *The French National Front*, 28–9.

28. Milza, *Fascisme français*, 303; 305.

29. Ibid., 301.

30. Shields, *The Extreme Right in France*, 70–2; Milza, *Fascisme français*, 302.

31. Shields, *The Extreme Right in France*, 70–2.

32. Winock, *Nationalisme, antisémitisme et fascisme en France*, 54.

33. Ibid., 75–88; Simmons, *The French National Front*, 32–3.

34. Shields, *The Extreme Right in France*, 78.

35. Ibid., 78–80; Simmons, *The French National Front*, 29–30.

36. Shields, *The Extreme Right in France*, 86–9; Simmons, *The French National Front*, 35.

37. Milza, *Fascisme français*, 309–21.

38. Ibid., 332.

39. Pascal Perrineau, 'Les étapes d'une implantation électorale (1972–1988)', in *Le Front national à découvert*, ed. Nonna Mayer and Pascal Perrineau (Paris: Presses de la Fondation Nationale des Sciences Politiques, 1989), 38.

40. Rousso, *The Vichy Syndrome*, 190.

41. Fysch and Wolfreys, *The Politics of Racism in France*, 105–6; Camus and Monzat, *Les Droites nationales et radicales en France*, 41–3.

42. Fysch and Wolfreys, *The Politics of Racism in France*, 103; 107.

43. Jean-Yves Camus, 'Origine et formation du Front national', in *Le Front national à découvert*, 31; Pascal Perrineau, 'Le Front national, 1972–2015', in *Histoire de l'extrême droite en France*, 247; Pierre-André Taguieuff, 'La métaphysique de Jean-Marie Le Pen', in *Le Front national à découvert*, 178–82.

44. Perrineau, 'Le Front national, 1972–2015', 248; Fysch and Wolfreys, *The Politics of Racism in France*, 112; Davies, *The National Front in France*, 33; Camus and Monzat, *Les Droites nationales et radicales en France*, 29; 267–8.

45. Ibid., 53–6.

46. Fysch and Wolfreys, *The Politics of Racism in France*, 107.

47. Perrineau, 'Le Front national, 1972–2015', 244. Duprat was an energetic activist in the post-war fascist movements Jeune Nation and its student wing the Fédération des Etudiants Nationalistes. Brigneau had been a member of Déat's RNP and was a former *milicien*, too.

48. Fysch and Wolfreys, *The Politics of Racism in France*, 108.

49. Pierre Milza, 'Le Front national: droite extrême … ou national-populisme?' in *Histoire des droites en France*, vol. 1, 694.

50. Perrineau, 'Le Front national, 1972–2015', 244.

51. Fysch and Wolfreys, *The Politics of Racism in France*, 143.

52. James Shields, 'The Front national: From systematic opposition to systemic integration?' *Modern & Contemporary France* 22, no. 4 (2014): 494.

53. Colette Ysmal, 'Sociologie des élite du FN (1979–1986)', in *Le Front national à découvert*, 109. Ninety-two out of 150 delegates responded to a questionnaire.

54. Ysmal, 'Sociologie des élite du FN (1979–1986)', 109.

55. Valérie Lafont, 'France: A two-centuries-old galaxy', in *Extreme Right Activists in Europe*, 101; Klandermans and Mayer, 'Links with the past', 19; Valérie Lafont, 'Les jeunes militants du Front National. Trois modèles d'engagement et de cheminement', *Revue Française de Science Politique* 51, no. 1–2 (2001): 178–9; Ralph Schor, 'Parler des étrangers. Les mots du Front national', *Cahiers de la Méditerranée* 54, no. 1 (1997): 117; Pierre Milza, 'Le Front national: droite extrême … ou national-populisme?' I, 701.

56. Catherine Fieschi, 'Rally politics and political organisation: An institutionalist perspective on the French far Right', *Modern & Contemporary France* 8, no. 1 (2000): 85–6; Perrineau, 'Le Front national, 1972–2015', 244–5; Milza, 'Le Front national: droite extreme … ou national-populisme?' 696; Camus, 'Origine et formation du Front national', 23–8.

57. James Shields, 'Radical or not so radical? Tactical variation in core policy formation by the Front national', *French Politics, Culture & Society* 29, no. 3 (2011): 80–3.

58. Shields, 'Radical or not so radical?' 83–4; Winock, *Nationalisme, antisémitisme et fascisme en France*, 61.

59. Fysch and Wolfreys, *The Politics of Racism in France*, 112; Camus, 'Origine et formation du Front national', 28.

60. Monica Charlot, 'L'émergence du Front national', *Revue française de science politique* 36, no. 1 (1986): 33; Perrineau, 'Front national (1972–1994)', 409; 411.

61. Christopher Husbands, 'Le Front national en région Ile-de-France, 1983–1989. Un vote des privilégiés?' *Les Annales de la recherche urbaine* 50 (1991): 119; 'Les idées que je defends? Les vôtres', says le Pen: Pierre-André Taguieffe, 'La rhétorique du national-populisme. Les règles élémentaires de la propaganda xénophobe', *Mots* 9 (1984): 115; Vergnon, *L'antifascisme en France*, 187; Charlot, 'L'émergence du Front national', 33.

62. Vergnon, *L'antifascisme en France*, 188.

63. Ibid., 187; 190.

64. Ibid., 188–9.

65. Perrineau, 'Les étapes d'une implantation électorale (1972–1988)', 42.

66. Fieschi, 'Rally politics and political organisation', 89n42; Camus, 'Origine et formation du Front national', 28.

67. Fiesch, *Fascism, Populism and the French Fifth Republic*, 19; Perrineau, 'Le Front national, 1972–2015', 253.

68. Charlot, 'L'émergence du Front national', 41–2; Early FN voters also reflect pied-noirs communities locations: Perrineau, 'Les étapes d'une implantation électorale (1972-1988)', 38–9; 43.

69. Charlot, 'L'émergence du Front national', 37–8.

70. Shields, 'Radical or not so radical?' 85–6.

71. Davies, *The National Front in France*, 20; 158–9; Piero Ignazi, 'Un nouvel acteur politique', in *Le Front national à découvert*, 69–72.

72. Davies, *The National Front in France*, 21–2.

73. Frédérique Matonti, 'Le Front national forme ses cadres', *Genèses* 10 (1993): 145; Fysch and Wolfreys, *The Politics of Racism in France*, 140–3.

74. Charlot, 'L'émergence du Front national', 37; Schor, 'Parler des étrangers', 120; 134; Arthur Goldhammer, 'Explaining the rise of the Front national: Political rhetoric or cultural insecurity?' *French Politics, Culture & Society* 33, no. 2 (2015): 139; *L'Alternative nationale. 300 mesures pour la renaissance de la France (Front national, programme de gouvernement)* 1993, 37; 45–7, quoted in Catherine Rodgers, 'Le Front national', in *French Political Parties: A Documentary Reader*, ed. N. A. Addinall (Cardiff: University of Wales Press, 1995), 80; Davies, *The National Front in France*, 33.

75. Schor, 'Parler des étrangers', 130–1.

76. Ibid., 121–35; Pierre-André Taguieffe, 'La rhétorique du national-populisme', 117; Tony S. Jugé and Michael P. Perez, 'The modern colonial politics of citizenship and whiteness in France', *Social Identities* 12, no. 2 (2006): 19; Davies, *The National Front in France*, 145–55; 158–9.

77. Guy Birenbaum, 'Le Front national à l'Assemblée (1986–1988): Respect et subversion de la règle du jeu parlementaire', *Politix* 5, no. 20 (1992): 99; Perrineau, 'Le Front national, 1972–2015', 258–60.

78. Buléon and Fourquet, 'Vote Front National 1984–2002', 454–5.

79. Anne Tristan, *Au Front* (Paris: Gallimard, 1987), 41.

80. Ibid., 40–1.

81. Buléon and Fourquet, 'Vote Front National 1984–2002', 455; Frédéric Royall, 'Regards croisés: La presse frontiste face aux mouvements des "sans" dans les années 1990', *French Politics, Culture & Society* 27, no. 1 (2009): 49; Schor, 'Parler des étrangers', 117–8; 123; Perrineau, 'Le Front national, 1972–2015', 254–5.

82. Husbands, 'Le Front national en région Ile-de-France', 123; Charlot, 'L'émergence du Front national', 39–40.

83. Shields, 'Radical or not so radical?' 86–8; Buléon and Fourquet, 'Vote Front National 1984–2002', 454; Sung Choi, 'The Muslim veteran in postcolonial France: The politics of the integration of Harkis after 1962', *French Politics, Culture & Society* 29, no. 1 (2011): 39; Jugé and Perez, 'The modern colonial politics of citizenship and whiteness in France', 18; Charlot, 'L'émergence du Front national', 42–3.

84. James Shields, 'The far right vote in France: From consolidation to collapse?' *French Politics, Culture and Society* 28, no. 1 (2010): 29; Perrineau, 'Le Front national, 1972–2015', 279–80.

85. Perrineau, 'Front national (1972–1994)', 410; Thierry Blöss, Judith Rouan and Gilles Ascaride, 'Le vote Front national dans les Bouches-du-Rhône: "Laboratoire" de l'alliance entre la droite et l'extrême droite?' *Revue française de science politique* 49, no. 2 (1999): 296; 307–8.

86. Shields, 'Radical or not so radical?' 88–9.

87. Blöss, Rouan and Ascaride, 'Le vote Front national dans les Bouches-du-Rhône', 308; Royall, 'Regards croisés', 51; Jean-Marie Donegani and Marc Sadouin, '1958–1992. Le jeu des institutions', in *Histoire des droites en France*, I, 458; Perrineau, 'Le Front national, 1972–2015', 255; Shields, 'The Front national', 494.

88. Perrineau, 'Front national (1972–1994)', 411.

89. Kevin Passmore, 'Femininity and the right: From moral order to moral order', *Modern & Contemporary France* 8, no. 1 (2000): 65–6.

90. Taguieuff, 'La métaphysique de Jean-Marie Le Pen', 176; Royall, 'Regards croisés', 48; Passmore, 'Femininity and the right', 65.

91. Davies, *The National Front in France*, 125–34.

92. Passmore, 'Femininity and the right', 66.

93. Tristan, *Au Front*, 61.

94. Lafont, 'Les jeunes militants du Front National'; 185.

95. Tristan, *Au Front*, 141; 146–7.

96. Perrineau, 'Les étapes d'une implantation électorale (1972–1988)', 50–1.

97. Tristan, *Au Front*, 209.

98. Perrineau, 'Front national (1972–1994)', 411; Perrineau, 'Le Front national, 1972–2015', 264; Perrineau, 'Les étapes d'une implantation électorale (1972–1988)', 49.

99. Perrineau, 'Le Front national, 1972–2015', 264; Davies, *The National Front in France*, 26–7.

100. Perrineau, 'Le Front national, 1972–2015', 266–7.

101. Perrineau, 'Front national (1972–1994)', 412; Perrineau, 'Le Front national, 1972–2015', 272–3; Milza, 'Le Front national crée-t-il une culture politique?' 40n1; Winock, *Nationalisme, antisémitisme et fascisme en France*, 62; Fysch and Wolfreys, *The Politics of Racism in France*, 142.

102. Société française d'enquête par sondage.

103. Winock, *Nationalisme, antisémitisme et fascisme en France*, 62; Perrineau, 'Le Front national, 1972–2015', 269–70.

104. Davies, *The National Front in France*, 5.

105. Perrineau, 'Le Front national, 1972–2015', 282.

106. Buléon and Fourquet, 'Vote Front National 1984–2002', 456.

107. Perrineau, 'Le Front national, 1972–2015', 283–4; Fiesch, *Fascism, Populism and the French Fifth Republic*, 19.

108. Tristan, *Au Front*, 29.

109. Lafont, 'France: A two-centuries-old galaxy', 93–5; 108.

110. Ibid., 106; Camus and Monzat, *Les Droites nationales et radicales en France*, 107.

111. Davies, *The National Front in France*, 6.

112. Blöss, Rouan and Ascaride, 'Le vote Front national dans les Bouches-du-Rhône', 295; Charlot, 'L'émergence du Front national', 41; Fiesch, *Fascism, Populism and the French Fifth Republic*, 25; Royall, 'Regards croisés', 48–9; Lafont, 'France: A two-centuries-old galaxy', 110–11.

113. Blöss, Rouan and Ascaride, 'Le vote Front national dans les Bouches-du-Rhône', 295.

Notes

114. Royall, 'Regards croisés', 48.

115. Fiesch, *Fascism, Populism and the French Fifth Republic*, 26; Shields, 'The Front national', 41; Perrineau, 'Le Front national, 1972–2015', 283–4.

116. Blöss, Rouan and Ascaride, 'Le vote Front national dans les Bouches-du-Rhône', 305.

117. Lafont, 'France: A two-centuries-old galaxy', 108; Blöss, Rouan and Ascaride, 'Le vote Front national dans les Bouches-du-Rhône', 307.

118. Shields, *The Extreme Right in France*, 278–9.

119. Perrineau, 'Le Front national, 1972–2015', 284–5.

120. Buléon and Fourquet, 'Vote Front National 1984–2002', 461.

121. Ibid., 461.

122. Shields, 'Radical or not so radical?' 90–1; Shields, 'The Front national', 496.

123. Boily, 'Aux sources idéologiques du Front national', 41–3.

124. Buléon and Fourquet, 'Vote Front National 1984–2002', 466; Jayson Harsin, 'Cultural racist frames in TF1's French *Banlieue* riots coverage', *French Politics, Culture & Society* 33, no. 3 (2015): 51; Perrineau, 'Le Front national, 1972–2015', 286–8.

125. Boily, 'Aux sources idéologiques du Front national', 44.

126. Buléon and Fourquet, 'Vote Front National 1984–2002', 464–5; Pamela M. Moores, 'The media prism and reflections on insécurité', *Modern & Contemporary France* 13, no. 4 (2005): 405–19; Richard J. Golsan, *The Vichy Past in France Today: Corruptions of Memory* (Lanham: Lexington Books, 2017), 23.

127. Moores, 'The media prism and reflections on insécurité', 414; Shields, 'The far right vote in France', 29.

128. Shields, 'The far right vote in France', 30.

129. Buléon and Fourquet, 'Vote Front National 1984–2002', 453.

130. Shields, 'The far right vote in France', 30.

131. Ibid., 30.

132. Presidential terms were reduced from seven years to five years in 2000.

133. Shields, 'The far right vote in France', 25–34, https://www.interieur.gouv.fr/Elections/Les-r esultats/Presidentielles/elecresult__presidentielle_2002/(path)/presidentielle_2002/FE.htm l; https://www.interieur.gouv.fr/Elections/Les-resultats/Presidentielles/elecresult__presiden tielle_2007/(path)/presidentielle_2007/FE.html (accessed 25 June 2018).

134. Harsin, 'Cultural racist frames in TF1's French *Banlieue* rots coverage', 51.

135. Vincent Martigny, 'Le débat autour de l'identité nationale dans la campagne présidentielle 2007: Quelle rupture?' *French Politics, Culture & Society* 27, no. 1 (2009): 30; 39n8; Aurelien Mondon, 'The Front national in the twenty-first century: From pariah to republican democratic contender?' *Modern & Contemporary France* 22, no. 3 (2014): 303; Florence Haegel, 'Nicolas Sarkozy a-t-il radicalise la droite française? Changements idéologiques et étiquetages politiques', *French Politics, Culture & Society* 29, no. 3 (2011): 62; 68; 73; Jeremy Ahearne, 'Cultural insecurity and its discursive crystallisation in contemporary France', *Modern & Contemporary France* 25, no. 3 (2017): 270.

136. Shields, 'Radical or not so radical?' 93; Shields, 'The Front national', 497; Shields, 'The far right vote in France', 36.

137. Shields, 'The far right vote in France', 27.

138. Perrineau, 'Le Front national, 1972–2015', 288.

139. Shields, 'The Front national', 47.

140. Davies, *The National Front in France*, 227.

141. Shields, 'The Front national', 499–500.

142. Goldhammer, 'Explaining the rise of the Front national', 138–9.

143. Shields, 'The Front national', 501; Dimitri Almeida, 'Exclusionary secularism: The Front national and the reinvention of *laïcité*', *Modern & Contemporary France* 2, no. 3 (2017): 249–50; 253; 259; Gabriel Goodliffe, 'From political fringe to political mainstream: The Front national and the 2014 municipal elections in France', *French Politics, Culture & Society* 34, no. 3 (2016): 130.

144. Ibid., 130.

145. Pascal Perrineau, 'The Great Upheaval: Left and right in contemporary French politics', in *France since the 1970s*, 37.

146. Goodliffe, 'From political fringe to political mainstream', 130; Davies, *The National Front in France*, 2–27.

147. Shields, 'The Front national', 502.

148. Ibid., 500–1; Goldhammer, 'Explaining the rise of the Front national', 139.

149. Almeida, 'Exclusionary secularism', 252; Winock, *Nationalisme, antisémitisme et fascisme en France*, 2014 edition, 68; Goodliffe, 'From political fringe to political mainstream', 126.

150. Goodliffe, 'From political fringe to political mainstream', 132.

151. Blöss, Rouan and Ascaride, 'Le vote Front national dans les Bouches-du-Rhône', 304; Goodliffe, 'From political fringe to political mainstream', 133; Davies, *The National Front in France*, 42–62.

152. Goodliffe, 'From political fringe to political mainstream', 141; Blöss, Rouan and Ascaride, 'Le vote Front national dans les Bouches-du-Rhône', 300.

153. Goodliffe, 'From political fringe to political mainstream', 132; Milza, 'Le Front national crée-t-il une culture politique?' 44.

154. Nick Hewlett, 'Voting in the shadow of the crisis: The French presidential and parliamentary elections of 2012', *Modern & Contemporary France* 20, no. 4 (2012): 407; 414; Nonna Mayer, 'The closing of the radical right gender gap in France?' *French Politics* 13, no. 4 (2015): 391; Shields, 'The Front national', 55.

155. Mondon, 'The Front national in the twenty-first century', 310–11.

156. Hewlett, 'Voting in the shadow of the crisis', 409; Mondon, 'The Front national in the twenty-first century', 303.

157. Ibid.

158. Shields, 'The Front national', 56.

159. Ibid., 62.

160. Hewlett, 'Voting in the shadow of the crisis', 415.

161. Goodliffe, 'From political fringe to political mainstream', 126; Shields, 'The Front national', 493.

162. Goodliffe, 'From political fringe to political mainstream', 129.

163. Ibid., 128; 136; Buléon and Fourquet, 'Vote Front National 1984–2002', 462–3; Fiesch, *Fascism, Populism and the French Fifth Republic*, 21–5; Martigny, 'Le débat autour de l'identité nationale dans la campagne présidentielle 2007', 27.

Notes

164. Shields, 'The Front national', 58–9.

165. Hewlett, 'The phantom revolution', 382. Le Pen won 7,678,491 votes and 21.3 per cent of vote in the first round. In the second round, she won 10,638, 475 and 33.9 per cent of vote.

Conclusion

1. Jenkins and Millington, *France and Fascism*, 73.

Appendix: The French allergy to fascism: A historiographical essay

1. René Rémond, *Une mémoire française. Entretiens avec Marc Leboucher* (Paris: Desclée de Brouwer, 2002), 82; 85–7; 134; 142; Samuel Kalman, 'René Rémond (1918–2007)', in *French Historians 1900–2000* ed. Philip Daileader and Philip Whalen (Oxford: Wiley-Blackwell), 501–13.

2. Kalman, 'René Rémond (1918–2007)', 504; Rémond, *La Droite en France*, 14; Angenot, 'L'immunité de la France envers le fascisme', 16; Passmore, *The Right in France*, 5–10.

3. Rémond, *La Droite en France*, 206–7.

4. Ibid., 207.

5. Ibid., 209–17.

6. Ibid., 215; 250.

7. Ibid., 215.

8. My italics.

9. Paul Chopine, *Six ans chez les Croix de Feu* (Paris: Gallimard, 1935), 164–71.

10. Ibid., 164–71; René Rémond, *Les Droites en France* (Paris: Aubier Montagne, 1982), 516.

11. Passmore, 'L'historiographie du "fascisme" en France', 475.

12. Rémond, *Une mémoire française*, 63.

13. Passmore, 'L'historiographie du "fascisme" en France', 487; Rémond, *Une mémoire française*, 73.

14. Rémond, *Une mémoire française*, 38–9; Kalman, 'René Rémond (1918–2007)', 501.

15. Rémond, *Une mémoire française*, 81.

16. Passmore, 'L'historiographie du "fascisme" en France', 487.

17. Rémond, *La Droite en France de 1815*, 229; Rémond felt little need to elaborate further on the history of Vichy in his 1982 edition: the *Etat français* garnered a mere 8 pages out of 360 in this edition (Rémond, *Les Droites en France* 231–9).

18. Rémond was writing, too, against the backdrop of the amnesties of those French convicted of collaboration. Dobry points this out in Michel Dobry, 'Avant-propos', in *Le mythe de l'allergie française au fascisme*, 8.

19. Philippe Machefer, *Ligues et fascismes en France (1919–1939)* (Paris: Presses Universitaires de France, 1974), 11–5.

20. Antoine Prost, *Les anciens combattants et la société francaise*, 3 Vols (Paris: Fondation nationale des sciences politiques, 1977), III, 217.

21. See for example Charles Willard, *Le Front populaire, la France de 1934 à 1939* (Paris: Editions Sociales, 1972).

22. George L. Mosse, 'The French Right and the working classes: Les Jaunes', *Journal of Contemporary History* 7, no. 3/4 (1972): 185–208; Ernst Nolte, *Three Faces of Fascism: Action Française, Italian Fascism, National Socialism* (London: Weidenfeld and Nicolson, 1965).

23. In his doctoral thesis, Brian Jenkins determined that the Croix de Feu was a combative extra-parliamentary expression of the rising fears of the conservative bourgeoisie'; 'The Paris riots of February 6th 1934: The crisis of the Third French Republic' (unpublished PhD thesis, University of London, 1979), 133.

24. Kalman, 'René Rémond (1918–2007)', 501–13.

25. Berstein, 'Une bien étrange approche de l'histoire', 17–33.

26. Sternhell, *La Droite révolutionnaire*, 409. See also Sternhell, 'Strands of French fascism', 479–501.

27. Zeev Sternhell, *Ni droite, ni gauche. L'ideologie fasciste en France* (Paris: Seuile, 1983).

28. Raoul Girardet, 'Notes sur l'esprit d'un fascisme français, 1934–1939', *Revue française de science politique* 3 (1955): 529–46.

29. Angenot, 'L'immunité de la France envers le fascisme', 25–7.

30. Jacques Julliard, 'Sur un fascisme imaginaire: à propos d'un livre de Zeev Sternhell', in *Fascisme Français?*, 69–93.

31. Milza, *Fascisme français*, 7–8.

32. See for example ibid., 35; Philippe Burrin, 'Le fascisme', I, 603–53.

33. Milza, *Fascisme français*, 36.

34. Burrin, 'Le fascisme', 630.

35. Julliard, 'Sur un fascisme imaginaire', 72; Jean-Noël Jeanneney, 'Introduction', in *Fascisme Français?*, 9–10; Michel Winock, 'Les limites de l'idéalisme historique', in *Fascisme Français?*, 33–49. See also Winock, *Nationalisme, antisémitisme et fascisme en France*, 269–70.

36. Berstein, 'Une bien étrange approche de l'histoire', 20–5.

37. Berstein, 'La France des années trente allergique au fascisme', 83–94.

38. Ibid., 89.

39. Ibid., 93.

40. Serge Berstein, 'Consensus politique et violences civiles dans la France du 20 siècle', *Vingtième Siècle* 69, no. 1 (2001): 52; 55.

41. René Rémond, *Notre Siècle de 1918 à 1988* (Paris: Fayard, 1988), 177–8.

42. Angenot, 'L'immunité de la France envers le fascisme', 35; Sternhell has continued this attack more recently in his memoirs, *Histoire et Lumières*. Zeev Sternhell, *Histoire et Lumières. Changer le monde par raison* (Paris: Albin Michel, 2014).

43. Angenot, 'L'immunité de la France envers le fascisme', 15–17.

44. Passmore, 'L'historiographie du "fascisme" en France', 498.

45. Milza, *Fascisme français*, 8n2.

46. Passmore, 'L'historiographie du "fascisme" en France', 469–99.

47. Jeanneney, 'Introduction', 5–15.

48. See for example Ibid., 5–15.

49. Robert Soucy, *Fascism in France: The Case of Maurice Barrès* (Berkeley, Los Angeles, London: University of California Press, 1972); *Fascist Intellectual: Drieu La Rochelle* (Berkeley, Los Angeles, London: University of California Press, 1979).

50. Soucy, *The First Wave*, xi.

51. Ibid., xi–xix.

52. Robert Soucy, *Le fascisme français, 1924–1933* (Paris: Presses universitaires de France, 1989).

53. Soucy, *The First Wave*, 43. In the French translation, this reference to La Rocque appears on page 74.

54. Burrin, *La Dérive fasciste*, 26; 61.

55. Ibid., 25.

56. Milza, *Fascisme Français*, 224–5.

57. Dobry, 'Février 1934': 511–33.

58. Ibid., 520.

59. Klaus-Jürgen Müller, 'French Fascism and modernization', *Journal of Contemporary History* 11, no. 4 (1976): 75–108.

60. Dobry, 'Février 1934': 530.

61. Ibid., 512.

62. Rémond, *Notre Siècle de 1918 à 1988*, 159; 216.

63. At that time, Sternhell had rejected the notion that the Croix de Feu-Parti Social Français was fascist, a position he would later change.

64. Irvine, 'Fascism in France', 295.

65. Robert Soucy, 'French fascism and the Croix de Feu: A dissenting interpretation', *Journal of Contemporary History* 26, no. 1 (1991): 159–88.

66. Soucy, *The Second Wave*.

67. Irvine, 'Fascism in France': 287.

68. Ibid., 287–9; 294–5.

69. Soucy, 'French fascism', 163; Soucy, *The Second Wave*, 309.

70. Soucy, 'French fascism', 163.

71. Passmore, 'Boy-scouting for grown-ups?' 531.

72. Ibid., 531–2.

73. Passmore, '"Planting the tricolor in the citadels of communism"', 814–51.

74. Winock, *Nationalisme, antisémitisme et fascisme en France* (1992). The book was updated in both 2004 and 2014. An English-language translation appeared in 1998: *Nationalism, Anti-Semitism and Fascism in France* (Stanford: Stanford University Press, 1998).

75. Winock, *Nationalisme, antisémitisme et fascisme en France* (2014), 240–5.

76. Ibid., 247–8.

77. Ibid., 256.

78. Ibid., 260.

79. Milza, 'Fascisme français', in *Dictionnaire historique de la vie politique française au XXe siècle,* 356–62.

80. Thomas, 'Les effectifs du Parti social français', 61–83.

81. Burrin, 'Le fascisme', 603–53.

82. Ibid., 632.

83. Ibid., 607.

84. Sternhell, 'Strands of French fascism', 494–6.

85. Berstein, 'Une bien étrange approche de l'histoire', 29–30. The 2012 re-edition of Sternhell's *Ni droite ni gauche* pictured a Croix de Feu parade on its front cover.

86. William D. Irvine, 'René Rémond's French Right: The interwar years', *Proceedings of the Fifth Annual Meeting of the Western Society for French History* 5 (1977), 301–9; Bingham, 'Defining French fascism, finding fascists in France', 537.

87. Ibid., 539; 542.

88. Bingham, 'Defining French fascism, finding fascists in France', 539–40; 542.

89. Dobry, ed., *Le mythe de l'allergie française au fascisme*; Brian Jenkins, ed., *France in the Era of Fascism: Essays on the French Authoritarian Right* (New York; Oxford: Berghahn, 2005).

90. Dobry, 'Avant propos', 12. See Jean-Paul Thomas's essay in response to the Dobry collection: Jean-Paul Thomas, 'Fascisme francais: Faut-il rouvrir un débat?' in *Un professeur en République. Mélanges en l'honneur de Serge Berstein*, ed. Rémi Baudouï, Jean Garrigues, Michel Leymarie, Didier Musiedlak and Guillaume Piketty (Paris: Fayard, 2006), 289–97.

91. Dobry, 'Avant propos', 11. Christophe Prochasson and Bertrand Joly described Dobry's collection as 'a punch in the face' in contrast to the usual 'kicks in the ankles' delivered by academics to their opponents: 'Du "fascisme" en France: un débat toujours continué. Deux points de vue critiques', *Revue d'histoire moderne et contemporaine* 54, no. 3 (2007): 186–93.

92. Brian Jenkins, 'Conclusion', in *France in the Era of Fascism*, 204.

93. Ibid., 214.

94. Michel Winock, 'Retour sur le fascisme français', *Vingtième Siècle* 90, no. 2 (2006): 8; 10.

95. Ibid., 8; 13; 27.

96. Robert Soucy, Francine Chase and Loïc Thommeret, 'La Rocque et le fascisme français: Réponse à Michel Winock', *Vingtième Siècle* 95, no. 3 (2007): 219.

97. Winock, 'En lisant Robert Soucy', 237–42.

98. Serge Berstein, 'Pour en finir avec un dialogue de sourds: A propos du fascisme français', *Vingtième Siècle* 95, no. 3 (2007): 243.

99. Ibid., 244–5.

100. Ibid., 245.

101. Kéchichian, *Les Croix-de-Feu*, 375–81.

102. Kennedy, *Reconciling France against Democracy*, 117.

103. Ibid., 118–19.

104. See for example: Downs, '"Nous plantions les trois couleurs"'; Koos, 'Fascism, fatherhood, and the family in interwar France'; '"Planting the tricolor in the citadels of communism"'; Sarnoff, 'An overview of women and gender in French fascism'; Sudda, 'Gender, Fascism and the right-wing'.

105. Geoff Read, *The Republic of Men: Gender and the Political Parties in Interwar France* (Baton Rouge: Louisiana State University Press, 2014).

106. Campbell, *Political Belief in France*.

107. Goodfellow, *Between the Swastika and the Cross of Lorraine*, 86–103.

108. Ibid., 161

109. Kalman, *French Colonial Fascism*.

110. Kestel, *La conversion en politique*.

111. Jenkins and Millington, *France and Fascism*.

112. François de La Rocque, *Pourquoi je suis républicain. Carnets de captivité* (Paris: Seuil, 2014).

113. Berstein, 'Une bien étrange approche de l'histoire', 17–33; Winock, 'Les limites de l'idéalisme historique', 33–52.

114. Jean-Paul Thomas, 'Croix de feu et PSF: les variations de Zeev Sternhell', in *Fascisme Français? La controverse*, ed. Berstein and Winock, 121.

115. Berstein and Winock, 'Conclusion', 237; 239.

116. Berstein and Thomas, eds, *Le PSF*.

117. Gilles Richard, 'Conclusion', in *Le PSF*, 331n18.

118. Berstein and Thomas, 'Introduction', in *Le PSF*, 11–12.

119. Passmore makes this point in 'L'historiographie du "fascisme" en France'.

120. Jackson is named among the consensus school historians in Soucy's 2007 response to Winock in *Vingtième Siècle*. Gordon is placed in the immunity school for his assertion that French wartime collaborationism failed due to 'the failure of fascism to sink deep roots into the French political community before or after 1940': Gordon, *Collaborationism in France*, 28.

121. In 1992, Burrin recognized that save for these historians' apparent agreement on the strength of interwar fascism, 'they differ … on nearly everything else'. See Burrin, 'Le fascisme', 608.

122. Jean-Paul Thomas, 'KENNEDY, Sean, *Reconciling France against Democracy. The Croix-de-Feu and the Part Social Français, 1927–1945*, Montreal, McGill-Queen's University Press, 2007, 384 p., 75 [dollars]', *Vingtième Siècle* 95, no. 3 (2007), 279–80.

SELECT BIBLIOGRAPHY

Archives Nationales, Pierrefitte-sur-Seine

BB[18]: Correspondance générale de la division criminelle
F[7]: Police générale
451 Archives privées: Fonds La Rocque

Archives de la Préfecture de Police, Paris

Series BA
Series DB

Newspapers and magazines

L'Action Française
L'Echo de Paris
L'Emancipation nationale
Le Flambeau
Gringoire
L'Humanité
L'Intransigeant
Je suis partout
Journal Officiel
Le Matin
Le National
L'Oeuvre
Le Petit Journal
Le Populaire
La Revue hebdomadaire et son supplément illustré
La Voix du combatant

Printed primary sources

9 février 1934. Journée rouge. Paris: Les Publications révolutionnaires, 1934.
Agapitidès, Sotiris. *Le Corporatisme en Italie.* Paris: Librairie Lipschutz, 1935.
Ansay, Armand. *La politique de crédit du fascisme de 1922 à 1932.* Paris: Recueil Sirey, 1935.
Bainville, Jacques. *Les Dictateurs.* Paris: Les Editions Denoël et Steele, 1935.
Belin, Jean. *My Work at the Sûreté.* London: George G. Harrap, 1950.
Bernadec, Christian. *Dagore. Les carnets secrets de la Cagoule.* Paris: France-Empire, 1977.

Select Bibliography

Bucard, Marcel. *Le Francisme. Paix, justice, ordre*. Paris, n.d.

Cambo, Francesco. *Autour du fascisme italien. Réflexions et commentaires sur quelques problèmes de politique contemporaine*. Paris: Plon, 1925.

Charbonneau, Henri. *Les mémoires de Porthos*. Paris: Les Editions du Clan, 1967.

Chopine, Paul. *Six ans chez les Croix de Feu*. Paris: Gallimard, 1935.

Comapolonghi, Luigi. *Avec l'Italie? Oui! Avec le Fascisme – Non!* Paris: Ligue des Droits de l'Homme, 1930.

Comité de Vigilance des Intellectuels Antifascistes. *Qu'est-ce que le fascisme? Le fascisme et la France*. Paris, 1935.

Ferro, Antonio. *Salazar, le Portugal et son Chef*. Paris: Editions Bernard Grasset, 1934,

Fontenay, Fernand. *La Cagoule contre la France. Ses crimes. Son organisation. Ses chefs. Ses inspirateurs*. Paris: Editions sociales internationales, 1938.

Guéhenno, Jean. *Diary of the Dark Years: Collaboration, Resistance and Daily Life in Occupied Paris*. Oxford: Oxford University Press, 2014.

Hirsch, Werner. *Leçons de courage. Comment les révolutionnaires allemands supportent la torture et la captivité*. Paris: Défense Editions, 1935.

Koestler, Arthur. *Scum of the Earth*. London: Eland, 2006.

La Rocque, Lieutenant-Colonel François de. *Service Public*. Paris: Editions Bernard Grasset, 1934.

La Rocque, Edith and Gilles de La Rocque. *La Rocque tel qi'il était*. Paris: Fayard, 1962.

Loustaunau-Lacau, Georges. *Mémoires d'un Français rebelle*. Paris: Laffont, 1948.

L'Italie sous la terreur. A bas le fascisme assassin! Paris: Editions du Secours Rouge International, 1926.

Massis, Henri. *Chefs*. Paris: Plon, 1939.

Parti. *Social Français. Une mystique. Un programme*. Paris, n.d.

Renaud, Jean. *La Solidarité Française attaque … .* Paris: Les Oeuvres Françaises, 1935.

Salazar, Antonio de Oliveira. *Doctrine and Action: Internal and Foreign Policy of the New Portugal, 1928–1939*, trans. by Robert Edgar Broughton. London: Faber and Faber, 1939.

Schreiber, Emile. *Le Portugal de Salazar*. Paris: Editiosn Denoël, 1938.

Trentin, Silvio. *Aux sources du fascisme*. Paris: Marcel Rivière, 1931.

Vries de Heekelingen, H. de. *Le Fascisme et ses résultats*. Paris: Social Editions, 1928.

Werth, Alexander. *The Destiny of France* London: Hamish Hamilton, 1937.

Secondary sources

Ahearne, Jeremy. 'Cultural insecurity and its discursive crystallisation in contemporary France', *Modern & Contemporary France* 25, no. 3 (2017): 265–80.

Alcalde, Ángel. *War Veterans and Fascism in Interwar Europe*. Cambridge: Cambridge University Press, 2017.

Almeida, Dimitri. 'Exclusionary secularism: The Front national and the reinvention of *laïcité*', *Modern & Contemporary France* 2, no. 3 (2017): 249–63.

Angenot, Marc. 'L'immunité de la France envers le fascisme: un demi-siecle de polémiques historiennes', *Etudes françaises* 47, no. 1 (2011): 15–42.

Arnold, Edward J., ed. *The Development of the Radical Right in France from Boulanger to Le Pen*. Basingstoke: Palgrave, 2000.

Aslangul, Claire. 'De la haine héréditaire à l'amitié indéfectible', *Revue historique des armées* 256 (2009): 3–13.

Atkin, Nicholas. *The French at War, 1934–1944*. Harlow: Longman, 2001.

Atkin, Nicholas and Frank Tallett, eds. *The Right in France, 1789–1997*. London; New York: IB Tauris, 1998.

Azéma, Jean-Pierre. 'La Milice', *Vingtième Siècle* 28, no. 4 (1990): 83–106.

Azéma, Jean-Pierre and François Bédarida, eds. *Le régime de Vichy et les Français.* Paris: Fayard, 1992.

Berstein, Serge. 'La France des années trente allergique au fascisme: A propos d'un livre de Zeev Sternhell', *Vingtième Siècle* 2, no. 1 (1984): 83–94.

Berstein, Serge. 'Consensus politique et violences civiles dans la France du 20 siècle', *Vingtième Siècle* 69, no. 1 (2001): 51–60.

Berstein, Serge. 'Pour en finir avec un dialogue de sourds: A propos du fascisme français', *Vingtième Siècle* 95, no. 3 (2007): 243–6.

Berstein, Serge and Odile Rudelle, eds. *Le modèle républicain.* Paris: Presses Universitaires de France, 1992.

Berstein, Serge and Jean-Paul Thomas. *Le PSF. Un parti de masse à droite.* Paris: CNRS Editions, 2016.

Berstein, Serge and Michel Winock, eds. *Fascisme Français? La controverse.* Paris: CNRS Editions, 2014.

Bingham, John. 'Defining French Fascism, finding Fascists in France', *Canadian Journal of History* 29 (1994): 525–43.

Birenbaum, Guy. 'Le Front national à l'Assemblée 1986–1988: Respect et subversion de la règle du jeu parlementaire', *Politix* 5, no. 20 (1992): 99–118.

Blatt, Joel. 'Relatives and rivals: The response of the Action Française to Italian Fascism, 1919–1926', *European History Quarterly* 11, no. 3 (1981): 263–92.

Blatt, Joel. 'The Cagoule plot, 1936–1937', in *Crisis and Renewal in France, 1918–1962,* ed. Kenneth Mouré and Martin S. Alexander, 86–104. New York: Berghahn Books, 2000.

Blinkhorn, Martin., ed. *Fascists and Conservatives: The Radical Right and the Establishment in Twentieth-Century Europe.* London; Boston: Unwin Hyman, 1990.

Boily, Frédéric. 'Aux sources idéologiques du Front national: le marriage du traditionalisme et du populisme', *Politique et Sociétés* 24, no. 1 (2005): 23–47.

Bourdrel, Philippe. *La Cagoule. Histoire d'une société secrète du Front populaire à la Ve République.* Paris: Albin Michel, 1992.

Braganca, Emmanuel. *La crise allemande du roman français.* Oxford: Peter Lang, 2012.

Brunelle, Gayle K. and Annette Finley-Croswhite. *Murder in the Metro: Laetitia Toureaux and the Cagoule in 1930s France.* Baton Rouge: Louisiana State University Press, 2010.

Brunet, Jean-Paul. *Jacques Doriot. Du communisme au fascisme.* Paris: Balland, 1986.

Buléon, Pascal and Jérôme Fourquet. 'Vote Front National 1984–2002, géographies et interprétations sucessives: Une equation politique', *Espace, populations, sociétés* 3 (2003): 453–467.

Burrin, Philippe. *La Dérive fasciste. Doriot, Déat, Bergery, 1933–1945.* Paris: Seuil, 1986.

Campbell, Caroline. *Political Belief in France, 1927–1945: Gender, Empire and Fascism in the Croix de Feu and Parti Social Français.* Baton Rouge: Louisiana State University Press, 2015.

Capdevila, Luc. 'The quest for masculinity in a defeated France, 1940–1945', *Contemporary European History* 10, no. 3 (2001): 423–45.

Cointet, Jean-Paul. *La Légion Française des Combattants. La tentation du fascisme.* Paris: Albin Michel, 1995.

Colas, Jean-François. *Les droites nationales en Lorraine dans les années 1930: Acteurs, organisations, réeseaux.* Lille: Atelier national de reproduction des thèses, 2002.

Dard, Olivier and Ana Isabel Sardinha-Desvignes. *Célébrer Salazar en France 1930–1974. Du philosalazarisme au salazarisme français.* Brussels: Pete Lang, 2018.

Davey, Owen Anthony. 'The origins of the Légion des Volontaires Français contre le Bolchevisme', *Journal of Contemporary History* 6, no. 4 (1971): 29–45.

Davies, Peter. *The National Front in France: Ideology, Discourse and Power.* London and New York: Routledge, 1999.

Deacon, Valerie. *The Extreme Right in the French Resistance: Members of the Cagoule and Corvignolles in the Second World War*. Baton Rouge: Louisiana State University Press, 2016.

Delporte, Christian. 'Méfions-nous du sourire de Germania! L'Allemagne dans la caricature française 1919–1939', *Mots* 48 (1996): 33–54.

Déniel, Alain. *Bucard et le francisme*. Paris: J. Picollec, 1979.

Dobry, Michel. 'Février 1934 et la découverte de l'allergie de la société française à la "révolution fasciste"', *Revue Française de Sociologie* XXX (1989): 511–33.

Dobry, Michel, ed. *Le mythe de l'allergie française au fascisme*. Paris: Albin Michel, 2003.

Douglas, Allen. 'Violence and fascism: The case of the Faisceau', *Journal of Contemporary History* 19, no. 4 (1984): 689–712.

Douglas, Allen. *From Fascism to Libertarian Communism: Georges Valois against the Third Republic*. Berkeley: University of California Press, 1992.

Downs, Laura Lee. '"Each and every one of you must become a *chef*": Toward a social politics of working-class childhood on the extreme right in 1930s France', *Journal of Modern History* 81, no. 1 (2009): 1–44.

Downs, Laura Lee. '"Nous plantions les trois couleurs": Action sociale féminine et recomposition des politiques de la droite française. Le mouvement Croix-de-feu et le Parti social français, 1934–1947', *Revue d'histoire moderne et contemporaine* 58, no. 3 (2011): 118–63.

Fiesch, Catherine. *Fascism, Populism and the French Fifth Republic*. Manchester: Manchester University Press, 2004.

Fillieule, Olivier and Danielle Tartakowsky. *La manifestation*. Paris: Presses de la Fondation Nationale des Sciences Politiques, 2008.

Fogg, Shannon L. '"They are undesirables": Local and national responses to Gypsies during World War II', *French Historical Studies* 31, no. 2 (2008): 327–58.

Fysch, Peter and Jim Wolfreys. *The Politics of Racism in France*. Basingstoke: Palgrave Macmillan, 2003.

Geiger, Wolfgang. *L'image de la France dans l'Allemagne nazie, 1933–1945*. Rennes: Presses Universitaires de Rennes, 2015.

Giolitto, Pierre. *Histoire de la Milice*. Paris: Perrin, 2002.

Goodfellow, Samuel Huston. *Between the Swastika and the Cross of Lorraine: Fascisms in Interwar Alsace*. De Kalb: Northern Illinois University Press, 1998.

Goodliffe, Gabriel. *The Resurgence of the Radical Right in France: From Boulangisme to the Front National*. Cambridge: Cambridge University Press, 2012.

Goodliffe, Gabriel. 'From political fringe to political mainstream: The Front national and the 2014 municipal elections in France', *French Politics, Culture & Society* 34, no. 3 (2016): 126–47.

Gordon, Bertram M. *Collaborationism in France during the Second World War*. Ithaca: Cornell University Press, 1980.

Griffiths, Richard. 'Fascist or conservative? Portugal, Spain and the French connection', *Portuguese Studies* 14 (1998): 138–51.

Guillon, Jean-Marie. 'La Légion française des combattants ou comment comprendre la France de Vichy', *Annales du Midi. Revue archéologique, historique et philologique de la France méridionale* 116, no. 245 (2004): 5–24.

Hedinger, Daniel. 'Universal Fascism and its global legacy: Italy's and Japan's entangled historu in the early 1930s', *Fascism* 2, no. 2 (2013): 141–60.

Hewlett, Nick. 'Voting in the shadow of the crisis: The French presidential and parliamentary elections of 2012', *Modern & Contemporary France* 20, no. 4 (2012): 403–20.

Hewlett, Nick. 'The phantom revolution: The presidential and parliamentary elections of 2017', *Modern & Contemporary France* 25, no. 4 (2017): 377–90.

Hoffman, Stanley. 'Collaborationism in France during World War II', *Journal of Modern History* 40, no. 3 (1968): 375–95.

Irvine, William D. *French Conservatism in Crisis: The Republican Federation of France in the 1930s*. Baton Rouge: Louisiana State University Press, 1979.

Irvine, William D. 'Fascism in France and the strange case of the Croix de Feu', *Journal of Modern History* 63, no. 2 (1991): 271–95.

Jackson, Julian. *The Politics of Depression in France, 1932–1936*. Cambridge: Cambridge University Press, 1985.

Jackson, Julian. *The Popular Front in France: Defending Democracy, 1934–1938*. Cambridge: Cambridge University Press, 1990.

Janeiro, Helena Pinto. 'Salazar et les trois France 1940–1944', *Vingtième Siècle* 62, no. 2 (1999): 39–50.

Jankowski, Paul. *Communism and Collaboration: Simon Sabiani and Politics in Marseille, 1919–1944*. New Haven: Yale University Press, 1989.

Jankowski, Paul. *Stavisky: A Confidence Man in the Republic of Virtue*. Ithaca; London: Cornell University Press, 2002.

Jenkins, Brian., ed. *France in the Era of Fascism: Essays on the French Authoritarian Right*. New York; Oxford: Berghahn, 2005.

Jenkins, Brian. 'The six février 1934 and the "survival" of the French Third Republic', *French History* 20, no. 3 (2006): 333–51.

Jenkins, Brian and Chris Millington. *France and Fascism: February 1934 and the Dynamics of Political Crisis*. Abingdon: Routledge, 2015.

Kalman, Samuel. *The Extreme Right in Interwar France: The Faisceau and the Croix de Feu*. Aldershot: Ashgate, 2009.

Kalman, Samuel. *French Colonial Fascism: The Extreme Right in Algeria, 1919–1939*. New York: Palgrave Macmillan, 2013.

Kalman, Samuel and Sean Kennedy, eds. *The French Right Between the Wars: Political and Intellectual Movements from Conservatism to Fascism*. New York: Berghahn, 2014.

Kéchichian, Albert. *Les Croix-de-Feu à l'âge des fascismes. Travail, famille, patrie*. Seyssel: Champ Vallon, 2006.

Kennedy, Sean. *Reconciling France against Democracy: The Croix de Feu and the Parti Social Français, 1927–1945*. Montréal; Ithaca: McGill-Queen's University Press, 2007.

Kestel, Laurent. *La conversion en politique. Doriot, le PPF et la question du fascisme français*. Paris: Raisons d'agir, 2012.

Klandermans, Bert and Nonna Mayer., eds. *Extreme Right Activists in Europe*. London and New York: Routledge, 2006.

Koos, Cheryl A. 'Fascism, fatherhood, and the family in interwar France: The Case of Antoine Rédier and the Légion', *Journal of Family History* 24, no. 3 (1999): 317–29.

Lafont, Valérie. 'Les jeunes militants du Front National. Trois modèles d'engagement et de cheminement', *Revue Française de Science Politique* 51, nos. 1–2 (2001): 174–98.

Lahousse, Gilles. 'De la solidarité française au parti du faisceau français: un exemple de radicalisation politique', *Vingtième Siècle* 58, no. 1 (1998): 43–54.

Larsen, Stein Ugelvik, Bernt Hagtvet and Jan Petter Myklebust., ed. *Who were the Fascists?* Oxford; New York; Oslo: Universitetsforlaget, 1980.

Lemmes, Fabian. 'Collaboration in wartime France, 194–1944', *European Review of History/ Revue européenne d'histoire* 15, no. 2 (2008): 157–77.

Levey, Jules. 'Georges Valois and the Faisceau: The making and breaking of a fascist', *French Historical Studies* 8, no. 2 (1973): 279–304.

Machefer, Philippe. 'L'Union des droites, le PSF et le Front de la liberté, 1936–1937', *Revue d'histoire moderne et contemporaine* 17, no. 1 (1970): 112–26.

Machefer, Philippe. *Ligues et fascismes en France 1919–1939*. Paris: Presses Universitaires de France, 1974.

Martigny, Vincent. 'Le débat autour de l'identité nationale dans la campagne présidentielle 2007: Quelle rupture?', *French Politics, Culture & Society* 27, no. 1 (2009): 23–42.

Mayer, Nonna and Pascal Perrineau., eds. *Le Front national à découvert*. Paris: Presses de la Fondation Nationale des Sciences Politiques, 1989.

Merglen, Albert. 'Soldats français sous uniformes allemands, 1941–1945: LVF et 'Waffen SS' français,' *Revue d'histoire de la Deuxième guerre mondiale* 108 (1977): 71–84.

Millington, Chris. *Fighting for France: Violence in Interwar French Politics*. Oxford: Oxford University Press, 2018.

Millman, Richard. *La question juive en France entre les deux guerres. Ligues de droite et antisémitisme en France*. Paris: Armand Colin, 1992.

Millman, Richard. 'Les croix-de-feu et l'antisémitisme,' *Vingtième Siècle* 38, no. 1 (1993): 47–61.

Milza, Pierre. *Italie fasciste devant l'opinion française*. Paris: Armand Colin, 1967.

Milza, Pierre, ed. *Les Italiens en France de 1914 à 1940*. Rome: Ecole française de Rome, 1986.

Milza, Pierre. *Fascisme français. Passé et présent*. Paris: Flammarion, 1987.

Mondon, Aurelien. 'The Front national in the twenty-first century: From pariah to republican democratic contender?' *Modern & Contemporary France* 22, no. 3 (2014): 301–20.

Muel-Dreyfus, Francine. *Vichy et l'éternel féminin. Contribution a une sociologie politique de l'ordre du corps*. Paris: Editions du Seuil, 1996.

Muller, Klaus-Jurgen. 'French fascism and modernisation,' *Journal of Contemporary History* 11, no. 4 (1976): 75–107.

Nobécourt, Jacques. *Le Colonel de La Rocque 1885–1946. Ou les pièges du nationalisme chrétien*. Paris: Fayard, 1996.

Ory, Pascal. *Les collaborateurs, 1940–1945*. Paris: Editions du Seuil, 1976.

Panicacci, Jean-Louis. 'Une section modèle? La Légion des Alpes-Maritimes,' *Annales du Midi. Revue archéologique, historique et philologique de la France méridionale* 116, no. 245 (2014): 91–110.

Parry, DLL. 'Counter-revolution by conspiracy', in *Crisis and Renewal in France, 1918–1962*, ed. Kenneth Mouré and Martin S. Alexander, 161–81. New York: Berghahn Books.

Passmore, Kevin. 'Boy-scouting for grown-ups? Paramilitarism in the Croix de Feu and the Parti Social Français,' *French Historical Studies* 19, no. 2 (1995): 527–57.

Passmore, Kevin. '"Planting the tricolor in the citadels of communism": Women's social action in the Croix de Feu and Parti Social Français,' *Journal of Modern History* 71, no. 4 (1999): 814–51.

Passmore, Kevin, ed. *Women, Gender and Fascism in Europe, 1919–45*. Manchester: Manchester University Press, 2003.

Passmore, Kevin. *The Right in France from the Third Republic to Vichy*. Oxford: Oxford University Press, 2013.

Passmore, Kevin. 'L'historiographie du "fascisme" en France,' *French Historical Studies* 37, no. 3 (2014): 469–99.

Paxton, Robert O. *Vichy France: Old Guard and New Order*. New York: Alfred A. Knopf, 1972.

Pellissier, Pierre. *6 Février 1934. La République en flammes*. Paris: Perrin, 2000.

Peschanski, Denis. 'Vichy au singulier, Vichy au pluriel. Une tentative avortée d'encadrement de la société 1941–1942,' *Annales. Economies, Sociétés, Civilisations* 43, no. 3 (1988): 639–61.

Philippet, Jean. *Le temps des ligues: Pierre Taittinger et les jeunesses patriotes 1919–1944*. Lille: Atelier nationale de reproduction des thèses, 2000.

Pinto, António Costa. 'Elites, single parties and political decision-making in Fascist-era dictatorships,' *Contemporary European History* 11, no. 3 (2002): 429–54.

Pinto, António Costa. 'Le salazarisme et le fascisme européen,' *Vingtième Siècle* 62, no. 1 (1999): 15–25.

Pollard, Miranda. *Reign of Virtue: Mobilizing Gender in Vichy France*. Chicago; London: University of Chicago Press, 1998.

Rémond, René. *La Droite en France de 1815 à nos jours. Continuité et diversité d'une tradition politique*. Paris: Aubier, 1954.

Rémond, René. *Les Droites en France*. Rev. edn. Paris: Aubier, 1982.

Rémond, René. *Une mémoire française. Entretiens avec Marc Leboucher*. Paris: Desclée de Brouwer, 2002.

Rudaux, Philippe. *Les Croix de Feu et le PSF*. Paris: Editions France-Empire, 1967.

Sarnoff, Daniella. 'Interwar fascism and the franchise: Women's suffrage and the ligues', *Historical Reflections/Réflexions Historiques* 34, no. 2 (2008): 112–33.

Schor, Ralph. 'Parler des étrangers. Les mots du Front national', *Cahiers de la Méditerranée* 54, no. 1 (1997): 117–37.

Shields, James G. 'Charlemagne's Crusaders: French collaboration in arms, 1941–1945', *French Cultural Studies* 18, no. 1 (2007): 83–105.

Shields, James G. *The Extreme Right in France: From Pétain to Le Pen*. Abingdon: Routledge, 2007.

Shields, James. 'The far right vote in France: From consolidation to collapse?', *French Politics, Culture and Society* 28, no. 1 (2010): 25–45.

Shields, James. 'Radical or not so radical? Tactical variation in core policy formation by the Front national', *French Politics, Culture & Society* 29, no. 3 (2011): 78–100.

Shields, James. 'The Front national: From systematic opposition to systemic integration?', *Modern & Contemporary France* 22, no. 4 (2014): 491–511.

Shirer, William L. *The Collapse of the Third Republic: An Inquiry into the Fall of France in 1940*. London: Literary Guild, 1970.

Shorrock, William I. 'France and the rise of fascism in Italy, 1919–1923', *Journal of Contemporary History* 10, no. 4 (1975): 591–610.

Sirinelli, Jean-François. *Histoire des droites en France*, 3 vols. Paris: Gallimard, 1992.

Sirinelli, Jean-François, ed. *Dictionnaire historique de la Vie Politique Française au XXe Siècle*. Paris: Presses Universitaires de France, 1995.

Soucy, Robert. *Fascism in France: The Case of Maurice Barrès*. Berkeley: University of California Press, 1972.

Soucy, Robert. *Fascist Intellectual: Drieu La Rochelle*. Berkeley: University of California Press, 1979.

Soucy, Robert. *French Fascism: The First Wave*. New Haven; London: Yale University Press, 1986.

Soucy, Robert. *French Fascism: The Second Wave*. New Haven; London: Yale University Press, 1995.

Soucy, Robert, Francine Chase and Loïc Thommeret. 'La Rocque et le fascisme français: Réponse à Michel Winock', *Vingtième Siècle* 95, no. 3 (2007): 219–36.

Sternhell, Zeev. *La Droite révolutionnaire, 1885–1914. Les origines françaises du fascisme*. Paris: Seuil, 1978.

Sternhell, Zeev. *Ni droite ni gauche. L'idéologie fasciste en France*. Paris: Seuil, 1983.

Sudda, Magali Della. 'Gender, Fascism and the right-wing in France between the wars: The Catholic', *Politics, Religion and Ideology* 13, no. 2 (2012): 179–95.

Taguieffe, Pierre-André. 'La rhétorique du national-populisme. Les règles élémentaires de la propaganda xénophobe', *Mots* 9 (1984): 113–39.

Tartakowsky, Danielle. *Les manifestations de rue en France 1918–1968*. Publications de la Sorbonne: Paris, 1997.

Tartakowsky, Danielle. *Les Droites et la rue. Histoire d'une ambivalence, de 1880 à nos jours*. Paris: La Découverte, 2014.

Thalmann, Rita. *Femmes et Fascismes*. Paris: Editions Tierce, 1986.

Thomas, Jean-Paul. 'Les effectifs du Parti social français', *Vingtième Siècle* 62, no. 1 (1999): 61–83.

Thomas, Jean-Paul. 'Les jeunes dans le mouvements Croix de feu-PSF', *Recherches contemporaines* 6 (2000–2001): 189–97.

Thomas, Martin, ed. *The French Colonial Mind: Violence, Military Encounters, and Colonialism.* Lincoln: University of Nebraska Press, 2011.

Torgal, Luis Reis. 'L'Etat Nouveau portugais: esquisse d'interprétation', *Pôle Sud* 22 (2005): 39–48.

Tournier, Maurice. 'Naissance du vocabulaire *fasciste* en France 1914–1945', in *Propos d'étymologie sociale. Tome II. Des mots en politique.* [online] Lyon: ENS Editions. http://boo ks.openedition.org/enseditions/1718?lang=fr.

Tumblety, Joan. 'Revenge of the fascist knights': Masculine identities in *Je suis partout*, 1940– 1944', *Modern & Contemporary France* 7, no. 1 (1999): 11–20.

Tumblety, Joan. *Remaking the Male Body: Masculinity and the Uses of Physical Culture in Interwar and Vichy France.* Oxford: Oxford University Press, 2013.

Vergnon, Gilles. *L'antifascisme en France de Mussolini à Le Pen.* Rennes: Presses Universitaires de Rennes, 2009.

Vervaecke, Philippe., ed. *A droite de la droite. Droites radicales en France et en Grande-Bretagne au XXe siècle.* Lille: Presses universitaires du Septentrion, 2012.

Vitkine, Antonin. *Mein Kampf. Histoire d'un livre.* Paris: Flammarion, 2009.

Weber, Eugen. *Action Française: Royalism and Reaction in Twentieth-Century France.* Stanford: Stanford University Press, 1962.

Weber, Eugen. *The Hollow Years: France in the 1930s.* London: Sinclair-Stevenson, 1995.

Wieviorka, Olivier. 'Guerre civile à la française? Le cas des années sombre 1940–1945', *Vingtième Siècle* 8, no. 1 (2005): 5–19.

Winock, Michel., ed. *La Droite depuis 1789: Les hommes, les idées, les réseaux.* Paris: Seuil, 1995.

Winock, Michel. 'Retour sur le fascisme français', *Vingtième Siècle* 90, no. 2 (2006): 3–27.

Winock, Michel. 'En lisant Robert Soucy: Sur La Rocque et les Croix-de-feu', *Vingtième Siècle* 95, no. 3 (2007): 237–42.

Winock, Michel. *Nationalisme, antisémitisme et fascisme en France.* Rev. edn. Paris: Editions du Seuil, 2014.

Winock, Michel. *Histoire de l'extrême droite en France.* Rev. edn. Paris: Points, 2015.

INDEX

Abetz, Otto   112, 119, 120, 121, 123, 125
Action Française
    anti-Semitism   9, 35, 57, 77, 147
    banning of   66
    and the Cagoule/OSARN   95, 97–8
    conflict with the Faisceau   22, 24–7
    and the crisis of February 1934   29, 35–6, 37,
        38, 39, 44, 105–6
    decline during the 1920s   28
    and Italian fascism   8, 14, 25–6, 28
    membership   16, 22, 28
    North Africa   19
    and Portugal   81, 82
    during the Second World War   113–14, 122
    violence   6, 14, 16, 24–5, 27, 36, 65, 66, 98
Algeria. *See* North Africa
Alibert, Raphaël   105, 114
Alliance Démocratique   70, 87
antifascism. *See also* Popular Front
    in France during the 1920s   6
    in France during the 1930s   9–10, 47, 62–3
        Comité de Vigilance des Intellectuels
            Antifascistes (CVIA)   9, 47
anti-Semitism   146–7, 152, 157, 162
    Action Française   9, 58, 77
    Cagoule/OSARN   99
    Crémieux decree   59, 89
    Croix de Feu   58–60
    FN   127, 137
    Francistes   33
    Poujadism   130–1
    PPF   88, 89, 120, 125
    PSF   77, 78
    Salazarism   115
    Solidarité Française   29, 33
    Unions Latines   19
    Vichy   108, 114, 115, 116
Arthuys, Jacques   20, 23, 27
Association Républicaine des Anciens Combattants
    (ARAC)   29, 38, 40

Bainville, Jacques   8
Bardèche, Maurice   129, 132
Barrès, Maurice   21, 81, 131, 154
    influence of   124, 128, 130
Barrès, Philippe   21, 23, 27
Belin, Jean   98, 102, 103, 105

Berstein, Serge   3, 152, 153–4, 160, 162–3
Blum, Léon   33, 45, 66, 71, 89, 91, 94, 110
    and anti-Semitism   77–8, 131
Boulanger, Georges   4, 9
Brasillach, Robert   35, 61, 83, 119
Bucard, Marcel   7, 23, 33, 34, 66, 119, 155

Cagoule/OSARN
    attempted coup   103–4
    and the crisis of February 1934   43, 95
    and the extreme right   97–100, 104
    financial resources of   96–7
    founding   95
    and the French army   96
    and Italian fascism   97
    membership   96, 97–100
    organisation   94, 95
    and the press   103–4
    strategy   93, 94–5, 102–3, 104
    violence of   101–2
    weapons   94–5
    and women   100
camelots du roi   6, 10, 14, 16, 18, 24, 26, 66,
    95, 99
Campbell, Caroline   64, 161
Cartel des gauches
    1924   14–15, 16, 17, 18, 23, 27
    1932   31
Catholicism
    as basis for a 'Latin' alliance   8, 28, 81, 82, 114
    conflict with the Action Française   28
    Croix de Feu   53, 54, 60, 160
    political activism   15–16, 23, 48
    PSF   77, 90, 91
        Social Catholicism   79
    Vichy   110
Charbonneau, Henri   98, 103, 132
Chautemps, Camille   29, 32, 35, 37, 94
Chiappe, Jean   94, 103
    and the crisis of February 1934   29, 37
Chirac, Jacques   129, 136, 137, 139, 140
collaboration   108
collaborationism   108–9
    divisions within   121–2
    number of sympathisers   119
communism
    antifascism   6, 9, 13, 14, 18, 24 , 45, 88

Cagoule/OSARN   93, 94, 95, 96, 99
Communist Party (of France)   5, 13, 15, 27, 44, 70, 102, 129, 134
    and the crisis of February 1934   31, 42
Croix de Feu   53, 62
FN   138, 139
Groupe de Défenses Antifascistes   6
PPF   69–70, 83–5, 87, 88
PSF   74–5, 80
Confédération Générale du Travail (CGT)   70, 84, 100
Corre, Aristide   95, 98, 99
Coty, François   52
    funding of the extreme right   17, 22, 33, 48
Croix de Feu   8, 10, 44, 109, 155
    antiparliamentarianism   55
    anti-Semitism   57–8, 59–60, 147
    auxiliary groups   50, 53–4
    and the conservative right   55–6
    and the crisis of February 1934   29, 36, 38, 39, 47, 51, 52
    Dispos/Disponibles   50, 62, 73, 74, 78, 146
    dissolution   65–6
    and fascism   47, 49, 61–2, 66, 149–51, 156–7
    and the FN   145
    founding   34, 48
    left-wing opposition to   47, 58, 62–3, 64, 66
    membership   34, 48, 50, 51, 52, 53
    and Muslims   60
    and Nazism   61–2
    North Africa   51, 59–60
    paramilitarism   50, 57–8
    political programme   38, 47, 51, 56
    relations with the Cagoule/OSARN   95, 96, 98, 99–100
    and René Rémond   149–51
    Republicanism   57, 66
    and Robert Soucy   156–7, 160
    social programme   54–5
    transformation into the PSF   71–9
    and veterans   48, 56
    violence   49–50, 60, 63–4
    and women   20, 53–4
    xenophobia   58–9, 60
CSAR. See Cagoule/OSARN

Daladier, Edouard
    and the crisis of February 1934   29, 30, 31, 37, 38, 39, 40, 41, 42, 43, 162
    opinion of La Rocque   65
    as Prime Minister in 1938   91
    resignation in 1934   42
Darnand, Joseph   107, 109, 124
    and the Cagoule   97
    leader of the Milice   105, 109, 118
    and the PPF   85

    and the SOL   117
Daudet, Léon   16, 24, 25, 26, 95
Déat, Marcel   38, 124
    career prior to 1940   110
    collaborationism   119, 125
    and the LVF   122
    and the RNP   111, 112, 120, 122, 127
    and the single party project   110, 111, 112
Deloncle, Eugène
    collaborationism   119, 120, 122, 123
    and the crisis of February 1934   43, 95
    as leader of the Cagoule/OSARN   43, 94, 95, 96, 97, 98, 99, 100, 102, 103, 104, 105
Déroulède, Paul   4–5, 6
d'Hartoy, Maurice   48
Dobry, Michel   6, 162, 163, 164
    the classificatory logic   3, 155–6
    the 'exchange of blows'   41
    the immunity thesis   3, 156, 159–60
Doriot, Jacques
    anticommunism   84, 87–8, 121, 122
    anti-Semitism   88–9
    and the Cagoule/OSARN   94
    career before the PPF   69, 83–5
    collaborationism   109, 111, 120–1
    fascism   88–9, 91–2
    and Italy   90
    as leader of the PPF   69
    and the LVF   122–3
    and Nazism   90
    personality cult   69, 89
    Vichy   109, 110, 111
Dormoy, Marx   88, 94, 103, 105
Doumergue, Gaston   30, 43, 45, 52
Drieu La Rochelle, Pierre   31, 84, 85, 89, 90, 154
Ducloux, Louis   41, 105
Duseigneur, Edouard   95, 97, 104

economic crisis of the 1930s
    effects in France   31–2, 45, 57–8
Etat Français. See Vichy

Faisceau
    decline   27, 28
    family policy   24
    founding   5, 20–1
    influence on successor movements   33
    and Italian fascism   14, 21, 25, 26, 28
    membership   22, 24
    plans for a Combatants' State   22, 23–4
    relations with the Action Française   22, 24–7
    violence   23, 24–5, 27, 145
    and women   24
family
    policy on   146

Croix de Feu 54, 55
Faisceau 23, 24
FN 128, 136
Jeunesses Patriotes 20
PPF 89
PSF 79
Vichy 108, 113, 114
fascism
definitions of 1, 2, 3, 4, 5, 10, 155,
    156-7, 158-9
and classificatory logic 3, 10, 156, 159,
    160, 162
essentialism of 3, 9, 124, 128, 156, 160,
    162
relational perspective 159, 162
denial of fascism's existence in France 1,
    149-50, 151-2, 153-4, 157-8, 163
Italian fascism
French admiration of 7, 22, 25, 26,
    93, 96
French opposition to 5, 14
French understandings of 14
Organizzazione per la Vigilanza e la
    Repressione dell'Antifascismo (OVRA)
    5, 97
reception in France 3-5, 25-6
sponsorship of French movements 33,
    86, 96
squadristi 3, 6, 25, 26, 62
universality of fascism 7
and violence 4, 6, 9, 14
and 'Latin civilisation' 4, 8, 19, 46, 61, 80, 97,
    114, 162
left-wing understanding as transnational
    9-10, 47, 62, 80, 103-4
use as a label 8, 9, 10, 25, 26, 27, 28, 66, 80, 86,
    88, 89, 128, 147, 148, 164
Fédération Nationale Catholique 16, 18, 48
Fédération Républicaine 17, 42, 77
and the crisis of February 1934 43
and the extreme right 6, 17, 55, 56, 70,
    87, 99
Ferry, Désiré 17, 55
Filliol, Jean 43, 95, 98, 99, 100, 101, 102, 103
Francistes 7, 10, 23, 34-5, 63, 119, 150, 151
Front National
anti-Semitism 137
and the conservative right 134, 136, 142
detoxification of the party's brand 141
and fascism 128, 134
founding 132
ideology 128, 133
and immigration 133, 134, 135, 139-40
and Islam 135, 139-40
membership 132-3, 136, 138, 139, 142
opposition to globalisation 141

secularism 141
split with Bruno Mégret 139
and Vichy 128
voters 135, 137, 138, 139, 140, 142
and women 136-7
Frot, Eugène 40, 42

Garrigoux, Jeanne 76, 107
Gressent, Alfred Georges. See Valois, Georges
Groupe de Recherche et d'Etude pour la
    Civilisation Européenne (GRECE)
    132, 134

Henriot, Philippe 118, 124
Herriot, Edouard 15, 32, 34
Hitler, Adolf
attempts to placate French opinion 46
attitude to France 7-8, 46
and France during the Second World War
    108, 121, 123
French opinion of 9, 10, 45-6, 47, 59, 61, 62,
    80, 88, 97, 116, 134

Irvine, William D. 3, 75, 156, 157, 158
Islam 19, 59-60, 89
Blum-Violette reforms 78, 89
and the FN 135, 139, 140, 141, 142, 147

Jean-Baptiste, Léon 97, 102
Jeantet, Gabriel 96, 101, 103, 107, 114, 132
Jenkins, Brian 128, 145, 152, 159, 162
Jeunesses Patriotes 10
and the Cagoule/OSARN 99
and the conservative right 17, 27
and the crisis of February 1934 29, 32, 36,
    37-8, 42
and the Croix de Feu 53, 55
dissolution 66
family policy 20
founding 5, 14, 16-17
and Italian fascism 14, 25
and the Ligue des Patriotes 14, 16-17, 20
membership 18-19, 22
and Nazism 46
North Africa 19
plans for a National Revolution 17
and veterans 19
and violence 6, 17-18, 26, 39
    murders at the rue Damrémont in 1925
    13-14
and women 19-20
Juif, Maurice 97, 102

Kestel, Laurent 10, 162, 163, 164

La Rocque, François de la

Index

antiparliamentarianism 49–50, 51, 52, 55, 70
anti-Semitism 58, 77–8
and the Cagoule/OSARN 104
career before leading the Croix de Feu 48–9
conflict with the PPF 87–8
and the conservative right 72
and the crisis of February 1934 36, 38, 39, 43, 47, 51–2
and dissolution of the Croix de Feu 65–6, 70, 78
and expansion of the Croix de Feu 50, 51, 54
and fascism 8, 66
and Italian fascism 61–2, 80
as leader of the Croix de Feu/PSF 34, 45, 48, 49
memoirs 162–3
and Michel Winock 157, 160
and Muslims 60, 78
and Nazism 8, 61, 80
and paramilitarism 56–7, 62, 74
and Portugal 80–2
and propaganda 73
and the Radical Party 72
Republicanism 8, 47, 56, 57, 66, 79–80, 91
Service Public (1934) 47, 56, 58, 64
and Spain 80
and Vichy 109–10, 111
and violence 49–50, 63–4, 73, 74–5
and women 50, 54
xenophobia 58–9
Laval, Pierre 117, 118, 120
and the Cagoule/OSARN 105
and collaborationism 119, 120
and the extreme right 55, 57, 64, 65
founding of the Vichy regime 108
and Italian fascism 46
and the National Revolution 112
as Prime Minister of the Third Republic 45
and the single party project 110–11
Lebecq, Georges 39, 40, 41
Lebrun, Albert 30, 31, 37, 42, 51
Légion des Volontaires Français contre le Bolchevisme (LVF)
founding 122
and masculinity 122–3
membership 123
motivations of recruits 123
social work 123
and women 123
Légion Française des Combattants 111, 124
and the National Revolution 115–16
in North Africa 116
as a potential single party 116–17
and social work 116
Le Pen, Jean-Marie

anti-Semitism 127, 137
election as a councillor in 1983 133–4
election to parliament in 1956 130
and the FN 132
political programme 134–6
and Poujadism 130
and the presidential election
1965 131
1974 133
1981 133
1988 137
1995 138
2002 129, 139–40
2007 140
split with Bruno Mégret 139
Le Pen, Marine
attempts to detoxify the FN 141
campaign for secularism 141
and the presidential election
2012 142
2017 129, 143
views on Islam 141
and views on the Second World War 127
Ligue des Patriotes 6, 14, 16, 17, 20

Marin, Louis 17, 42, 72
Marion, Paul 90, 114, 117, 119
Maurras, Charles 7, 16, 28, 61
and the Cagoule/OSARN 95
conflict with the Faisceau 22, 24, 25, 27
and fascism 26, 28
and the FN 128
and Poujadism 138
and Salazarism 81
Vichy 113, 114, 115, 124
Maurrasianism. *See* Maurras, Charles
Mégret, Bruno 136, 139
Mein Kampf
French publication 7–8, 46
Milice Française
founding of 117
membership 118
and violence 118–19
Milza, Pierre 154, 155, 158
on the FN 128, 130, 131, 153
on the PPF 70
on Vichy 115, 118, 124
Mitterrand, François 134, 137
Molle, Jules 19, 59, 99, 162
Moreau, Marie-Thérèse 19–20
Morocco. *See* North Africa
Mouvement Social Révolutionnaire (MSR) 105, 119, 120
Muslims. *See* Islam

Mussolini, Benito   1, 6, 10, 22, 26, 33, 56,
      61, 62
   French admiration of   4, 5, 7, 14, 26, 28, 46,
      61, 90, 116
   a 'French Mussolini'   4, 5, 21
   relations with Hitler   7, 80, 81

National Front (1934)   52, 64
National Front (1972-present). *See* Front National
Nazism   7–8, 9, 33, 46, 62, 81, 115, 119, 147
North Africa
   Action Française in   19
   anti-Semitism in   59–60, 77–8, 88–9
   and the Cagoule/OSARN   99
   the Croix de Feu in   51, 53, 59–60, 64
   and the FN   135
   Islam   60, 78
   the Jeunesses Patriotes in   19
   the Légion in   116, 117
   the PPF in   86, 88–9, 111, 121
   the PSF in   72, 77–8, 80
   the SOL in   117
   and the Spanish Civil War   71, 80
   the UDCA in   130
   Vichy   113

Ordre Nouveau   132–3
Organisation Secrète d'Action Révolutionnaire
      Nationale (OSARN).
      See Cagoule/OSARN

Parti Démocrate Populaire   6, 87
Parti Populaire Français (PPF)
   activists post-war   129, 133, 145
   anti-Semitism   78, 88–9, 147
   and the Cagoule/OSARN   95, 98, 99
   collaborationism   121
   and fascism   70, 88–9, 91, 155, 157
   financial resources of   85–6
   founding   69, 85
   Freedom Front against Communism   87–8
   and the LVF   122–3
   membership   86, 121
   and Muslims   89
   and Nazism   89, 120
   opposition to   69–70
   political programme   69, 85, 89–90
   and the PSF   87, 112
   and Vichy   110–11, 114, 121, 125
   and violence   85, 117, 121
   and women   86
   work of Laurent Kestel on   162
Parti/Progrès Social Français (PSF)   8
   anti-Semitism   77–8, 147
   and the Cagoule/OSARN   98, 99, 100

conflict with the PPF   87–8
conflict with the Radical Party   70, 72, 91
and the conservative right   70, 72
continuity with the Croix de Feu   73–4, 78
and the elections of 1940   91
and the FN   133, 142
founding   70
and Italian Fascism   80
left-wing opposition to   80
membership   71–3
and Muslims   78
and paramilitarism   74–5, 78–9
political programme   76–7, 79
and Portugal   80–3
Propaganda Flying Squads (Equipes Volantes
      de Propagande)   73, 74, 78, 79
recent scholarship on   163
Republicanism   79–80
social work   75–6
Syndicat Professionel Français (SPF)   72–3
Vichy   109–10, 111
and women   76, 146, 161
and xenophobia   77
Parti Républicain National et Social (PRNS)
      66, 87
Passmore, Kevin   3, 115, 151, 154, 157, 159, 163
Paxton, Robert O.   2, 115, 153
Pétain, Philippe   1, 3, 117, 121
   advocates an armistice with Germany in
      1940   108
   appointment to the Ministry of War in
      1934   42
   and the Cagoule/OSARN   96, 105
   and the Croix de Feu-PSF   109, 111
   and the FN   127
   as leader of Vichy   108, 109, 110, 122
      and the single party project   110–11,
      125
   and the National Revolution   112, 113
   and the PPF   111, 125
   and Salazarism   114
Phalanges Universitaires   18, 19
Poincaré, Raymond   15, 16, 27, 28, 81
Popular Front   8, 31, 44, 45, 47, 63, 64, 70, 73
   election of   66, 69, 85, 93
   end of   91
   and the FN   133
   and the Spanish Civil War   71
   and Vichy   107
   and violence   85
   and xenophobia   77
Poujade, Pierre   129–31, 134
Poujadism   129–31
Pozzo di Borgo, Joseph   48, 95
Préval, Antoinette de   50, 54, 76

Index

Pucheu, Pierre
  and the crisis of February 1934   43
  and the PPF   86, 89, 90, 121
  at Vichy   114, 117, 119
Pujo, Maurice   24, 27

Radical Party   32
  antifascism   6, 31, 44, 45
  and the Cagoule/OSARN   98
  and the crisis of February 1934   35–6, 42
  and the extreme right   17, 26, 65, 87, 157
  and the PSF   72, 91
Rassemblement National   127. *See also*
      Front National
Rassemblement National Populaire (RNP)   124,
      125, 127
  anti-Semitism   122
  conflict with Deloncle   120
  and fascism   120, 155
  founding   111–12, 119
  membership   120
  and women   120
Rebatet, Lucien   109, 119
Rémond, René   82, 83
  and the historiography of French fascism   1–3,
      149–52, 154, 155, 156
Renaud, Jean   8
  and Italian Fascism   8, 33
  as leader of the Solidarité Française   33, 34
  and Nazism   33
  and Portugal   83
Reynaud, Paul   43, 108

Salazar, António de Oliveira
  comparison with the PSF   82–3
  Estado Novo   81–3, 114
  and fascism   82–3, 115
  French admiration of   8–9, 80–2, 114, 116, 134
  Vichy   114–15
Sarkozy, Nicolas   140, 142
Service d'Ordre Légionnaire (SOL)   117
Shields, James G.
  on the FN   128, 131, 140, 141–2
  on Vichy   112
Shirer, William   30, 42, 49
Socialist Party   6, 9, 10, 15, 26, 31, 32, 37, 40,
      84, 110
  antifascism   6, 53
  and the Cagoule/OSARN   99
  and the FN   134, 135, 138, 140
  and the Popular Front   45, 57, 67
social work
  as an outlet for female activism   11, 146, 161
    in the Croix de Feu   53–5, 57
    in the FN   142

  in the Francistes   33–4
  in the Jeunesses Patriotes   19–20
  in the Légion   116
  in the LVF   123
  in the Milice   118
  in the PPF   86, 90, 111
  in the PSF   75–7, 110
Solidarité Française   8, 10, 33, 147
  and the Cagoule/OSARN   98
  and the crisis of February 1934   29, 36, 37–8, 40
  decline   52
  North Africa   85
Soucy, Robert   3, 14, 154–7, 160, 163, 164
Spanish Civil War   71, 97
Stavisky, Serge Alexandre
  Stavisky Affair   29, 31, 35–7, 41, 51
Sternhell, Zeev
  and the Croix de Feu   158
  and the historiography of French fascism   2, 3,
      152–4, 155, 159, 163, 164

Taittinger, Pierre
  and the Cagoule/OSARN   96
  career   16–17
  and the conservative right   17, 19, 27
  and the crisis of February 1934   38, 39, 43
  founding of the PRNS   66
  and the French Empire   19
  and Italian Fascism   25
  as leader of the Jeunesses Patriotes   13, 14
  and the PPF   87
  and violence   18
  and women   20
Thorez, Maurice   45, 84
totalitarianism
  and collaborationism   125
  supposed French rejection of   8, 80, 82, 114
  supposed Portuguese rejection of   81, 82–3, 114
Tunisia. *See* North Africa

Union de Défense des Commercants et Artisans
      (UDCA)   129–30
Union des Comités d'Action Défensive (UCAD)   95
Union Fédérale   34, 80
Union Nationale des Combattants (UNC)   34
  and the crisis of February 1934   29, 37,
      38, 40–1
  and the extreme right   19, 23, 35, 39, 48,
      72, 119
Unions Latines   19, 59, 99, 162

Valois, Georges   5, 7, 48
  career   21–22
  conflict with the Action Française   22, 24–7
  and fascism   26

ideas of   23
  as leader of the Faisceau   21, 22, 28
  and veterans   23
veterans   15, 17, 45. *See also* UNC; Union Fédérale
  and Adolf Hitler   61
  and the Cagoule/OSARN   97, 98, 104
  and the crisis of February 1934   29, 31, 32, 34, 38, 40–1, 162
  and the Croix de Feu   8, 34, 48, 49, 54, 56
  and the Faisceau   21, 22, 23, 24
  and fascism   150, 152, 163
  and Italian fascism   4, 5, 7, 80
  and the Jeunesses Patriotes   19
  and the Légion   115, 118
  in Portugal   82
  and the PSF   72, 82
  and the RNP   119
  and the Solidarité Française   33
Vichy
  admiration of Salazar   114–15
  fall of France in 1940   108–9
  and fascism   2–3, 114–15, 124–5
  founding   108
  in historiography   2–3
  National Revolution   2, 108, 112–15
    anti-Semitism   108
    and the collaborationists   109, 122, 125
    foreign influences on   114–15
    and gender   108
    and the Légion   115–16, 124
    and the Milice   118
    and the PSF   110, 112
  single party project   109–12
violence   16, 49, 99–100, 136–7
  between antifascists and leaguers   13–14, 18, 62–4, 74–5, 85
  Cagoule/OSARN attacks   93–4, 97, 101–2
  at Clichy in 1937   75
  and the crisis of February 1934   38–41, 84
  between the Faisceau and Action Française   24–7

during January 1934   36
killing of Marius Plateau   16, 26
and the Légion Française des Combattants   116
MSR attacks   105
murders at the rue Damrémont   13–14, 18, 25
paramilitarism   21
  and the Action Française   16
  and the Croix de Feu   49, 50, 62, 73, 74, 78, 146
  and the Faisceau   22
  and the Francistes   33
  and the Jeunesses Patriotes   17–18
  and members of the Cagoule/OSARN   98–99
  and the Milice   117–18
  and the PSF   73–4
  and the Solidarité Française   33
between political activists and the police   69–70, 74, 80, 84

Winock, Michel   3, 157, 160, 163
Women   11, 146, 161
  in the Cagoule/OSARN   100
  in the Croix de Feu   50, 53–5, 157, 161
  in the Faisceau   22, 24
  in the FN   136–7
  in the Jeunesses Patriotes   19–20
  in the Légion   116, 117
  in the LVF   123
  'natural' abilities of   20, 54, 96, 108, 146
  in the PPF   88
  in the PSF   76–7, 109, 157, 161
  in the RNP   120
  Vichy   113

xenophobia   57–60, 63, 77, 130, 133–4, 136, 140, 142, 146–7

Ybarnégaray, Jean   55, 65, 66

Lightning Source UK Ltd.
Milton Keynes UK
UKHW022210161219
355495UK00003B/142/P